D1082998

Asian/Oceanian Historical Dictionaries
Edited by Jon Woronoff

Asia

1. *Vietnam*, by William J. Duiker. 1989. *Out of print. See No. 27.*
2. *Bangladesh*, 2nd ed., by Craig Baxter and Syedur Rahman. 1996
3. *Pakistan*, by Shahid Javed Burki. 1991
4. *Jordan*, by Peter Gubser. 1991
5. *Afghanistan*, by Ludwig W. Adamec. 1991
6. *Laos*, by Martin Stuart-Fox and Mary Kooyman. 1992
7. *Singapore*, by K. Mulliner and Lian The-Mulliner. 1991
8. *Israel*, by Bernard Reich. 1992
9. *Indonesia*, by Robert Cribb. 1992
10. *Hong Kong and Macau*, by Elfed Vaughan Roberts, Sum Ngai Ling, and Peter Bradshaw. 1992
11. *Korea*, by Andrew C. Nahm. 1993
12. *Taiwan*, by John F. Copper. 1993. *Out of print. See No. 34.*
13. *Malaysia*, by Amarjit Kaur. 1993. *Out of print. See No. 36.*
14. *Saudi Arabia*, by J. E. Peterson. 1993
15. *Myanmar*, by Jan Becka. 1995
16. *Iran*, by John H. Lorentz. 1995
17. *Yemen*, by Robert D. Burrowes. 1995
18. *Thailand*, by May Kyi Win and Harold Smith. 1995
19. *Mongolia*, by Alan J. K. Sanders. 1996
20. *India*, by Surjit Mansingh. 1996
21. *Gulf Arab States*, by Malcolm C. Peck. 1996
22. *Syria*, by David Commins. 1996
23. *Palestine*, by Nafez Y. Nazzal and Laila A. Nazzal. 1997
24. *Philippines*, by Artemio R. Guillermo and May Kyi Win. 1997

Oceania

1. *Australia*, by James C. Docherty. 1992
2. *Polynesia*, by Robert D. Craig. 1993. *Out of print. See No. 39.*
3. *Guam and Micronesia*, by William Wuerch and Dirk Ballendorf. 1994
4. *Papua New Guinea*, by Ann Turner. 1994
5. *New Zealand*, by Keith Jackson and Alan McRobie. 1996

New Combined Series

25. *Brunei Darussalam*, by D. S. Ranjit Singh and Jatswan S. Sidhu. 1997
26. *Sri Lanka*, by S. W. R. de A. Samarasinghe and Vidyamali Samarasinghe. 1998
27. *Vietnam*, 2nd ed., by William J. Duiker. 1998
28. *People's Republic of China: 1949–1997*, by Lawrence R. Sullivan, with the assistance of Nancy Hearst. 1998
29. *Afghanistan*, 2nd ed., by Ludwig W. Adamec. 1997
30. *Lebanon*, by As'ad AbuKhalil. 1998
31. *Azerbaijan*, by Tadeusz Swictochowski and Brian C. Collins. 1999
32. *Australia,* 2nd ed., by James C. Docherty. 1999
33. *Pakistan*, 2nd ed., by Shahid Javed Burki. 1999
34. *Taiwan (Republic of China)*, 2nd ed., by John F. Copper. 2000
35. *Laos*, 2nd ed., by Martin Stuart-Fox. 2001
36. *Malaysia*, 2nd ed., by Amarjit Kaur. 2001
37. *Papua New Guinea*, 2nd ed., by Ann Turner. 2001
38. *Tajikistan*, by Kamoludin Abdullaev and Shahram Akbarzedeh. 2002
39. *Polynesia,* 2nd ed., by Robert D. Craig. 2002

Historical Dictionary of Polynesia

Second Edition

Robert D. Craig

Asian/Oceanian Historical Dictionaries, No. 39

The Scarecrow Press, Inc.
Lanham, Maryland, and London
2002

SCARECROW PRESS, INC.

Published in the United States of America
by Scarecrow Press, Inc.
4720 Boston Way, Lanham, Maryland 20706
www.scarecrowpress.com

4 Pleydell Gardens, Folkestone
Kent CT20 2DN, England

British Library Cataloguing-in-Publication Information Available

Library of Congress Cataloging-in-Publication Data

Craig, Robert., D. 1934–
Historical dictionary of Polynesia / Robert D. Craig.—2nd ed.
p. cm. – (Asian/Oceanian historical dictionaries ; no. 39)
Includes bibliographical references and index.
ISBN 0-8108-4237-8 (alk. paper)
1. Polynesia—History—Dictionaries. I. Title. II. Series.

DU510 .C73 2002
996'.003—dc21 2001054169

The paper used in this publication meets the minimum requirements of American National Standard for Information Sciences—Permanence of Paper for Printed Library Materials, ANSI/NISO Z39.48-1992.
Manufactured in the United States of America.

CONTENTS

EDITOR'S FOREWORD

The *Historical Dictionary of Polynesia*, unlike most others in these series, deals not with one country but over a dozen, as well as related countries and assorted islands. What links them together, aside from location, are cultural and historical ties which form a similar, if infinitely varied background. This book can, therefore, explore numerous common themes and variations on those themes. It can examine how each state or island has evolved and developed up to the present. It can also consider how they fit in with one another and the rest of the world. For Polynesia, an essential part of this rest consists of two similar groupings in the Pacific Ocean—Micronesia (on which there is already a volume) and Melanesia (being written).

If it is useful for parts of Polynesia to know more about one another, it is even more helpful for outsiders to know more about them. Polynesia was once remote both geographically and practically. That is no longer true. It is increasingly easy to visit, to invest and trade, to get to know people and places. But many of us have not realized this and, when we do want to learn more, we may not know where to look. Well, this historical dictionary is certainly an excellent starting point. As noted, it tells us much about the region, both past and present. It sheds light on political, economic, social, and cultural aspects. It highlights noteworthy leaders and institutions. No less important, it provides a detailed bibliography that covers the region as a whole and each component part.

It takes an exceptional knowledge of Polynesia to draw the many strands together. No one could have done it better than Robert D. Craig. He is personally familiar with the region, having traveled widely and frequently over many years. He has also taught others about Polynesia as founder and editor of the journal *Pacific Studies*, publications editor of the Institute for Polynesian Studies, professor of Pacific history at the University of Guam, and until recently director of the Pacific Rim Studies Center at Alaska Pacific University (Anchorage).

Finally Dr. Craig has written extensively, including a *Historical Dictionary of Oceania*, a *Historical Dictionary of Honolulu and Hawai'i*, and this second edition of the *Historical Dictionary of Polynesia*, which substantially expands on the already extremely useful first edition.

Jon Woronoff
Series Editor

PREFACE

Writing a second edition to any publication gives the author the opportunity to update and polish previous material, to add new information since the last edition, and to make corrections that bypassed the author, several readers, and the editors in the earlier work. Hopefully, this has all been accomplished.

In this edition, every entry dealing with contemporary events was updated where necessary, a few entries were discarded, and many new ones were added. This substantially increased the size of the new volume. The total number of pages would have been much longer, but by using a different font size, we were able to keep the book within the size limits set by the publisher.

Many of the concerns and problems discussed in the first edition still remain. To cover as broad a geographical area in the Pacific Ocean as Polynesia with its many islands and independent states poses a challenge to any researcher. The simple matter of how much space to allot to each island group was difficult. Other questions needed to be asked. For example, is the history of Hawai'i more important than the Cook Islands or Tuvalu? Or, should New Zealand and Hawai'i be given greater treatment than let's say Tokelau or Easter Island simply because their historical data are more readily available? How do you provide enough detailed information in the main entries for each of the 14 island states[1] so that the entries are more than just chronological listings of names, dates, and places? All these endless decisions had to be made at every turn.

---

1. American Sāmoa, Cook Islands, Easter Island, French Polynesia, Hawai'i, Nauru, New Zealand, Niue, Pitcairn, Sāmoa, Tokelau, Tonga, Tuvalu, and Wallis and Futuna. Perhaps some time in the not too distant future, a separate historical dictionary can be published for each of these island nations. To date, two have been published by Scarecrow Press—one for Hawai'i (*Historical Dictionary of Honolulu and Hawai'i*, 1993) and one for New Zealand (*Historical Dictionary of New Zealand*, 1996).

The introduction in the current volume continues to remain very general. However, the main entries for each island group, when read in conjunction with the many other related entries scattered alphabetically throughout the volume, will flesh out the details of each of the islands' history. An updated bibliography provides a wide selection of published materials for further investigation.

A note in the bibliography comments on the great assistance the Internet has been in the gathering of data for this revised dictionary. Library research continues to be a must, but now that island newspapers, journals, magazines, and in some cases databases are on-line, it makes one's work a lot simpler and less expensive. I continue to offer my heartfelt thanks to the many librarians throughout the Pacific Rim on whom I call for assistance from time to time. A special thanks is offered to Riley Moffat at the Institute for Polynesian Studies (Hawai'i), to Karen Peacock and Lynette Furuhashi at the University of Hawai'i Pacific Collection, to Efi Rex and Mark Perkins at the SPC library in Nouméa, and to Brian Hawkins at the University of Alaska—Anchorage interlibrary loan department. I also offer thanks to the other librarians and Pacific friends who so swiftly sent returns to my "emergency" e-mail requests. I could not have completed as many of the entries without their help.

Robert D. Craig
San Diego, California

ACRONYMS AND ABBREVIATIONS

$	Monetary amounts in this volume are in U.S. dollars unless indicated otherwise by the common designations: $A for Australian dollars, $F for Fijian dollars, $NZ for New Zealand dollars, and so forth.
ABCFM	American Board of Commissioners for Foreign Missions
ACP	African, Caribbean, and Pacific States
ADB	Asian Development Bank
ADF	Asian Development Fund
AIDAB	Australian International Development Assistance Bureau
ANZUS	Security Treaty between Australia, New Zealand, and the United States
APEC	Asia and Pacific Economic Cooperation
ASAO	Association for Social Anthropology in Oceania
ASPA	Association of South Pacific Airlines
ASG	American Sāmoa Government
AusAID	Australian Agency for International Development
CBE	Commander, Order of the British Empire
CCOP/SOPAC	Committee for Coordination of Joint Prospecting for Mineral Resources in South Pacific Offshore Areas
CDP	Christian Democratic Party (Sāmoa)
CEDIP	Compañía Explotadora de la Isla de Pascua
CIP	Cook Islands Party
CIPA	Cook Islands Progressive Association
CMS	Church Missionary Society

CPAS	Center for Pacific and Asian Studies
CPIS	Center for Pacific Islands Studies, University of Hawai'i
CSPCP	Conference of South Pacific Chiefs of Police
CSPS	Center for South Pacific Studies
DAP	Democratic Alliance Party (Cook Islands)
DBE	Dame Commander, Order of the British Empire
ECAFE	United Nations Economic Commission for Asia and the Far East
EEC	European Economic Community
EEZ	Exclusive Economic Zone
EFO	Établissements Français de l'Océanie (French Polynesia)
ESCAP	United Nations Economic and Social Commission for Asia and the Pacific
ESFO	European Society for Oceanists
EU	European Union
EWC	East-West Center
FFA	Forum Fisheries Agency
FLP	Front de Libération de la Polynésie (Tavini Huira'atira Party in French Polynesia)
GCMG	Grand Cross, Order of St. Michael and St. George
GEIC	Gilbert and Ellice Islands Colony
HRPP	Human Rights Protection Party (Sāmoa)
IMF	International Monetary Fund
JPS	*Journal of the Polynesian Society*
JSS	Cook Islands/Niue/New Zealand Joint Shipping Service
KBE	Knight, Order of the British Empire
KCB	Knight Commander, Order of the Bath

LMS	London Missionary Society
MRG	Mouvement des Radicaux de Gauche (Wallis and Futuna political party)
NASA	National Aeronautics and Space Administration
NCDS	National Centre for Development Studies
NFZ	Nuclear Free Zone
NOC	National Olympic Committee (Oceania)
NP	National Party (New Zealand)
NPP	Niue People's Party
NZMFT	New Zealand Ministry of Foreign Affairs and Trade
OBE	Officer, Order of the British Empire
OECD	Organization for Economic Cooperation and Development
OHA	Office of Hawaiian Affairs (Hawai'i)
PACOM	Pacific-Asian Congress of Municipalities
PAMBU	Pacific Manuscripts Bureau
PARTA	Pacific Regional Trade Agreement
PCC	Pacific Conference of Churches
PCC	Polynesian Cultural Center (Lā'ie, Hawai'i)
PFL	Pacific Forum Line
PIC	Pacific Islands Conference
PIDP	Pacific Islands Development Program (East-West Center)
PIF	Pacific Islands Forum
PILOM	Pacific Islands Law Officers Meeting
PIM	*Pacific Islands Monthly*
PINA	Pacific Islands News Association
PIPA	Pacific Islands Producers' Association
PITDC	Pacific Islands Tourism Development Council
PPP	Pacific People's Partnership

PVS	Polynesian Voyaging Society
PWRB	Pacific Women's Resource Bureau
RCT	Regional Committee on Trade
RDPT	Rassemblement Démocratique des Populations Tahitiennes (French Polynesian political party)
RPR	Rassemblement pour la République (Tā hō'ē ra'a Huira'atira Party in French Polynesia; also Wallis and Futuna political party)
SEATO	Southeast Asia Treaty Organization
SIDS	United Nations Small Island Developing States
SIS	Smaller Island States
SNDP	Sāmoa National Development Party (Sāmoa)
SOPAC	South Pacific Applied Geoscience Commission
SPATC	South Pacific Air Transport Council
SPBEA	South Pacific Board for Educational Assessment
SPC	Secretariat for the Pacific Community (formerly the South Pacific Commission)
SPEC	South Pacific Bureau for Economic Cooperation
SPECTEL	South Pacific Regional Telecommunications Meeting
SPF	South Pacific Forum
SPFFA	South Pacific Forum Fisheries Agency
SPHS	South Pacific Health Service
SPICIN	South Pacific Islands Criminal Intelligence Network
SPJC	South Pacific Judicial Conference
SPLMC	South Pacific Labor Ministers Conference
SPRCAC	South Pacific Regional Civil Aviation Council
SPRSC	South Pacific Regional Shipping Council
SPTO	South Pacific Tourism Organization (formerly the Tourism Council of the South Pacific)
THP	Tahoera'a Huira'atira Party (French Polynesia)

UDF	Union pour la Démocratie Française (Wallis and Futuna political party)
UDO	Union pour la Défense de l'Océanie (French Polynesia)
UFP	Université Française du Pacifique
UN	United Nations
UNDP	United Nations Development Program
UNFPA	United Nations Population Fund
UPD	Union Populaire Locale (Wallis and Futuna political party)
U.S.	United States of America
USP	University of the South Pacific
UTD	Union Tahitienne Démocratique (French Polynesia political party)
VAT	Value-Added Tax

CHRONOLOGY

B.C.

1300 Colonization of Tonga by Lapita settlers.

1000 Settlement of Sāmoa.

A.D.

200 Lapita culture ends in Tonga and Sāmoa. Settlement of the Marquesas Islands.

450 Settlement of Easter Island and the Society Islands.

650 First settlement of Hawai'i.

700 Beginning of the construction of Easter Island monuments.

850 Settlement of the Cook and Austral Islands.

900 Settlement of New Zealand and beginning of its Moa culture.

925 Traditional date of Kupe's voyage to New Zealand.

950 Establishment of the Tu'i Tonga dynasty in Tonga.

1000 Beginning of the Middle Period of Easter Island monument building.

1100 Expansion period of ancient Polynesian culture.

1200 Settlement of the Chatham Islands. Construction of the Tongan trilithon, the Ha'amonga-a-Maui, in Tongatapu. Second settlement of Hawai'i.

1250 Tonga conquers Sāmoa, 'Uvea, Futuna, and Rotuma.

1300 Sāmoa chief Karika lands on Rarotonga (Cook Islands) and establishes chiefly line.

1350 Traditional fleet of canoes arrive in New Zealand from the Society Islands.

1400 Beginning of the classical period of ancient Polynesian culture.

1450 Tongan settlement of Wallis Island.

1470 Establishment of the Tui Ha'a Takalaua dynasty in Tonga.

1500 Salamasina rules as queen (Tupu'o Sāmoa) of Sāmoa.

1568 First European (Alvaro de Mendaña) sights Polynesia—the island of Nui in Tuvalu.

1595 Mendaña visits Marquesas, sights Pukapuka in the northern Cook Islands.

1610 Establishment of the Tui Kanokupolu dynasty in Tonga.

1616 W. C. Schouten and Jacques LeMaire visit Futuna and Tonga.

1680 Beginning of the late period of Easter Island monument building.

1722 Jacob Roggeveen sights Sāmoa and Easter Island.

1765 John Byron first sights Tokelau islands (Atafu).

1767 Samuel Wallis lands on Tahiti and Wallis islands. Philip Carteret lands on Pitcairn Island.

1769 Captain James Cook visits Tahiti.

1774 Cook visits Niue.

1778 Cook lands on and visits Hawai'i.

1779 Cook is killed in Hawai'i.

1787 Lapérouse loses crew in Sāmoa. First shipload of convicts sent to Australia.

1789 *Bounty* Mutiny occurs.

1797 London Missionary Society Protestant missionaries arrive in Tahiti, Tonga, and Marquesas.

1799 Civil War breaks out in Tahiti and Tonga.

1803 Pomare I of Tahiti dies.

1810 Kamehameha I of Hawai'i establishes domination over Hawai'i.

1815 Pomare II accepts Christianity; Russian intrusion into Hawai'i.

1819 Kamehameha I dies; Hawaiian *kapu* system abolished. De Peyster sights Tuvalu. Pomare Law Code promulgated.

1820 American Board of Commissioners for Foreign Missions Protestant missionaries arrive in Hawai'i. Thaddeus von Bellinghausen surveys Tuamotu islands.

1821 LMS Protestant missionaries in the Cook Islands.

1822 Wesleyan missionaries in Tonga.

1824 Kamehameha II visits England and dies there.

1826 Wesleyan missionaries arrive in Tonga.

1827 French Catholic missionaries arrive in Hawai'i.

1829 John Adams dies on Pitcairn.

1830 LMS Protestant missionaries arrive in Sāmoa; Malietoa Vai'inupo of Savai'i becomes king.

1834 French Catholic missionaries in Mangareva.

1836 Catholic missionaries land on Tahiti and are expelled. Commercial agreement between France and Hawai'i.

1837 Catholic Marist missionaries in Wallis and Futuna.

1838 U.S. (Wilkes) Expedition to Sāmoa (1838–42). New Zealand Company formed. Pitcairn constitution established (women given vote).

1839 U.S. Commercial Treaty with Sāmoa. Catholics recognized in Hawai'i.

1840 Kamehameha III establishes constitutional monarchy in Hawai'i. Treaty of Waitangi in New Zealand.

1841 Chief Malietoa Vai'inupo dies in Sāmoa; civil war ensues.

1842 France annexes the Marquesas and establishes protectorate over Tahiti, its dependencies, and over Wallis and Futuna.

1843 Captain George Paulet seizes Hawai'i, but annexation is revoked by British government. First Mormon missionaries to Pacific (French Polynesia).

1844 Pritchard Affair in Tahiti.

1845 Tāufa'hāu becomes King George I of Tonga. Land Wars begin in New Zealand.

1847 George Pritchard becomes first British consul in Sāmoa.

1848 Great Mahele (land division) in Hawai'i.

1850 First modern law code for Tonga.

1852 George I gains supremacy in Tonga.

1854 King Kamehameha III dies in Hawai'i.

1856 Godeffroy & Son commercial agency established in Āpia

1860 Peruvian blackbirders carry off Tuvaluans to work in mines and plantations.

1861 LMS Protestant missionaries arrive in Tuvalu from the Cook Islands. Protestantism introduced into Tokelau.

1862 Tongan law code established.

1863 King Kamehameha IV dies in Hawai'i. King Charles Te Moana of Nuku Hiva dies.

1864 Catholic Christianity introduced to Easter Island. William Stewart begins cotton plantation on Tahiti.

1865 First Chinese laborers arrive in Hawai'i.

1868 First Japanese laborers arrive in Hawai'i.

1870 LMS Protestant missionaries arrive in Tuvalu.

1872 United States signs treaty with Sāmoans regarding Pago Pago harbor. King Kamehameha IV dies in Hawai'i.

1873 Malietoa Laupepe recognized king of Sāmoa.

1874 King Lunalilo of Hawai'i dies.

1875 Tongan Constitution promulgated.

1876 Reciprocal trade treaty between Hawai'i and the United States. Niue assembly elects Matai Tuitogia as king.

1877 Queen Pomare IV of Tahiti dies.

1878 First Portuguese laborers arrive in Hawai'i.

1879 Britain establishes naval station in Sāmoa; Bismarck Agreement.

1880 France annexes Tahiti and dependencies; Teraupo'o Wai (1880–97) in French Polynesia. Shirley Baker becomes prime minister of Tonga.

1881 Lackawanna Agreement controlling affairs in Sāmoa.

1883 Kalākaua and Kapi'olani of Hawai'i crowned.

1885 Free Church of Tonga established.

1886 Kalākaua seeks Pacific confederation. Seventh-Day Adventists on Pitcairn.

1887 France announces formal protectorate over Wallis Island. Tataaiki selected king of Niue.

1888 Great Britain establishes protectorate over Cook Islands. Chile annexes Easter Island.

1889 Hurricane in Sāmoa (March); Britain, United States, and Germany sign Berlin Act providing for condominium rule of Sāmoa. British protectorate over Tokelau.

1890 Basil Thomson becomes prime minister of Tonga.

1891 Kalākaua dies, Lili'uokalani becomes queen of Hawai'i. John Ballance (Liberal Party) becomes prime minister of New Zealand.

1892 Gilbert and Ellice Islands (Tuvalu) become British protectorate.

1893 Revolution in Hawai'i, Sanford B. Dole becomes president of Hawaiian republic. George Tupou II becomes king of Tonga. Richard Seddon (Liberal Party) becomes prime minister of New Zealand.

1894 Republic established in Hawai'i.

1895 Queen Lavelua of Wallis Island dies.

1898 United States annexes Hawai'i, Dole becomes first governor.

1899 Anglo-German Agreement divides Sāmoa between Great Britain and the United States. Niue protectorate established by Great Britain. Robert Louis Stevenson settles in Western Sāmoa.

1900 New Zealand annexes the Cook Islands. France annexes the Austral Islands. Niue placed under New Zealand administration. Wilhelm Solf becomes governor of Western Sāmoa. Treaty of Friendship between Tonga and Great Britain.

1901 Britain gains control over Tonga's external affairs and annexes Cook Islands. Queen Elisabeth Vahekehu of Nuku Hiva dies.

1905 Reform Party established in New Zealand. Tongan-British treaty brings Tonga within British Empire.

1908 Mau revolt in Western Sāmoa; men deported to Mariana Islands.

1910 Labour Party formed in New Zealand.

1911 Queen Makea Takau of Cook Islands dies.

1913 Wallis and Futuna become French colonies.

1914 World War I begins. New Zealand seizes Western Sāmoa.

1916 Gilbert Islands, Ellice Islands, and Tokelau become British colonies.

1918 Influenza epidemic. Sālote becomes queen of Tonga.

1920 League of Nations mandate given to colonial powers for control of Pacific islands. Hawaiian Land Trust established.

1924 Union of Free Church of Tonga and the Wesleyan church.

1925 Administration of Tokelaus transferred to New Zealand.

1929 *Mau* uprising in Āpia, Western Sāmoa, against New Zealand administration.

1935 Michael Savage (Labour Party) becomes prime minister of New Zealand.

1940 Peter Fraser (Labour Party) becomes prime minister of New Zealand.

1941 Japan bombs Pearl Harbor in Hawai‘i; United States declares war.

1942 United States establishes military bases on Funafuti.

1945 End of World War II.

1946 Legislative Council formed in Cook Islands. Democratic Party (backed by labor) wins elections in Hawai‘i.

1947 Tahitians revolt for more say in government. Western Sāmoa prepares for independence. South Pacific Commission established.

1948 Tokelau Act gives full sovereignty of the islands to New Zealand.

1949 Sidney Holland (National Party) becomes prime minister of New Zealand.

1951 Administration of American Sāmoa transferred to the Department of the Interior.

1952 Easter Island granted local civilian government. ANZUS Pact signed.

1953 C. Larsen, resident commissioner on Niue, murdered. Social Credit Party of New Zealand formed.

1954 Father Pierre Chanel canonized.

1957 Western Sāmoan Amendment Act. Pouvana'a becomes vice president of French Polynesia. Walter Nash (Labour Party) becomes prime minister of New Zealand.

1958 Tāhō'ēra'a Huira'atira Party formed in French Polynesia.

1959 Hawai'i becomes 50th U.S. state. Wallis and Futuna become French territories. Matā'afa becomes prime minister of Western Sāmoa.

1960 Constitutions for both American and Western Sāmoa. Keith Holyoake (National Party) becomes prime minister of New Zealand.

1961 Wallis and Futuna become an overseas territory of France.

1962 Western Sāmoa becomes first Pacific island nation to become independent.

1963 First French nuclear tests on Moruroa atoll. Death of Tupua Tamasese Mae'ole, joint head of state of Western Sāmoa.

1964 Cook Islands constitution established.

1965 Cook Islands become independent; Albert Henry becomes first premier. Queen Sālote of Tonga dies; Tāufa'āhau Tupou IV becomes king.

1966 Niue Act establishes elections; Robert Rex becomes premier.

1967 Tuvalu's constitution established.

1968 University of the South Pacific established in Suva. National Women's Committee formed in Western Sāmoa.

1970 Tonga becomes independent. Tupua Tamasese Lealofi becomes prime minister in Sāmoa.

1971 South Pacific Forum organized.

1972 Matā'afa becomes prime minister of Western Sāmoa.

1974 Niue gains self-government.

1975 Gilbert and Ellice Islands separated; Ellice Islands become Tuvalu. Tamasese's second term as prime minister of Western Sāmoa. Robert Muldoon (National Party) becomes prime minister of New Zealand.

1976 Western Sāmoa joins the United Nations. Tonga establishes diplomatic relations with the Soviet Union. Tupuola Efi becomes prime minister of Western Sāmoa.

1977 French Polynesia gains internal autonomy; Francis Sanford becomes vice president. Tavina Huira'atira Party founded in French Polynesia. Ta'atira'a Polynesia Party formed in French Polynesia.

1978 Exclusive Economic Zone (EEZ) established. **3 January:** Peter Coleman becomes first Polynesian governor of American Sāmoa. **25 July:** Thomas Davis becomes prime minister of Cook Islands. **October:** Independence of Tuvalu; Toaripi Lauti becomes prime minister.

1979 **Feruary:** Tuvalu signs Treaty of Friendship with United States.

1980 **November:** Peter Coleman reelected governor of American Sāmoa.

1981 Dr. Tomasi Puapua elected prime minister of Tuvalu.

1982 **3 June:** Gaston Flosse becomes vice-president of French Polynesia. **13 April:** Va‘ai Kalone (Human Rights) becomes prime minister of Western Sāmoa, then Tupuola Efi (18 September), and then Tofilau Eti (31 December).

1983 Tourism Council of the South Pacific formed. **March:** Geoffrey Henry becomes prime minister of Cook Islands but resigns in August. **August:** Thomas Davis becomes prime minister of Cook Islands. New Zealand and United States ratify treaty regarding U.S. claims to Tokelau.

1984 French Polynesia gains internal autonomy. **January:** Sergio Rapu Haoa becomes Easter Island's first indigenous governor. **26 July:** David Lange (Labour Party) becomes prime minister of New Zealand. **14 September:** Flosse becomes president of French Polynesia. **November:** A. P. Lutali elected governor of American Sāmoa.

1985 Treaty of Rarotonga establishes nuclear free zones in Pacific nations. Puapua reelected prime minister of Tuvalu. Disintegration of ANZUS Pact. **July:** *Rainbow Warrior* blown up in Auckland harbor.

1986 Tonga signs a five-year fishing agreement with thc United States. **January:** Cook Islands declare themselves a neutral country. **April:** Flosse reelected president of French Polynesia. Civil unrest in Wallis and Futuna against French administrator. **November:** Tuvalu approves new constitution; John Waihe‘e elected governor of Hawai‘i.

1987 Université Française du Pacifique established in French Polynesia. Niue People's Party established. Dispute in Wallis and

Futuna over claims to throne of Sigave. **February:** Flosse resigns as president of French Polynesia, succeeded by Jacques Teuira. **June:** New Zealand Labour Party gains majority of seats in House. **July:** Dr. Pupuke Robati becomes prime minister of Cook Islands. **October:** Dock workers' strike in Tahiti. **9 December:** Alexandre Léontieff becomes President of French Polynesia.

1988 Aggie Grey dies in Western Sāmoa. Tofilau Eti elected prime minister of Western Sāmoa. Roger Dumec appointed French administrator of Wallis and Futuna. Tonga signs friendship treaty with the United States. Tongan Supreme Court upholds 'Aikilisi Pohiva's claim against the government for dismissing him as minister of education in 1985. **June:** New Zealand Labour Party gains majority of seats in House. **July:** Dr. Pupuke Robati becomes prime minister of Cook Islands. **November:** Peter Coleman elected governor of American Sāmoa.

1989 **January:** Geoffrey Henry becomes prime minister of Cook Islands. **March:** Manihiki Island threatens succession from Cook Islands. American Sāmoa announces severe financial deficit. French prime minister Rocard visits Wallis and Futuna to intervene between French administrator and local territorial assembly. **June:** Niue experiences severe food shortage, Rex's government receives no-confidence vote. **September:** Commoners in Tongan Legislative Assembly boycott meetings. **October:** Bikenibeu Paeniu becomes prime minister of Tuvalu and Naama Latasi becomes first woman member of Tuvaluan cabinet. Jacobo Hey becomes governor of Easter Island. Tonga announces plans for the establishment of a university. Henderson Island included in the U.N. "World Heritage List" as a bird sanctuary.

1990 **January:** Tokelau elects three *faipule* (atoll presidents)—Peniuto Semisi, Salesio Lui, and Kuresa Nasau. **February:** Cyclone Ofa rips through the South Pacific. **August:** Agreement between French Polynesia and Cook Islands regarding EEZ conflict. Robert Pommies appointed new French chief administrator of Wallis and Futuna. Rex reelected premier of Niue. New Zealand announces midyear that it planned to deport all illegal residents. **October:** James Bolger (National Party) becomes prime minister of New Zealand; Sāmoa grants vote to women. **November:** Daniel Akaka elected to replace U.S. Senator Spark Matsunaga who died in July.

1991 **March:** Mass demonstration against Tongan government's sale of passports to foreigners. **April:** Flosse becomes president of French Polynesia; massive demonstrations in Pape'ete against proposed taxes; Tofilau Eti Alesana elected prime minister of Western Sāmoa (fourth term). **May:** French prime minister Rocard visits New Zealand and apologizes for *Rainbow Warrior* bombing. American Sāmoa pressures U.S. Congress for social security insurance privileges. First female cabinet member selected (Fiame Naomi) in Western Sāmoa. **June:** New Zealand reduces aid payments to Niue; Tonga announces plans to build an oil refinery and power station by 1993. **October:** Cook Islands prime minister Geoffrey Henry visits France, signs treaty of cooperation, and negotiates loans for utility improvements. **December:** Hurricane Wasa hits French Polynesia and cyclone Ofa devastates the Sāmoas; dockworkers' strike cripples Tahiti and French Polynesia.

1992 **January:** Governor Waihe'e of Hawai'i elected chair of Democratic Governors' Association. **February:** Ruling New Zealand National Party loses popularity at polls but retains control of government. **March:** A. P. Lutali announces candidacy for governor of American Sāmoa against Peter Coleman. Ethnic Hawaiians and part Hawaiians push sovereignty issue at the approach of 1993 (100th anniversary of overthrow of monarchy). **April:** France announces moratorium on nuclear tests in the Pacific for the remainder of 1992; political and economic unrest plagues French Polynesia as a result; South Pacific Forum Fisheries Agency signs new 10-year treaty with United States **May:** Arson cripples Cook Islands' communications network. **June:** Six arrested. Western Sāmoa celebrates 30th anniversary of independence. **3 November:** Construction begins on the Royal Tongan International Airport Hotel. Lutali elected governor of American Sāmoa.

1993 **March:** Niueans elect Terry Coe, its first *palagi* (European), to its territorial assembly. **27 May:** A group of Nauruan women protest against the government's bad investments abroad by staging a sit-in on Nauru's airstrip. **July:** A taro blight devastates Sāmoa's staple food crop. **19–20 August:** The People's International Tribunal meets in Hawai'i and finds the U.S. government guilty on eight counts of wrongs to the Hawaiian people.

1994 **January:** The Republic of Nauru claims to have been swindled out of $1.2 million by an accountant in its Melbourne office. **March:** A three-week demonstration protests against Sāmoa's value-added goods and services tax. **24 May:** Cook Islanders reelect Sir Geoffrey Henry as prime minister in landslide election. **October:** Tonga's first political party, the Tonga Democratic Party, is formed. **7 October:** Nauru's chief accountant pleads guilty of fiscal malfeasance and agrees to make restitution of money stolen. **4 November:** Democratic Party candidates sweep the elections in American Sāmoa and Hawai'i.

1995 **20 June:** Volcanic eruptions under the Pacific form a new Tongan island. **5 September:** France detonates its first nuclear explosion in the current series. **6–7 September:** Antinuclear and pro-independence activists in Pape'ete, Tahiti, go on rampage, injuring 13, and resulting in damages of $27.6 million. **2 October:** The South Pacific Forum suspends France as a dialogue partner because of its continued nuclear testing in the Pacific. **3 November:** Queen Elizabeth signs New Zealand's Waikato Raupatu Claims Settlement Act. **22 November:** Lagumot Harris elected president of Nauru after defeating Bernard Dowiyogo. **17 December:** The Anglican diocese of Polynesia ordains its first indigenous female priest, Sereima Lomaloma. **19–26 December:** Tahitian Public

Services (TPS) employees in charge of garbage collection go on strike in Pape'ete.

1996 **29 January:** French President Jacques Chirac announces an end to France's nuclear testing in the Pacific. **31 January:** The French National Assembly votes to increase autonomy in French Polynesia. **23 February:** Frank Lui is reelected premier of Niue. **28 February:** New Zealand's National Party forms a coalition government with the United New Zealand Party. **21 March:** Sir Michael Hardie Boys becomes governor-general of New Zealand, replacing Dame Catherine Tizard. **22 March:** UNESCO formally declares Easter Island a Cultural Patrimony of Humanity. **25 March:** The United States, France, and Great Britain sign protocols to the South Pacific Nuclear Free Zone Treaty (Treaty of Rarotonga) in Fiji. **21 April:** Forty youths, called the Messengers of the Moai of Peace, besiege the Easter Island court and gain custody of their leader Mateo Tuki Atau. **12 May:** French Polynesia's anti-independence Tāhō'ēra'a Huira'atira party wins 22 of the 41 seats in the Territorial Assembly, and the pro-independence party wins 11. **17 May:** Tofilau Eti is reelected Sāmoan prime minister. **19 July:** A 20-foot tidal wave hits the southern coast of the Society Islands resulting in $11.6 million in damages. **5 September:** France is readmitted as a member of the South Pacific Forum. **19 September:** Tongan journalist and pro-democracy Member of Parliament Pohiva jailed for contempt. **4 October:** The New Zealand government settles with the South Island's Ngai Tau tribe for compensation in the amount of $NZ 170 million. **12 October:** New Zealand elections result in the National Party winning four seats, Labour 37, New Zealand First 17, and the Alliance 13. **7 November:** A no-confidence vote (9–7) in Nauru results in the resignation of President Lagumot Harris and the reinstallation of Bernard Dowiyogo. **30 November:** A severe fire on Easter Island destroys one *moai* and damages 46 others. **3 December:** A judge in Hawai'i upholds same-sex marriages.

1997 **7 February:** The South Pacific Commission celebrates its 50th anniversary. **20 February:** A statewide teachers' strike (first in 24 years) in Hawai'i is averted. **2 March:** The U.S. Navy announces a $500 million project to develop Ford Island (450 acres) at Pearl Harbor, Hawai'i. **6 March:** Western Sāmoa introduces legislation to drop "Western" from its name. **19–20 April:** Vandals spray hate messages on thousands of grave sites at the National Cemetery of the Pacific in Honolulu. **15 May:** Students and parents in Hawai'i demonstrate against the Bishop Estate trustees for mismanagement. **8 July:** Hawai'i law awards reciprocal health benefits to couples that cannot legally marry. **19 July:** The Australian government is embarrassed over insults to Pacific island nations and leaders in its AUSTEO briefing paper. **31 July:** Pacific leaders object to the *Pacific Teal* ship carrying 40 canisters of nuclear waste through Pacific waters from France to Japan. **9 August:** Prominent Hawai'i citizens urge the state to investigate actions of members of the Bishop Estate Trust and in September they call for their removal. **19 August:** Sāmoan chiefs march on Parliament to protest the sharp increase in prices and cost of living. **13–14 September:** Japan hosts its first Pacific Island nations summit in Tokyo. **12 October:** New Zealand elects members to Parliament under a new system of proportional representation. **20 October:** The South Pacific Commission approves changing its name to Secretariat of the Pacific Community. **30 October:** Five thousand demonstrators march through the streets of Āpia, Sāmoa, protesting the high cost of living and charging corruption in the government. **17 November:** Pitcairn islanders announce plans to build their first airport. **21 November:** The New Zealand government settles the historic Māori land claim. **12 December:** Hawai'i's H-3 freeway opens after 20 years of controversy—at a price tag of $1.3 billion. **20 December:** Hawai'i's supreme court announces that it will no longer appoint trustees to the Bishop Estate. **21 December:** The Sāmoan government announces the loss of 150 passports, presumably sold illegally by immigration authorities.

1998 **1 January:** French Polynesia introduces a value-added tax. **16 Januay:** Two thousand demonstrators march on Sāmoa's government house to protest allegations of government corruption. **14 February:** Political demonstrations in Pape'ete by 2,500 members of the pro-independence party. **8 March:** American Sāmoa Government employees are asked to take a 25 percent wage cut to reduce government debt. **5 May:** Tonga's Crown Prince Tupouto'a resigns ministerial posts to pursue business interest. **24 May:** Gaston Flosse's ruling party in French Polynesia wins 25 of the 41 seats in the territorial elections. **11 June:** The new Hawaiian convention center opens in Honolulu. **19 June:** Nauru elects Bernard Dowiyogo as prime minister for his fifth term. **22 June:** Angry villagers in Sāmoa kill hundreds of cattle and threaten a police station over a land dispute. **23 June:** France announces the dissolution of its Center for Atomic Energy. **8 July:** France officially closes its nuclear test site on Moruroa. **8 August:** Hawaiian groups begin a torchlight marathon around O'ahu to mark the 100th anniversary of the annexation of Hawai'i by the United States. **17 August:** Australia ratifies the South Pacific no nuclear dumping treaty. **18 September:** King of Tonga suspends Parliament to investigate speaker's mismanagement of government funds. **27 September:** Flosse elected senator from French Polynesia. **15 October:** King of Tonga appoints youngest son, Prince 'Ukukalala Lavaka Ata, as minister of foreign affairs. **17 October:** Sāmoan chiefs in Salamumu village torture five men and destroy their homes for practicing a different religion than Methodism. **21 October:** A French court finds Hirohiti Tefa'arere guilty of inciting the 1995 riots in Pape'ete. **2 November:** China opens diplomatic relations with Tonga and Cook Islands. **23 November:** Tofilau Eti Alesana resigns as Sāmoa's prime minister. **19 December:** Tonga ends its practice of selling passports to foreigners; the Vatican clarifies a ruling regarding the use of the hula during church service.

1999 **4 January:** A renovated airport is reopened at Ha‘apai, Tonga. **11 February:** A French task force (FATF) reports Russian organized crime (money laundering) observed in Sāmoa, Nauru, and the Cook Islands. **26 February:** Nauru announces a civil service reduction of 50 percent by 2001. **9 March:** European Union (EU) begins negotiations regarding free trade with Sāmoa, Tonga, and Tuvalu. **11 March:** Pro-democracy party in Tonga wins five of the nine commoners seats in Parliament. **19 March:** Niue Premier Frank Lui loses seat in elections and position in government. **26 March:** Sani Elia Lakatani elected premier of Niue. **13 April:** Prime Minister Bikenibeu Paeniu receives a no-confidence vote in Tuvalu. **27 April:** Ionatana Ionatana selected prime minister of Tuvalu; Nauru president Bernard Dowiyogo loses position after 10 years in office. **28 April:** Nauru Parliament elects René Harris as its new president. **27 May:** The French cabinet approves a draft bill to expand local autonomy for French Polynesia. **29 June:** Sir Geoffrey Henry returns as prime minister of Cook Islands. **16 July:** Sāmoan minister of works, Luagalau Levaula Kamu, assassinated. **29 July:** Cook Islands elect Dr. Joe Williams its new prime minister. **2–4 August:** First international conference on the Samoan language held in Pago Pago. **18 August:** Primary schools in Wallis and Futuna open after a seven-week strike. **19 August:** American Sāmoa recognizes English and Samoan as its two official languages. **13 August:** United Nations grants American Sāmoa an "observer seat" status. **12 September:** Division in the Evangelical Church in French Polynesia over the use of breadfruit and coconut water instead of bread and wine in the communion. **14 September:** Nauru and Tonga accepted as members of the United Nations. **16 September:** *Honolulu Star Bulletin* newspaper announces it will close publication after 117 years on 30 October. **5 October:** Pacific Islands Forum ratifies a free trade area for the Pacific to be effective within two years. **8 October:** Hubert Coppenrath consecrated as new archbishop of Polynesia. **10 October:** King of Tonga signs a bilateral trade agreement with China. **12 October:** French senate in Paris endorses constitutional amendment to grant French Polynesia status of "overseas country" and its own autonomy. **23 October:** Niue frees its four prisoners and closes its jail in celebration of 25 years of self-rule. **29 October:** Tourism Council of the South Pacific changes its name to South Pacific Tourism Organization. **2 November:** Pa Ariki is reelected president of Cook Islands' House of Ariki for her seventh term. **6 November:** First opera in the Tahitian language, *Ui no Fa'aoe* [*King of Fa'aoe*], opens at the Cultural Center in Pape'ete. **18 November:** Cook Islands Prime Minister Joe Williams resigns; Dr. Terepai Moate becomes new prime minister.

2000 **4 January:** King of Tonga appoints his youngest son, Prince 'Ulukalala Lavaka Ata, prime minister. **10 January:** French military forces begin withdrawing from French Polynesia after 37 years. **14 February:** Legislative bill introduced to change current *matai* (chiefly) succession law in American Sāmoa. **11 March:** Flosse resigns as mayor of Pirae, French Polynesia, after 37 years of uninterrupted service. **16 March:** Tonga signs a defense agreement with China. **4 April:** Don McKinnon, New Zealand's foreign minister, becomes secretary-general of the British Commonwealth Secretariat. **9 April:** French Polynesian women granted full salary during maternity leave. **12 April:** Harris reelected as president of Nauru but loses to Bernard Dowiyogo six days later. **17 April:** American Sāmoa Flag Day celebrates 100 years of U.S. administration. **June:** *Pacific Islands Monthly* magazine ceases publication after 70 years. **21 July:** Hawaiian rights bill introduced into the U.S. Congress. **3 August:** Rosalia Tisa Fa'amuli is first woman to enter the political race for governor of American Sāmoa. **16 August:** Easter Island holds a lottery to return 604 acres of land back to 280 of its residents. **17 August:** A judge rules that non-Hawaiians can be appointed to Hawaiian Affairs' positions. **24 August:** A U.S. federal report suggests native Hawaiians gain control over surplus Hawaiian lands and federal recognition of Hawai'i's indigenous people. **30 August:** Niue's premier Sani Lakatani installed as chancellor of the University of the South Pacific in Fiji. **1 September:** Tuvalu becomes a full member of the Commonwealth as well as the 189th member of the United Nations. **24 September:** Jeremy Harris reelected mayor of Honolulu. **26 September:** Native Hawaiian Bill passes the U.S. House of Representatives. **28 September:** Sāmoa's crackdown on money laundering results in $14 million seized. **16 October:** Niueans vote to retain their free association relationship with New Zealand. **30 October:** The South Pacific Forum changes its name to Pacific Islands Forum. **1 December:** Cook Islands government ratifies the Waigani Convention. **8 December:** Prime Minister Ionatana Ionatana dies in Tuvalu. **13 December:** The French senate in Paris approves the increase in the number of seats in French Polynesia's territorial assembly; the Native Hawaiian recognition bill dies in the U.S. Senate. **December:** Tisimasi Heafala appointed *kivalu*, the equivalent of prime minister, in Wallis and Futuna.

2001 **8 January:** French Polynesia establishes a news media agency, called the Agence Tahitienne de Presse, to report on news for overseas audiences. **18 January:** Five Pacific island countries—the Cook Islands, Nauru, Niue, Palau, and Vanuatu—warned about money laundering from the Organization for Economic Cooperation and Development (OECD). **24 January:** A New Zealand book alleges Tongan royal family involved in international drug smuggling and corruption. **30 January:** U.S. banking system slaps sanctions on Niue for alleged money laundering. **18 February:** American Sāmoan governor closes doors to large-scale immigrant labor workforce as a result of Daewoosa Sāmoa garment factory closure scandal. **23 February:** Faimalaga Luka named new prime minister of Tuvalu. **3–23 March:** Elections in Sāmoa returns the Human Rights Protection Paty (HRPP) to power. **5 April:** Chinese president Jiang Zemin pays an official visit to French Polynesia. **6 May:** Elections in French Polynesia return

Flosse and his party to power. **30 May:** Kurt Meyer, former New Zealand high commissioner to Niue, is appointed high commissioner to the Cook Islands. **29 June:** An appeals court in Paris clears French Polynesia President Gaston Flosse of earlier graft charges. **1 July:** Tonga announces that children born to Tongan woman married to foreigners will immediately be granted citizenship, reversing previous policy of recognizing only father's citizenship. **4 July:** King of Tonga unveils a Tongan–Japanese peace monument near the royal palace at Nuku'alofa, Tonga. **10 July:** Prime Minister Helen Clark predicts that New Zealand will inevitably become a republic. **20 July:** New Zealand announces it will accept Tuvaluans who are being forced from their island as a result of rising ocean waters. **29 July:** Cook Islands Deputy Prime Minister Norman George sacked after altercations between him and the prime minister. **26 July:** Marquesas islands express intentions to remain French should the rest of French Polynesia becomes independent. **31 July:** Wallis and Futuna celebrate 40 years as a French territory.

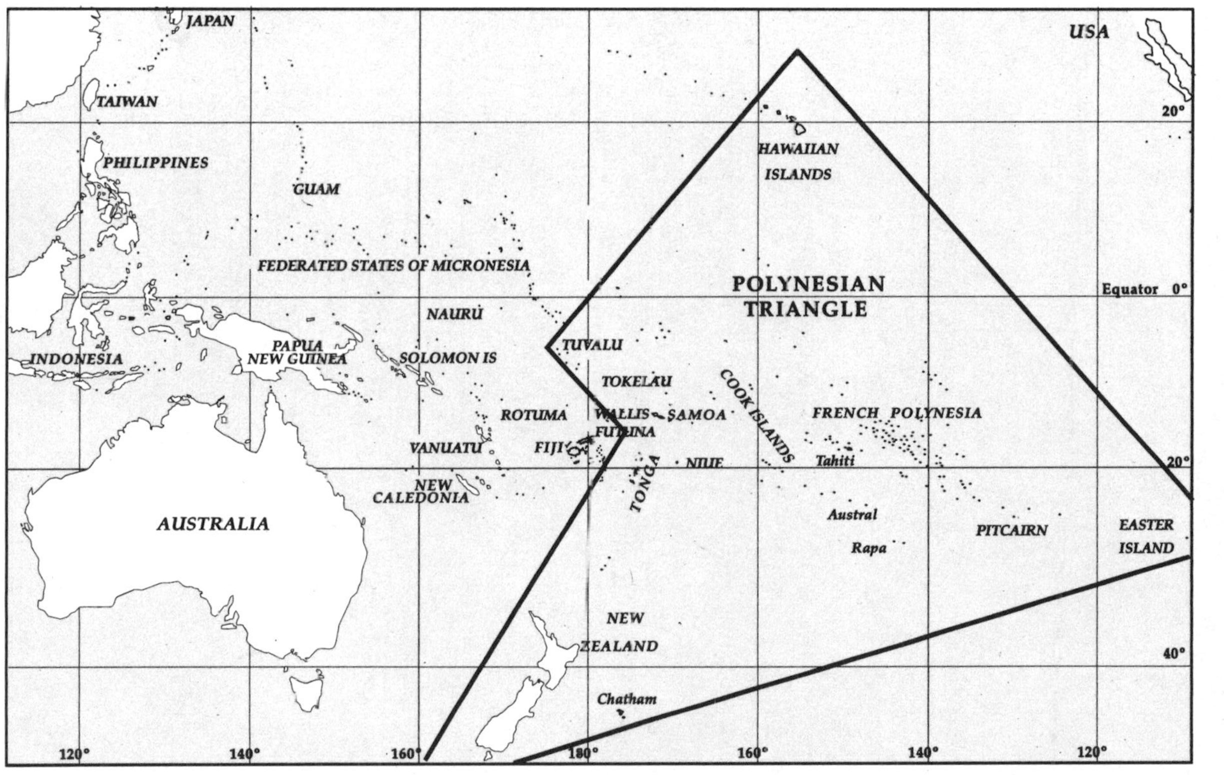
JAPAN
USA
TAIWAN
20°
HAWAIIAN
ISLANDS
PHILIPPINES
GUAM
FEDERATED STATES OF MICRONESIA
POLYNESIAN
TRIANGLE
Equator 0°
NAURU
PAPUA
NEW GUINEA
INDONESIA
SOLOMON IS
TUVALU
TOKELAU
COOK ISLANDS
ROTUMA
WALLIS
FUTUNA
SAMOA
FRENCH POLYNESIA
VANUATU
FIJI
TONGA
NIUE
Tahiti
20°
NEW
CALEDONIA
AUSTRALIA
Austral
PITCAIRN
EASTER
ISLAND
Rapa
NEW
ZEALAND
40°
Chatham
120°
140°
160°
180°
160°
140°
120°

INTRODUCTION

The term Polynesia refers to a cultural and geographical area in the Pacific Ocean, an area bounded by what is commonly referred to as the Polynesian Triangle—from Hawai'i in the north to New Zealand in the southwest to Easter Island in the southeast (refer to the frontispiece map). Thousands of islands are scattered throughout this area, most of which are currently included in one of the modern island states of American Sāmoa, Cook Islands, French Polynesia, Hawai'i, New Zealand, Sāmoa, Tonga, Tokelau, Tuvalu, and Wallis and Futuna. Some—Easter Island, Nauru, Niue, and Pitcairn, for example—still remain only isolated islands. With the exceptions of Hawai'i and New Zealand, all are inhabited by a majority population of Polynesian descent, a population that first began the settlement of these islands some three thousand years ago.

Pre-European History

It originated in southeast Asia when, about 3000 B.C., Mongoloid-type peoples began to expand into Melanesia (in the southwest Pacific) where they picked up certain physical characteristics—a tall, heavy build, for example—before moving further eastward into the Tongan and Sāmoan islands about 1200 B.C. Here in western Polynesia, they developed their unique social and cultural characteristics that would distinguish them from Micronesians and Melanesians, the two other major cultural groups in the Pacific basin. Pushing out in their large, double-hulled, ocean-going canoes, these ancient Polynesians sailed vast distances to reach the Marquesas Islands by the second century before Christ, and from the Marquesas they settled other islands in an area referred to as eastern Polynesia—Hawai'i, Cook Islands, Tuvalu, Tokelau, French Polynesia (Society Islands), Easter Island, and New Zealand. In some instances, islands were settled several times by new waves of immigrants from neighboring archipelagos. Their migration is regarded as one of the most daring navigational exploits in all of human history. By A.D. 1000, almost all of the islands and atolls within this triangle were inhabited, and for the next six hundred years, these island people developed, in relative isolation, complex political, social, religious, and cultural characteristics that formed a sophisticated and unique Neolithic society.

Having no written language, Polynesians passed down through generations of time their oral traditions, most of which have been lost with the exceptions of a few volumes recorded in the 19th century by European missionaries and scholars, or later by indigenous writers educated by Westerners. These stories provide tales of gods and heroes that rival any classical Greek and Roman mythology, but unfortunately, they provide less detail on the specific history of their own ancient society.

Throughout the pre-European period, never did any one island chief assume a position of dominance over an entire chain of islands, but in some cases (Hawai'i, for example) the process of assimilation of such power had begun by the time of European contact in the late 18th century. Numerous district chiefs and their retainers controlled their island society, a society consisting primarily of commoners who held little or no social, political, religious, or land tenure rights. The great high chiefs were frequently regarded as semidivine and were carried about on a dais so that their person would not touch objects belonging to subordinates. Otherwise, the property would become theirs. Commoners' daily life consisted of subsistence agriculture and fishing to provide for their daily needs and for the levies demanded by their social and religious superiors. Women made tapa clothing, wove mats, and pursued some types of agricultural operations befitting their sex. Intertribal warfare was frequent, and commoners avoided traveling outside their districts for fear of losing their lives. Leisure time activities in the evenings consisted of listening to learned storytellers, swimming, dancing, and playing various games. All in all, island life was generally hard and precarious, not the idyllic "noble-savage" stereotype that the 19th-century Europeans described in their romantic novels and journals. The basis of this society, however, collapsed almost immediately upon European contact. The introduction of an iron nail, for example, drastically changed the patterns of labor and the economic systems within the islands. By mid-19th century, writers in the more Western-influenced islands were complaining that the old order had pretty much disappeared.

European Exploration

Although the Spanish explorer Mendaña was the first European to sight a Polynesian island (1568), it was almost two hundred years before any other European visited these islands. By 1800, however, almost every major island within the area had been sighted and surveyed by the famous explorers William Shouten, Jacob LeMaire, Abel Tasman, Jacob Roggeveen, John Byron, Samuel Wallis, Louis-Antoine de Bougainville, James Cook, and Jean-François Lapérouse, to mention only a few. For two hundred years after 1500, Spain so dominated the Pacific that it was frequently referred to as "The Spanish Lake." But with the defeat of the Spanish Armada in 1588 and with the subsequent decline of Spain's importance in Europe, her domination of the Pacific collapsed as England and France began more extensive exploratory voyages south of the equator, an area of little concern to imperial Spain. Consequently, the Spanish language is unknown in Polynesia today (aside from Easter Island), whereas the languages of the new European powers—English and French—remain the two dominant languages spoken by bilingual Polynesians.

Western Immigrants

The European explorers actually spent relatively little time in the islands. They were there for scientific and ethnographic exploration, for establishing ports of call for subsequent voyages, and for the glory and prestige of their native homelands. It was not until the arrival of permanent settlers that a wholesale destruction and restructuring of island life began. Beachcombers provided some of the first permanent influences on island politics. Beginning in 1790, John Young and Isaac Davis were influential advisors to the rising power of chief Kamehameha in Hawai'i. Others exercised similar influence elsewhere—Will Mariner and George Vason in Tonga and Peter Hagerstein in Tahiti.

Protestant missionaries from London first arrived in the islands in 1797, and because they provided little of what the islanders desired from Westerners—arms, ammunition, tools, and technical knowledge—their process of conversion was extremely slow. In some instances, 15 to 20 years passed before any substantial progress was made. This progress came only as a result of the important high chiefs finally being convinced of the power and superiority of the Christian god, and it frequently involved civil war between district chiefs to enforce the conversion of others to the new religion. The ultimate result was, of course, that all of Polynesia became Christian and along with it came the destruction of not only the old gods and religions, but a whole lifestyle as well. Puritanical rulers outlawed dancing, nudity, prostitution, abortion, alcohol, adultery, murder, and the numerous other Christian "sins." Missionaries who had come to proselytize and convert were now summoned by the rulers to assist them in the establishment of a new order—Shirley Baker in Tonga, Hiram Bingham in Hawai'i, John Williams in the Cook Islands and Sāmoa, and George Pritchard in Tahiti and Sāmoa. Through this process, the Protestant missionaries set out to create a kingdom of God on earth among the "savages of the Pacific." They were eventually confronted, of course, not only by Catholic opposition, but by indigenous rulers, who wished to maintain their independence and control of their own island states, and by immigrant settlers, who, because of their economic interests, opposed the policies of both the rulers and their missionary advisers. These conflicts were usually resolved only through the intervention of foreign warships and the eventual seizure of the islands by England, Germany, France, and the United States.

Foreign settlement in the islands was piecemeal, except in New Zealand where there was a determined and planned effort at colonization. Children and grandchildren of missionary families remained in the various islands to establish themselves in commercial enterprises that were to dominate the island economy in the last half of the 19th century. The early sandalwood trade that flourished between 1800 and 1820 invited outside entrepreneurs to set up shop in the islands. They were the middlemen between the visiting ships and the local population. They exchanged island produce (taro and other root crops, fruit, vegetables, pork, fish, water, as well as female entertainment) for iron, textiles, arms, munitions, and building supplies and generally meddled in island politics. As whaling became a dominant feature of the island economy (1820–1850), these middlemen exercised a powerful influence over island politics—John C. Jones and Richard Charlton in Hawai'i, Jacques-Antoine Moerenhout in Tahiti, Theodor Weber and the Godeffroys in Sāmoa. Individuals such as these challenged authority and demanded changes in the law to afford them the right to own land and property in the islands. Land alienation had begun.

By mid-century, the Polynesian population in all of the islands had dwindled to less than half of what it had been earlier. It simply could not cope with Western diseases (measles, whooping cough, elephantiasis, tuberculosis, influenza, and venereal diseases) that swept the islands. Civil war with new forms of destructive weapons accounted for additional loses.

Accompanying the whaling boom in the 1840s and 1850s, came Western demand for coconut oil and sugar, both commodities easily obtained in the islands. Coconut palms were planted everywhere mid-century, and the production of copra in the 20th century still remains a major economic endeavor in the smaller islands. Sugar production became paramount primarily in Hawai'i where sufficient land was available and where substantial markets were close at hand (mainland United States). Both commercial endeavors caused social and political upheavals within the islands.

Westerners came to control the process from production to refining, and Asians were brought in to augment the dwindling Polynesian population that was unwilling to work according to Western standards. Chinese (1865), Japanese (1868), and Portuguese (1878) were imported to work in the sugar fields in Hawai'i, and by 1900, the indigenous Hawaiians made up only 20 percent of the total population. A similar situation occurred in New Zealand where a steady stream of immigrants from Australia after 1840 brought with them thousands of sheep that were to dominate the economy there. The discovery of gold attracted additional immigrants, and by 1900, the Māori population dwindled to less than 6 percent of the total population of the islands. The remaining Polynesian islands, however, retained their ethnic identity, and currently (2001), Polynesians are by far the largest majority within the island nations of American Sāmoa (90 percent), Cook Islands (81 percent),

Easter Island (60 percent), French Polynesia (77 percent), Sāmoa (90 percent), Tonga (90 percent), and Wallis and Futuna (97 percent).

Late Nineteenth-Century Imperialism

Accompanying the commercial exploitation of the islands in the late 19th century was the international competition of Western nations for aggrandizement of their empires. As a result, by about 1900 no Pacific island group remained independent. Long under the hungry eyes of Great Britain, France, and the United States, the independent kingdom of Hawai'i fell to a group of U.S. businessmen in 1893 who pressed for and gained U.S. annexation in 1898. A tripartite control of Sāmoa among Great Britain, Germany, and the United States (1887–1899) eventually left the islands splintered and divided between Germany and the United States. Britain, however, gained concessions elsewhere, as she pressed and established control over the Cook Islands (1888), Tokelau (1889), Tonga (1900–1905), Tuvalu (1892), Pitcairn (1898), and of course New Zealand (1840). France's expansion in Polynesia followed her Catholic missionaries, who caused disruption in the status quo of Protestant-dominated islands wherever they went. Subsequent squabbles between England and France led to international crises and decisions being made in the European capitals of Paris and London regarding the future political status of the island states. Consequently, France gained Tahiti (a protectorate in 1847, annexation in 1880) and her surrounding island groups—the other Society Islands (1880), the Marquesas (1880), the Tuamotus and Gambiers (1881), Wallis and Futuna (a protectorate in 1842, annexation in 1887), and the Australs (1900), all of which currently make up an area called French Polynesia.

Colonial Administration

Colonial administration of the islands by the imperial Western powers generally reflected that same policy (or lack thereof) which had originally led to empire consolidation. That policy depended both upon the attitudes of the metropolitan capital and the personalities of the resident administrators whom the home offices had appointed, and at no time did the imperial governments discuss the moral rightness of their gaining and controlling these islands and their people.

For the most part, Germany approached her Pacific empire with forthright intelligence and efficiency, and she was fortunate to have Wilhelm Solf as administrator in Sāmoa (1900–1910). Although Germany regarded the islands as an integral part of the German world, Solf respected local customs and set himself between the commercial interests of the settlers and the Sāmoans. When World War I broke out in 1914, however, Germany's control over her Polynesian empire collapsed. Supporting their mother country of Great Britain, New Zealand troops pushed in and seized the islands, and after the war, they were awarded to New Zealand by the League of Nations under a Class "C" mandate. They continued under New Zealand jurisdiction until their independence in 1962.

Britain, who eventually gained the largest Pacific empire (including vast territories in Melanesia), ruled the islands in somewhat of an ad hoc manner, but one that generally reflected a paternalistic and humanitarian style, a style that created enemies on all fronts. Most of the islands directly under British rule, however, were located in Melanesia—Fiji and New Guinea—and the only Polynesian island group that was directly involved with the British colonial office was Tonga. The other British possessions (Cook Islands, Niue, Tokelau, and Sāmoa) were placed under the jurisdiction of New Zealand who, surprisingly, became the largest empire holder in the South Pacific.

New Zealand immigrants from Great Britain had gained self-government in 1852, and during the last half of the 19th century, their government attempted a policy of assimilation and miscegenation in the hopes that the dwindling Māori population would be absorbed into the society. Laws were passed that provided for legal equality, and in general, the government mediated difficulties between the Māori and the British colonials. But dispossessed of their land and the loss of a Māori identity, tribes united between 1850 and 1880 to fight against their encroaching enemies. By century end, government legal equality had not brought with it social and economic equality, and the late 19th century saw the Māori groups attempting other more peaceful measures to assist in their struggle.

New Zealand's administration of her other island groups did not reflect the same policy as the Māoris at home. New Zealand military officers assigned to Sāmoa in the 1920s did not consider preparing the islands for eventual self-rule, nor did they understand the Sāmoans and their dislike of foreign administrators. As a result, organized opposition (the *Mau* movement) broke out between 1926 and 1936, and several individuals were killed in the confrontations. Although the Cook Islanders remained generally passive until World War II, they were likewise ruled by administrators who generally considered Cook Islanders as their wards.

U.S. policy, on the other hand, was pragmatic and unpretentious. Hawai'i was regarded as an outright possession or territory, one to be settled and developed similar to the other mainland territories that had eventually became legitimate states of the union. Neither France, Great Britain, nor Germany had similar policies regarding their Pacific possessions. American Sāmoa, on the other hand, was placed under administration of the U.S. Navy (1900–1951), and being so far from the U.S. mainland, it was left pretty much to itself until after World War II.

France's policy in her Polynesian possessions was one of benign neglect. Between 1882 and 1914, over 22 administrators were sent to govern Tahiti and the surrounding islands. Little change came about in the lives of the islanders, and few French found permanent emigration to the islands inviting. World War II, however, was to have far-reaching effects upon the islands and their governments. Because French Polynesians allied with the Free French movement of Charles de Gaulle, after the war they were granted French citizenship, local assemblies, and regarded as inhabiting overseas territories, all of which brought them into a closer relationship with metropolitan France than ever before.

Toward Independence and Self-Government

World War II brought all the islands into closer contact with the rest of the modern world both as a result of islanders serving their mother country in the front lines in Europe and as a result of U.S. GIs being stationed on the Pacific islands. After the war, worldwide anti-colonial sentiment brought pressures upon the metropolitan countries to grant self-government to their former colonies. The colonies themselves were no longer satisfied to remain under the tutelage of their imperial rulers. Sāmoans petitioned the United Nations for self-rule, and the Cook Islanders organized labor demonstrations against the New Zealand administration. As a result, Britain, New Zealand, and Australia adopted a policy of eventual self-determination for the islands. France, on the other hand, only reluctantly began discussions of granting some self-government to her Polynesian islands. Over the next two decades, negotiations, meetings, agreements, and concessions between the metropolitan governments and the islands eventually led to the independence or the gaining of internal autonomy of Sāmoa (1962), American Sāmoa (1965), Cook Islands (1965), Niue (1965), Tonga (protectorate lifted in 1970), French Polynesia (1977), Tokelau (1977), and Tuvalu (1978). Hawai'i became a legitimate U.S. state in 1959, and Wallis and Futuna became an overseas territory of France in 1961. Those Polynesian islands once within the British empire, however, wished to join The Commonwealth of Nations rather than become totally independent on their own primarily because of their minuscule size and the precarious nature of their economy.

Contemporary Polynesia

During the last four decades, these newly independent Polynesian states (except U.S. territories) have adopted parliamentary forms of government, but forms that have been adapted somewhat to their particular island's character. Subsequent changes in governments and constitutions have come about relatively orderly when compared to the turbulence experienced by many postcolonial entities elsewhere in the world. Politics and issues in the islands continue to be dominated by personalities, a traditional trait that has survived the two centuries of Western influence and one that creates lively campaigns and debates. Political parties are relatively new, and the allegiance to an institution or idea almost unknown. As a result, leaders frequently turn to their family or kinship groups for support, and consequently, allegations of nepotism and corruption frequently fill the columns in the local newspapers.

The governments continue to face serious economic and social problems. The islands are generally lacking in those natural resources to allow them to compete in the world economic system, yet their societies have come to expect an ever-increasing standard of living that they witness through the medium of television or the Internet. Imports far exceed exports, and all governments pursue foreign aid in one form or another. Economic independence did not accompany the political independence of the islands. On the contrary, the islands are as dependent upon their metropolitan powers as they were decades ago. Several of them are even listed by the United Nations as being among the poorest in the world, although it must be pointed out that their quality of life is much higher than one would find among other poorer nations.

Since World War II, the island states have united in numerous cooperative organizations to assist in solving their mutual problems. In 1947, for example, they created a South Pacific Commission (since 1998 called the Secretariat of the Pacific Community) whose purpose has been to offer advice and give assistance to member nations, and since then, other similar organizations have been formed. Finding themselves without sufficient economic resources, the new island governments realized that they alone could not support the programs that their countries needed—buildings, communication and transportation lines, schools and universities, and so forth—so they reluctantly accepted the continued membership of the colonial powers in the SPC. Consequently, the metropolitan countries continue to contribute substantial funds to the SPC's annual budget (Australia 33.3 percent, the United States 16.8 percent, New Zealand 16.1 percent, France 13.9 percent, and the United Kingdom 12.2 percent, and others 7.9 percent).

Rapid population expansion in the 1960s and 1970s created major problems for these land-poor islands. Since then, this expansion has been reduced significantly through family planning efforts and through emigration, primarily to New Zealand, Australia, Hawai'i, and the continental United States (in that order). It is estimated that more Cook Islanders and Niueans live in New Zealand and that more American Sāmoans live in Hawai'i and California than in their own homelands. The situation is similar throughout most of Polynesia. Remittances sent back by these emigrants to their families play a major role in the gross domestic income for the small island states, and most of them have come to rely upon these funds for a major part of their support. Emigration alleviated the population problem, but it also has created a brain drain from the islands. Polynesian students graduating from universities (usually abroad) frequently find no appropriate jobs for themselves when they return home, or they find that they are not accepted in a political system based on social and genealogical titles. As a result, they emigrate to an urban center (Auckland, Sydney, Honolulu, Los Angeles, or Pape‘ete) where they can find rewarding employment. Their home islands suffer further loss. The recent establishment of local universities in Tahiti and Sāmoa (with one planned in Tonga) may help alleviate some of this loss.

Land problems continue to plague all of the islands. The smaller islands and atolls lack arable land, and consequently most of their agriculture continues to be on a subsistence level without promise of much further development. New Zealand and Hawai‘i, on the other hand, have substantial land, but their problems center on claims to lands their indigenous peoples assert were confiscated from them over a hundred years ago. Māoris and Hawaiians are currently resorting to court battles to press these claims. Land problems are further aggravated by the traditional custom of collective land tenure that continues to exist in many of the islands. Families who own such land are reluctant to partition it or to sell it, and as a result, much of it lies idle and unproductive. Island governments will need to exercise whatever creative energies they can muster to settle their land problems expeditiously and fairly.

The ability of the Polynesian states to solve their particular problems rests in the character of their peoples. Long admired as being warm, amicable, and generous, they approach their mutual problems in a unique collegiality that has come to be called "The Pacific Way." Perhaps the islands' greatest contribution to world civilization may be the way in which they respect each other's culture and the way in which they cooperate and solve problems through nonconflictive discussion and consensus. The continued adherence to these traits and the pride they take in their traditional cultures will make them resistant to the undesirable forces that could so easily change their unique Polynesian way of life.

THE DICTIONARY

-A-

‘ĀI‘A ‘ĀPI (“New Nation or Nouveau Terre”). A political party in **French Polynesia**, headed by **Émile Vernaudon**, who has served as president of the territorial assembly since 1991 and who is the mayor of Mahina. Having split off from the Te ‘Ē‘a ‘Āpi Party in March 1982, it is a “centrist” party, represents the Polynesian element within the population, favors greater autonomy from **France**, and opposes the current government headed by **Gaston Flosse**, although it has aligned with Flosse’s party, the **Tāhō‘ēra‘a Huira‘atira**, in a coalition government since 1991. It gained seven of the 41 seats in the territorial assembly in the March 1991 elections and five seats in the 1996 elections. In the May 2001 elections, however, it received less than 5 percent of the votes and no seats in the assembly. Its loss is attributed to the rise of another pro-autonomy party, the **Fetia ‘Āpi**. *See also* TE ‘Ē‘A NO MĀ‘OHI NUI.

AIDS (Acquired Immunodeficiency Syndrome). A contemporary fatal disease that has become a major worldwide epidemic. AIDS is caused by the human immunodeficiency virus (HIV) that kills or impairs cells of the immune system and destroys the body’s ability to fight infections and certain cancers. Individuals diagnosed with AIDS are susceptible to life-threatening diseases called opportunistic infections, which are caused by microbes that usually do not cause illness in normal people. The first reported AIDS case in the Pacific was in 1985 (1981 in the United States). Since then there have been slightly over 2,000 cases, 84 percent of which come from the combined states of **New Zealand** (669) and Papua New Guinea (1,031), a Melanesian country. Of the 758 cases reported mid-2000 in Polynesia, 669 cases, or 88 percent, come from New Zealand and 74 (10 percent) from **French**

Polynesia. The only other Polynesian states to report AIDS cases are **Sāmoa** (6 cases), **Tonga** (8 cases), and **Wallis and Futuna** (1 case).

AKAKA, DANIEL KAHIKINA (1924–). First U.S. Senator of Polynesian (Hawaiian) ancestry and the only Chinese American member of Congress. Born in Honolulu, **Hawai'i**, on 11 September 1924, Akaka graduated from the Kamehameha School for Boys, served in the Pacific War during World War II, and for nearly 20 years had a successful career in education as a schoolteacher, principal, and state official. As a Democrat, he later served for 13 years in the U.S. House of Representatives (1976–1990) before being sworn in on 15 May 1990 to serve in the seat vacated by the late Senator Spark M. Matsunaga. His initiatives include protection of Hawai'i's fragile environment, prevention of drug abuse, promotion of diversified agriculture for the state, preservation of Hawai'i's sugar industry, and strengthening programs that help native Hawaiians (the Native Hawaiian Educational Act and the Hawaiians Health Act). In 1993, he assisted in pushing a joint resolution through the U.S. Congress that formally apologized to the Hawaiian people for the 1893 revolution that overthrew **Queen Lili'uokalani** from the throne, an act that led to the U.S. annexation of the Hawaiian islands. He also authored a bill that would allow indigenous Hawaiians the right to form a government. His popularity remains strong among his constituents. In the November 2000 elections, Akaka received 67.7 percent of the votes over his opponent, Republican John Carroll, who received 22.8 percent of the votes.

AKARURU, INATO (1937–). Deputy prime minister of the **Cook Islands**, Akaruru was born on 31 March 1937 on Pukapuka where he attended primary school. As a founding member of the Cook Islands Party, he was first elected to Parliament in the general elections of 1967 and has held numerous positions in the government ever since. He has served as deputy prime minister and minister of energy, foreign affairs, customs, immigration, inland revenue, and director of the Rarotonga Electricity Authority. He is married to Rebecca Akaruru and they have nine children.

ALESANA, TOFILAU ETI (1924–1999). Prime minister of **Sāmoa** (1982–1985 and 1988–1998), the longest serving head of state in the Pacific. Born on 4 June 1924 in the village of Vaitogi, **American Sāmoa**, of missionary parents, Alesana and family moved to Sāmoa in 1930. During World War II, he served in the U.S. Army; and in 1947, he moved to his mother's family in Savai'i (Sāmoa) where he gained the chiefly (*matai*) title Va'aelua. In 1957, he was elected as a member of the legislative assembly and a year later was appointed health minister. Alesana was a member of the constitutional committee that led to Sāmoa's independence (1962) from **New Zealand**. He was elected again to the legislative assembly in 1967, but failed to win election in the 1973–1975 assembly. In 1977, he won election again and served until his retirement in November of 1998. In 1979, he and Va'ai Kolone formed the **Human Rights Protection Party (HRPP)** at a time when there were no political parties in Sāmoa. As a member of the HRPP, he became prime minister between 1982 and 1985 and then again from 1988 until 1998. He is credited with major infrastructure developments in Sāmoa during his administration—introducing needed tax reforms (albeit sometimes unpopular), universal suffrage (before only chiefs could vote), and legislation to change the country's name to Sāmoa (previously Western Sāmoa). After a long illness, he died of cancer on 19 March 1999, leaving his wife Pitolua To'omata and 14 children.

ALEXANDER TURNBULL LIBRARY. A unit of the national library system in Wellington, **New Zealand**, primarily noted for its Pacific collection, which was originally donated to the state by John Horsburgh Turnbull upon his death in 1918. The library now houses over a quarter of a million volumes and thousands of maps, manuscripts, documents, paintings, and drawings.

ALOFI ISLAND. *See* WALLIS AND FUTUNA.

AMERICAN BOARD OF COMMISSIONERS FOR FOREIGN MISSIONS (ABCFM). A Congregationalist organization, formed in Boston, Massachusetts, that sponsored missionary activities throughout the world from 1820 to 1863. In the Pacific, its activities were primarily aimed first at **Hawai'i** and then Micronesia. Its organization resembled those established by other similar groups such as the **London Missionary Society** and the **Church Missionary So-**

ciety. Volunteers to the Pacific included not only ordained ministers, but physicians, teachers, carpenters, printers, farmers, and any other occupation that they felt might be needed to "civilize" the "heathen nations." ABCFM activities ended when the Congregational Christian and the Evangelical and Reformed Churches merged into the United Church of Christ, but it continued to function as the United Church of Christ, Board of World Ministries. *See also* ROMAN CATHOLIC CHURCH IN OCEANIA; MORMON CHURCH IN POLYNESIA.

AMERICAN SĀMOA. An unincorporated and unorganized territory of the **United States**, consisting of six islands in the Sāmoan group—Tutuila, Ta'ū, Olosega, Ofu, 'Aunu'u, and Rose—and **Swains Island**, a coral atoll lying 338 km (210 mi) northwest of Tutuila. The area of the islands is 194.8 sq km (76.1 sq mi) with a population of 65,446 (2000 census, an increase of about 39 percent since 1990). Over 90 percent of the population is of Polynesian descent speaking both the Sāmoan and English languages. Ninety percent of the people also live on Tutuila where Pago Pago is the chief administrative center. American Sāmoans are U.S. nationals who may apply for full citizenship after six months' residence in one of the 50 U.S. states. It is estimated that an additional 85,000 Sāmoans live in **Hawai'i** or on the U.S. mainland.

Flora, Fauna, Natural Resources: The volcanic islands are located in the southern tropics (14° south latitude, 169° to 171° west longitude) and thus have a wet and warm climate. Mount Piao averages 50 cm (200 in.) of rainfall a year and is commonly referred to as "The Rainmaker." The rich volcanic soil supports a lush vegetation of **taro**, **coconut palm**, and **breadfruit** on the coast and a rain forest further inland. The highest peak is mount Matafao, 703 m (2,303 ft), located on Tutuila.

Prehistory: Culturally and politically, these islands were anciently part of **Sāmoa**, their neighboring islands to the west. For their prehistory, see the entry on Sāmoa.

Modern History: The first European to visit these islands was Jacob Roggeveen in 1722; the French explorer **Bougainville** stopped on Ofu and Olosega briefly in 1768; and when Jean-François Lapérouse and his men anchored on Tutuila in 1787, a dozen of them were massacred by the islanders. By the turn of the century, however, the islands had become a haven for **beachcombers**, escaped convicts, and runaway sailors. **Great Britain** became the first active European country to intervene in island affairs.

In 1830, Tahitian missionaries were landed under the direction of the **London Missionary Society**, but it was only with the arrival of the Reverend Archibald Murray in 1836 that significant progress was made. Within a year of his arrival, most of the islanders had been converted to Protestant Christianity.

The first U.S. involvement in Sāmoa came as a result of the **Wilkes' Expedition** to the South Pacific (1838–1842). Among other things, Captain Charles Wilkes surveyed the magnificent harbor at Pago Pago and appointed a provisional American consul to Sāmoa before his departure. During the next 40 years, internal civil war raged among the Sāmoans over control of their ruling titles. At the same time, the growing interest in the strategic position of the islands by the Western powers of Great Britain, **Germany**, and the United States led to an international rivalry that eventually saw them divided between Germany and the United States. U.S. interest in the fine harbor of Pago Pago developed as a result of its expanding trade with Asia during the 1860s and 1870s. The harbor could provide an excellent refueling and refurbishing station for U.S. ships on their way across the Pacific.

On 4 February 1872, Commander Richard W. Meade of the USS *Narragansett* signed an agreement with High Chief Mauga that allowed the establishment of a naval station in Pago Pago harbor in return for U.S. protection of the Sāmoan people. The agreement essentially helped to discourage British and German interest in these islands. U.S. President Ulysses S. Grant appointed Colonel **Albert B. Steinberger** to investigate conditions in the islands. Steinberger overstepped his authority by establishing a new government in Sāmoa with himself as prime minister. Within a year (1875), he was ousted by both the British and American representatives in the islands.

The next several years saw the escalation of imperial competition for Sāmoa. Discussions on this subject were held at a Washington Conference in 1887, and a Berlin Act signed 14 June 1889 established a three-power condominium rule of Sāmoa. Finally, an Anglo-German Agreement between Great Britain and Germany on 14 November 1899 and a tripartite convention in December among the three powers settled the problem. By its terms, Germany received the islands lying west of 170° longitude (Sāmoa) and the United States received the islands lying east of the demarcation (American Sāmoa); in April 1900, a deed of cessation was signed by the United States and the Sāmoan chiefs. In April 2000, American Sāmoa celebrated its centennial anniversary as a U.S. territory.

Until 1951, administration of American Sāmoa fell under the jurisdiction of the U.S. Navy who left the internal governance of the islands to the discretion of the local chiefs and Sāmoan custom (*fa'a Sāmoa*). The two treaties of cession (1900 and 1904) were eventually approved by the U.S. Congress in 1929. Technically, American Sāmoa remains an unorganized and unincorporated territory of the United States, and there has never been a move by Congress to make Sāmoa a state of the union. (Sāmoan culture regarding land tenure and chiefly titles is incompatible with the U.S. constitution.) Neglect and the prohibition of land sales to non-Sāmoans have helped to preserve the traditional Sāmoan way of life, but that life has been drastically shaken since World War II.

In 1951, the administration of the islands was transferred to the Department of the Interior. A governor was appointed by the Interior, and a senate (elected only by chiefs, or *matai*) and a house of representatives were established. Because of international criticism of the islands' neglect in the early 1960s, congressional appropriations rose from a meager $1.3 million in 1959 to $13 million by 1963, and by the mid-1990s had grown to $33 million.

Governor H. Rex Lee's administration (1961–1967) saw the establishment of a new airport, roads, schools, a luxury hotel in Pago Pago, a fisheries cannery, new harbor facilities, an impressive educational television system, and numerous other innovations. **Tourism** boomed. All of this increased the acceptance of Western ideas and institutions, lifestyles, and way of living. Many emigrated to Hawai'i or to California or joined the armed forces, and as a result, over 65,000 American Sāmoans live on the U.S. west coast and over 20,000 in Hawai'i.

A constitution, promulgated in 1960 and revised six years later, provides the legal basis for Sāmoa's government. A Future Political Status Study Commission, created by the assembly in 1969, recommended that no change be made in American Sāmoa's relationship with the United States. It did recommend the popular election of its own governor, popular election of its senators, and representation in the U.S. Congress by a delegate-at-large. Plebiscites regarding the election of its own governor, held three consecutive years between 1972 and 1975, however, rejected the notion, primarily because of suspicion among the Sāmoans that one chiefly family might obtain the appearance of a paramount chief—a situation that in the 19th century had produced incessant wars. Declining economic conditions and dissatisfaction with Governor John M. Haydon, however, promoted a reversal of the vote by 1976. **Peter Tali Coleman**, a highly respected Sāmoan government official, became its first elected governor, a position he held from 1978 to 1984 and then again from 1988 to his defeat in November 1992. (The Sāmoan constitution prohibits three consecutive terms as governor.)

In the 1984 elections, **A. P. Lutali** became American Sāmoa's new governor with Eni Hunkin as his lieutenant governor. Lutali's administration was characterized by a move toward revitalizing the economy's private sector, opposing nuclear testing in the Pacific, cleaning up the islands, establishing additional tourist sites, developing a youth fitness program, and looking more toward the Pacific than to Washington.

Lutali lost the 1988 governor's election to the ever-popular Peter Coleman, and **Eni Hunkin Faleomavaega** won in a run-off election for American Sāmoa's delegate to the U.S. House of Representatives. (In October 1988, the previous delegate, Fofō Sunia, had been found guilty in a U.S. court for mismanaging his office payroll and was sentenced to five to 15 months in prison for fraud.) Faleomavaega has introduced legislation in the U.S. House of Representatives to create a federal commission to examine the territory's political status, and he has charged the federal government to clean up Pago Pago Harbor of the toxic lead released from ships sunk 30 years ago in the harbor. In the November 1992 elections, Lutali defeated Coleman, receiving 53 percent of the votes, while Faleomavaega retained his congressional seat, receiving 65 percent of the votes. Lutali's lieutenant governor, **Tauese P. Sunia**, a Democrat, successfully ran for governor in 1996 and in 2000, although the results in 2000 were close enough to be contested by his opponent Peter Reid.

Both Lutali's and Sunia's administrations were plagued with financial problems that still remain unsolved. Annual deficits during the past decade have sometimes dismayed U.S. federal agencies which often had to absorb some of the fiscal shortfalls. In 1990 the total deficit was $17 million and by 1998 had grown to over $55 million. A U.S. commission in 1995 investigated allegations of corruption and fraudulent use of public funds, and its report was critical of the American Sāmoan government (ASG). American Sāmoa's financial problems can be attributed to the public's ever-growing demand for governmental services, American Sāmoa's limited economic resources and tax base, frequent natural disasters—droughts and hurricanes, for example—the islands remote location from the U.S. mainland, and unpaid taxes by individuals and businesses alike. The government often proposes increasing taxes—a sales tax (rejected in 1986 and 1999), import taxes, and tobacco and alcohol taxes (as it did in 1998)—but they are usually unpopular. (American Sāmoans pay an average of 2 percent taxes whereas mainland U.S. citizens pay about 35 percent.) The government also initiated a 25 percent pay cut among government workers in 1998 for four weeks. That savings netted nearly $500,000. The government's annual operating budget has grown from $113 million in 1990 to nearly $200 million in 2001. The U.S. federal government's grant-in-aid averages approximately $33 million a year. In 1998, the federal government created a Financial Advisory Commission, whose chair is former governor John Waihe'e of Hawai'i, to help the islands reduce their deficit and to become more self-sufficient.

Financial relief came in 1999 when the Master Tobacco Plan settlement awarded American Sāmoa $29 million over 25 years. The ASG negotiated with the U.S. government for immediate payment of $18 million in exchange for its relinquishment of claim to the rest. In 1999, Governor Sunia maintained that his three-year term had substantially held down government costs and reduced debt, but still in 2000 a congressional committee threatened to reduce funding if ASG did not implement financial reforms by 2001.

In 1999 and 2000, heated debates regarding gambling and illegal overspending by the legislature's jubilee committee took center stage. A controversial gambling bill, that would have allowed casinos, passed the senate in January 1999 by 13 to 2, but was unanimously defeated in the house on 16 March 2000. Poker machines received the same fate after the high court declared them illegal. In January 1999, the senate began investigations into the legislature's overspent budget ($500,000) for its jubilee celebration in 1998. The yearlong investigation led to numerous accusations and rebuttals, and to the firing of the main financial officers and the suspension of numerous employees over the issue. As a result, a house investigation committee (HIC) was formed for the purpose of reviewing government operations and its financial institutions. The HIC was closed on 11 January 2001.

In April 2000, American Sāmoa observed its 100th anniversary of being a U.S. territory. A weeklong celebration in Pago Pago with parades, traditional songs and dances, and political speeches was attended by dignitaries from many Pacific island states including the king of **Tonga**, the prime ministers of Sāmoa and **Tuvalu**, the governors of Guam and the Northern Marianna Islands, as well as numerous dignitaries from the U.S. federal government and military.

Government: American Sāmoa's 1967 constitution provides for an elected governor who has executive power for all operations within the territory of American Sāmoa and who has veto power over the legislature (*fono*) which consists of the senate and a house of representatives. The 18 members of the male-dominated senate are elected by local chiefs (*matai*) for a term of four years. The 20 members of the house of representatives are elected by popular vote every two years. The *fono* meets twice a year to discuss and pass legislation.

The judicial system consists of the high court presided over by a chief justice, currently **Michael Kruse**, the first ethnic Sāmoan ever to be appointed to the high court of American Sāmoa. The lands and title division hears cases involving land or *matai* titles, both of which are ruled by Sāmoan rather than U.S. law. American Sāmoa sends one nonvoting delegate to the U.S. House of Representatives who is popularly elected every two years.

Many indigenous traditions (*fa'a Sāmoa*) continue in the islands. Especially important is the concept of '*aiga* (extended family). Each '*aiga* is headed by a *matai* who exercises almost complete control over the life of the village, including land. Ninety percent of the land is communal and cannot be sold, only leased under certain circumstances. This collective rather than individual way of thinking dominates many facets of the island's society.

Economy: American Sāmoa's economy is strongly tied to that of the United States, and a substantial part of the government's 2001 operating budget ($33.1 million out of a total of $198.8 million) comes from a grant-in-aid from the Department of the Interior, the islands' biggest employer (48 percent of the workforce). Tuna canning is the second highest employer (33 percent of the workforce), but most of the workers in the two factories (COS Sāmoa and StarKist) come from neighboring **Sāmoa**. In 1999, tuna exports, which accounts for approximately 90 percent of all exports, amounted to $400 million. The annual per capita income is only $3,039, and the minimum wage has just been increased from $2.50 to $3.97. An unemployment rate of 16 percent in the mid-1990s has been reduced to approximately 10 percent. Tourism, a vital economic part of other Polynesian countries, is practically lacking in American Sāmoa. The great distance from the mainland United States and the island's lack of sufficient tourist infrastructure, such as hotels, tour agencies, and so forth, prevent it from being a major tourist attraction.

ANGLO-GERMAN AGREEMENT OF 1899. A settlement between **Great Britain** and **Germany** regarding the disposition of the Sāmoan Islands. A **Berlin Act**, 14 June 1889, had failed to bring a resolution to the problem of internal civil war in Sāmoa and the rivalry among the three great powers over control of the islands. Negotiations carried out during the last quarter of 1899 involved Joseph Chamberlain (representing the British) and Count Hatzfeldt, the German ambassador. Britain relinquished her rights in Sāmoa for recognition of her position in **Tonga** and the Solomon Islands. The agreement was officially signed on 14 November, and a subsequent conference held in December allowed German control over the western islands (Savai'i and 'Upolu) and U.S. control over the eastern islands (the Manu'a group and Tutuila). By 1900, the two powers had officially annexed the islands to their respective governments. *See also* AMERICAN SĀMOA; SAMOA; WEBER, THEODOR.)

ANZAC DAY (Australian and New Zealand Army Corps Day). A national holiday celebrated on 25 April each year in both countries to commemorate the landing of **Australian** and **New Zealand** soldiers at Gallipoli during World War I.

ANZUS PACT. A tripartite security treaty ratified by **Australia, New Zealand**, and the **United States** on 29 April 1952, to coordinate defense in the Pacific region. The treaty stipulates that the parties will "consult together whenever in the opinion of any of them the territorial integrity, political independence or security of any of the parties is threatened in the Pacific" (Article 3). Until the 1980s, meetings were held annually and rotated among the three capitals to discuss mutual security issues, and the alliance appeared to work fairly harmoniously.

In 1985, however, a crisis occurred as a result of the **New Zealand Labour Party's** ban on nuclear-powered or nuclear-carrying ships visiting her ports—the New Zealand Nuclear Free Zone. In 1986, the United States claimed that this rendered the ANZUS treaty inoperable and took unilateral actions to reduce its defense relations with New Zealand. Relations since have been strained while New Zealand has proposed new defense strategies to make her more reliant upon Australia and other South Pacific countries.

As late as January 1992, U.S. President George H. Bush reiterated the importance of the pact to the United States, however, no substantial headway was made in its resurrection. More recently, however, Prime Minister **Jim Bolger** agreed to lift the ban on nuclear-powered vessels while continuing the ban on nuclear arms. *See also* NUCLEAR FREE ZONE TREATY.

AOTEAROA. The **Māori** name for **New Zealand** meaning "Land of the Long White Cloud," a name given to these islands by Hine-te-aparangi, wife of the famous Polynesian explorer Kupe who first visited the islands about A.D. 925.

ARI'I TA'IMA'I, PRINCESS (1821–1897). A high-ranking Tahitian chiefess whose *Memoirs* by U.S. historian Henry Adams were published in 1901. Her memoirs shed light on 19th-century Tahitian history and the **Pomare** royal family. She married Alexander Salmon, and their daughter, **Marau**, married the heir apparent Teri'i Tari'a (1839–1880) who became King Pomare V in 1877. The monarchy ended when the French annexed the islands in 1880, and Princess Ari'i Ta'ima'i continued to live in Pape'ete until her death in 1897. *See also* FRENCH POLYNESIA.

ARIKI. A **Māori** term to indicate the hereditary paramount chiefs in **New Zealand** and the **Cook Islands**. In **Hawai'i**, the term is *ali'i* and in **Tahiti**, *aliki*.

ARIKI, PA UPOKOTINI (MARIE) (1947–). President of the House of Ariki (a forum of paramount chiefs in the **Cook Islands**, an annually elected position she has held since 1994. Born in September 1947, she received her education at the Ngatangia School and Tereora College (Rarotonga), and the Newton Central School in Auckland, **New Zealand**. She assumed the position of Pa Ariki upon the death of her mother Pa Tapaeru (the highest ranking traditional leader in the Cook Islands) in 1990. She is the Takitumu paramount chief or "queen," and she has been active in community and state affairs throughout her life. She is the mother of Noeline Teaurima, Princess Salamasina, and Prince Samuela Napa. *See also* DAVIS, PA TEPAERU ARIKI.

ARIYOSHI, GEORGE RIYOICHI (1926–). Elected governor of the state of **Hawai'i** from 1974 to 1986, the first person of Asian ancestry to be elected governor in the **United States**. Born on 12 March 1926, in Honolulu, Ariyoshi attended McKinley High School, Michigan State University (BA 1949), and the University of Michigan Law School (JD 1952). While practicing law in Honolulu, Ariyoshi was elected a member of the Hawai'i House of Representatives (1954–1958) before Hawai'i became a state of the United States. After statehood, Ariyoshi served as state senator (1959–1970) and then as lieutenant governor (1970–1973) under **John A. Burns**. He became governor of the state for three terms (1974–1986), and he never lost an election in the three decades he was in politics. Problems Ariyoshi had to face as new governor were a fragmented Democratic Party, land and housing shortages, and public health issues. In the 1990s, Ariyoshi became president of the Prince Resorts Hawai'i and 'Aina Kamali'i, the holding company that is part of the Seibu Group in **Japan**. He also served as chairman of the board of governors for the **East-West Center**.

ASIA FOUNDATION. A private U.S. grant making organization that provides assistance to over 30 Asian and Pacific island nations in strengthening representative government, effective legal systems, human rights, market economies, and independent and responsible media. During 1990–1992, the foundation supported activities in the Polynesian states of the **Cook Islands**, **Nauru**, **Tonga**, **Tuvalu**, and **Sāmoa** at a cost of $505,683. Its total budget for all programs for 1990–1991 was $35 million. By the end of the 1990s, however, the foundation downsized its aid to Pacific island nations. In 1997, for example, it spent a grand total of only $156,884 (less than 1 percent) in the Cook Islands for a national disaster program. Its address is 46 California Street, San Francisco, California, 94104, and its **Internet** address is http://www.asiafoundation.org/.

ASIAN DEVELOPMENT BANK (ADB). A regional bank established in December 1966 by the **United Nations** to reduce poverty by providing economic assistance in the region in the form of loans to its 31 (now 59) **Economic and Social Commission for Asia and the Pacific** (ESCAP) member nations. Its related objectives are to foster economic growth, to support human development, to improve the status of **women**, and to protect the environment. Included in its member nations are the Polynesian states of the **Cook Islands**, **New Zealand**, **Tonga**, **Sāmoa**, and **Tuvalu** A special Asian Development Fund (ADF) was established in 1974 to provide assistance to the least-developed member countries. By 1999, the bank has lent some $77.3 billion to the various Asian and Pacific island countries (Cook Islands $24.5 million, **Nauru** $2.3 million, Tonga $47.8 million, Sāmoa $97.4 million, and Tuvalu $4.6 million). Approximately 60 percent of the bank's capital is provided by 15 developed countries outside the region—in Western Europe, the **United States**, and Canada—and by member nations of **Japan**, **Australia**, and **New Zealand**. The ADB headquarters is located in Manila, although "resident mission" offices will soon be established in 13 Asian countries and a "regional mission" in the South Pacific. Its **Internet** site is http://www.adb.og.

ASSOCIATION FOR SOCIAL ANTHROPOLOGY IN OCEANIA (ASAO). An international organization dedicated to comparative studies of the Pacific. It holds annual meetings (usually in February) with a special format designed to facilitate discussion and development topics for publication. It sponsors publications (monograph series and a special publication series), and its members are active in an electric bulletin board (ASAO) hosted by the University of Illinois at Chicago. Details on the association and how to join its bulletin board can be found on the **Internet** at http://www.soc.hawaii.edu/asao/pacific/hawaiki.html.

ASSOCIATION OF SOUTH PACIFIC AIRLINES (ASPA). An airlines established in 1979 by the **South Pacific Bureau for Economic Cooperation (SPEC)** that provides cooperation among the 17 member airlines for aviation development within the region.

ATA, ʻULUKALALA LAVAKA (1959–). Prime minister of **Tonga** since 3 January 2000, and the youngest son of **King Tāufaʻāhau Tupou IV** and Queen Halaevalu Mataʻaho. Born 12 July 1959, Crown Prince Lavaka received a master's degree in defense studies from the University of New South Wales and a master's degree in international relations from the University of Bond (1998). He was commander of Tonga's navy and defense services (1991–1995). He entered Parliament as a minister of foreign affairs and defense (October 1998) taking over Crown Prince Tupoutoʻa's responsibilities. According to tradition, the appointment as prime minister by the king will be for life. As prime minister, he also holds the portfolios of marine, fisheries, agriculture, and forestry. The new prime minister maintains similar views as his father regarding the fledgling democratic movement within Tonga.

'ATENISI INSTITUTE. A unique, private, and independent institute in **Tonga** comprising a high school, performing arts foundation, and a university. Founded in 1965 by Dr. 'I. Futu Helu, the institute bases its core curriculum on classical and traditional subjects—philosophy, logic, art, and literature—and declares that "knowledge can effectively be put to better use if theory precedes practice and not vice versa." 'Atenisi is the Tongan word for Athens, the ancient center of classical learning in Greece. The university awards associate and bachelor's degrees, and in 1991 limited postgraduate studies were introduced leading to the master's and doctorate degrees. In the mid-1970s, the institute enrolled approximately 1,300 students. The current enrollment is about 500. An elaborate graduation program, held in late November, includes traditional Tongan dancing, feasting, and gift giving. Its Website is located at: http://www.kalianet.to/atenisi/index.html.

ATOLL. Defined as a ring of coral islands or islets encircling a lagoon which has free access to the open sea. Technically atolls are not islands although many of them (Wake, Midway, and Johnston, for example) have erroneously been called islands in the past. (See Appendix A for a listing of the islands and atolls in **Polynesia**.)

AUSTEO REPORT ("Australian Eyes Only" Report). A 93-page confidential document accidentally left lying on a table at the July 1997 South Pacific Forum Economic Minister's Meeting, held in Cairns, **Australia**, that contained disparaging remarks on island governments and their leaders. The document was picked up by two journalists and its contents published in various media all of which caused great embarrassment to the Australian government. The document inferred that the Pacific island states were tropical "basket cases," and several leaders were called crooks and incompetents. *Time* magazine listed it as one of the top 10 scandals of 1997. Although the Australian government launched an investigation into the matter, it never issued a formal apology to any of the island leaders.

AUSTRAL ISLANDS. One of the five major island groups belonging to **French Polynesia**. This group consists of five inhabited islands and several uninhabited islands lying in a chain 1200 km (800 mi) long and 640 km (375 mi) south of **Tahiti**—Tubuai, Rurutu, Raivavae,

Rapa, Rimatara, Maria, and Marotiri (Bass Island). The total population numbers 6,563 (1996 census), representing 3 percent of the population of French Polynesia, on a landmass of 164 sq km (63 sq mi). Most of the islands are fertile and grow tropical **coconuts**, **breadfruit**, oranges, bananas, **taro**, coffee, and vanilla, which make their way to the markets in Pape'ete, Tahiti. The Austral Islands send two deputies to represent them in the autonomous territorial assembly in Pape'ete.

AUSTRALIA. A South Pacific nation (non-Polynesian) that contributes substantially to the development of its neighboring island states primarily through its **Australian International Development Assistance Bureau**. Australia and **New Zealand** both provided leadership in the formation of the earliest South Pacific regional organizations—the South Pacific Health Services in 1946 and the South Pacific Commission, now called the **Pacific Community**, in 1947, for example. Interested in providing defense security to the area after World War II, Australia, New Zealand, and the **United States** signed the **ANZUS treaty** of 1952. In fiscal year 1999, Australia contributed $84.7 million in assistance to the South Pacific region (not including Papua New Guinea) compared to $52.5 million from New Zealand and to $12.4 million from the United States. Australia's aid in 1999 included $1.1 million to the **Cook Islands**, $580,000 to **Nauru**, $580,000 to **Niue** and **Tokelau**, $7.16 million to **Sāmoa**, $6.45 to **Tonga**, $1.6 million to **Tuvalu**, and $1.16 to French territories. *See also* AUSTRALIAN AGENCY FOR INTERNATIONAL DEVELOPMENT.

For further details on Australia, refer to James C. Docherty's *1999 Historical Dictionary of Australia* (second edition), published by Scarecrow Press.

AUSTRALIAN AGENCY FOR INTERNATIONAL DEVELOPMENT (AusAID). An administratively autonomous agency within the Foreign Affairs and Trade Portfolio of the Australian government responsible for the management of the official government overseas aid program. Its central office is located in Canberra with state offices in Sydney, Brisbane, Melbourne, Adelaide, and Perth. Its objective is to assist developing countries to reduce poverty and achieve sustainable development. Its total aid budget for 1998–1999 was $955 million, out of which $84.7 million was budgeted for the Pacific island states (excluding Papua New Guinea). Further information can be found at its Website at http://www.ausaid.gov.au. *See also* AUSTRALIA.

AUSTRALIAN INTERNATIONAL DEVELOPMENT ASSISTANCE BUREAU (AIDAB). Renamed the **Australian Agency for International Development** in 1995.

- B -

BAKER, SHIRLEY WALDEMAR (1836–1903). A Methodist minister who became **Tonga's** first prime minister (1880–1885) under **King George Tupou I**. Born in London in 1836, Baker emigrated to **Australia** in 1850 where he embraced Methodism and felt called to become a missionary. He was sent to Tonga in 1860 where he formed a friendship with the king who requested him to assist in the modernization of his kingdom.

Among other achievements, Baker designed Tonga's flag, wrote its 1875 constitution, balanced its budget, and created the Free Church of Tonga. He essentially paved the way for Tonga to be recognized by other powers as a "civilized" nation and to free Tonga from imperial powers that threatened the island nations in the 19th century. In doing so, Baker made numerous enemies, and he was blamed for much of the violence that accompanied his reforms. He was dismissed in 1890 by the king who was under pressure by the British and by Baker's enemies. Although deported in 1890, Baker returned to Tonga but was never able to regain his status and fortune. He died of a heart attack in November 1903.

BARET, JEANNE (1744–1788). The first woman to circumnavigate the world (1767–1773). She hired on as a "male valet" aboard a ship captained by the famous French navigator **Louis-Antoine de Bougainville**. It was not until the ship arrived in **Tahiti** that her sexual identity was detected. She later spent time in Madagascar assisting the researcher Philibert Commerson in his botanical work and then returned to her home in France. *See also* FRENCH POLYNESIA.

BATAILLON, PIERRE-MARIE (1810–1877). The first Roman Catholic bishop of central Oceania. In December 1836, a group of Marist (Society of Mary) missionaries left **France** for the conversion of the people of the western Pacific. In 1837, Bataillon and Brother Joseph Luzy landed on Wallis Island where by 1842 they had converted the entire population. Bataillon was appointed Bishop of Central Oceania (New Caledonia, New Hebrides, Fiji, **Tonga**, **Sāmoa**, **Tokelau**, **Wallis and Futuna**), and he opened the first seminary in Oceania to train native clergy. He died on Wallis Island on 10 April 1877. *See also* ROMAN CATHOLIC CHURCH IN OCEANIA; WALLIS AND FUTUNA.

BEACHCOMBER. A person of non-Oceanic origin who settled in the Pacific islands prior to any other organized, intensive colonization in the late 18th and early 19th centuries. **Polynesia** was a particularly attractive area because of the climate, the hospitality of the people, and the frequency of European ships visiting the islands. Most of the beachcombers were deserters from either **whaling** vessels or trading ships; a few were shipwrecked. Their importance lies in the fact that these individuals became the first intensive contact the islanders had with Western culture and that a few of them wrote accounts of their island experiences. Because of the beachcombers' superior technical knowledge, it is not surprising that the indigenous chiefs came to rely on their expertise in everyday matters—including the art of making war. Their long-range influence, however, was minimal. They were few in number, and their residence in the islands was limited to a few months or a few years. It is only with the arrival of the Christian missionaries that the greatest influence upon island life was to occur. *See also* CAMPBELL, ARCHIBALD; DAVIS, ISAAC; DIAPER, WILLIAM; HAGERSTEIN, PETER; MARINER, WILLIAM; ROBARTS, EDWARD; VASON, GEORGE; YOUNG, JOHN.

BERLIN ACT OF 1889. An agreement reached by the governments of **Great Britain**, the **United States**, and **Germany** regarding the political status of the Sāmoan Islands. Friction for control of these islands as well as internal civil war in **Sāmoa** precipitated the need for some discussion on the subject. A preliminary conference in 1887 had failed to produce any substantial agreement.

After the devastating 1889 hurricane that destroyed several warships in Āpia harbor, a conference was convened in Berlin and a formal nine-page act agreed upon. The agreement addressed judicial procedures, reorganization of public finance, importation of arms and ammunition, alcoholic beverages, and especially land claims. The net result of the agreement was a three-power condominium administration of the islands through their respective consuls located in Āpia.

Internal civil war continued, and it became apparent by 1899 that the system was not working. The **Anglo-German Agreement of 1899** divided the islands between the United States (the islands of Manu'a and Tutuila becoming **American Sāmoa**) and Germany, who gained control of the western islands consisting of 'Upolu, Manono, Apolima, and Savai'i.

BEST, ELSDON (1856–1931). A **New Zealand** scholar whose works regarding the traditional **Māori** culture are unsurpassed. He was born near Wellington, and for numerous years he worked as a road foreman and health inspector in the Urewere Country where he came into personal contact with the Māori groups there. He learned their language, heard their legends, and then wrote numerous books and papers regarding Māori history and lore. His best known are *The Maori as He Was, The Maori* (both published in 1924), and *Tuhoe, the Children of the Mist* (1925).

BINGHAM, HIRAM (1789–1869). A pioneer missionary to **Hawai'i** representing the **American Board of Commissioners for Foreign Missions (ABCFM)**. Bingham was born on 30 October 1789, in Bennington, Vermont, and graduated from Andover Theological School (1816–1819). When the ABCFM proposed to send a contingent of Christian missionaries to Hawai'i, they chose Bingham and Asa Thurston to head the delegation.

Arriving in the islands in 1820, the missionaries set about constructing a written language for the Hawaiians, building schools, and generally attempting to establish a Christian commonwealth there. They did so by converting the influential elements within the royal family. In 1824, chiefess **Ka'ahumanu** and her husband, Kalanimoku, as regents for the young **Kamehameha II**, established Christian laws that forbade many of the practices of the Hawaiians and foreigners alike.

Bingham's adamant support of those puritanical laws and his dogmatic personality created enemies in many quarter

When his wife Sybil became ill in 1839, they left the islands. Bingham's autobiographical work, *A Residence of Twenty-One Years in the Sandwich Islands* (1847), provides a valuable insight into early Hawaiian history as well as into Bingham's personality. Bingham's son Hiram II (1831–1908) became an ABCFM missionary to the Gilbert Islands (Micronesia), and his grandson Hiram III (1875–1956) became a member of the U.S. Senate (1924–1932) during which time he secured passage of a number of bills that assisted Hawai'i's economy and medical services.

BISHOP, CHARLES REED (1822–1915). An educator, banker, and philanthropist in **Hawai'i**. Born in New York, he visited Hawai'i in 1846 as a tourist. He decided to stay in the islands where he worked as a janitor until he became the founder and president of the Bishop National Bank. He married Bernice Pauahi, a member of the royal family, and throughout his life was active in community affairs. Much of his energies went into the establishment of the Kamehameha Schools, the Honolulu Library, the Hawaiian Historical Society, the O'ahu College, and the development of homes for girls and boys. He was active in numerous civic projects. After his wife's death, he retired to California where he died on 7 June 1915. *See also* BISHOP MUSEUM.

BISHOP MUSEUM, BERNICE PAUAHI. One of the world's finest institutions for scientific research, publication, and the preservation and exhibition of Pacific antiquities. Located in Honolulu, **Hawai'i**, the museum was founded by **Charles Reed Bishop** in 1889 as a memorial to his wife, Chiefess Bernice Pauahi Bishop, the last survivor of the founding dynasty of the Hawaiian monarchy. The museum has sponsored numerous expeditions to the Pacific islands, and these findings have been published in hundreds of monographs, occasional papers, bulletins, and reports. Its extensive library provides materials for scholars and students interested in researching all aspects of Pacific cultures and peoples.

BISMARCK AGREEMENT OF 1879. An agreement reached among the consuls of **Great Britain**, the **United States**, and the commander of the **German** warship *Bismarck*, anchored in the port of Āpia, to bring an end to the raging civil war among the **Sāmoans**, to restructure a new government, and to provide security for the European residents in the islands. According to the agreement, **Mālietoa** Talavou was to become king (*tupu*) and Mālietoa Laupepa was to serve as regent. A council was to be established to assist the king in enforcing the laws, and an executive council consisting of three Europeans was to advise the government. The agreement lasted less than a year when civil war broke out again. Hostilities and the insecurity of European residents eventually led to the **Anglo-German Agreement of 1899**. *See also* AMERICAN SĀMOA; SĀMOA.

BLACKBIRDING. A practice in the 19th century of "persuading" Pacific islanders to work on colonial plantations elsewhere in the Pacific—Queensland, (**Australia**), Fiji, and Peru, for example. The "persuasion" frequently took the form of kidnapping. *See also* LABOR TRADE.

BLIGH, WILLIAM (1754–1817). A British navigator whose sailing exploits have been immortalized in literature and cinema. Bligh was sent to **Tahiti** aboard the HMS *Bounty* to obtain **breadfruit** cuttings for the West Indies where they were to become a staple food for the black slaves. En route from Tahiti, on 28 April 1789, a mutiny broke out headed by Fletcher Christian, the master's mate. Bligh and 18 crewmen were set adrift in a ship's launch, and they survived a 5,820-km (3,637-mi) journey to Timor in the East Indies. They arrived in England where Bligh faced a courtmartial, but the court exonerated him. He later returned to Tahiti (1791–1793) to complete his assignment of taking breadfruit to the West Indies.

Ironically, the islanders in the West Indies did not like the breadfruit as a staple food and refused to eat it. Bligh later commanded several ships and received numerous commendations. He was courtmartialed and reprimanded again in 1805 for his oppression and abusive language, but in 1806 he was appointed governor of New South Wales, **Australia**. Another mutiny deposed him in 1810, and he returned to England in 1811 where he was promoted twice before his death in 1817. *See also* FRENCH POLYNESIA.

BOLGER, JAMES B. (1935–). Head of the **National Party of New Zealand** and prime minister from October 1990 until he retired in December 1997. Born of Irish immigrants, Bolger grew up on a Taranaki dairy farm (North Island), then moved to Te Kuiti where he has been engaged in sheep and cattle farming since 1965 and where he became interested in politics. His career includes parliamentary undersecretary (1975) in several ministries, and then in 1977 he became minister of fisheries and associate minister of agriculture during which time he assisted in negotiations that established **New Zealand's** 200-mile **exclusive economic zone (EEZ)**. From 1978 to 1984, he served as minister of labor and is best remembered as introducing Saturday shopping and voluntary unionism.

Bolger was elected leader of the National Party and leader of the opposition on 26 March 1986 in place of Jim McLay. Criticisms against the **Labour Party** over the rise in student fees and the sale of state assets led to a substantial victory of Bolger's National Party in the October 1990 elections. National obtained 68 seats, while Labour returned only 28. Under his leadership, the New Zealand economy was transformed from having the lowest growth rate among the 29 nations of the Organization for Economic Cooperatoina and Development (OECD) to having one of the strongest. In the 1996 elections, Bolger formed a coalition government with the New Zealand First Party. He retired in December of 1997 and was appointed minister of state and associate minister of foreign affairs and trade. In April 1998, he was appointed New Zealand ambassador to the **United States**.

BOUGAINVILLE, LOUIS-ANTOINE DE (1729–1811). French explorer who conducted **France's** first around-the-world sea voyage (1766–1769). He was one of the first Europeans to visit the Tuamotu Islands (now part of **French Polynesia**) and **Tahiti** (1768) where he claimed the islands for France, although he was unaware that the British Captain Samuel Wallis had been there just the previous year. Bougainville's description of the islands in his *Nouvelle Cythère* gave material for subsequent writers to create the romantic concept of the "noble savage" and the myth of the mirage of the South Seas. Napoleon Bonaparte honored him with the titles of senator and count for his contributions to France. An island in the Solomons and the beautiful flower, Bougainvillea, were named after him. He died in Paris on 31 August 1811. *See also* BARET, JEANNE; FRENCH POLYNESIA.

***BOUNTY* MUTINY.** *See* BLIGH, WILLIAM.

BOYS, SIR MICHAEL HARDIE (1931–). Governor-general of **New Zealand** from 1996 to 2001. Born to Justice Reginald and Edith May (Bennett) Hardie Boys in Wellington, Sir Michael attended Hataitai School, Wellington College, and Victoria University where he earned a BA, LLB, and a Doctor of Laws (1997). He practiced law in Wellington for numerous years before being appointed judge of the high court (1980). In 1989, he became an honorary bencher of Gray's Inn, London, a council member of the Wellington District Law Society (1978–1979) and its president in 1979, judge of the high court (1980–1989), and a member of the court of appeal (1989–1995). He was knighted (GCMG) in 1995 and then appointed governor-general on 21 March 1996. He has been active in numerous community and church activities throughout his life. He married Edith Mary Zohrab in 1957, and they are the parents of four children. Upon his retirement in 2001, he was replaced as governor-general by **Dame Silvia Cartwright**.

BREADFRUIT (*Artocarpus altilis*). A staple food throughout all of **Polynesia**, more important, however, in its less economically developed nations. Breadfruit trees are propagated through shoots and root cuttings and meticulously cared for until they reach a size not easily damaged, usually two to three feet in height. Afterwards, they require little or no care, except perhaps for an occasional pruning. The trees (resembling the oak tree) grow to immense size with numerous branches that have pinnate leaves over 16 inches in length. The trees bear fruit almost year-round and thus provide a staple, starchy food for the island peoples' diet. The large round or pear-shaped fruit (resembling what Americans would call a large hedge-apple) is picked from the tree and cooked in a variety of ways—either whole over an open flame, in an oven, or boiled—and then peeled and the insides eaten. The taste is pleasant, and numerous recipes today continue to make it a major food item in Polynesia. *See also* BLIGH, WILLIAM; COCONUT PALM; TARO.

BRUAT, ARMAND JOSEPH (1796–1855). The first governor of French Oceania. Born in Alsace, Bruat entered the French naval academy and distinguished himself in the line of duty at Navarino (1827) and in Algeria (1830). In 1843, he was appointed French commissary to **Queen Pomare IV** of **Tahiti**. Upon his arrival in Tahiti, he became embroiled in the bitter rivalry between the established English Protestants and the "intruding" French Catholics, a rivalry subsequently referred to as the Pritchard Affair. Bruat had **George Pritchard**, the English consul, expelled from the islands in 1844, suppressed a Tahitian uprising, and established Tahiti and the **Society Islands** as a French protectorate, the **Établissements Français de l'Océanie**, with himself as its first governor. After peace had been restored to the islands, Bruat returned to **France** in 1847 where he continued to serve his country until he died at sea in 1855. One of Pape'ete's main streets, Avenue Bruat, is named in his honor. *See also* FRENCH POLYNESIA; POMARE.

BUCK, PETER HENRY (TE RANGI HIROA) (ca. 1880–1951). New Zealand administrator, politician, and leading expert on the subject of **Polynesia**. Born to an Irish father and **Māori** mother, he was reared by his mother's family and he identified himself with that heritage. After gaining a reputation as an athlete during his school days at Te Aute College and Otago University, he became medical officer for Māori health between 1905 and 1908, served in World War I as a medical officer, and then returned as director of the Division of Māori Hygiene between 1919 and 1927. His work in physical anthropology during the 1920s is well-known, and as a result, he was appointed professor of anthropology at Yale University and later became director and president of the board of trustees of the **Bishop Museum** in Honolulu. He wrote numerous books, articles, and scientific monographs including *Vikings of the Sunrise* (1938), *Anthropology and Religion* (1939), *The Coming of the Maori* (1949), as well as ethnographic works on the **Cook Islands** and **Sāmoa**.

BURNS, JOHN ANTHONY (1909–1975). Elected governor of the state of **Hawai'i** from 1962 to 1974. Born on 30 March 1909 at Fort Assinneboine, Montana, Burns was educated in Honolulu, attending the University of Hawai'i. He became a member of the Honolulu police department between 1934 and 1945 (as captain between 1941 and 1945) until he founded his own business, Burns & Company Real Estate. Of plain and simple speech and common background, he and his friends were responsible immediately after the war for the establishment of the power of the Democratic Party in the islands. He was elected Hawai'i's delegate to the U.S. Congress in 1956 and reelected in 1958. A long-time supporter of the national Democratic Party, he was appointed personal representative of President John F. Kennedy to the **South Pacific Commission** Conference in 1962, and later that year was elected governor, Hawai'i's second elected governor since attaining statehood in 1959. He was elected two more times—in 1966 and 1970.

His administration is noted for the social, economic, and educational advances made by the new state government. Burns made Hawai'i the political and economic crossroads of the Pacific. The community college system, the **East-West Center**, the new state Capitol building, all are attributed to his energy and enthusiasm. Although he gained the nickname "Stone Face," he was highly respected and honored throughout his life. He died of cancer on 5 April 1975 at the age of 66.

- C -

CAMPBELL, ARCHIBALD (1787–?). A sailor from Scotland, who settled as a **beachcomber** on O'ahu, **Hawai'i**, for 10 months between 1809 and 1810, and whose book, *A Voyage Round the World from 1806 to 1812*, provides an early account of the rule and character of **King Kamehameha I**. Although Campbell returned to Scotland eventually to immigrate to the **United States**, he never returned to Hawai'i.

CARTER, GEORGE ROBERT (1866–1933). Hawai'i's second territorial governor from 1903 to 1907. Diplomat, businessman, and banker, Carter was responsible for establishing a firm financial basis for the new territory and for the establishment of the five county governments in the islands.

CARTWRIGHT, DAME SILVIA (1943–). Appointed **New Zealand's** 18th governor-general in April 2001 for a five-year term. Her appointment means that New Zealand's top five political leaders—prime minister, leader of the opposition, attorney general, chief justice, and governor-general—are all held by women. Cartwright was born on 7 November 1943 and reared in Dunedin of working-class parents, Mont and Eileen Poulter. She was one of six children. She graduated from Otago University in 1967 and practiced law in Dunedin, Rotorua, and Hamilton before becoming a district court judge in 1981. She was appointed the first female chief judge of the district court and is best known for heading the commission of inquiry into the treatment of cervical cancer and other related matters at National Women's Hospital. Her report marked a turning point in medical ethics. In 1989 she was created D.B.E. She replaced **Sir Michael Hardie Boys** who had been governor-general since 1996.

CATHOLIC CHURCH. *See* ROMAN CATHOLIC CHURCH IN OCEANIA.

CENTER FOR PACIFIC AND ASIAN STUDIES (CPAS). Located at the University of Nijmegen, the Netherlands, it was established in 1991 originally as the Center of Pacific Studies. Its name change came in 1999. The center currently employs a staff of 25 senior and 14 junior members. Its aims are to advance basic and applied research in Asia and the Pacific, offer courses and coordinate teaching programs within its field of interest, and provide information about these geographical regions. The center publishes a biannual *Oceania Newsletter* which includes reports on research projects, short articles on topical issues, and announcements of workshops, seminars, and conferences. Its Website, http://www.kun.nl/cps/, provides copies of its newsletter, a bibliographical database (searchable), as well as **Internet** bookmarks to other Pacific sources.

CENTER FOR PACIFIC ISLANDS STUDIES (CPIS). Located at the University of Hawai'i—Mānoa campus—in Honolulu, the center was established in 1950 to coordinate much of the Pacific-related activity at the university. It celebrated its 50th anniversary in November 2000. It currently provides academic programs (both undergraduate and graduate), sponsors the publication of monographs and working papers, and has developed an extensive outreach program to promote greater awareness and understanding of the region. Conferences, seminars, and workshops are frequently held to bring together educators, government officials, business persons, and the general public. Its first two directors were Leonard Mason and Norman Meller. Professor Robert C. Kiste, its current director, has been its prime motivator since 1978, and the CPIS boasts an enviable list of over 30 distinguished scholars who teach in the academic disciplines throughout the university. It is the only university in the **United States** to offer a master's degree in Pacific island studies. Its **Internet** Website is http://www.hawaii.edu/cpis.

CENTRAL POLYNESIAN LAND AND COMMERCIAL COMPANY (1871–1895). A land scheme devised by San Francisco speculators in which they planned to purchase cheaply approximately 200,000 acres of land during **Sāmoa's** civil wars (1869–1873) and then to sell them at a profit. All land claims of the company were eventually rejected by a land claims commission between 1891 and 1894, and the company was liquidated the following year. *See also* AMERICAN SĀMOA; WEBB, WILLIAM HENRY.

CENTRE FOR SOUTH PACIFIC STUDIES (CSPS). Located at the University of New South Wales (**Australia**), the center was established in 1987. It collects, collates, and distributes information about the peoples and places of the South Pacific as well as coordinates university programs and seeks funding for them from outside agencies. Its *Newsletter* reaches some 4,000 individuals and institutions in over 60 countries around the world. Its current director is professor Grant McCall, an **Easter Island** scholar from the University of New South Wales. The center's **Internet** Website is located at http://www.arts.unsw.edu.au/southpacific/CSPS_Welcome.html#Welcome.

CHANEL, PIERRE (1803–1841). Polynesia's first and only Roman Catholic saint. Born in **France**, Pierre Chanel joined the Marists (Society of Mary) in 1819, and in 1837 was sent to the Pacific under the direction of **Bishop Jean-Baptiste François Pompallier**. After visiting **Tahiti**, he and Father Delorme were sent to **Futuna** to attempt the conversion of the islanders to Christianity. On 28 April

1841, a dispute broke out between the factions on the islands, and chief Musumusu, thinking Chanel was usurping his authority, surrounded Chanel's lodgings, entered, and clubbed him to death. Bishop Pompallier immediately visited the island, strengthened the missionary contingent, and by 1843 the whole island had been converted to Roman Catholicism. Father Chanel was beatified on 14 November 1889, canonized on 12 June 1954, and his relics were returned from Paris in 1976 to be interred in a small chapel erected to his honor at Poi on the northeast coast of Futuna. *See also* ROMAN CATHOLIC CHURCH IN OCEANIA; WALLIS AND FUTUNA.

CHATHAM ISLANDS. An island group in the South Pacific Ocean, lying approximately 860 km (533 mi) east of Christchurch, **New Zealand**, politically belonging to New Zealand and administered by a resident commissioner appointed by the Department of Māori and Island Affairs in Wellington. The current mayor is Patrick Smith. The group is made up of 10 volcanic-formed islands with a total landmass of 963 sq km (372 sq mi). Two of the islands, Chatham and Pitt, are inhabited with approximately 750 residents, most of whom are of European origin with some New Zealand **Māoris** who replaced the indigenous **Moriori** who died out in 1933. The islanders have been trying to gain additional autonomy from New Zealand for a number of years, especially the right to manage their own rich fisheries. In January of 2000, a subtribe on the island announced plans to declare the islands a sovereign state and assume control over the fishing grounds, the major contention between it and the New Zealand government. Export of wool and breeding sheep are still an essential part of the islands' economy. International notoriety came to the islands as a result of their being the first inhabited landmass in the world to greet the first dawn of the new millennium on 1 January 2000.

CHEVRON, JOSEPH (1808–1884). First Catholic missionary to **Tonga** As a member of the French Marists (Society of Mary), Chevron first visited Tonga in 1837, but he was opposed by the Protestant (Wesleyan) advisors to **King George Tupou** I who forced him to leave. Chevron returned to Tonga in 1842, arriving at Pangaimotu, an island near Nuku'alofa harbor. Opposition to the growth of the new religion broke out in open war between 1852 and 1855, and it was only through the intervention of French warships that Catholic adherents were granted tolerance of belief. The first Catholic church was built at Mu'a in 1847 and a school established in 1855. After 42 years of work in Tonga, Father Chevron died on 6 October 1884. *See also* ROMAN CATHOLIC CHURCH IN OCEANIA.

CHRISTIAN DEMOCRATIC PARTY (CP). *See* SĀMOA NATOINAL DEVELOPMENT PARTY.

CHURCH MISSIONARY SOCIETY (CMS). Founded in England in 1799 as a world evangelical society, the CMS became the agency for the establishment of Anglicanism in **New Zealand**. The **Reverend Samuel Marsden**, who headed the Anglican mission in Australia, contacted the society regarding missionary work in New Zealand. Marsden landed several members of the CMS (Thomas Kendall, William Hall, and John King) at Rangihoua in the Bay of Islands in 1814, but it was not until the arrival of the **Reverend Henry Williams** in 1823 that any substantial headway was made. Assistance was provided by other notable CMS missionaries—William Williams (Henry's brother), Robert Maunsell, William Colenso (a printer and **Māori** scholar), George Clarke, A. N. Browne, Octavius Hadfield, and Richard Taylor—who arrived shortly thereafter. *See also* LONDON MISSIONARY SOCIETY; MORMON CHURCH IN POLYNESIA; ROMAN CATHOLIC CHURCH IN OCEANIA.

CLARK, HELEN (1950–). Prime minister of **New Zealand** since 27 November 1999. Born in 1950 in Hamilton, New Zealand, Clark attended Te Pahu Primary School, Auckland's Epsom Girls' Grammar School, and entered the University of Auckland in 1968 where she studied politics and became active in political issues of the day—the Vietnam War, apartheid in South Africa, and nuclear testing in the Pacific. She joined the **Labour Party** in 1971 and won election to Parliament in 1975. Currently, she is the longest-serving woman member of New Zealand's Parliament. Between 1984 and 1987, she was chair of the foreign affairs and defence select committee when New Zealand declared itself nuclear free and pursued a more independent foreign policy. When Labour came to power in 1987, she became a member of cabinet holding several ministerial positions—conservation, housing, labor, and health. As health minister, she sponsored anti-tobacco legislation. She was deputy prime minister between August 1989 and October 1990, and she became leader of the Labour Party and the opposition in 1993. In the 1999 elections, Labour won and Clark assumed the position of prime minister and maintained that Labour's win was because "National has moved away from the values of rural people and is listening too much to financial interests in the big cities."

COCONUT PALM (*Cocos nucifera*). A tree common to almost every island and atoll in the Pacific and every part of which supplies some sort of everyday need for island peoples. The seeds (nuts) of the palm were most likely brought first to the islands by the early Polynesian settlers, and because their production requires little or no effort, the trees spread rapidly throughout the island groups. The tree matures in five or six years at which time it starts bearing fruit (nuts), lives to be between 60 and a hundred years old, and attains a height of 60 to 75 feet (20–25 meters). The tall, slender trunks are used for house poles, fence posts, or wood carvings; the leaves for thatching, woven baskets and mats, or other ornaments; the shells of the nut for bowls and bottles; the husks for sennit (rope); and the meat inside the nut for food and oil products. **Copra** production became important in the 19th century, but has grown less so as a result of the use of petroleum oil and detergents. *See also* BREADFRUIT; TARO.

COLEMAN, PETER TALI (1919–1997). Governor of **American Sāmoa** from 1956 to 1961, 1977 to 1985, and 1989 to January 1993. Born on 8 December 1919, in American Sāmoa, Coleman attended St. Louis College (Honolulu) and Georgetown University (Washington, D.C.) and served in the U.S. Army in the Pacific (1940–1946) having attained the rank of captain.

In 1951, he began his long political career in the Department of the Interior, Washington, and the following year was appointed public defender in American Sāmoa. After a short appointment as attorney general (1955), he was appointed as governor of the territory (1956–1960), then transferred to the U.S. Trust Territories (Micronesia) as district administrator (1961–1966), and subsequently deputy high commissioner from 1969 to 1977. He returned to American Sāmoa to enter the gubernatorial elections in 1978 for the Republican Party. He became American Sāmoa's first elected governor in 1978, a position he held until 1984 (he could not legally run for a third consecutive term), and was reelected again in 1988. His public career spanned the entire last half of the 20th century, and he has placed his personal stamp upon American Sāmoa's history. He was recipient of the 1997 American Sāmoan Governor's Humanitarian Award and gained the chiefly title Uifa'atali from his home village of Pago Pago. He died on 28 April 1997 in Honolulu, leaving his wife Nora and 12 children.

COLONIAL POWERS. A term that refers to those Western nations that gained possession of Pacific island nations during the 19th century and that subsequently governed them into the 20th century. In **Polynesia**, those powers were **France**, **Germany**, **Great Britain**, and the **United States**. With the exception of Germany, which lost its Pacific islands in 1914, they continue to have a strong presence in Polynesia.

COMITÉ POUVANA'A. One of the first political parties to emerge after World War II in **French Polynesia**. Its founder, **Marcel Pouvana'a a Oopa**, appealed to the **Tahitian** population in the elections of 1949 for more internal autonomy for the islands. The party won 62 percent of the votes. Soon afterwards, it joined with the Union of Volunteers to form the **Rassemblement Démocratique des Populations Tahitiennes (RDPT) party**.

COMMITTEE FOR COORDINATION OF JOINT PROSPECTING FOR MINERAL RESOURCES IN SOUTH PACIFIC OFFSHORE AREAS (CCOP/SOPAC). *See* SOUTH PACIFIC APPLIED GEOSCIENCE COMMISSION.

COMMONWEALTH (BRITISH). A voluntary association of 54 independent sovereign states, including **Great Britain** and most of its former dependencies (nearly one-quarter of the world's population). Polynesian members of the Commonwealth include **New Zealand**, **Tonga**, and **Sāmoa**; dependencies include the **Cook Islands**, **Niue**, **Tokelau**, and **Pitcairn Island**; special members are **Nauru** and **Tuvalu**, not represented at meetings of the Commonwealth Heads of Government. Meetings are held every two years after which a communiqué is released that provides the consensus of discussions of the meetings. The Commonwealth association also provides numerous resource organizations for its members. Located at Marlborough House in London, it celebrated its 50th anniversary in July 1999.

Prior to 1952, the organization was called the "British Commonwealth," but after the accession of Queen Elizabeth II to the throne, the adjective British was tacitly dropped and the current appropriate designation is simply the "Commonwealth."

CONFERENCE OF SOUTH PACIFIC CHIEFS OF POLICE (CSPCP). An informal organization founded in 1970 in Suva, Fiji, aimed at improving police services among the newly emerging Pacific island states, while at the same time providing for exchange of information and expertise on international crime in the area.

There are currently 17 member nations—Fiji, Kiribati, **Nauru**, Solomon Islands, **Tonga**, **Tuvalu**, Vanuatu, **Cook Islands**, **New Zealand**, Papua New Guinea, **Sāmoa**, **American Sāmoa**, **Australia**, **French Polynesia**, New Caledonia, and the Northern Mariana Islands. Meetings are held annually in different locations that last approximately five days during which time training courses are provided, papers presented, and discussions held regarding drugs, alcohol, and general police affairs. In 1987, the South Pacific Islands Criminal Intelligence Network (SPICIN) was created with headquarters now in American Sāmoa.

COOK ISLANDS. An internally self-governed state in free association with **New Zealand** and a member of the **Commonwealth**, it consists of 13 inhabited and two uninhabited islands located between **American Sāmoa** to the west and **French Polynesia** to the east. These islands are spread over approximately 2 million sq km (750,000 sq mi) of ocean and are geographically divided into the Northern Cook Islands (six coral atolls) and the Southern Cook Islands (nine volcanic islands). The total landmass consists of 237 sq km (91.5 sq mi) with the main administrative center, Avarua, located on the island of Rarotonga (67 sq km) in the southern group.

Population: The total population of 14,300 (2001 estimate) is primarily of Polynesian descent (81.3 percent full blood), half of whom live on Rarotonga. (Cook Islanders have New Zealand citizenship, and more of them live in New Zealand than in their home islands.) English is the official language, but Cook Island **Māori** is also spoken. The climate is tropical and warm, moderated by southwest trade winds. Average rainfall measures 2,030 mm (80 in.) a year. The islands produce bananas, **breadfruit**, **coconuts**, mangoes, pandanus, sweet potatoes, **taro**, and yams. Citrus fruit, pineapples, cotton, and coffee have been introduced.

Religion: Approximately 70 percent belong to the Cook Islands Christian Church (formerly the London Missionary Society), 15 percent are Roman Catholic, and the remaining divided between other Protestant groups—Seventh-Day Adventist, Latter-day Saints (Mormons), and so forth.

Prehistory: Until European contact, the islands existed separately and independently. Archaeological sites on Rarotonga have produced Sāmoan-type adzes dated approximately A.D. 950, possibly the oldest inhabited site in the islands. Traditions maintain that the islands were settled by invaders from **Tahiti** and **Samoa** in the 13th century, but even at that time there were earlier inhabitants in the islands, possibly having come from the **Marquesas**. These early Polynesians established a highly stratified society not unlike those found in their neighboring island groups. (Refer also to the **Introduction** and the entry on **Ancient Polynesian Culture**.)

Modern history: The first European to sight any of the islands (Pukapuka) was Alvaro de Mendaña in 1595; the explorer Pedro Quirós landed on Rakahanga in 1606; and **James Cook**, after whom the islands are named, explored five of the southern islands in the 1770s. First continuous European contact with the islanders came only with the introduction of Christianity in 1821 by Papehia, a Polynesian missionary from Rā'iatea, Society Islands, who was landed on Rarotonga by **John Williams** of the **London Missionary Society (LMS)**. By 1827, Papehia had converted a good portion of the island—Papehia was Polynesian, he had married the chief's daughter, he converted the important chiefs (*ariki*), and he had Western technology to prove the superiority of his god's power. Williams returned to the islands in 1827, learned the language, and devised a writing system. Other English missionaries arrived, and in 1834, Williams left to begin his missionary work in Sāmoa.

Christianity brought a wholesale restructuring of the islands' culture. Villages were formed, Christian legal codes proclaimed, **women's** status enhanced, and schools founded, all of which led to the establishment of a more peaceful order in the islands. Handicrafts were taught, and the surplus goods and crops were traded to outsiders, a situation that by 1870 had also brought more European settlers with their undesirable influences upon the islands. The brisk commerce and trade had also caused a rapid decline in church membership (from one-half to one-fourth) and the introduction of other Christian denominations.

Dominant in the change that came to the islands was the continuous role that the *ariki* (chiefs) played in the new order. No single chief gained the power and prestige that resulted in kingship and unification of the islands as emerged in the other Polynesian groups—**Hawai'i** and **Tahiti**, for example—although in the late 19th century, **"Queen" Makea Takau** dominated affairs around Avarua, the growing political and economic center of the islands.

Growing threat of French intrusion into the South Pacific caused Makea to petition **Great Britain** for protection, an act accomplished in October 1888 and an authority that extended to all of the islands in the southern group. British Resident Administrator Frederick J. Moss clashed with the newly established executive council, whereupon Moss was withdrawn and replaced in September 1898 by Lieutenant Colonel W. E. Gudgeon who essentially was responsible for the establishment of law and order, for the development of production and commerce, for the elimination of the LMS's theocratic rule over the people, and for the gradual introduction of Western political concepts.

Encouraged by Gudgeon, the Council of Ariki petitioned for annexation to New Zealand in 1900 so they might become part of the British Empire. Formal annexation took place on 11 June 1901, and Gudgeon was appointed resident commissioner with executive responsibility for the Cook Islands. Wholesale reorganization of the islands' government ensued. New Zealand took charge of the Cook Islands' finance and the appointment and dismissal of officials. *Ariki* courts were abolished, the Rarotonga Council became advisory, island councils became elective (franchise over 21), and centralized authority was assumed by the resident commissioner.

By the time Gudgeon retired in 1909, he was disliked by a good number of the paramount chiefs. A New Zealand investigation team visited the islands in 1910 and again in 1911, the result of which was the Cook Island Act of 1915 which codified most of the laws in the islands. Between 1912 and 1935, island administrators primarily emphasized the development of medical, educational, and vocational programs with little or no interest in the advancement of political awareness that would eventually lead to self-government.

Dissatisfaction with New Zealand administration and the first signs of Cook Island nationalism appeared during World War II when U.S. troops stationed in Aitutaki openly accused New Zealand of neglecting the islands. In 1943, dissatisfied Cook Islanders on Aitutaki organized a group called Cook Islands Progressive Association (CIPA). In 1944, a similar group was formed on Rarotonga by Ua Turua, Tautu Aneru, and Arona, with Dr. T. R. A. Davis as advisor; and by 1945, a group had been formed in Auckland (New Zealand) where numerous Cook Islanders had emigrated to work. Labor disagreements resulted in violent clashes in 1947 and 1948 between the workers who had joined the CIPA and the New Zealand administration.

With the establishment of the **United Nations** and its insistence that colonial powers should ensure the political, economic, and social development of non-self-governing territories, New Zealand moved toward some form of independence for the Cook Islands. A legislative council, consisting of representatives from all the islands, was established in 1946 with the resident commissioner as president. During the 1950s, developments in the economy, society, education, medical care, and politics all quickened. A legislative assembly with extended powers was formed in 1957, and by 1962, the islanders announced to the United Nations Trusteeship Council their intent of having internal self-government within three years.

A new constitution was promulgated in 1964, and general elections for the legislative assembly held on 20 April 1965. **Albert Royle Henry**, head of the Cook Islands Party (CIP), became the first premier (and was reelected in 1968, 1971, 1974, and March 1978). The newly-elected legislative assembly chose internal self-government in free association with New Zealand rather than complete independence or integration into any other Pacific island nation. New Zealand would provide financial assistance, defense, support in external affairs, and the Cook Islanders would retain their New Zealand citizenship.

A constitutional amendment act in 1980–1981 revised the earlier constitution. Currently, executive powers are exercised by a cabinet consisting of the prime minister (premier before 1980) and eight ministers responsible to Parliament (legislative assembly before 1980) which is made up of 25 members elected every five years (every four years before 1980). A House of Ariki (formed in 1965) consists of 15 hereditary chiefs (*ariki*) who hold only advisory positions in the government (its current president is Margaret Makea Karika Ariki).

Also formed in 1965, the Cook Islands Party dominated politics until 1978 when, in July of that year, Sir Albert Henry and associates were arraigned on corruption charges. It was revealed that Cook Island expatriates were flown to the islands to vote in the March elections with their fares being paid from public funds, thus assuring the continued domination of the CIP. Henry lost his seat in Parliament, his position as prime minister, and his British title. He later died on 1 January 1981.

Henry's position in the government was assumed by **Dr. Thomas Davis**, leader of the **Democratic Party (DP)**, a position he held until the March 1983 elections at which time his party lost to **Geoffrey Henry**, a cousin of the late Albert Henry and subsequent head of the CIP. In the same elections, Ms. Fanaura Kingstone became the first woman elected to the Cook Islands Parliament since self-government. She was subsequently appointed as minister of internal affairs and postmistress general. Henry's government was short-lived. On a constitutional technicality, Parliament was dissolved in August and new elections held in November. This time, the Democratic Party returned to power with Thomas Davis again as prime minister, but by 1984, it was apparent that his support was weak and, as a result, he reshuffled his cabinet giving three positions to the CIP and appointing Geoffrey Henry as deputy prime minister.

The coalition lasted only 12 months. Henry was dismissed and the CIP withdrew its support from Davis's government. By 1987, Davis's strength had diminished, and in July, Parliament voted a unanimous no confidence in his government. His anti–New Zealand stance and his budgetary proposals had played against him. He was succeeded as prime minister by Dr. Pupuke Robati, a prominent member of the CIP as well as a member of Davis's cabinet.

The general elections of January 1989 returned the CIP to power, having won 12 of the 24 seats in Parliament. Geoffrey Henry again became prime minister and governed the country for 10 years until his resignation in July of 1999. (The CIP overwhelmingly won 20 of the 25 seats in Parliament in the March 1994 elections.) During the first years the CIP was in power, it attempted to make a positive contribution to the islands. Roads were repaired, telecommunications and the port were upgraded, the power system was expanded, and numerous other improvements made. By the mid-1990s, however, the government was being criticized on all sides. Various government scandals had caused a lack of faith by the public. The 1992 Wine-Box Affair (the Cook Islands banks used by New Zealand tax evaders) and the 1994 "Letters of Guarantee" (the Cook Islands government issuing loan guarantees far above its ability to guarantee) were only two of several scandals. By 1995, **tourism** was down, the government was overborrowing, the national debt was a staggering $160 million ($5 million was reasonable), government businesses were not doing well, taxes were high (value-added tax at 10 percent and personal income tax at 37 percent), the gross domestic product (GDP) slowed, and Cook Islanders were emigrating in droves.

Many causes were to blame but all seemed to reflect back on the government. The government was overspending and overborrowing. The public sector was bloated, and it is estimated that 95 percent of the households in the Cook Islands relied to some extent on government salaries or aid or both. Government employees worked few hours and with little initiative, and government officials siphoned money off for personal gain. Public funds and labor went to support local churches activities and in some cases church construction.

The **Asian Development Bank** became concerned, sent in representatives to investigate, and made several suggestions. Complying with their recommendations, Prime Minister Henry announced a severe restructuring of finances in April of 1996. He ordered a 50 percent reduction of government employees, a 60 percent reduction in the number of government departments and ministries, and announced a drastic privatization program to aid the islands' austere economy. The pay of all government workers was reduced 15 percent in March and then another 50 percent in June. Demonstrations, strikes, and civil service ineffectiveness all resulted. Henry sold off government-owned hotels, television stations, printing works, businesses, and the like. A mass exodus ensued, and it is estimated that within 18 months, approximately 36 percent of the population left the islands.

In April of 1997, the prime minister published "Vision 2005," a government plan whose key goals were to improve the economy through tourism, agriculture, marine resource developments, offshore financial services, and local industries and services. Its aim was to reduce the national debt by 30 percent and to build a national reserve of at least $33 million. The public, however, remained disillusioned both with the government for what it had done and for the opposition for having allowed it. In the face of constant criticism in 1998 from the press and the House of Ariki, the prime minister reshuffled his cabinet, even giving away his prized financial portfolio. The government's annual budget for 1998–1999 was announced at $23.2 million. A trade agreement with China in December 1998 resulted in $450,000 in Chinese aid for developments in the outer islands.

The elections and subsequent events in 1999 ended the 10-year rule of the CIP. The CIP gained only 10 seats in the June election versus the Democratic Alliance Party's (DAP) 11, and the New Alliance Party's four. Henry resigned as head of the CIP and Dr. Joe Williams (a CIP member) allied with Norman George (NAP) and gained the necessary votes to be elected prime minister (13 to 12). A court decision over the Pukapuka parliamentary seat ended in November when the court declared the CIP the winner, but that decision was appealed. Parliament now hung in the balance, especially after Williams dismissed two of his cabinet members. A number of Parliament members gathered around Dr. Terepai Maoate, a well-respected member of the DAP, and announced their intent to call on Williams to resign. On 18 November, Williams conceded, having ended the 10-year rule of the CIP, and Maoate was elected prime minister. Maoate promptly proposed that the new government establish a code of conduct of honesty and integrity for its officials and then adjourned Parliament until March 2000.

During the following year, the new government took positive steps to eliminate some of the islands' problems. Several government agencies were abolished, prices were slashed on electrical surcharges, tariff cuts were made, a national pension system proposed, and financial assistance to the outer islands provided, all of which were applauded by the House of Ariki, the chamber of commerce, and even the opposition CIP.

Economy: After several years of severe economic recession, the Cook Islands economy is rebounding. Although the per capital income is relatively high ($6,900) for a Pacific island nation, the islands continue to have limited resources and a shortage of skilled labor. Commercial agriculture ventures have generally failed despite the fact that much of the islands' landmass is arable. Subsistence farming is the norm on the outer islands. Export crops consist of papaya, **copra**, pineapple, **coconut**, vanilla, and coffee, most of which are sold to New Zealand. Marine resources offer a great potential for economic growth both for fishing in the maritime **exclusive economic zone (EEZ)** as well as the sale of fishing licenses to foreign fleets. The black pearl industry continues to be a vital segment of the economy, and there is current discussion regarding expanding that market to Suwarrow atoll.

In the last three years, the successful tourism market has prompted the government to give greater impetus to this industry. The number of tourists in 2000 hit 72,994, the most profitable year in Cook Islands' history, 30 percent over 1999's figure of 55,559. (Compared to 39,984 arrivals in 1991.) Prime Minister Maoate now maintains that tourism is the key to Cook Islands' future. A hotel room shortage is being felt, but a new 75-room resort is being built on Aitutaki Island and a foreign investor is purchasing the government-initiated 206-room hotel on Rarotonga. Critics argue, however, that the islands should reduce the number of tourists since their water disposal systems cannot handle more.

A good portion of the islands' economy also comes from aid from New Zealand ($3.1 million in 2000) and **Australia** ($1.3 million in 2001) and from remittances sent back to the islands from expatriates living abroad.

COOK ISLANDS/NIUE/NEW ZEALAND JOINT SHIPPING SERVICE (JSS). An arrangement entered into in 1975 among the **Cook Islands**, **Niue**, and **New Zealand**, establishing a shipping service among these island groups on a regular basis "to ensure the optimum economic development of the three countries." Its steering committee is composed of the ministers of transport who meet annually to review matters of general policy, rates, and schedules. The Cook Islands Line currently operates two ships between Auckland (New Zealand), the Cook Islands, and **Tahiti**. New Zealand subsidizes the operation through its Ministry of Foreign Affairs, and it receives benefits from the high-quality fresh produce coming from the Cook Islands and Tahiti.

COOK, JAMES (1728–1779). The most renowned Pacific navigator of all time. Born in Yorkshire, England, on 27 October 1728, Cook joined the British navy and saw military action in 1756 in Newfoundland against the French. Cook's reputation as a cartographer and scholar came as a result of his mapping the coastline of Newfoundland.

In 1768, when the Royal Society of Britain desired to send a scientific expedition to the Pacific, Cook was chosen to head it. Accompanying him on this three-year voyage was the botanist Joseph Banks. While Cook charted coastlines of new lands and recorded ethnographic data concerning the indigenous peoples, Banks and his colleagues collected samples of the various flora found in these new lands.

Cook's second voyage (1772–1775) attempted to find that illusive *Terra Australis* (southern continent), but without success. He was more successful in the "rediscovery" and locating of islands which had not been scientifically established by previous European explorers. Cook's third voyage (1776–1779) attempted to find a Northwest Passage between the Pacific and Atlantic Oceans. After visiting the **Society Islands**, Cook headed northward and "discovered" the Hawaiian islands, naming them the **Sandwich Islands** after his friend and patron, the Earl of Sandwich. Cook set out toward Alaska, but because of foul weather, he had to return to Kealakekua Bay, **Hawai'i**, for repairs of his ship. Here he met his death on 14 February 1779 in a skirmish with the Hawaiian followers of chief Kalani'ōpu'u. His second-in-command, Captain James Clerke, continued the voyage but without finding the

Northwest Passage. Cook's achievements are still unparalleled in the history of Pacific exploration.

COPPENRATH, HUBERT (1930–). Catholic archbishop of Pape'ete, **French Polynesian**, since the retirement of his brother **Archbishop Michel Coppenrath** in 1990. Born on 18 October 1930 in Pape'ete, Monsignor Coppenrath attended secondary school in Poitiers, **France**, where he also studied law. After military service, he entered the seminary and was ordained a priest in 1958. He returned to Pape'ete where he became a parish priest (1967), then vicar-general, and then coadjutor (1997) under his brother. He is considered an authority on the **Tahitian** language and is a member of the Tahitian Academy. His Tahitian grammar helped prepare the way for a new dictionary for that language, and his translation of the New Testament into Tahitian is used also by non-Catholics.

COPPENRATH, MICHEL (1924–). Catholic archbishop of **French Polynesia** from 1973 until 1999. Born in Pape'ete, Coppenrath joined the French Resistance during World War II, obtained a law degree, and then entered the seminary in Paris in 1950. He was consecrated bishop of Pape'ete in 1968, and then archbishop. Under his direction, the church gained new religious orders, erected new churches and schools, and has seen a renewed vitality. He retired on 4 June 1999 due to ill health and was succeeded as archbishop by his brother **Hubert Coppenrath**.

COPRA PRODUCTION. A commercial activity in the Pacific that originated and flourished in the 19th century but has since diminished in importance in the more commercially developed island nations. Copra production is the process of growing and harvesting of the coconut and the subsequent drying of its meat and the extraction of the oil therefrom.

The oil has many uses—soaps, margarine, explosives, cosmetics, perfumes, and other products. The **coconut palm** (*Cocos nucifera*) flourishes on almost all of the Pacific islands and atolls, and its cultivation requires little or no human assistance. To obtain copra, the nuts (fruit) are collected, split in two, and the meat dug out and either laid out in the sun or smoked until the moisture level is reduced to about 14 percent. In islands where no extraction plants exist, the dried meat is collected in gunnysacks and shipped to the nearest factory sometimes thousands of miles away. In the 19th century, plantations of coconut palms were established on hundreds of islands in the Pacific by companies similar to the J. C. Godeffroy and Son of Hamburg who first established a factory in Āpia, **Sāmoa**, in 1856. Many of these plantations are still standing.

The discovery of oil in the 19th century and then the use of detergents in the 20th century have contributed to the decline in importance of copra. As a result, copra prices have fluctuated drastically, and in some island groups it is not economically profitable to continue the industry. In the last 15 years production has declined even further as a result of the reputation coconut oil has gained as a saturated fat and the effect of cholesterol upon one's health. Currently, 91 percent of the copra produced in **Polynesia** comes from three island nations: Sāmoa (54 percent), **French Polynesia** (26.5 percent), and **Tonga** (10.3 percent). Although copra production in Polynesia dropped 11 percent between 1995 and 2000, it still remains the essential backbone of the economy on many of the smaller islands and atolls. *See also* COCONUT PALM.

COUNTERPART INTERNATIONAL (originally the Foundation for the Peoples of the South Pacific). A nonprofit organization established in the **United States** in 1965 to aid and assist indigenous peoples of the South Pacific in their basic needs development. In 1992, it became global to assist other developing countries and moved its headquarters from New York to Washington, D.C. It has established 30 regional offices around the world. In the Pacific, they are located in Sydney, **Australia**; Nadi and Suva, Fiji; Port Moresby, Papua New Guinea; Honiara, Solomon Islands; Nuku'alofa, **Tonga**; and Āpia, **Sāmoa**. Its founder and president, Elizabeth Bryant Silverstein, was honored in 1999 by receiving the Visionary Global Leadership Award from former First Lady Hillary Rodham Clinton. Its **Internet** address is http://www.counterpart.org.

- D -

DAMIEN, FATHER JOSEPH (1840–1889). A Belgian priest who served as a missionary in **Hawai'i** for six years before volunteering to work among the eight hundred lepers who had been abandoned on the island of Moloka'i. Damien served alone as priest, minister, physician, counselor, house builder, sheriff, and undertaker to them until some assistance arrived in 1884. Afterwards, Damien discovered that he too had contracted leprosy, but he worked diligently until a month before his death in 1889.

DAVIDSON, JAMES WIGHTMAN (1916–1973). Regarded as the "Father of Pacific History," Davidson was born on 1 October 1915 in **New Zealand**. He received his Ph.D. from Cambridge (1942), spent four years in the British navy, then accepted a post at Cambridge, and later became a professor of Pacific history at the Australian National University for 23 years. More than any other single individual, Davidson assisted **Sāmoa** in its movement toward independence (1962) as well as helping with the drafting of the **Cook Islands** constitution and acting as an adviser to the of Micronesia. His publications include *Samoa Mo Samoa: The Emergence of the Independent State of Western Samoa* (1967), and he assisted in the founding of the scholarly *Journal of Pacific History*.

DAVIS, ISAAC (ca. 1757–1810). A **beachcomber** from England who lived in **Hawai'i** from 1790 until his death in 1810. He and another beachcomber, **John Young**, became intimate advisors to **King Kamehameha I**, and foreign visitors to the islands held both in high esteem for their integrity and positive influence over the king. Davis was poisoned, however, in 1810 by enemies who disliked his meddling in royal affairs.

DAVIS, PA TEPAERU ARIKI (1923–1990). The highest ranking traditional leader in the **Cook Islands** until her death in February 1990 and one of the strongest voices for **women's** and indigenous rights in the Pacific. She received the title Pa Ariki at the age of nine and spent much of her early childhood in **New Zealand**. She married

Tom Davis, who later became prime minister of the Cook Islands, and for the last 10 years of her life, she was the elected president of the House of Ariki, the highest traditional position in the Cook Islands. Her death was marked by two days of official mourning in the islands, the only such official mourning ever recognized there. Several months after her death, her daughter, Marie Napa, was officially installed as the new Pa Ariki. *See also* ARIKI, PA UPOKOTINI (MARIE).

DAVIS, SIR THOMAS ROBERT ALEXANDER HARRIES (1917–). Premier of the **Cook Islands** from 1978 to March 1983 and again from November 1983 to 1987. Born on 11 June 1917, Davis was educated in **New Zealand**, in **Australia** (School of Tropical Medicine), and later the Harvard School of Public Health where he received a master's of public health degree in 1952. His public health service included surgeon specialist in the Cook Islands Medical Service (1945–1948); member of the **South Pacific Commission** (1950–1952); member of the Harvard School of Public Health (1952–1955); a one-year residence in Fairbanks, Alaska (1955–1956); army service (1956–1963); and private medical practice (1974–1978) just prior to being elected premier of the Cook Islands in 1978. He was created KBE by Queen Elizabeth II in 1980.

His Democratic Party gained votes as a result of **Sir Albert Henry** (premier 1965–1978) flying voters in from New Zealand at government expense. Davis lost his seat in Parliament in the March 1983 elections, primarily because of the general belief that the constitutional changes introduced (life of Parliament from four to five years) were designed to secure pension benefits for incumbent ministers, that excess government travel funds were being used by Davis's ministers, and that Davis was growing increasingly remote from his constituency. Davis won back his seat in the November elections, and became prime minister once again. Davis boasts of having turned the Cook Islands economy around, reduced emigration out of the country, increased **tourism** dramatically, reformed the tax structure, and initiated a more independent Cook Islands foreign and trade policy. Because of a whole series of problems among which were his age (70), his anti-New Zealand policy, and his difficult personality, he was unanimously voted out of office in 1987. His autobiography, *Island Boy: An Autobiography*, appeared in 1992.

DEMI(S). A French term currently used in everyday speech in **French Polynesia** to indicate an individual of mixed (usually Polynesian and European) descent as opposed to ***mā'ohi*** to indicate a Polynesian or ***popa'ā*** a Caucasian. *See also HAOLE; PĀKEHĀ; PALAGI.*

DENGUE FEVER. A flu-like virus transmitted by a mosquito bite that causes mild influenza, muscle aches, exhaustion, rashes, severe headache, high fever, gum bleeding, and sometimes death. The disease frequently becomes epidemic in proportion throughout the tropics. No dengue vaccination has been developed, although scientists in Thailand report positive progress. In recent years, public health authorities have emphasized disease prevention and mosquito control through community efforts to reduce larval breeding sources. The disease was first reported in 1779–1780 in Asia, Africa, and North America. During most of the last two hundred years, the disease has been benign, but serious epidemics break out frequently in intervals of 10 to 40 years. A global pandemic of dengue began in Southeast Asia shortly after World War II. In the Pacific, dengue viruses were reintroduced in the early 1970s after an absence of more than 25 years. The most recent outbreaks occurred in **Sāmoa**, **Cook Islands**, and Fiji during 1997 and claimed 14 lives, and in **French Polynesia** in 2001. Thousands of dollars were spent spraying and cleaning up mosquito infested areas.

DeROBURT, SIR HAMMER (1923–1992). The first president of **Nauru**. DeRoburt was born on Nauru on 25 September 1923 and educated at Geelong Technical College in **Australia**. He returned to Nauru where he became a schoolteacher from 1940–1942. During World War II, he survived the **Japanese** invasion and forced labor (1942–1946), and after the war he became an administrator in Nauru's public service (1947–1951). He was elected to Nauru's council in 1955 and then head chief of Nauru in 1965. He was elected president four times (1968–1976, 1978–1986, 1986, and 1986–1989). He served as second chancellor of the **University of the South Pacific** from 1973 to 1976 and received an honorary doctorate from there in 1976. DeRoburt was created Officer, Order of Grand Cross of St. Michael and St. George

(GCMG) and received the Order of the British Empire (OBE) from Queen Elizabeth for his exemplary diplomatic service. He died in July of 1992.

DIAPER, WILLIAM (1820–1891). An infamous **beachcomber** who lived on several southwest Pacific islands—**Sāmoa**, **Tonga**, and several Melanesian islands—as a wanderer and vagabond. He also went by the aliases John Jackson and "Cannibal Jack." His surviving autobiographical writings reveal his intelligence, tolerance, exuberance, and enthusiasm for life. He was known to have left 38 children and 99 grandchildren. His works include: *Cannibal Jack, The True Autobiography of a White Man in the South Seas* (London: Faber and Gwyer, 1928); and John Jackson, "Narrative by John Jackson of his Residence in the Feejees," in J. E. Erskine, ed., *Journal of a Cruise Among the Islands of the Western Pacific* (London: John Murray, 1853).

DOLE, SANFORD BALLARD (1844–1926). First and only president of the Republic of **Hawai'i** (1893–1900) and then the first governor of the U.S. Territory of Hawai'i (1900–1903). Born in Honolulu in 1844 of immigrant parents from Maine, Dole became a lawyer and was appointed to the Hawai'i Supreme Court in 1886. After the revolution that overthrew **Queen Lili'uokalani** in 1893, Dole was elected president of the new republic and pressed U.S. President William McKinley for annexation. When annexation came in 1900, Dole became Hawai'i's first territorial governor. He served as U.S. district judge from 1903 until retirement in 1916. He died on 9 June 1926.

DOWIYOGO, BERNARD (1946–). President of the Republic of **Nauru** intermittently since December 1976. Born 14 February 1946, Dowiyogo studied law at the Australian National University and at the age of 28 entered Nauru's Parliament from Ubenide. He served as secretary of the Nauru General Hospital, general manager of the Nauru Co-Op Society, minister of justice, minister of external affairs, chairman of the Bank of Nauru, and leader of the Nauru Party. In December of 1976, he was elected president of Nauru, and according to the *Guinness World Records*, he was the youngest person (age 30) to be president of an independent republic. To date, he has served as president on five different occasions: 1976–1978, 1989–1995, 11–26 November 1996, 1998–1999, and from 20 April 2000 to 30 March 2001.

DUPETIT-THOUARS, ABEL AUBERT (1793–1864). French admiral responsible for seizing the **Marquesas** and **Society Islands** for **France** between 1838 and 1844. During his round-the-world voyage between 1836 and 1839, Dupetit-Thouars learned of the difficulties the newly arrived French Catholic priests were having in establishing their religion in Protestant-dominated **Tahiti**. In 1838, he set out from Valparaiso, Chili, landed two Catholic priests in the Marquesas Islands, and arrived in Tahiti during a heated conflict among the **London Missionary Society** (LMS) missionaries, the ruler, **Queen Pomare IV**, and the two Catholic priests. Backed up by his warships, Dupetit-Thouars demanded redress from the queen, a 21-gun salute to the French flag, and religious tolerance for the Tahitians.

Dupetit-Thouars returned to France only to be ordered back to the Pacific where he took possession of the Marquesas in April and May 1842. He arrived in Tahiti where French opposition by the LMS missionary **George Pritchard** almost caused an international conflict between **Great Britain** and France. Dupetit-Thouars annexed the islands outright, appointed a French governor (Joseph Bruat), and left. He was promoted to vice admiral in 1843, elected deputy from Marne-et-Loire in 1849, and died in Paris in 1864. His four-volume work, *Voyage autour du monde sur la frégate la Venus pendant les années 1836–1839* (Paris: Gide, 1840–64), provides firsthand details regarding the incident.

DUTROU-BORNIER, JEAN-BAPTISTE (?–1877). A French entrepreneur who settled on **Easter Island** in 1866 and established the foundations for a prosperous agricultural undertaking at Mataveri. His forced labor, his self-invoked title of king, and his rape of women resulted in many of the islanders migrating to **Tahiti** and eventually led to his murder in 1877.

- E -

EAST-WEST CENTER (EWC). (Center for Cultural and Technical Interchange between East and West). An internationally recognized center for Pacific studies, located in Honolulu on the Mānoa campus of the

University of Hawai'i (but independent of the university), it was created in 1960 and is primarily supported by U.S. federal funds. This funding, however, has declined through the years, and the EWC must rely more on public and private donations, foundations, and corporations. Its main purposes are to provide scholarship and grants to students and scholars from the **United States** and the Pacific basin to come to the university to study, to encourage the growth and development of academic programs at the university that deal with Pacific subjects, and to gather and disseminate information regarding contemporary Pacific issues through publications, seminars, and conferences. Its 18-member international board of governors consist of five appointees of the U.S. secretary of state, five by the governor of **Hawai'i**, five from Asia and the Pacific, the governor of Hawai'i, the president of the university, and the associate directory of educational and cultural affairs of the U.S. Information Agency. The center maintains three residence halls on campus for visitors, and its current president is Charles E. Morrison who was appointed on 1 August 1998. Its **Internet** address is http://www.east west center.org/.

EASTER ISLAND. Known in the local Polynesian dialect as *Rapanui* or *Te Pito te Hunua* (The Navel of the World), it is officially known by its Spanish name, *Isla de Pascua*, a dependency of Chile since 1888. In May of 1996, UNESCO declared Easter Island a "Cultural Possession of Humanity," and the current Chilean government views Easter Island favorably as an important geopolitical outpost. The volcanic-formed island of 158 sq km (60 sq mi) lies 27° 9' south latitude and 109° 26' west longitude, about 3,200 km (2,000 mi) west of the South American continent and 2,000 km (1,130 mi) southeast of **Pitcairn Island**. Its highest peak, Mount Terevaka, reaches a height of 510 meters (1,673 feet). The principal community on Easter Island is Hanga Roa. The island population is estimated to be nearly 3,700 with an additional 600 Rapanui living in Chile, 200 in **French Polynesia**, and over 50 in the **United States**. Approximately 60 percent of the island population is of Polynesian extract, and 50 percent under the age of 29. Spanish is the official language, but English, French, and German are understood by a few islanders.

Climate, Fauna, and Flora: The climate of Easter Island is subtropical with an average rainfall between 125 cm and 150 cm (50 to 60 in.) per year. There are no streams on the island; drinking water comes from three lakes located in the craters of the mountains. Vegetation is sparse and principally consists of tall grass that covers most of the island. A few acacia trees (called *miro Tahiti*) provide wood carving materials for local sculptors. Cultivated crops include sweet potatoes, sugar cane, bananas, yams, and tobacco. Sheep, cattle, and horses, introduced by Europeans, provide the only animals on the island. Abundant fish and lobsters are available in the coastal waters offshore.

Pre-European History: The island was most likely first settled by **Marquesans** around A.D. 450 with perhaps contacts and settlers from the South American continent. Rapanui tradition ascribes the first settler as Hotu Matu‘a whose followers were called Hanau Momoka (“short ears”). The Hanau Eepe (“long ears”) arrived sometime after, and the two groups remained rivals upon the island. Pre-European Rapanui developed one of the most highly evolved technologies of Neolithic culture in the world. This resulted in the carving of thousands of structures on the island—*ahu* (religious edifices) and *moai* (monolithic stone statues), some weighing over 20 tons. The culture also produced a written script, *kohau rongorongo*, something unique among any of the other Polynesian islands. Feuding between the kinship groups on the island characterized the last several hundred years before the arrival of the Europeans and resulted in the toppling of many of the stone images and the introduction of cannibalism.

Modern History: Dutch navigator Jacob Roggeveen sighted the island on Easter Sunday in 1722, thus the reason for the modern nomenclature. Other Europeans made their way to the island—Felipe Haedo “annexed” the islands to Spain in 1770, **James Cook** of England arrived in 1774, and the French navigator Jean-François Lapérouse in 1786. Other ships arrived on the island bringing Western influence, disease, and devastation. Others, looking for cheap labor, decimated the population through **blackbirding**. Between 1862 and 1863, for example, an estimated 1,500 islanders were taken by Peruvian entrepreneurs to work as slaves in the guano mines in the Chincha Islands or in the sugar plantations along the coast of Peru. Few ever returned.

Roman Catholic Christianity was introduced in 1864 by **Father Eugene Eyraud**, who converted every individual on the island before his death in 1868. Soon after, several foreign entrepreneurs attempted commercial enterprises on the island. **Jean-Baptiste Dutrou-Bornier**, a Frenchman, settled on the island in 1866 and established the foundations for a prosperous agricultural undertaking at Mataveri. His harsh tactics led to his murder in 1877. John Brander, an Englishman from **Tahiti**, established a sheep ranch operation on the island in 1869.

By 1877, the population had dropped from an estimated 4,000 at contact to only 110 individuals. In 1888, the island was annexed to Chile by Captain Policarpo Toro because of the island's strategic location and because of its possible commercial value. The Tahitian-based sheep ranch operation gave way to a Chilean operation owned by Enrique Merlet and then the Williamson-Balfour Corporation, under the designation of Compañía Explotadora de la Isla de Pascua (Easter Island Exploitation Company), or the CEDIP, with Merlet as its manager, and the islanders exploited of their land and labor. (The CEDIP essentially remained the major governing power on Easter Island until its demise in 1952.)

On occasion, the indigenous population has revolted against their Chilean overlords. In 1900, they rioted after the last Rapanui king (Riro) was murdered (possibly by Merlet). Again in 1914, a prophetess named Angata led an uprising against their colonial overlords. Order was restored only with the arrival of the Chilean warship *Baquedano.* Bishop Rafael Edwards arrived on the island in 1916 to investigate the shocking reports of squalid living conditions of the Rapanui. Edwards's reports suggested that the CEDIP was a feudal overlord and that the Rapanui were no more than slaves. Depositions collected by company officials and foreign visitors, however, rejected these allegations. A court case against the company in 1927 was eventually dropped, and the company continued to conduct island affairs until 1952. Revocation of the company leases in 1952 resulted in the affairs of the island being administered through the navy with an appointed civilian governor aided by a mayor and a council of elders.

As other Pacific island nations became independent in the 1950s and 1960s, the Easter Islanders themselves sought a greater degree of control and recognition from Chile. A French expedition in the early 1960s criticized the navy's administration of the Easter Islanders and the fact that by 1964 Easter Islanders still had no vote in government affairs at any level, and membership in the advisory body was subject to approval by the military governor. Protests were sent to the president in Chile, and the islanders elected a mayor (Alfonso Rapu) against the threat of the military governor. French and Chilean warships appeared in the harbor, but any confrontation was thwarted by the call for new elections, the extension of the franchise to include **women**, and the introduction of a secret ballot. Easter Island was granted the status of a civil department within the province of Valparaiso, and since 1966, the Chilean government has spent millions of dollars on Easter Island.

Sheep raising remained the chief industry until 1967 when the island's first airport was built, and as a result, **tourism** and government employment have replaced it as the island's economic mainstay. In 1985, the **United States** concluded an agreement with the Chilean government to establish a $9 million space shuttle emergency landing and rescue site on the island (opened late 1987). The Mataveri airport expansion project created approximately 150 construction jobs. Since then, jet airplane service connects the island with Valparaiso and Tahiti with two flights per week. During the 1990s, the levels of social and health services, utilities, communications, transportation, and housing have all been upgraded. Money was allocated for the repaving of roads (especially the one from Hanga Roa to Anakena, 16 km away, in 1996), the repaving of the airstrip and upgrading the tower and terminal building ($12.2 million in 1996), and the building of an old people's home (1998), a new pier, school, and an art gallery (1999). A new antenna in 1996 now allows direct television broadcasts from Chile; new telephone area codes and the installation of hundreds of telephones have made communications to and from the island more accessible. **Internet** was introduced in January 1998, but service is expensive. Customers pay a $47 monthly fee, and they must also pay a $.05 minute telephone charge.

Most of the funding of the recent projects has come from grants from the Chilean government. The island's working budget for 1997 was $1.54 million, but even at that, the governor feared that expenses would exceed the government's income. (The islanders pay no taxes.)

Other support comes from grants from foreign countries; international cultural agencies; United Nations Educational, Scientific, and Cultural Organization; and tourists. During the first half of 1993, a full-length Hollywood film, *Rapa Nui*, was filmed on the island. The filming had only a temporary impact upon the economy, although islanders were able to learn new skills and increase their incomes, while at the same time businesses flourished. The main economic impact of the 1990s, however, was the rapid increase in tourism. In 1990, only 4,961 tourists visited the island. By 1999, the number had soared to 21,434. The effects upon a small island such as this are overwhelming. The intrusion of foreign (primarily Western) influences has created social and cultural problems that the local government and residents will need to address.

A major grievance of most Rapanui today centers on land. They resent the fact that they were herded off their property and claim they never sold or gave their land away to the CEDIP or its subsequent Sasipa organization that lays claim to over 40 percent of the island. That changed, however, in 1997 when the government announced that hundreds of parcels of property would be returned to the Rapanui. On 16 August 1999, 1,500 hectares (about 600 acres) were restored by means of a lottery. Each recipient received five hectares, and future allocations may be forthcoming.

The island government is headed by a governor who is appointed from Valparaiso. Since 1984 this position has always been held by an islander. The current governor is Enrique Pakarati Ikia, an engineer, who was appointed in September 2000 after the resignation of former Governor Jacobo Hey Paoa. A council of elders was first formed in 1983 to advise the governor, and its spokesman assumes responsibilities for providing authority on the customs and traditions of the Rapanui. The municipality of Hanga Roa holds elections every four years to elect six town councilors, one of whom becomes the mayor by election. In October 1996, that office was won by Petero Edmunds Paoa. *See also* ENGLERT, SEBASTIAN; RAPU, SERGIO; ROUTLEDGE, KATHERINE PEASE; TUKI, LUCIA.

EASTER ISLAND FOUNDATION. A California-based nonprofit organization, founded in 1989 for the purpose of establishing an endowment to support a library on **Easter Island**. The nucleus of the library is the collection of anthropologist William Mulloy who devoted much of his life to the study of the island. The foundation accepts donations to this cause, and it also sponsors a publication series of books related to Easter Island whose proceeds go to support the foundation. Its current director is Dr. Georgia Lee, and its Website can be located at http://www.netaxs.com/~trance/eif.html.

ECONOMIC AND SOCIAL COMMISSION FOR ASIA AND THE PACIFIC (ESCAP). A **United Nations** commission, founded in 1947 (as the Economic Commission for Asia and the Far East, ECAFE, but changed to ESCAP in 1974), to encourage the economic and social development of Asia and the Pacific islands. The **Polynesian** nations of **Nauru, New Zealand, Tonga, Tuvalu, Sāmoa**, and **French Polynesia**—represented by **France**—are members; associate members include the **Cook Islands, Niue**, and the Territory of **American Samoa**. ESCAP provides a wide range of developmental programs to member governments such as aid in increasing agricultural development, regional planning, international trade, beneficial use of natural resources, and transport and communication support. It also provides database statistics for demography and family planning. Its main office is located in Bangkok, Thailand.

EDUCATION IN THE PACIFIC. Education has been a major concern of all island governments since the introduction of literacy by the missionaries in the early 19th century. One of the first tasks undertaken by the missionaries was to create a written language for the islanders, and secondly they had to instruct them to read and write. Their primary reason, of course, was to facilitate understanding of the precepts found in the holy Bible and to "civilize" the indigenous peoples.

The development of a vernacular language and elementary literacy were accomplished in a surprisingly short time. Since **Tahiti** was the first field of endeavor, it was there that the first works appeared in the vernacular languages. **Henry Nott** and John Davies published their *Te Aebi no Taheiti* (*Tahitian Alphabet*) in 1810, and **William Ellis** established the first printing press in the South Pacific on the island of Mo'orea in 1816. Its first run was a spelling primer with 2,600 copies. Schooling in the 1820s and 1830s became compulsory by law in **Ha-**

wai'i. Later in **Tonga**, the missionaries could not keep up with the demand for schools and books published in their own languages. Within 10 years after conversion, the majority of the population in most of the island groups could read and write, an accomplishment which had not yet been attained by even the more progressive nations of the world, yet it was an education limited and subordinated to the goals of the church.

During the colonial regimes in **Polynesia**, educational policies were seen as a way to assimilate colonial peoples into particular cultures—British, German, American, or French—and to produce a malleable population. In most cases, however, colonial schools were few and far between. As Pacific peoples have become independent in the last half of the 20th century, they have seen education as a priority and as a vehicle for social mobility, but the educational systems left by the colonial powers are not always compatible with traditional cultures.

Debate continues between the countryside and the capital city and between professional and vocational training over which educational system is best for a particular country as well as what language of instruction should be used. Should the colonial language be continued (English or French, for example) or should the indigenous language be the mode of instruction? The result of this dilemma produces graduates who are bilingual but whose expertise in either language is not on a par with others. At the same time, Western education continues to undermine the traditional cultures. While parents insist that their children master the imperial culture in order to get ahead in the modern age, they lament the fact that many of their children find jobs not in their home villages or islands but in far off cosmopolitan cities such as Auckland, Sydney, Honolulu, or Los Angeles. As Pacific nations have to reduce their annual budgets for education, they have hard choices to make. *See also* 'ATENISI INSTITUTE; NATIONAL UNIVERSITY OF SĀMOA; UNIVERSITÉ FRANÇAISE DU PACIFIQUE; UNIVERSITY OF THE SOUTH PACIFIC.

EFI, TAISI TUPUOLA TUFUGA (also known as Tui-atua Tupua Tamasese Efi) (1938–). A Sāmoan politician, member of Parliament since 1965, prime minister from 1976 to 1982, and until 1991, the leader of the opposition, the **Sāmoa National Development Party (SNDP)**. Born on 1 March 1938, Efi was educated at St. Joseph's College in Āpia, **Sāmoa**, and at Victoria University in Wellington, **New Zealand**. He was first elected to Parliament (*fono*) in 1965 and served as the minister of works, civil aviation, marine, and transportation from 1970 to 1973.

When elected prime minister in 1976, he was seen as a youthful force that could move ahead further than his predecessor. He himself had high optimism of cleaning up the corruption and inefficiency in the previous government. He was reelected in 1979, but his administration soon became unpopular as a result of economic disasters, his tight controls over the economy that many referred to as "Tupuola's socialism," a public servants' strike that crippled the government from April to July 1981, and scandals in his own government. He lost the election in 1982 to Va'ai Kolone, head of the **Human Rights Protection Party (HRPP)**.

Efi returned as prime minister from October to December 1982 as a result of Kolone losing his majority in Parliament. In 1990, he took the title Tui-atua and the name Tupua Tamasese Efi.

ELLIS, WILLIAM (1794–1872). A missionary for the **London Missionary Society** in the Pacific. Ellis served in the **Society Islands** for six years (1816–1822) during which time he learned Tahitian, introduced the first printing press into the South Pacific, and gathered extensive ethnographic data that were to be published after his return to **Great Britain**.

After leaving **Tahiti**, Ellis spent two years in **Hawai'i** where he assisted the missionaries from the **American Board of Commissioners for Foreign Mission** in their conversion of the Hawaiians. Returning to England, Ellis published his Hawaiian notes under the title *A Tour Through Hawaii*, a work that went through five editions by 1828. In 1842, he published his *Polynesian Researches*, a publication that included material about the other South Pacific islands—Tahiti, Huahine, **New Zealand**, and several other Polynesian islands.

After his Pacific adventures, Ellis was active in Madagascar where again his publications have been recognized as outstanding ethnographic source materials. He died on 2 June 1872 at Hoddesdon, Hertfordshire.

ENGLERT, SEBASTIAN (1888–1969). An Easter Island anthropologist, born near Augsburg, **Germany**, he became a Capuchin monk and settled on **Easter Island** in 1936. He studied the ancient Polynesian dialect spoken on Easter Island, although by then in corrupted form, and published a grammar and text on the language. His influence on the islanders was tremendous, and his other published works remain a major source for Easter Island ethnography. *See also* EYRAUD, EUGEN.

ENVIRONMENT. Pacific islanders live in fragile environments and ecosystems. Their limited arable lands have always forced them to have a close relationship with their encircling ocean both for food and transportation. Changes in the character of that ocean can be devastating, especially to atolls that rise just a few feet from sea level. Because changes in the Pacific Ocean have occurred at a significantly faster rate in the last 30 to 40 years, many of the Pacific nations have become alarmed over the future of their island homes. A significant major loss has been reef destruction brought about by overfishing, pollution, bleaching, and rapid population growth. Eighty percent of islanders' animal protein intake comes from fish, and should the reefs disappear, it will take away an integral part of the islanders' way of life.

Another change has been in what is called global warming caused by greenhouse gas emissions. The International Panel on Climate Control predicts that the increase in global warming within the coming years will bring about the demise of several Pacific island nations. Its forecasts predict a rise in the sea level between 50 cm (1 foot 7-1/2 inches) and one meter (3 feet 3 inches) over the next 100 years. By then, the Polynesian state of **Tuvalu**, which sits only three feet above sea level, will not even be a speck on the map. Other Pacific countries stand to lose hundreds of their islands as well. During the last decade, numerous international conferences have been held regarding these issues, and they have appealed to the industrialized nations to take greater steps in reducing their gas emissions. The 1997 Kyoto Protocol, for example, is a bold attempt by the **United Nations** to protect the environment. The large, industrialized nations, however, dispute the proposed reductions in emissions from fossil fuels, and even among scientists disputes exist regarding the actual cause of our global warming. Moreover, in 2001 the new U.S. administation of George W. Bush refused to ratify the Kyoto Protocol. Hopefully, the next decade will bring about positive steps to alleviate the deterioration of not only our Pacific islands but our own continental environments as well.

ÉTABLISSEMENTS FRANÇAIS DE L'OCÉANIE (EFO) (French Oceanic Establishments). French name given to the various Pacific protectorates acquired by **France** in the mid-19th century. The EFO originally included all of France's Pacific island possessions, but in 1860 New Caledonia and **Wallis and Futuna** were made separate entities. Finally in 1957, the EFO was renamed the Overseas Territory of French Polynesia. *See also* FRENCH POLYNESIA.

EUROPEAN SOCIETY FOR OCEANISTS (ESFO). Located at Vienna University (Austria), it was established in 1992 during the first European colloquium on Pacific studies. It is a professional association which addresses itself to reseachers with a regional interest in Oceania, including the Pacific islands, Papua New Guinea, Irian Jaya, **Australia**, and **New Zealand**. The society is an interdisciplinary organization, and membership is open to all academic researchers in the social sciences and humanities from around the world. ESFO hopes to be an information network by organizing biannual conferences which have been held in Nijmegen (1992), Basel (1994), Copenhagen (1996), Leiden (1999), and Vienna (2002). Its Website, http://cc.joensuu.fi/esfo, contains detailed information regarding the society, membership lists, bibliographies, and other Websites to aid in Oceania research.

EUROPEAN UNION (EU). A union, consisting of the nations of western Europe, that works toward and oversees the economic and political integration of these nations. The EU had its beginnings in 1957–1958 as the European Economic Community (EEC), and its success led to the formation of the EU in November 1993 (the Maastricht Treaty). The group of African, Caribbean, and Pacific (ACP) states of the EU was created in February 1975 at the conclusion of the first Lomé Convention (Lomé, Togo). The Polynesian states of **Tonga**, **Sāmoa**, and **Tuvalu** were Pacific members of the convention. Under the Lomé Convention, the ACP states were given special aid, price supports, and trade concessions. When the successsor of the Lomé Convention expired in 2000, meetings were conducted between the EU and the ACP regarding their future status. In the meantime, representatives from the EU's other trading partners insisted that if the EU concluded a reciprocal trade agreement with the ACP states, the other members of the **Pacific Forum** should also be included. The EU and the ACP representatives met on 8 June 2000 and signed a new partnership agreement between them. Two weeks later, the EU announced that it would include all 14 forum island states in the agreement. Those additional six states are the **Cook Islands**, the Federated States of Micronesia, the Republic of the Marshall Islands, **Nauru**, **Niue**, and Palau. *See also* PACIFIC REGIONAL FREE TRADE ZONE.

EXCLUSIVE ECONOMIC ZONE (EEZ). A two-hundred mile (370-km) band of sea extending from the shoreline of a nation which claims exclusive rights over it—exploring, exploiting, conserving, and managing all nonliving and living resources. The zone was established by the international Territorial Sea and Exclusive Economic Zone Act signed on 1 April 1978. Although the bordering nations have the exclusive rights to resources within the EEZ, they cannot limit high seas freedom of navigation, overflight, laying of submarine cables and pipelines, or other internationally lawful uses of the sea. The EEZ provides the small Polynesian nations with vital economic resources otherwise not available to them—primarily in fish extraction. Several of these nations sell rights to foreign vessels to extract fish from their waters thus bringing in to their government's treasury money not otherwise available. *See also* UNITED NATIONS CONVENTION OF THE LAW OF THE SEA.

EYRAUD, EUGEN (1820–1868). One of the first **Catholic** missionaries to **Easter Island** (1864), responsible for the conversion of the island to Roman Catholicism. Hearing that Peruvian slave traders had carried off hundreds of Easter Islanders in the early 1860s, Bishop Étienne Jaussen of **Tahiti** demanded French intervention. He also sent Father Eyraud to the island to convert the islanders and to look after their needs. Through his efforts, houses were built, fruit trees and berry bushes were planted, and before his death on 14 August 1868, every individual on the island had been converted to Christianity. His companion, Father Hippolyte Roussel, created a dictionary and catechism in their Rapanui language. *See also* ENGLERT, SEBASTIAN.

- F -

FA'A SĀMOA. A Sāmoan term meaning "the Sāmoan way," or the attempt to retain as much as possible a traditional way of doing things. **Sāmoa** has preserved more of its pre-European culture than most of the other **Polynesian** states despite the modern pressures for change and adoption of Western culture. *See also* MĀORITANGA.

FALEOMAVAEGA, ENI FA'AUA HUNKIN (1943–). American Sāmoa's elected representative (Democrat) to the U.S. House of Representatives since 1988. Born on 15 August 1943 in Vailoatai, American Sāmoa, Faleomavaega (his chiefly title adopted in 1988) served in the United States Army in Vietnam (1966–1969), received a bachelor's degree from Brigham Young University (Provo, Utah), and a law degree from the University of California at Berkeley. He is married to Hinanui Cave (from **Tahiti**), and they have five children.

Faleomavaega began his career in Washington, D.C., working for the delegate from American Sāmoa (1973–1974), then as an assistant counsel, Committee on Interior and Insular Affairs in the U.S. House of Representatives. In 1984, he was elected as American Sāmoa's lieutenant governor under **A. P. Lutali**, and then in 1988 its delegate to the House of Representatives. Described as "the most adventurous congressional candidate since Davy Crockett," Faleomavaega hopes to end the many years of what he calls "colonial abuse" in his home islands by working to secure a status of free association with the **United States**, similar to the situation which exists between the **Cook Islands** and **New Zealand**. His other aim is to make American Sāmoa less dependent on Washington by diversifying the islands' economic infrastructure. Likewise, he pushed through a bill calling for the distribution of $4 million a year in scholarships for American Sāmoans to attend U.S. colleges or universities. His popularity is indicated by the election results in American Sāmoa which ranged from 65 percent in 1992 to 86 percent in 1998. In November of 2000, he won in a runoff election having garnered 61 percent of the votes.

FARE VANA'A. An academic academy established in Pape'ete, **French Polynesia**, in 1975 to safeguard and to enrich the **Tahitian** language. The academy comprises some 20 authorities on the language. It sponsors the publication of edited works and the translation of world literature into that language, promotes the teaching of Tahitian in all forms of expression—songs, public addresses, and newspapers—as well as making it a tool of scholarly research. The first "official" Tahitian grammar book appeared in 1985 and an expanded dictionary appeared in 1987 and again in 1999.

FARRINGTON, WALLACE RIDER (1871–1933). Appointed governor of the Territory of **Hawai'i** from 1921 to 1929. Born and educated in Maine, Farrington came to Hawai'i in 1891 as a newspaper editor. As Hawai'i's sixth appointed governor, Farrington promoted social, political, economic, and educational rights for the Hawaiians. He founded the College of Hawai'i (which later became the University of Hawai'i) and secured federal money for various development projects in the islands. He died on 6 October 1933.

FASI, FRANK FRANCIS (1920–). Mayor of the city and county of Honolulu, **Hawai'i**, from 1969 to 1994 (except for one term, 1981–1985). Born in Hartford, Connecticut, on 27 August 1920 to immigrant Italian parents, Fasi obtained his bachelor's degree in history at Trinity College (1942), served as a Marine during World War II, and settled in Hawai'i after the war was over where he established the Frank F. Fasi Supply Company. He was elected to the Democratic National Committee (1952–1956) and to the Hawai'i Territorial Senate (1958–1959). First elected city councilman (1965–1969), he was then elected mayor, a position he held for over 20 years despite many attempts by the opposition to bring him down. His exuberant and flamboyant style of politics is frequently referred to as Fasicrat, Fasician, or simply Fasi. He is one of the few Hawaiian politicians who has been responsible for the rapid economic growth of the islands since statehood, and it would be difficult to name another individual who has left a greater mark on Honolulu. He unsuccessfully ran for governor in 1994 and 1998 and again for mayor in 2000. He is married to Joyce Kono Fasi, and they have 11 children.

***FAUTUA*.** "Adviser," a political position in **Sāmoa**, created in 1912 by the German governor **Wilhelm Solf** to end bitter rivalry among various factions of the Sāmoan chiefly families for the position of *tafa'ifā* (paramount chief). The first two advisers were Tupua Tamasese Lealofi and Mālietoa Tanumafili I. When independence was declared on 1 January 1962, the two *fautua*, Tanumafili Mālietoa II and Tupua Tamasese Mea'ole (died 1963), were named joint heads of state, thus ending the title.

FESTIVAL OF SOUTH PACIFIC ARTS. A regional competition established by the South Pacific Commission (now called the **Pacific Community**) in 1972 and held every four years thereafter in which individuals from the South Pacific island nations come together to compete in traditional and contemporary drama, music, dance, literature, and art. The festivals provide opportunities for Pacific islanders to share in and encourage the development, conservation, continuation, and display of the evolving cultures of the Pacific basin. A South Pacific Arts Council supervises the organization and designates the site for the next festival. The sixth Festival of Pacific Arts was held in Rarotonga, **Cook Islands**, in 1992, the seventh in Āpia, **Sāmoa**, in 1996, and the eighth in Nouméa, New Caledonia, in 2000 with a theme "Pacific Cultures on the Move Together." Over 2,500 participants from 27 nations contributed to the festival in Nouméa. Further details about the festival can be found on the **Internet** at http://www.festival-pacific-arts.org. *See also* SOUTH PACIFIC GAMES.

FETIA 'ĀPI. A pro-autonomy political party in **French Polynesia** headed by Boris Léontieff that promotes greater autonmy from **France**, but not independence like its rival party the **'Āi'a 'Āpi**. The new Fetia 'Āpi party gained one seat in the 1996 elections and seven in the 2001 elections. It is considered a third voice in current French Polynesian politics. *See also* TĀHŌ'ĒRA'A HUIRA'ATIRA; TAVINI HUIRA'ATIRA.

FLOSSE, GASTON (1931–). President of **French Polynesia** from 1982 to 1987 and then from April 1991until the present time. Born on 24 June 1931 at Rikitea, Gambier Islands, French Polynesia, Flosse studied in Pape'ete and then in France (Lyon). In 1958 he became politically active and helped form a unit of the Union Tahitienne Démocratique (UTD) party in the **Marquesas Islands**. In 1962, Flosse became secretary to Rudy Bambridge, a prominent political figure, and on 5 May 1963, was elected to the district council of Pirae (town east of Pape'ete). In 1965, he was elected its first mayor, a position he held until his resignation in May of 2000. His optimism and organizational ability led to his rise as president of the **Tāhō'ēra'a Huira'atira Party** and finally to the position of president of the government (1982–1987 and again from 1991–). Flosse dominated politics during the 1990s, gained greater internal autonomy concession from Paris, and won elections in 1991, 1996, and again in 2001. Although he seeks greater autonomy for French Polynesia, he does no go as far as seeking full independence from **France**. He was tried and convicted on several charges of corruption and abusing his political influence for personal gain, but this does not seem to diminish his popularity.

FORUM FISHERIES AGENCY (FFA). *See* SOUTH PACIFIC FORUM FISHERIES AGENCY.

FOUNDATION FOR THE PEOPLES OF THE SOUTH PACIFIC. *See* COUNTERPART INTERNATIONAL.

FRANCE. A colonial power whose entrance into the Pacific in the first half of the 19th century resulted by 1900 in the annexation of several Polynesian archipelagoes—the **Marquesas**, the **Tuamotus**, the **Society Islands**, the **Austral Islands**, and **Wallis and Futuna**—all of which still remain part of France's overseas territory. Considering France's other Pacific territories in Melanesia, for example, and the introduction of the 200-mile **exclusvie economic zone (EEZ**) around these islands, France controls more ocean than any other nation.

After the loss of its empire during the Napoleonic Wars (1812–1815), France was anxious to reestablish its honor and glory, and by 1840, it was rivaling its Pacific competitors—**Great Britain**, the **United States**, and **Germany**—in maritime trade, the **whaling** industry, scientific expeditions, and religious (Catholic) proselytizing. France's ventures into **Hawai'i** from 1836 to 1843 were thwarted by both Great Britain and the United States, and an attempt to colonize **New Zealand** (1839) was rebuffed by the British who were already firmly established there. As a result, France looked elsewhere, and in June 1842, French **Admiral Abel Dupetit-Thouars** sailed into the

Pacific and annexed the less protected Marquesas Islands, the first outright act of Western imperialism in the Pacific. By 1900, France had seized not only an extensive Polynesian territory, but the Melanesian islands of New Caledonia and the New Hebrides (Vanuatu) as well. (Vanuatu became independent in May of 1980, and New Caledonia maintains its ties with France regulated by the Nouméa Accord signed on 5 May 1998.)

Until after World War II, France administered **French Polynesia** directly through French-appointed governors. Agitation for internal autonomy, however, resulted in more self-government being granted to the islands in 1977, 1984, 1996, and again in 2001. France's extensive nuclear testing on the **Moruroa atoll** from 1966 until 1996 and the resultant increase in the islanders' standard of living have generated French Polynesia's economic dependency upon France as well as France's wish to remain in the Pacific. France maintains a seat in the **South Pacific Forum** and the **Pacific Community** and besides the financial support given to its overseas Pacific territories and to the Pacific Community, it also contributes funds and grants to other Pacific island nations. *See also* NUCLEAR TESTING.

FRASER, PETER (1884–1950). Prime minister of **New Zealand** between 1940 and 1949 as a member of the **Labour Party**. Born in Scotland, Fraser immigrated to Auckland in 1910 where, as a member of the working class, he became active in the trades union and socialist movements. He helped unify these groups into an organized Labour Party, and was elected to Parliament from 1918 until his death in 1950. When Prime Minister **M. J. Savage** died in 1940, Fraser became prime minister and held this position through World War II until the **National Party** came into power in 1949. He gained recognition as a result of his skilled administration and leadership, received honorary degrees from numerous universities, and was highly respected by the **Māori** community.

FREAR, WALTER FRANCIS (1863–1948). Governor of the Territory of **Hawai'i** from 1907 to 1913. As a lawyer, Frear was appointed circuit judge in 1893 by **Queen Lili'uokalani**. After U.S. annexation of Hawai'i as a territory in 1900, Frear was appointed chief justice of its supreme court (1900–1907) and was responsible for the revision and annotation of the Hawaiian laws. In 1907, President Theodore Roosevelt appointed him governor, a position he held until 1913. Hawai'i's stable judiciary system remains his legacy. He returned to law from 1913 until 1934. He died on 22 January 1948.

FREE TAHITI PARTY. Also known as the Tahitian People's Independence Party, a radical political party in **French Polynesia**, active primarily in the early 1980s, and headed by Charlie Ching, who spent time in prison for his antigovernmental demonstrations and who is currently retired. The party advocated complete freedom of the islands from **France**.

FRENCH POLYNESIA. An overseas territory of **France** located in the southeastern corner of the Pacific, consisting of approximately 130 islands divided into five major groups: the **Society Islands**, Tubuai (or the Austral Islands), the **Marquesas**, the **Tuamotu Archipelago**, and the Gambier Islands. The Society Islands are made up of the Windward Group (**Tahiti**, Mo'orea, Maiao, Tetiaroa) and the Leeward Group (Bora Bora, Rā'iatea, Huahine, Taha'a, Maupiti, Tupai, Manuae, Mopelia, Temiromiro). The Gambier Islands, southeast of Tahiti, consist of Mangareva, Taravai, Aukena, Agakauitai, Akamaru, Makaroa, Manui, and Kamaka. The Austral Islands, located 1,600 km (1,000 mi) southeast of Tahiti, include Raivavae, Tubuai, Ruruta, and six smaller atolls or islets. The Marquesas Islands, located 1,450 km (906 mi) northeast of Tahiti, consist of some 13 islands, are divided into a northern group (the largest of which are Nuku Hiva, Ua Huka, Ua Pou) and a southern group (the largest of which are Hiva Oa, Fatu Huku, Mohotani, and Fatu Hiva). The Tuamotu Islands comprise approximately 78 coral atolls east of the Society Islands. The total landmass of French Polynesia is 4,014 sq km (1,544 sq mi).

The entire population numbers 219,521 (1996 census, but estimated to be 228,786 in 1999) and is approximately 77 percent Polynesian, 14 percent European, and 9 percent Chinese Asian. A breakdown on population for the island groups is as follows:

Island Group	Population
Windward Islands	162,686
Leeward Islands	26,838
Tuamotus-Gambiers	15,370
Marquesas	8,064
Australs	6,563

The official languages are French and Tahitian, although Marquesan and Tuamotuan dialects are spoken in those island groups. Over two-thirds of the population live on the island of Tahiti where Pape'ete is the chief administrative center. The territory is an integral part of the French Republic and is represented in Paris by a senator and two deputies. France is represented in the islands by a high commissioner appointed from Paris. The executive branch of the local government is headed by a president, elected by a majority vote of the territorial assembly, consisting of 41 (raised to 49 in May 2001) elected representatives from the various districts in the islands. The president then chooses members for a council of ministers.

Climate, Fauna, and Flora: Generally, the climate of French Polynesia is tropical, hot, and humid, but cooled by trade winds. The average monthly temperature is between 20°C (68°F) and 29°C (84°F) with the rainy season occurring between November and April. The average rainfall is about 165 cm (65 in) a year. Dense subtropical flora grows along the coast and in the valleys. Besides grasses and shrubs, **coconut**, mango, **breadfruit**, ironwood trees, bougainvillea, and frangipani are common. Land animals, other than domesticated ones, hardly exist. The islands, however, are supplied by a rich sea life with over 300 species of fish living in the lagoons and surrounding ocean.

Pre-European History: The first settlers into these islands came from the west—**Sāmoa** or **Tonga**—about the second century B.C. The Marquesas were the first settled, and from there groups subsequently settled a good portion of Eastern Polynesia—the Society Islands, the Austral Islands, Mangareva, the Tuamotus, **Hawai'i** to the north, and then on to the **Cook Islands** and **New Zealand** to the southwest. A closely related Eastern Polynesian culture subsequently developed in these island groups. (*See also* ANCIENT POLYNESIAN CULTURE.)

Modern History: Although Ferdinand Magellan hit upon Pukapuka in the Tuamotus in 1521 and Alvaro de Mendaña landed in the Marquesas in 1595, there were no other known European visits to these islands until the British explorer Samuel Wallis visited Tahiti in 1767. Afterwards, French explorer **Louis-Antoine de Bougainville** (1768) and English explorer **James Cook** (1768–1769) left vivid accounts of the tropical splendor of the islands and of the warm welcome of their Polynesian inhabitants. As a result, these islands became a favorite stopover for subsequent ships plying the South Pacific. Matavai Bay and then the port of Pape'ete became the most popular landing places on Tahiti.

As a result, **Pomare**, the Tahitian chief who controlled this district of the island, gained prominence over all the others. Firearms and trade with the white foreigners gave him the prestige and armed force necessary to subdue the other chiefs who eventually acknowledged him "king" over the island. The Pomare family ruled a quasi-independent kingdom until the French established a protectorate in 1847 and then formally annexed the islands in 1880.

The islands were Christianized by representatives of the **Protestant London Missionary Society** who first arrived in 1797. When French Catholic priests Caret and Laval landed upon the islands in 1836, there followed six years of intrigue and war that eventually led to the French protectorate in 1847.

After Queen Pomare IV died in 1877, she was succeeded by her less able son Pomare V who ceded his kingdom to France. Shortly thereafter, France obtained the Marquesas (1880), the Gambiers (1881), the Australs (1900), and Rapa (1901). These formed the **Établissements Français de l'Océanie (EFO)** ruled by a French governor appointed from Paris to Pape'ete, the recognized capital of the colony.

During World War I, Pape'ete was heavily damaged by the German ships *Scharnhorst* and *Gneisenau*, and over a thousand French Polynesian troops served in the war in Europe. The depressions of the 1920s inflamed a growing animosity against the outdated governmental structure. Popular demonstration forced the governor to rescind an unpopular tax bill in 1922, and through the ballot box (1932), they ousted a government-sponsored candidate (Gratien Candace) as their representative in Paris. The government was forced to establish an old advisory council consisting of 13 members, seven of whom were elected.

During the 1930s, worldwide interest in the islands developed as a result of the films *Taboo* (1928) and *Mutiny on the Bounty* (1934), participation in world fairs and exhibits (1931), and more so the first boatload of American tourists from California in 1934. French Polynesia joined Charles de Gaulle's Free French movement in World War II as 300 of its volunteers saw action in North Africa, Italy, and France. Bora Bora became a naval air base for some 5,000 American troops whose money and ideas were to have far-reaching influence after the war.

After the war, local nationalism spurred the organization of the party Comité Pouvana'a (later the Rassemblement Démocratique des Populations Tahitiennes, the RDPT), headed by **Marcel Pouvana'a a Oopa**, which pressed for more freedom from France. He continued to be elected as the islands' representative to the French Parliament (1949, 1952, and 1956). Finally, in 1957, the territory gained considerable local power as the EFO was reorganized and Pouvana'a became vice president of a new territorial assembly. Demonstrations and riots in 1958 led to Pouvana'a's arrest and imprisonment for attempted murder, arson, and illegal possession of firearms. A new jet airport was opened at Fa'a'a in October 1960, and Hollywood producers began the filming of *Mutiny on the Bounty* with Marlon Brando.

In 1963, the French began nuclear testing on the **Moruroa atoll**, and to handle the large influx of French nationals, the Pape'ete harbor was enlarged. Opposition to the new French onslaught began anew under the leadership of **Francis Sanford** who had been the liaison officer assigned to the American military on Bora Bora during World War II.

Finally, on 22 July 1977, the French National Assembly voted to grant a new status of autonomy to French Polynesia, and Francis Sanford became the vice president of the territorial assembly (essentially, the prime minister). After the elections of 1982, the **Tāhō'ēra'a Huira'atira Party (THP)**, a Gaullist party led by **Gaston Flosse**, in conjunction with the **'Āi'a 'Āpi Party (New Nation Party)** and later the Pupu Here 'Āi'a Party, advocated even further reforms. They wished to see greater territorial autonomy (but not total independence from France) for the islands. Ultimately, the French National Assembly approved a new statute in September 1984 that created a local government whose responsibilities included increased internal autonomy over education, health, public works, agriculture, fisheries, and **tourism** and whose president, elected from among the members of the territorial assembly, is in essence the chief executive of the territory. Gaston Flosse was the first president of the council of ministers elected by the assembly, and he has held this postion ever since (except during the four years 1987–1991).

In the heated elections of March 1986, Flosse's party gained 22 of the 41 seats in the territorial assembly. Flosse was elected president again, and in the same elections, he won a seat as deputy to the French Parliament in Paris where he was appointed junior minister of South Pacific affairs. Opposition voices accusing him of misuse of public funds and corrupt electoral practices forced him in February 1987 to resign his position to Jacques Teuira, a trusted colleague, rather than to his contender **Alexandre Léontieff**. A dock workers' riot in October (brought about after a year of trouble with the dock workers due to the government's attempt to reduce the number of workers on Moruroa) resulted in numerous arrests after a state of emergency had been declared and police reinforcements in the form of French Legionnaires were flown in from Moruroa atoll, New Caledonia, and Paris. By December, opposition to Flosse's style of politics and his misuse of government funds forced a change in government.

The **Te Ti'arama party**, led by Alexandre Léontieff, formed a new government from a strange coalition of the dissidents of Flosse's own party as well as members from the center-left and the moderate, pro-independence party, the **'Ia Mana**. Surprisingly, the party gained substantial support in the April 1988 elections (with 23 seats won in the assembly). Léontieff's government remained in power until the 1991 elections when Flosse's party made a strong comeback (31.5 percent of the votes), but he could form a government only with the backing of **Émile Vernaudon's** 'Āi'a 'Āpi Party, an alliance that only lasted five months.

In May 1989, the new government announced a serious financial deficit (approximately $73.4 million) inherited, it said, from the previous Léontieff government. In June, the Flosse-Vernaudon coalition introduced drastic increases in taxes on gasoline, tobacco, beef, and electricity, as well as major cuts in the public sector (which employed 36 percent of the island population). On 10 July, an angry citizen response took the form of massive demonstrations in Pape'ete with roadblocks that essentially cut the capital off from the rest of the island. French high commissioner **Jean Montpezat** sent in well-armed gendarmes to prevent a recurrence of the 1987 riot, and within 24 hours the government had rescinded its tax proposals and cuts in employment, based on the high commissioner's promise of additional French subsidies to cover the shortfall.

Since then, the history of French Polynesia has essentially been dominated by several complex and intertwining factors. First, French Polynesia's desire to gain further autonomy from France; second, political infighting led by powerful and charismatic leaders (several of whom were convicted of illegal dealings); third, France's nuclear testing and the impact it has had upon the islands; and, fourth, French Polynesia's precarious economy which is based primarily upon large-scale funding by Metropolitan France.

The statute of 1984 paved the way for further discussions and conferences regarding French Polynesia's status. A Development Charter conference was held in July of 1992 at which time the participants proposed priorities for reform. A 10-year "Pact for Progress" was signed between France and French Polynesia on 14 May 1992, and in June, Deputy Léontieff succeeded in getting an amendment passed in France that would essentially make altering the territory's statutes (laws) by France almost impossible. During that same month, President Flosse unilaterally began substituting the local term "Tahiti Nui" for the name of French Polynesia in all of his communiqués. The renewal of nuclear testing by France in the Pacific provoked widespread island protests culminating in the violent riots in Pape'ete on 6 September 1995 (details below). Flosse pressed France again regarding additional internal autonomy, and the territorial assembly adopted essentially a "wish list" in November and forwarded it to Paris. After being drastically amended, the "Institutional Act" (sometimes referred to as the Territorial Constitution) passed and came into force on 12 April 1996. It essentially extended the territory's control over fishing, shipping, mining, international transportation, and the **exclusive economic zone (EEZ)**. It failed, however, to allow the territory to make Tahitian an official language, to control immigration, and to regulate television and radio transmission.

A change in political leadership in France in 1997—the coming to power of the Socialist Party—created a cooling attitude in Paris regarding the further autonomy of French Polynesia. Flosse was not as welcomed, and the French government insisted that French Polynesia was merely part of France and must abide by France's laws. In September 1997, the French Overseas Territories' Secretary of State Jean-Jacques Queyranne visited Tahiti and when Flosse proposed more autonomy, the secretary responded negatively. Although Flosse did not propose full independence from France, he became provoked over France's attitude. He defiantly attended a Smaller Island States meeting in the Cook Islands, used the Tahitian flag, and spoke at the opening ceremonies in Tahitian. The main source of contention at this time was over France's membership in the **European Union (EU)**. As a part of France, French Polynesia was required to accept all the ramifications that meant—free immigration into the islands by Europeans as well as affording them with equal employment opportunities. Flosse demanded internal control over such matters, but Queyranne again responded negatively. (Two months later, however, France granted New Caledonia, its other Pacific island territory, those same demands.)

In May of 1998, Flosse announced to the territorial assembly that he was drafting a new status document that would essentially make French Polynesia an overseas country rather than territory. A conference on the issue was held in November, and in April of 1999, Flosse went to Paris where he proposed a timetable for the approval process. Local objections to the proposal were soon heard, primarily from the opposition parties which saw the process as being dictatorial without much input from the local constituents. Nevertheless, the proposal went to Paris where it passed the French national assembly unanimously on 10 June. As of mid-2001, however, the senate has not yet discussed the issue. The French national assembly adjourned in February 2000 without acting on the matter. It is possible that changes will be made in the document before it actually becomes law.

Politics during the 1990s were characterized by rancorous disagreements between and within political parties and by court convictions of French Polynesia's major government leaders. Although Flosse's Tāhō'ēra'a Huira'atira party maintained its control throughout the decade, it was only through coalition with sometimes old enemies. Flosse formed his government in 1991 with the help of Vernaudon, and that lasted only five months. By early 1992, the disgruntled Vernaudon closed the territorial assembly doors for months and prevented it from meeting. Then on 1 April, a court convicted Flosse of corruption—the first conviction of a local politician—but allowed him to remain in office. In the 1993 elections for the two seats to the National Assembly in Paris, Flosse and Jean Juventin barely won. The losers, Léontieff and Vernaudon, never made it to the second round of votes, and the surprise candidate was Oscar Temaru, the radical pro-independence leader, who gained his largest percentage ever. In 1994, Juventin, who had allied with Flosse in 1991, now deserted him and joined the opposition. Mimicking Vernaudon, Juventin as speaker of the house disrupted the sessions and refused to convene it for months. As a result, a split in his party occurred. Raymond Van Bastolaer and Tinomana Milou Ebb left and formed a new party, the Te Avei'a Mau. Ebb aligned himself with Flosse and became president of the assembly. Juventin and Léontieff both were convicted of corruption and of receiving kickbacks from a Japanese investor. Juventin was sent to prison in Paris, and Flosse was judged for "passive corruption."

The 1996 elections returned Flosse's party to power, again winning 22 of the 41 seats, and the pro-independence parties gains were better than anticipated. In March of 1997, a judge annulled the May 1996 elections of 11 territorial councilors for electoral fraud, most of them being from Flosse's own party. New elections in 1998, however, showed that corruption and convictions mattered little in local elections. There were few changes in the makeup of the assembly as a result of the new vote. Meanwhile, Alexandre Léontieff who had been fighting two corruption charges received a three-year prison sentence. Flosse stood for election for senator from French Polynesia and won the seat in September 1999. He held three political hats—mayor of Pirae, president of French Polynesia, and senator to Paris until he resigned his mayoral position in March 2000. In the May 2001 elections, Flosse's party gained 28 assembly seats out of 49, the Tavinai Huira'atira 13, and the Fetia 'Āpi seven seats. Flosse retained his position of president, and on

18 May, Lucette Taero was elected president of the territorial assembly, the first woman ever to hold that position. She had been minister of employment prior to her election.

From 1966 to 1996, France detonated 181 underground and atmospheric nuclear explosions on Mururoa atoll in French Polynesia for testing purposes. An influx of French personnel to administer this program brought an extensive increase in revenues to French Polynesia. Over the years, it created a standard of living higher than any of French Polynesia's neighbors, but not without its price, the main one of which is the islands' economic dependence upon metropolitan France. When France announced the moratorium of its testing on 8 April 1992, panic broke out in Pape'ete. Speculating that France would pull out all its resources from the islands and lay off hundreds of islanders, the newspapers announced the end of the world. This came at a time of an already serious economic recession in the islands. A round of discussions was held, and France agreed to a 10-year pact of progress and promised not to diminish its usual funding to French Polynesia. When French President Jacques Chirac announced the resumption of nuclear tests on 13 June 1995, however, opposition to the tests was unanimous, not only by French Polynesians, but by its neighbors and the whole world. Fearing the impact it would have upon tourism as well as upon its relations with other South Pacific neighbors, islanders staged a long two-week demonstration in downtown Pape'ete. The demonstrations reached a fevered pitch on 6 September. A women's airport sit-in turned into a violent mêlée of burning buildings and automobiles that disrupted Pape'ete for two days. The damage was estimated at $40.2 million. The testing and riots also caused tourists to stay away in droves. When France declared a moratorium on all testing in January 1996, French Polynesia again extracted concessions, both for guaranteed funding (an additional $190 million annually) as well as concessions to its internal autonomy. Continued French subsidies though assures the islands' continued dependence upon France. Although Flosse wishes to see more internal autonomy for the islands, he and the majority of French Polynesians fear France might withdraw all of its financial support from the islands should they demand independence.

Economy: Excluding the U.S. territories in the north Pacific, French Polynesia has the highest per capita income ($18,100 in 1998) of all the Pacific island states. Economically on par with New Zealand, French Polynesia is no longer considered as having a developing economy, primarily because of four decades of French investment. The territorial government plays a major role in the economic life of the islands, and its spending dominates the economy. Its annual budget for the year 2001 amounted to approximaely $800 million, a 10 percent increase over 2000.

French Polynesia's main industry is tourism. The islands' exotic volcanic islands, lagoons, and climate all contribute to its reputation as a South Seas paradise. During the past decade, the number of tourists has risen from 139,705 in 1989 to approximately 210,800 in 1999. Since the slump in 1996, the number of tourists has consistently risen, reaching a peak in 1999. The opening of new hotels since 1997, the increase in luxury liners, the commencement of the new Tahiti Nui Airlines, and the positive world economy have all contributed to this phenomenon. Tourism brings in more than $390 million to the islands' economy. The Tahitian black pearl industry ranks second to tourism. This industry, which had its beginnings back in the 1960s, now supplies more than 75 percent of the world market. Fifty-five percent ($142 million in 1999) of French Polynesia's total annual exports comes from pearls, most of which are sent to Japan. Other than pearls, agriculture (coconuts, vegetables, fruit, vanilla, and coffee) and fishing are the next main exports. Japanese and Korean fishing vessels pay licenses to fish within the islands' EEZ. This industry has the potential for considerable growth within the next five years. Sixty boats are now under contract, while Flosse says that 50 more can be expected by 2006. Similar to the other Pacific island nations, French Polynesia's trade deficit is high. Total exports, for example, amount to only 22 percent of total imports.

FRIENDLY ISLANDS. *See* TONGA.

FRONT DE LIBÉRATION DE LA POLYNÉSIE (FLP). Known in Tahitian as **Tavini Huira'atira**. A pro-independence political party in **French Polynesia** headed by **Oscar Temaru**.

FUTUNA ISLAND. *See* WALLIS AND FUTUNA.

- G -

GAUGUIN, PAUL (1848–1903). A French artist who abandoned everything in 1891 to sail to **Tahiti**, **French Polynesia**, where he hoped to gain inspiration for his "primitive" type of painting. He spent several years in Tahiti and then in the **Marquesas**, but was never able to satisfy his yearning for the primitive art of ancient **Polynesia**. He died on 7 May 1903 in the Marquesas. His paintings only became popular well into the 20th century. A small museum is dedicated to him at Papeari on the island of Tahiti. He is buried on Hiva Oa, an island in the Marquesas.

GERMANY. A colonial power whose once vast empire in the Pacific during the 19th and early 20th centuries included not only islands in **Polynesia**, but in Micronesia and Melanesia as well. In 1857, the German firm of J. C. Goddefroy and Son established a trading center in Āpia, **Sāmoa**, and from there it expanded into every major island group in the Pacific. By 1879, it was exporting millions of dollars worth of **copra**, cotton, and pearl shells. After Germany's unification in 1870 and the inauguration of Otto von Bismarck's imperialist policy in 1884, Germany vigorously entered the international competition for overseas territories, and because of the already existent plantation settlements throughout the Pacific, it was rather simple for the soldier and politician to follow the merchant.

Germany's only territorial acquisition in Polynesia was in Sāmoa where, by 1885, over 98 percent of its exports were in German hands. Violent civil wars over indigenous titles and a fierce three-way struggle among Germany, **Great Britain**, and the **United States** for control of the islands ultimately led to the **Anglo-German Agreement of 1899**. Germany received the Sāmoan islands (Savai'i and 'Upolu) lying west of 170° longitude, and those to the east (Tutuila and the Manu'a group) fell to the United States.

Because of competent colonial management and efficient working methods, Sāmoa became self-sufficient, and by 1908, its governor received no further imperial subsidies from Berlin. Germany's colonial rule in Sāmoa, however, lasted only until 1914. Within a few weeks of the outbreak of World War I, the entire German empire in the Pacific collapsed. **New Zealand** troops captured Sāmoa, **Australia** seized New Guinea, and **Japan** took Germany's Micronesian islands in the North Pacific.

Even though the German political presence in the Pacific ended at the beginning of the 20th century, Germans continue to be a visible part of the **tourists** who currently visit the islands. Numerous German South Pacific travel, cultural, and academic groups exist that help to disseminate information about the area. German scientists conduct research in the area, and the German government has contributed funds for various cultural and restoration projects. *See also* AMERICAN SĀMOA; BERLIN ACT OF 1899; BISMARCK AGREEMENT OF 1879; KRÄMER, AUGUSTIN FRIEDRICH; LACKAWANNA AGREEMENT OF 1881; *MAU* OF PULE; NELSON, OLAF FREDERICK; SOLF, WILHELM HEINRICH; TUI MANU'A; TUPU'O SĀMOA; WEBER, THEODORE.

GIBSON, WALTER MURRAY (1822–1887). A colorful adventurer who became premier of the kingdom of **Hawai'i** during the reign of **King Kalākaua**. As a young man, Gibson had already sought fame and fortune in the California gold fields, Mexico, Central and South America, the south Atlantic, and the Dutch East Indies. When the Utah **Mormons (Church of Jesus Christ of Latter-day Saints)** were having difficulty with the U.S. government, the newly converted Gibson presented himself before church president Brigham Young and proposed an Asian mission that would bring the gospel to all the Pacific basin nations.

Gibson's first stop was in Hawai'i where he found the church in disarray because of the lack of mainland missionaries assigned to the islands. Gibson self-appointed himself leader and moved the "saints" to the island of Lāna'i, where he amassed a considerable fortune by keeping the church contributions made by the members and by selling church offices. After approximately three years, church officials from Utah visited the island to investigate allegations from local church members. Gibson refused to hand over the lands and moneys, whereupon he was excommunicated.

Gibson left Lāna'i, traveled extensively to recruit laborers for work in Hawai'i, and eventually made his way into Hawaiian politics.

After being elected to the Hawaiian legislature, Gibson befriended King Kalākaua and eventually was chosen as the king's premier. Gibson's empire building, his emphasis upon re-establishing Hawaiians to be in control of their own islands, and his unorthodox way of doing things created powerful enemies in the government. After five years and a depleted royal treasury, Gibson was forced out of Hawai'i by a group of white reformers. He made his way to San Francisco where he died in 1887.

GOLDIE, CHARLES FREDERICK (1870–1947). One of **New Zealand's** best-known artists whose paintings of **tattooed Māoris** are known worldwide. Born in Auckland, Goldie studied art in Paris from 1892 to 1898 and then returned to his home country where he worked until his death in 1947. His paintings, known primarily for their historical value, hang in numerous international galleries.

GREAT BRITAIN. A colonial power whose extensive empire in **Polynesia** in the 19th and 20th centuries included the **Cook Islands**, **New Zealand**, **Niue**, **Pitcairn**, **Tokelau**, **Tonga**, **Tuvalu**, and **Sāmoa**

British exploration of the Pacific in the late 18th century led to the annexation of **Australia** in 1770 and the establishment of a penal colony there in 1787. At the same time, British explorers were claiming territories in other parts of the Pacific. For example, Samuel Wallis claimed **Tahiti** in 1767 and George Vancouver did the same in **Hawai'i** in 1794, but these claims were later withdrawn. It was only in 1840 that England took formal possession of another Pacific territory—New Zealand. By this time, international competition in the Pacific with **France**, **Germany**, and the **United States** had become brisk, and the independence of Polynesia was being threatened. Eventual annexation of the islands came in the late 19th century as a result of negotiations among (and in) London, Paris, Washington, and Berlin rather than in Honolulu, Pape'ete, or Āpia. By 1900, every major island group had lost its independence to one of these Western powers.

Administration of Britain's possessions in Polynesia—the Cook Islands, Sāmoa, Pitcairn, Tokelau, and Niue—eventually fell to New Zealand, while Tonga remained a British protectorate and Tuvalu became part of the Gilbert and Ellice Islands Colony. By 1978, most of these colonial possessions had negotiated self-government or independence or both and had been accepted as members of the **Commonwealth**. This status, plus the fact that Australia and New Zealand tend to dominate the "new Pacific," results in British influence remaining strong in the islands.

GREY, AGGIE (1898–1988). A South Pacific entrepreneur whose fame comes from her management of a hotel establishment in Āpia, **Sāmoa**, she was born Aégnes Genevieve Swann to William J. Swann whose Lincolnshire family migrated to **New Zealand** in the 1860s. In 1889, William established a business in Āpia and married a Sāmoan girl named Pele. They had three daughters—Maggie, Aggie, and Mary. Aggie first married Gordon Hay-MacKenzie (four children), and after his death she married businessman Charles Grey in 1926 (three children). Aggie's hotel became a popular spot with the GIs during World War II. Her notoriety as being the model for James Michener's fictional character "bloody Mary" brought almost every South Pacific traveler to Āpia to stay in her little hotel. *Pacific Islands Monthly* magazine editor R. W. Robson wrote some 35 years ago, "she is famous . . . for having taken a ramshackle old building and turning it, by her lovable personality and a genius for management, into a colorful Āpia institution and an exceedingly pleasant place in which to live."

GREY, SIR GEORGE (1812–1898). British statesman and scholar, he was appointed governor of **Australia** (1841–1845), of **New Zealand** (1845–1854), of Cape Colony (1854–1859), and then recalled home to England. He returned to New Zealand a second time as governor from 1861 to 1867. After serving as premier of New Zealand from 1877 to 1879, he returned to London where he died on 19 September 1898 and was buried in Saint Paul's Cathedral. Grey was respected by all who had dealings with him. His book, *Polynesian Mythology*, published in 1855 in **Māori** and English, remains a landmark in ethnographic studies of Pacific peoples. He was knighted KCB in 1848.

- H -

HAGERSTEIN, PETER (ca. 1757–1810). A Swede who was a **beachcomber** in **Tahiti** from 1793 until his death in 1810. Deserting George Vancouver's ship, the HMS *Daedalus* in 1793, "Peter the Swede" became an influential mediator between **King Pomare II** and the arriving Christian missionaries of the **London Missionary Society** in 1797. He also was influential in establishing the early pork trade between Tahiti and New South Wales, **Australia**. *See also* FRENCH POLYNESIA.

HALL, JAMES NORMAN (1887–1951). A famous U.S. writer who collaborated with **Charles B. Nordhoff** in writing numerous novels regarding the South Pacific—*Faery Lands of the South Seas* (1921), *Mutiny on the Bounty* (1932), *Men Against the Sea* (1933), *Pitcairn Island* (1934), *The Hurricane* (1936), *Dark River* (1938), and *No More Gas* (1940), several of which have been made into motion pictures. Hall died on 5 July 1951 at his home in Aure, **Tahiti**, **French Polynesia**.

HALL, JOHN WAYNE "JACK" (1916–1971). An organized union activist whose name is synonymous with the rise of the working class in **Hawai'i**. Hall was a young merchant seaman when he arrived for the first time in Hawai'i in 1935. He quickly became involved in organizing the territory's workers despite being labeled a troublemaker and being threatened by their employers. He urged the islanders to unite as a working class, to strike against the major island companies, and to elect pro-labor candidates to state offices.

The strike he organized in 1940 continues to be the longest in Hawai'i's history (298 days). When wartime martial law was lifted in 1944, many of the workers took other jobs or moved to the mainland. The International Longshoremen's and Warehousemen's Union (ILWU) appointed Hall as regional director in 1944. During the 1950s, the union leaders were accused of communist leanings as they led the workers in strikes against their bosses. Eventually, Hall left Hawai'i (1969) to become vice president of the ILWU in San Francisco where he died in 1971.

HAOLE*.** A Hawaiian word that traditionally meant any "foreigner," but today it is used in colloquial speech to refer primarily to Caucasians. Depending on the tone used, it may also be used as a derogatory expression. It is similar to the word ***pākehā in **New Zealand Māori**, ***palagi*** in **Sāmoan**, and ***popa*‘ā** in **Tahitian**.

HARRIS, RENÉ (1948–). President of **Nauru** between 1999 and 2000 and again since his election on 30 March 2001. Born on 11 November 1948, Harris was educated at Geelong College and at the Swinburne Technical College, Victoria, **Australia**. He has been chairman of the Nauru Phosphate Company and manager of the former Nauru Pacific Line. He was also a founding member and director of the *Nauru Post*, a national weekly magazine, and he has served continuously in Nauru's Parliament since his first election in 1977. Harris is married with five children and four grandchildren.

HAWAI‘I. One of the 50 states of the **United States** of America. The state of Hawai‘i consists of eight major volcanic islands located in the central northern Pacific Ocean (from largest to smallest, they are: Hawai‘i, Maui, O‘ahu, Kaua‘i, Moloka‘i, Lāna‘i, Ni‘ihau, and Kaho‘olawe) and 124 minor islands with a total landmass of 16,770 sq km (6,450 sq mi). The population consists of Caucasians (36.8 percent), Japanese (22.3 percent), Filipino (15.2 percent), Hawaiian (12.5 percent), Chinese (6.2 percent), and other (7 percent). Of the total population of 1,211,537 (2000 census), approximately 884,000 live on the island of O‘ahu where Honolulu, the capital city, is located. Since Hawai‘i is the military command center of the U.S. Pacific forces, approximately 41,361 military personnel and their dependents (44,350) are stationed in the islands and contribute to its economy, however, the number has decreased by 25 percent since 1990. English and Hawaiian are the two principal languages, but numerous other languages are also spoken including Filipino, Japanese, and Chinese.

Climate, Fauna, Flora: The climate of the Hawaiian islands is classified as semitropical with mild and equable temperatures and humidity. Summers (May to October) are dry with accompanying northeast trade winds, and winters (November to April) bring cooler, wetter weather to the islands. The islands' flora varies from the tropical, wet, windward sides of the islands to the desert cacti on the leeward sides of the islands. Land fauna is relatively scant with most of the animals being introduced by the Europeans since their first visits to the islands in 1778. The ocean surrounding the islands is rich in sea life with 20 percent of the 700 species of fish found only in Hawaiian waters.

Pre-European History: The original inhabitants of the islands, the Polynesians, first settled the Hawaiian islands in approximately A.D. 650 from their homeland in the **Marquesas Islands**, located in the South Pacific. Another wave of immigrants came from **Tahiti** in approximately A.D. 1200. They brought with them in their large double-hulled canoes their animals and plants for food. Over the next six hundred years, they established a complex society and culture based upon subsistence agriculture and fishing. Each of the island districts was ruled over by a chief whose rank and status were determined by genealogy. At the time of European arrival, several high-ranking chiefs had begun to extend their authority over their neighboring islands.

Modern History: Captain **James Cook** and his crew were the first known Europeans to sight the islands (18 January 1778). He named them the **Sandwich Islands** after the Earl of Sandwich, one of the patrons of his third and last voyage. After spending several weeks in the islands, Cook turned northward where he explored the Arctic region trying to find a possible water route through North America. Cook returned to Hawai'i in November for a winter rest. Amicable relations between the Europeans and the Hawaiians collapsed when Cook demanded that Chief Kalani'ōpu'u be taken aboard his ship as a hostage. A scuffle broke out between the two groups, and Cook was slain on 14 February 1779.

Shortly thereafter, the young chief **Kamehameha** unified the islands under his rule, and his family ruled the islands as a monarchy until it was overthrown in 1893. (See the chronological list of Hawaiian monarchs in Appendix B.) The 19th century saw drastic changes in all aspects of the islands' government, society, religion, economy, and culture. Calvinist missionaries from the Boston-based **American Board of Commissioners for Foreign Missions** first reached the islands in 1820, but it was not until the conversion of chiefess **Ka'ahumanu** in 1824 that the religion began to flourish. Within a short time, the royal family had initiated Christian laws that were to govern the society—against murder, theft, breaking the Sabbath, polygamy, drinking alcoholic beverages, and so forth. The missionaries also introduced literacy, and by 1831 numerous schools were opened with some 50,000 students enrolled. Meanwhile, the many European and American immigrants brought diseases not known in early Hawai'i. As a result, by 1890, less than one-tenth of the original indigenous population survived.

Similar to other island nations in the Pacific in the 19th century, Western imperialists threatened the precarious independence of the island state of Hawai'i. Although British explorer George Vancouver had secured a cession of the islands in 1794, it was never ratified in London. Treaties with England in 1836 and **France** in 1837 gave Hawai'i a most-favored-nation status. Fearing a French takeover of the islands, British commander **George Paulet** impulsively seized the islands for **Great Britain** on 25 February 1843, but several months later, British Rear Admiral **Richard Thomas** restored their independence. By the 1850s, the economy of the islands was tied directly to foreign trade and especially to the American **whaling** industry, and in 1854, the American sector of the population unsuccessfully pressed the government of the United States to annex the islands. The decline in whaling (1860s) led to the rise of sugar as the major industry in the islands. This precipitated the need for an additional labor supply. As a result, thousands of workers—other Pacific islanders, Chinese (1865), **Japanese** (1868), and Portuguese (1878)—were imported to work the fields.

Meanwhile, American businessmen in the islands complained of the political instability of the monarchy and called for reform and control of the government. The result was a palace revolution that overthrew **Queen Lili'uokalani** on 17 January 1893, and that installed an American-dominated republican form of government. **Sanford B. Dole**, the new president, pressed for annexation by the U.S. Congress, an act that was eventually passed in 1898 and that took effect on 14 June 1900. Hawai'i became a U.S. territory with Dole as its first appointed governor.

During the first half of the 20th century, Hawaiian history was characterized by the growth and development of the sugar industry, the efforts of the plantation business interests to gain control over the economy, the efforts of the Republican Party to gain control of the government, and the rise of organized labor. Production of sugar increased from 153,000 tons to over one million tons annually. Population also increased drastically from 154,000 to more than 423,000 with the Japanese becoming the largest ethnic group (40 percent) while the ethnic Hawaiian percentage dropped from 24.5 to 15. Business consolidation saw the emergence of the "Big Five" that controlled the economy—Alexander and Baldwin, C. Brewer & Company, Theodore H. Davies and Company, Castle and Cooke, and American Factors.

The bombing of Pearl Harbor by the Japanese on 7 December 1941 brought the United States into World War II. Hawai'i became a staging center for the Pacific War, and over a million U.S. troops passed through the islands on their way to the war front in Asia. Martial law was immediately imposed, and although there was little threat of any further attacks, civil authority was not restored until 1944, and then only by an appeal to the U.S. Supreme Court.

By 1946, organized labor had expanded its influence enough to be a major element in politics. In 1946, the Political Action Committee of the International Longshoremen's and Warehousemen's Union (ILWU) was responsible for the success of the Democratic Party. Since then, the Democratic Party has essentially dominated Hawaiian politics. (In 1986, Patricia Saiki became the first Republican elected in Hawai'i to the U.S. House of Representatives since statehood in 1959.) After a long struggle that had begun earlier in the 20th century, Hawai'i was admitted to the Union as the 50th state on 21 August 1959.

Government: Similar to the other U.S. states, executive powers are vested in a governor, elected every four years, and in a bicameral legislature of 51 representatives elected for two-year terms and 25 senators elected for four-year terms. Hawai'i elects four members to the U.S. Congress—two senators and two representatives.

After Statehood: The first state elections in 1959 returned Territorial Governor **William F. Quinn** to government (the state's only Republican governor) for a three-year term. Hiram L. Fong, a Hawaiian Chinese lawyer and businessman, became the first U.S. senator of Asian ancestry; while **Daniel K. Inouye** became the first U.S. representative (later senator) of Japanese ancestry. Governors **John A. Burns** (1962–1974), **George R. Ariyoshi** (1974–1986), **John Waihe'e** (1986–1994), and **Benjamin J. Cayetano** (1994–) have all been Democrats.

Statehood brought with it an accelerated growth in the economy, population, and international prestige as the islands soon became the political and economic crossroads of the Pacific. Hawai'i's rapidly increasing population (632,772 in 1960 to 1,211,537 in 2000) and tourism (109,000 tourists in 1955 to 6,975,866 in 2000) have created the need for extensive highrise apartments, condominiums, and hotels, all of which eat away at the islands' small available land and destroy the islands' natural beauty—the state's chief tourist attraction. (O'ahu is the most densely built-up of any Polynesian island).

Economy: The per capita income for employees in Hawai'i is slightly less than that of their mainland counterparts, although the cost of living is approximately 34 percent higher. To local Hawaiians, this disparity is called "the paradise tax." The inflated price of land contributes much to this disparity. Indigenous Hawaiian organizations—the **Ka Lāhui Hawai'i**, for example—maintain that both the state and federal governments administer land which in reality belongs to them, and they are currently pressing for land and monetary settlements. Land problems are expected to continue well into the 21st century.

The dominance of sugar and pineapples in Hawai'i's postwar economy has given way to the growth of the tourist industry. By 1966, income from **tourism** (one million tourists) had surpassed the total production of sugar and pineapples combined and had become the islands' major industry, and by 1992 the number of tourists peaked at 7.5 million (6.9 million in 2000). The resultant increase in hotels, timeshare condominiums, pavement, and concrete has given rise to numerous problems for the current government, the greatest of which are land use, population density, and water. (For additional information on the state of Hawai'i, see the author's volume *Historical Dictionary of Honolulu and Hawai'i*, published by Scarecrow Press in 1998.)

HAWAIKI/HAVAIKI. A Polynesian word used anciently to mean an original homeland or island from which the emigrants left, and as such, when the voyagers landed in a new island group, they would generally name one or more of the islands with this name. In **French Polynesia**, for example, several islands were anciently known as Hawaiki (Fakarava and Rā'iatea). The **Sāmoans** have their Savai'i, the Rarotongans their Avaiki, the **Tongans** their Habai, and of course the Hawaiians their **Hawai'i**. Confusion occurred during modern times when scholars inquired of islanders regarding their origin, and the reply would most frequently be "Hawaiki," an expression that led Westerners to identify wrong migration patterns of the early Polynesians.

HEILALA FESTIVAL. A colorful 10-day celebration in **Tonga** that annually celebrates the king's birthday (July 4th) with a public display of traditional music and dance, parades, choral festivals, fishing tournaments, and competitive sports, ending with a Miss Heilala beauty pageant. The festival in 2001 marked King Tāufa'āhau Tupou IV's 83rd birthday. The capital of Nuku'alofa decorates every possible structure and sponsors all kinds of carnival rides. The event had its beginnings in 1979 when the Tonga Tourist Association hoped to attract tourists, celebrate the king's birthday, and preserve Tonga's culture and tradition all at the same time. The name "*heilala*" was supplied by the king and is the name of Tonga's national flower.

HEKE-POKAI, HONE (ca. 1810–1850). A famous **New Zealand Māori** leader who opposed British settlement in his native land. He was one of the first, however, to sign the **Treaty of Waitangi** between **Great Britain** and the Māori chiefs (1840). His rebellion took the form of cutting down the flagpoles holding the British flag. A final confrontation occurred in 1845 and 1846 when a British contingent seized Heke's forces while they were holding Sunday religious services. The defeat ended his further attempts at revolt.

HEKE (RANKIN), HONE (1869–1909). A prominent **New Zealand Māori** political leader in the late 19th century, great-grand nephew of the famous **Hone Heke-Pokai**. The young Hone became a member of Parliament and was one of the most influential leaders of the **Young Māori Movement** until his death in 1909. He was responsible for the Māori Lands Administrative Act and the Māori Council Act of 1900 that established Māori councils on a local level.

HENRY, ALBERT ROYLE (1906–1981). Premier of the **Cook Islands** between 1965 and 1978. Born on 11 June 1906, Henry was the son of a minor chief, Geoffrey Henry, and his wife, Metua of Aitutaki, and a descendant of the early missionary Henry Royle who arrived in Aitutaki in 1839. An exceptionally bright student, Henry won a scholarship to study in **New Zealand** when 13 years of age, but the administration would not permit him to accept it because of his age. His father sent him anyway, and when he returned in 1923, he became a schoolteacher at the age of 18. He later became headmaster, but resigned over a salary dispute and joined A. B. Donald's, a local trading company.

During World War II, he and his family moved to New Zealand where he took numerous jobs to support them. For 14 years, he was an interpreter for Cook Islanders in the Auckland courts out of which grew his interest in Cook Island politics and affairs. As the Cook Islands neared self-government (1965), he formed New Zealand branches of the Cook Islands Progressive Association and the Cook Islands–New Zealand Society (later his Cook Islands Party). Returning to the islands in 1964, he organized a campaign and his party won 14 of the 22 seats in the 1965 elections. His sister Marguerite Story stood for him in the elections until he met the three-year residency requirement.

Henry's administration carved out a national identity for the new government of the Cook Islands. He represented it enthusiastically in the South Pacific Commission, now called the **Pacific Community**, and was one of the founders of the **South Pacific Forum**. He became a prominent figure in the South Pacific in its self-governing infancy, and his personality "has been a vital ingredient in the flavor of the South Seas." His downfall came in the elections in 1978, when his party flew Cook Islanders from New Zealand to vote for it in the elections using government money. In 1979, a court battle ended in his being fined for conspiracy and fraud. He was stripped of his knighthood which he had received from Queen Elizabeth II when she visited the island in 1974. After that, he lived quietly in Rarotonga until his death on New Year's Day 1981.

HENRY, GEOFFREY ARAMA (1941–). Successor to his cousin **Albert Royle Henry** as leader of the Cook Islands Party and prime minister of the **Cook Islands** in 1983 and again from 1989 to 1999. Born on16 November 1940, Henry first ran for Parliament in 1964 as an independent candidate for Aitutaki. After his term was over in 1967, he returned to **New Zealand** to continue his education, receiving a bachelor's of art in education at Victoria University.

While at law school, he was called home by Albert Henry to work in the government. He established the external affairs department and became assistant secretary of the premier's department, head of education and justice (1972), minister of finance and post-master general (1973–1978). In 1981, Geoffrey Henry was chosen as president of the Cook Islands Party on a platform of "parliamentary consultative system." In the general elections of March 1983, Henry held a narrow margin (13 to 10) in Parliament. A technicality in the constitution forced him to resign in August and called for new elections in November. His narrow majority had dwindled, and the Democratic Party under the leadership of **Sir Tom Davis** came to power from 1983 to 1987.

In the elections of January 1989, Henry was returned to office, with a small majority, but was able to maintain his position of prime minister until he resigned on 30 July 1999. Henry's decade of leadership reflected recessional economic problems found elsewhere in the world, and Henry's government often became the object of severe criticism. In April of 1996, however, he announced a severe restructuring of the government's departments and ministries which seems to have helped resolve some of Cook Islands' economic problems. In June 1992, he was made Knight Commander of the Order of the British Empire (KBE). He was succeeded as prime minister by **Dr. Joe Williams**.

HENRY, TEUIRA (1847–1915). A linguist and scholar of the Tahitian language. She was born in **Tahiti** on 27 January 1847 of a prominent missionary family, granddaughter of both the **Reverend John M. Orsmond** and the **Reverend William Henry**. Well educated in English, French, and Tahitian, Henry taught school for over 20 years. She was responsible for the reconstruction of her grandfather's (J. M. Orsmond) lost manuscript dealing with ancient Tahitian society and culture. The extensive manuscript was published posthumously by the **Bernice P. Bishop Museum** in Honolulu under the title *Ancient Tahiti* (1928). Henry died on 23 January 1915 in Pa'ea, Tahiti.

HENRY, WILLIAM (1770–1859). One of the original missionaries of the **London Missionary Society (LMS)** to assist in the conversion of **Tahiti** and **Mo'orea**—currently **French Polynesia**—to Protestant Christianity. Born in Ireland on 21 June 1770, Henry arrived in Tahiti with his other British LMS colleagues in March 1797. During the turbulent years of civil war on the island, most of the missionaries and wives moved to Sydney, **Australia**. In 1800, Henry rejoined the mission, however, and was involved in the early conversion of the islands. He baptized nearly a thousand islanders before ill health forced him to leave Tahiti (1842) for Australia. He eventually returned to England where he died on 1 April 1859.

HERE ʻĀIʻA ("Patriots' Party"). A political party in **French Polynesia**, founded in February 1965 by John Teariki, advocating complete autonomy from **France** for the islands and an end to France's nuclear testing in the Pacific. Its popular leader during the early 1990s was Jean Juventin, the mayor of Papeʻete, who claimed about 8,000 members, including the Chinese and *māʻohi* (Polynesian) groups within the islands. In September of 1991, it joined forces with **Gaston Flosse's Tāhōʻēraʻa Huiraʻatira party** in an effort to strengthen Flosse's government. A rupture between them, poor leadership by Juventin, and in-fighting within the party essentially led to its demise. Jeventin was convicted of corruption and bribery charges in November of 1996 and sentenced to 18 months in prison.

***HŌKŪLEʻA*.** A double-hulled canoe, 62-feet long, built between 1973 and 1975 by the Polynesian Voyaging Society in an attempt to resurrect the ancient art of canoe making and canoe navigating. The numerous voyages made by the *Hōkūleʻa* have not only provided a wealth of information about Polynesian navigation and migration, but have inspired Polynesians throughout the Pacific with a pride and awareness in their native cultures. The *Hōkūleʻa's* maiden voyage—round-trip to **Tahiti** and back in 1976—commemorated the bicentennial celebration of the **United States** as well as the first long-distance voyage of Hawaiians since the 12th century.

Artist Herb Kane designed the canoe, architects Warren Seaman and Rudy Choy drew up the plans, and Curtis Ashford was the shipwright. Micronesian navigator Mau Piailug guided the *Hōkūleʻa* some 2,400 miles to Tahiti and then back without modern instruments by using celestial bodies and swells of the ocean, the way the ancient Polynesians had done when they discovered Hawaiʻi in the eighth century.

Construction of a companion canoe—the *Hawai'iloa*—was begun in 1991 in an attempt to use (as much as possible) traditional construction materials. The 57-foot *Hawai'iloa* was designed by Rudy Choy, Barry Choy, and Dick Rhodes. Other assistants were Nainoa Thompson (master canoe carver), Wright Bowman, Jr., and Wally Froiseth. It was completed in 1993 and officially launched in July 1994. In 1995, the two canoes sailed together to the **Marquesas** in the South Pacific and then to the U.S. Pacific Northwest.

Hōkūle'a's most recent accomplishment was its sail from Hawai'i to **Easter Island** from 15 June to 9 October 1999. It returned to **Hawai'i** in February 2000 in time to celebrate its 25th anniversary in March.

HOLLAND, SIR SIDNEY GEORGE (1893–1961). Prime minister of **New Zealand** from 1949 until 1957 representing the **National Party**. The son of a member of Parliament from Christchurch (Henry Edmund Holland), Sidney Holland represented the political views of the business and middle classes. He entered Parliament in 1935, became leader of the National Party in 1940, and served in various capacities in the government during World War II.

Holland capitalized on the country's dissatisfaction with the **Labour Party's** continual policy of wartime restrictions, and as a result, he and the National Party won the elections in 1949. He returned numerous businesses to private ownership and imposed strict regulations regarding unions and arbitration. Holland took a firm stand against a waterside workers' union strike in early 1951 by using military forces to break up the strike. When he called a special election for 1951, he was returned to power with a larger majority (50 seats for National, 30 seats for Labour). Holland was knighted and retired in 1957 because of ill health. He was succeeded by Keith Holyoake who barely lost the elections to Labour (39 to 41).

HOMOSEXUALITY. Traditional **Polynesian** societies looked indifferently upon homosexual behavior and in some instances even encouraged it, especially when the oldest child was male. In that case, the boy was reared as a female to help take care of his younger siblings. The **Hawaiian** and **Tahitian** word "*māhū*" (half man, half woman) is used to refer to homosexuals, "*fa'afine*" (gay men) and "*fa'atama*" (lesbians) in **Sāmoan**, and "*fakafafine*" or "*fakaleiti*" (gay men) and "*fafine tangata*" or "*fakatangata*" (lesbians) in **Tongan**. Western colonization and Christianity brought with them the stigma against the practice, but it survived despite the repression. Currently, most island groups have given gays and lesbians an acceptance at home unheard of overseas. Gays and lesbians often hold important positions within the community primarily because of their strong work ethic and because they are perceived as making positive contributions to their families and society. The advance of **AIDS** has caused concern within some quarters, however, and recently there has been a growing number of altercations against gays, including crackdowns by island authorities.

HONGI HIKA (ca. 1777–1828). A fierce **New Zealand Māori** warrior who befriended the first Christian missionaries to New Zealand. He visited England from 1820 to 1821 and decided to establish his sovereignty over all of New Zealand. He sold land for muskets which he used in his ferocious warfare against the neighboring tribes through the south and central North Island region. Thousands were slain before the chief himself was shot and died. The resultant depopulated areas allowed easier British settlements in subsequent years.

HUI NA'AUAO. A coalition of approximately 40 Hawaiian organizations, created in 1991 under a grant ($364,061) from the federal administration for Native Americans to promote awareness of Hawaiian sovereignty and self-determination. The coalition claims that the federal government, which administered **Hawai'i** as a U.S. territory from 1898 until 1959, illegally used the lands seized in the overthrow (1893) of **Queen Lili'uokalani** for other purposes without compensation.

The coalition's key ally has been Democratic Senator **Daniel Inouye** who has promised to introduce legislation in the U.S. Congress to create an independent Hawaiian government within the framework of the federal and state governments that allow Hawaiians to bring lawsuits against the federal government. Not all Hawaiians, however, agree that the actions of the coalition are representative of the majority of the 40,000 native Hawaiians and 160,000 part Hawaiians who live in the islands. Its current director is Kunani Nihipali. *See also* KA LĀHUI HAWAI'I; OFFICE OF HAWAIIAN AFFAIRS.

HUMAN RIGHTS PROTECTION PARTY (HRPP). Sāmoa's first political party, formed in 1979 under the leadership of Va'ai Kolone, Tofilau Eti, and La'ulu Fetauimalemau as opposition against Prime Minster **Tupuola Efi**. In the February 1982 elections, the HRPP party gained enough seats to select Va'ai Kolone as prime minister, but only to lose his position because of an election irregularity in September of that year. It won its third successive victory at the polls in 1988, winning 25 seats in the 49-member legislative assembly (*fono*); in 1991 with 30 seats; and then in 1996 with 24 seats (43.5 percent of votes). The party is currently headed by Prime Minister **Tuila'epa Sailele Malielegaoi**.

- I -

'IA MANA TE NUNA'A ("Power to the People"). A current political party in **French Polynesia**, headed by Jacques (Jacqui) Drollet, that advocates self-managed socialism and independence from **France** for the islands. Founded in November 1975, the party achieved its first success in the May 1982 elections when it gained three seats in the territorial assembly (J. Drollet, J. Van Bastolaer, and P. Atger), but only to lose them in the 1991 elections. It has held no seats in the assembly during the last decade, but it does represent some 9 to 10 percent of the electorate, primarily in Pape'ete.

INOUYE, DANIEL K. (1924–). Democratic congressman and senator from the state of **Hawai'i** for over 40 years. Of **Japanese** descent, Daniel K. Inouye was born on 7 September 1924 in Honolulu, where he attended public schools. In March 1943, he enlisted in the armed forces where he served in the 100th Infantry Battalion in Europe. Highly decorated, he returned home and entered law school. He became deputy public prosecutor for the City and County of Honolulu and was elected to the Territorial House of Representatives in 1954.

After statehood (1959), he became Hawai'i's first elected congressman; he has served as one of Hawai'i's senators since his election in 1962. He delivered the keynote address at the 1968 Democratic National Convention, served on numerous party committees, and gained national exposure and respect as a member of the Senate Watergate Committee (1973–1974). In January 1989, he was appointed chairman of the Senate Democratic Steering Committee, responsible for Senate committee assignments. Elections results indicate his extreme popularity in the islands—1962 (69 percent), 1968 (83 percent), 1974 (83 percent), 1980 (78 percent), 1986 (74 percent), 1992 (57 percent), and 1998 (76.4 percent).

INSTITUTE FOR POYNESIAN STUDIES. A scholarly organization founded in 1979 primarily through the efforts of Robert D. Craig, Jerry K. Loveland, and Jay Fox, at that time professors at the Brigham Young University–Hawai'i Campus, Lā'ie, **Hawai'i**. It currently publishes the scholarly journal *Pacific Studies* and other monographs dealing with Polynesian island nations and sponsors seminars, conferences, and other timely discussions of island societies. Its current executive administrator is Vernice Wineera, who has been associated with the Institute since its beginning. *See also* POLYNESIA.

INTERNET. A late 20th-century revolution in telecommunications that one Pacific journalist called "God's gift to the Pacific." It compares in magnitude to the introduction of television, telephone, wireless radio, and electricity, and similar to these other inventions, it brings the outside world much closer to the isolated Pacific islands. In fact, the Internet brings far more benefits to the dispersed island people than it does to those living in populous Los Angeles, Melbourne, and London. Children in those urbanized cities have numerous libraries within a short distance from their homes and can take advantage of them; in the Pacific, however, children do not have that luxury. In many instances, books and other resources are just not there. The Internet can help fill this void. The Internet also allows subscribers to communicate freely to individuals around the world as well as bringing global markets within their reach. In this regard, it truly is a modern, unique phenomenon.

Major obstacles, however, prevent the Internet's expansion in many of the islands. The biggest is money. Most of the islands remain just above the poverty level, and only a handful of homes are equipped with computers that can access the Internet. Governments, universities, public schools, and libraries, however, are pushing forward to supply these resources, and at least the Internet will become available to the local people in that way.

Several Pacific island governments have experimented with marketing their domain names to help raise money for their budgets. **Tuvalu** with its *.tv* ("television") domain name and **Niue** with *.nu* ("new"), for example, are selling domain names on the world market to raise money. For a couple of years, Tuvalu also was renting out its lines to host an international telephone sex Website. (It no longer is doing that, however.)

To researchers, journalists, and scholars throughout the Pacific, the Internet has been a godsend. Data that once could only be accessed via distant libraries or through the postal system can now be obtained immediately right from one's own home. Sources such as government databases, newspapers, books, journals, and the like are all available within a click of a computer.

Despite the fact that Websites change URL numbers frequently, a list of the most important Websites as of this writing is listed in sections "N" and "O" of the bibliography.

IONATANA, IONATANA (1937–2000). Prime minister of **Tuvalu** from April 1999 until his death on 8 December 2000. Ionatana (Tuvaluan for Jonathan) was born on the capital atoll of Funafuti, a descendant of an Irish trader known as O'Brien. In 1956, Ionatana entered public service. He joined the police force and rose to become chief of police in 1976. In 1977, Ionatana became government secretary and the top advisor to the cabinet. He was later elected to Parliament. In 1998 as minister of education, he entered a leadership struggle with former prime minister Bikenibeu Paeniu and as a result became prime minister. Although holding this office just under two years, Ionatana won international recognition for his deep concerns over climate change and the impact it might have on his low-lying atoll, for leading Tuvalu's efforts to become a member of the **United Nations** and a full member of the the **Commonwealth**, and for his development of Tuvalu as a self-sufficient country through the selling of its *.tv* **Internet** suffix.

ISLA DE PASCUA. Official Spanish name of **Easter Island**.

- J -

JAPAN. Second to **Australia**, Japan is the South Pacific nations' greatest financial donor. Although Japan's interest in Oceania dates back several centuries, it is only in the 19th and 20th centuries that this interest has taken a more aggressive approach. In the 1800s, Japanese laborers emigrated to **Hawai'i** and New Caledonia (a Melanesian country); and by 1890, Japan's trade and exploration included Micronesia in the North Pacific. When **Germany's** North Pacific empire fell during World War I (1914–1918), Japan took the opportunity to seize its vast Micronesian possessions not primarily for what they contained economically but as stepping stones toward a larger Pacific empire eastward and southward, a southward movement that could have threatened **Polynesia**.

In 1937, Japan invaded China and World War II broke out in the Far East. By mid-1941 Japanese forces had expanded their military operations from China into South-East Asia, and by March of 1942 they had added Indonesia's large oilfields and much of New Guinea into Japan's expanding Greater East Asia Co-Prosperity Sphere. Just what were the outer limits of Japan's expanding empire is not known. Its movements southward suggests at least Melanesia and Australia, and from there a logical conclusion would have been the Polynesian islands lying eastward. The strike on Pearl Harbor (Hawai'i) on 7 December 1941 formally brought the **United States** into the war and a halt to Japan's northward advances. The battles of Midway in the north (May 1942) and Guadalcanal (August 1942) in the south became the turning points of the war. By 1945, Japan's continual retreat suggested the end was near. Only after two U.S. **nuclear** explosions on Japanese soil (Hiroshima and Nagasaki, 6 and 9 August 1945), did Japan finally surrender unconditionally.

The war brought an end to Japan's imperial designs on the Pacific, and for the next 25 years, Japan had little interest in the Pacific islands where the Western powers were still firmly entrenched. By the 1970s and 1980s, however, Japan became increasingly interested in Oceania once more—for economic and security reasons. In the 1980s, Prime Minister Yasuhiro Nakasone explicitly included the Pacific island nations in Japan's commitment to the building of an Asia-Pacific Community, and the official Japanese Kuranari Doctrine (1987) further elevated the importance of the Pacific islands.

Since 1988, nearly every Pacific island nation and regional organization has received financial support from Japan. Its contribution to the **South Pacific Forum Secretariat**, for example, has amounted to approximately $6.7 million since 1988, and Japan's contributions to individual Polynesian nations include the building of the **National University of Samoa** ($14.2 million), the improvement of **Tonga's** water supply ($1 million), road improvements in **Tuvalu** ($83,000), numerous grants-in-aid to the **East-West Center** (Hawai'i), and contributions to the building of a Pacific Islands Center in Tokyo (1996). In addition to grants-in-aid, Japan remains one of the most important trade partners for several Polynesian states, and that trade is expected to expand exponentially over the next several years. Another source of Japanese revenue for the Pacific island nations is **tourism**. Although most Japanese tourists flock to the North Pacific destinations of Guam, the Northern Marianas, and Hawai'i, their presence in the South Pacific is vital to the region's tourist economy and their numbers have grown rapidly over recent years.

In October 1997, Japan organized its first summit ever with the South Pacific Forum. Several Pacific leaders in attendance remarked that the summit proved to be far more successful than had been initially expected although a former U.S. ambassador to the Pacific critically pointed out that Japan's interests include fishing rights, deep seabed mining rights, and voters in the United Nations. A second summit (Pacific Island Leaders Meeting—"PALM 2000") was held in Tokyo on 20 April 2000 with an agenda that included three main topics—sustainable development of the Pacific islands, global and regional issues of common concern, and Japan–South Pacific Forum partnership. A formal statement regarding the environment was also issued, and the two sides agreed that future summits would be held every two or three years. It is anticipated that although Japan's role in the Pacific islands will continue to expand, it will adopt a low profile and its motivations will primarily reflect its national interests.

JARNAC, CONVENTION OF. An agreement entered into on 19 June 1847 between **France** and **Great Britain** regarding the independent status of the leeward **Society Islands**—currently **French Polynesia**. When the French established a protectorate over **Tahiti** in 1842, independence of the leeward islands was in question, and a civil war broke out that lasted until 1846. The document recognized the independence of the leeward islands (Bora Bora, Huahine, Rā'iatea, and so forth) and that no ruler of either the leeward islands or Tahiti would ever rule over the entire chain. When the French moved in and annexed the leeward islands in 1880, diplomatic correspondence between the two countries resulted in a reciprocal agreement that Great Britain would recognize France's annexation while at the same time France would withdraw from the New Hebrides.

JUDD, GERRIT PARMELE (1803–1873). Originally from New York, Judd became a medical missionary to **Hawai'i** in 1828 and ultimately one of the most influential advisors to **King Kamehameha III** as translator, interpreter, and minister of finance and foreign affairs.

JUDD, LAWRENCE McCULLY(1887–1968). Appointed governor of the Territory of **Hawai'i** from 1929 to 1934 and later governor of the Territory of **American Sāmoa** for one year in 1953. Judd's major contributions to Hawai'i are the public parks and playgrounds that dot the islands' landscapes and the reduction of state spending. He died on 4 October 1968.

JUVENTIN, JEAN (1928–). Current political figure in **French Polynesia**. Born on 9 March 1928 in Pape'ete, Juventin had a career in teaching before entering politics in 1965. He became a prominent member of the Pupu Haere 'Ā'i'a political party headed by Jean Teariki, and then became a member of the city council of Pape'ete in 1966 before a quarrel with Mayor Tetua Pambrunin in 1974. With a coalition of supporters, Juventin was elected mayor of Pape'ete in 1977, then territorial counselor in 1977, deputy of French Polynesia from 1978 to 1986, and finally president of the territorial assembly in December 1987. In 1991, he joined forces with **Gaston Flosse** in an effort to strengthen Flosse's government only to split from Flosse in 1994. He unsuccessfully attempted to topple Flosse's government and as president of the assembly refused to convene it for three months. Meanwhile, a rift in his own party left him essentially without support. These events, plus the fact that he was convicted of bribery and corruption charges, led to the demise of his power; however, he currently is leader of the newly formed Polynesian Union Party.

- K -

KA LĀHUI HAWAI'I. A **Hawaiian** native organization primarily designed to bring about self-government for the native Hawaiian people. Formed in 1987 at a constitutional convention, it held another convention in 1989 in which officers were elected and a constitution ratified. **Helena Salazar** was chosen Ali'i Nui (high chief); and **Mililani Trask**, a Hawaiian lawyer, was elected Kia'āina (governor) for a four-year term. The primary objective of the organization is to secure recognition of a sovereign state for the Hawaiian people within the framework of the **United States** federal government in order to resolve land and other entitlement claims of the Hawaiian people against the federal government. The organization has over 3,000 members. *See also* OFFICE OF HAWAIIAN AFFAIRS.

KA'AHUMANU (1772–1832). Favorite wife of **King Kamehameha I** of **Hawai'i**, premier (*kahui nui*) from 1819 to 1832, and then queen regent during the minority of King Kamehameha III. She assisted in the destruction of the religion and taboos of ancient Hawai'i and aided the Protestant missionaries in their conversion of the islanders to Christianity.

KALĀKAUA, DAVID (1836–1891). King of **Hawai'i** from 1874, selected by the legislative assembly upon the death of his predecessor, **King Lunalilo**. Educated, talented, and artistic, Kalākaua helped to revive an interest in the ancient Hawaiian culture. His visit to Washington, D.C., and the subsequent reciprocity treaty with the **United States** brought prosperity back to his kingdom. His popularity, however, diminished as he became more imperialistic and extravagant while his cabinet ministers became more greedy and corrupt. In November 1890, the king sailed to California because of his sickness. Unfortunately, his condition grew worse, and he died on 20 January 1891 in

San Francisco. He was succeeded to the throne by his sister, **Lili'u-okalani**, the last monarch of Hawai'i.

KAMEHAMEHA. Name of the ruling monarchs of **Hawai'i** from 1795 to 1872.

Kamehameha I (1795–1819), the Great, consolidated his position as high-chief of the Big Island, and then began his territorial expansion until, by 1810, he had united the islands under his personal political control and founded a dynasty. As a result of his dominant personality and shrewd business sense, he amassed a fortune during his lifetime. His wife, **Ka'ahumanu**, bore him two sons, Liholiho and Kauikeaouli, both of whom succeeded him as rulers of the island state.

Kamehameha II (Liholiho) ruled for five years (1819–1824) during which time the traditional taboos were overthrown, Christianity introduced, and education begun. In 1824, Kamehameha II and his wife, Kamāmalu, both died from measles while on a state visit to England. Upon his death, his brother Kauikeaouli ascended the throne as Kamehameha III (1825–1854). During his minority, his mother Ka'ahumanu (d. 1832) and then his half-sister Kinau were regents for him. After assuming control of the government in 1833, Kamehameha III ruled until his death at the age of 41 in 1854. Hawai'i's first written constitution was granted, the old feudal order abolished, land redistributed (the Great Māhele), and education and finances placed on a sounder basis.

Kamehameha IV (1854–1863) was the grandson of Kamehameha I through his mother Kinau. Departing from the democratic nature of his predecessor, he brought an air of aristocracy and elegance to the Hawaiian throne. He and his wife Queen Emma expressed real concern for the plight of their dying race. Financial support resulted in the building of Queen's Hospital in Honolulu. During his short reign of nine years, both the **whaling** and sugar industries flourished and brought prosperity to the islands. Significant improvements were also made in foreign affairs. His death came unexpectedly in 1863 when he died of complications of asthma, leaving no direct heir to succeed him.

His elder brother, Prince Lot, came to the throne as Kamehameha V (1863–1872). His stern and powerful character dominated politics during his nine-year reign. He firmly believed in paternalistic rule and felt what he was doing was in the long run best for his people. As a result, some of his policies aroused firm opposition. Being a bachelor, his death ended the direct Kamehameha line. His refusal to choose a successor threw the selection of the new monarch to the legislative assembly, an action that took several weeks to conclude. Its choice was **William Charles Lunalilo**, a descendant of the brother of King Kamehameha I.

KAVA. A nonalcoholic, euphoria-producing drink commonly found in most of the Polynesian islands (except **New Zealand** and **Easter Island**). It is produced by pulverizing (chewing or pounding) the root of the *piper methysticum* (member of the pepper plant) and mixing it with water. After the mixture is strained, the drink resembles muddy water. The euphoric effects of the kava generally take the form of sedation and loss of muscular control and unlike alcohol do not distort thinking. In some islands, elaborate ceremonial regulations surround its use and indicate a strict hierarchy of social order; in others, it is used without such distinctions and ceremonies. Governmental attempts have frequently been made to restrict the use of the drink, but it continues to be used and enjoyed by many islanders.

Until recently, kava was relatively unknown outside of the South Pacific. During the 1990s, Western and Asian pharmaceutical companies learned of its soothing abilities and began buying it to use in pills and tonics. Kava bars sprung up in many large cities, and its popularity has brought greater attention to the physical effects upon the human body. In 1997, the **Australian** government put restrictions upon its import and forbade its shipment by mail. In New Zealand, the drink is being attacked by the Department of Social Welfare which claims its use is creating major social problems. Legal battles have begun in California courts where opponents are attempting to compare it with alcohol when it comes to drinking and driving.

KAWĀNANAKOA, ABIGAIL KINOIKI KEKAULIKE (1926–). Great grandniece of **Queen Lili'uokalani** and heir apparent to the **Hawaiian** throne should the monarchy be restored. Kawānanakoa graduated from Notre Dame (1943) and attended the University of Hawai'i (1945). Heiress to the Campbell estate, she became a rancher and volunteer worker in numerous humanitarian and philanthropic organizations in the islands, including director and president of the Friends of 'Iolani Palace (one of the last visible remains of the Hawaiian monarchy in the islands). *See also* KA LĀHUI HAWAI'I.

KERMADEC ISLANDS. Three main islands—Raoul, Macauley, and Curtis—with a total landmass of 33 sq km (13 sq mi), located approximately 1,000 km (625 mi) northeast of Auckland between **New Zealand** and **Tonga**. The islands were annexed to New Zealand in 1887 and are currently inhabited by a 12-man meteorological survey team that measures the numerous earthquakes in the islands. The islands are also designated as a wildlife refuge habitat for marine animals and sea birds.

KING, SAMUEL WILDER (1886–1959). Appointed governor of the Territory of **Hawai'i** from 1953 to 1957. Born in Honolulu, King graduated from the U.S. Naval Academy in 1910 and returned to Hawai'i where he served in various positions in the government. In 1934, he was elected delegate to the U.S. Congress for eight years. As governor of the state, King's major contribution was his untiring effort in preparing the islands for statehood. Highly respected by his colleagues, he died on 12 March 1959.

KINGI, WIREMU (ca. 1795–1882). A **New Zealand Māori** chief (Te Rangitake), who became one of the first converts to Christianity and who befriended the early British immigrants to the land. By the late 1840s, however, his attitude changed as he became alarmed at further British settlements. When Governor Gore Brown ignored the Māori land rights in 1859, war broke out (the Taranaki Land Wars), and Kingi worked as a pacifist against the injustices done to his people. Eventually, the government recognized its error and in 1926 awarded £5,000 annually to the Taranaki Trust Board (an advisory body of representatives elected to the New Zealand government every three years by the various Māori tribes). *See also* LAND WARS.

KIWI (*Apterygidae*). A primitive bird unique to **New Zealand** and the national symbol of the country. This nocturnal bird is found throughout the country, is unable to fly, and has no breastbone. It nests on the ground and lays eggs much larger to the relative size of the bird than those of any other species of bird. The male incubates the eggs which take about 75 days to hatch. New Zealanders are frequently referred to as kiwis.

KIWIFRUIT (*Actinidia chinensis*). A subtropical fruit indigenous to China but which has become one of **New Zealand's** major export commodities. Commonly known as the Chinese gooseberry, the fruit grows on vines and takes years before it matures. Their popularity has resulted in their production being launched in other countries, and competition from areas such as California now threatens New Zealand's markets in the **United States**.

KRÄMER, AUGUSTIN FRIEDRICH (1865–1941). A German scholar of Pacific ethnography. Having studied medicine in Tübingen and Berlin, Krämer joined the imperial navy and served on two expeditions to the South Pacific (1893–1895 and 1897–1899) most of which time was spent in **Sāmoa**. He returned to the Pacific twice, from 1906 to 1907 and 1909 to 1910, as an anthropologist during which time he gathered volumes of scientific and ethnographic data. Among his most famous publications is the two-volume work *Die Samoa-Inseln* (1902–1903) which provides detailed information on traditional Sāmoan society in the late 19th century.

KRUSE, LEALAIALOA F. MICHAEL (1948–). The first ethnic Sāmoan to be appointed (1987) to the high court of **American Sāmoa**. All previous appointments had been *palagis* (Caucasians). Kruse received his AB degree from Victoria University in Wellington, **New Zealand**, then his law degree from George Washington Law School in Washington, D.C. He joined the law firm of Kruse, Sunia, and Ward in Pago Pago where he practiced for 11 years before being appointed to the high court position by U.S. Interior Department Secretary Donald Hodel.

- L -

LABOR TRADE. A system of indentured labor that replaced slavery in the 19th century, sometimes referred to as "**blackbirding**." When **Great Britain** abolished slavery in 1833, her colonies that had relied upon cheap plantation labor to this point had to find other means of providing this same labor.

In 1847, Benjamin Boyd, an entrepreneur from New South Wales, took on two shiploads of Pacific islanders from the Loyalty Islands and the New Hebrides (Vanuatu) to assist on his sheep farm, but the experiment was unsuccessful. Meanwhile, the demand for labor grew as traders in **sandalwood**, **whalers**, ship captains, and plantation owners all needed lots of cheap manual labor.

The result was a system of "recruiting" islanders that assumed a form not much different than slave trading. A sea captain would visit an island village, induce islanders to sign on as plantation workers elsewhere in the Pacific with promises of great wealth and adventure, and then "sell" them to plantation masters at some distant land or island. Their experiences in the new land seldom produced the promised rewards. They frequently were paid in arms and munitions which contributed to the brutal civil wars that raged on many of the home islands, or they were abandoned in their new land.

The largest importer of island labor was Queensland in **Australia**. It is estimated that over 60,000 islanders worked in that colony during the last half of the 19th century. The most flagrant misuse of the system came from Peru during 1862 and 1863 when some 33 ships sailed the Pacific looking for prospective laborers to work in its coastal plantations. Many prospects were lured on board ship with flagrant misrepresentations of salaries and rewards or they were forcibly kidnapped. Of the 3,634 islanders (including **women** and children) recruited in this fashion, almost none ever made their way back to their native homelands. It was only with the intervention of the French and the insistence of the British that it be checked in their territories that this system was eventually abandoned.

LABOUR PARTY. A **New Zealand** political party, founded in 1910 from various tradesgroups and labor councils, it maintains a socialist view of providing an adequate standard of living to its citizens, and is currently one of the two major political parties in New Zealand. Its first national victory came in 1935 when its leader **Michael Joseph Savage** became prime minister and controlled the government until 1949. Subsequent governments (1957–1960, 1972–1975, 1984–1990) have attempted to deal with the various economic crises of the last 50 years.

In the 1990 elections, Labour won 28 Parliament seats while its longtime rival, the **National Party**, received 68 seats and came to power. Labour lost both the 1993 and 1996 elections. In 1993, **Helen Clark** replaced Michael Moore as Parliament leader and in the 1999 elections, Labour won a significant victory (49 seats to National's 39). As a result, Clark became Labour's first female prime minister in New Zealand's history.

LACKAWANNA AGREEMENT OF 1881. An agreement reached among the three powers—the **United States**, **Britain**, and **Germany**—on 21 July 1881 regarding the internal civil unrest in **Sāmoa**. The agreement attempted to end the civil wars between the **Tupua** and **Mālietoa** families and to provide for security of the European residents in the islands. According to the agreement, Mālietoa Laupepa was to be king and Tupou Tamasese Titimaea was to be vice king with the seat of the government to be at Mulinu'u. The new government was little supported by the district chiefs who continued to use government taxes to purchase arms and munitions for protection and offensive attacks against their rivals, and the German consulate and commercial representatives supported intrigues against the Mālietoa administration. By 1888, the new system had collapsed and internal warfare had once again resumed in Sāmoa. *See also* ANGLO-GERMAN AGREEMENT OF 1889.

LAND WARS IN NEW ZEALAND. Sometimes referred to (inaccurately) as the **Māori** Wars, they occurred periodically from 1845 to about 1870 between the indigenous Māoris and the new settlers, the British. The main reasons for the outbreaks of violence were primarily over ownership of land and the desire among the Māoris to retain their independence and racial identity. The outbreaks between 1860 and 1861 are referred to as the Taranaki Wars and those between 1863 and 1864 as the Waikato Wars. *See also* HEKE, HONE; NEW ZEALAND; WIREMU KINGI.

LANGUAGES (POLYNESIAN). Consist of some 30 languages spoken throughout the Pacific island nations that make up **Polynesia**. Together, they form a close relationship that resembles the relationship found in the Romance languages of Europe (French, Spanish, Italian,

Portuguese, and so forth). But the Polynesian languages are derived from a minor branch of a larger Austronesian family group spoken throughout much of the Pacific basin and Asian rim (Melanesia, Micronesia, Indonesia, Philippines, Madagascar, South Vietnam, and the Malaya peninsula). This minor branch is further divided into Proto-Tongic (**Tongan** and **Niuean**), Proto-Sāmoic (**Sāmoan** and its numerous neighboring island languages), and Proto-Central Polynesian (**Easter Island**, **Hawaiian**, **Marquesan**, **Māori**, **Tuamotuan**, **Tahitian**, and Rarotongan).

Numerous cognates exist in these languages (*manu*—for bird, for example—is found in almost all of the Polynesian languages), and as a result, speech is frequently understood from one island to another. When the Christian missionaries created a written language for these island groups in the 19th century, they did so by using the Roman alphabet with its Latin pronunciation for the various consonants (b, f, h, k, l, m, n, p, r, s, t, w) and vowels (a, e, i, o, u). A reverse apostrophe (‘) before a vowel or between vowels indicates a glottal stop—*o‘o* in Hawaiian, for example, is pronounced similar to the English "Oh, oh." (It most likely was a k sound in its earlier linguistic development.) The glottal stop and the macrons above vowels (ā, ē, ī, ō, ū, for example) were frequently omitted in earlier texts, but in the last decade, they are appearing as the result of the revival of interest in the purity and the accurate recording of the Polynesian languages.

Because of their past colonial history, a large percentage of the Polynesian peoples are bilingual. Unfortunately in Hawai‘i and **New Zealand** where the colonial immigrants outnumbered the indigenous peoples, the Hawaiian and the New Zealand **Māori** languages almost died out. They have had a revival since the 1970s, however, and greater attention is being given to their survival. *See also* EDUCATION IN THE PACIFIC.

LAPITA CULTURE. A term to designate the prehistoric Polynesian culture that existed from about 1500–500 B.C., primarily in western **Polynesia—Tonga** and **Sāmoa**. Unique Lapita motifs on ceramic potsherds, found in numerous sites, indicate a Melanesian connection, especially from Fiji. In Sāmoa and Tonga, ceramic pottery ceased being made sometime after the turn of the Christian era, while the Fijian style was replaced about 500 B.C. by other types of Melanesian pottery. The word Lapita generally refers to the entire culture as reconstructed from archaeological finds—house sites, adzes, fishhooks, chisels for **tattooing**, and so forth. It is generally recognized that the Lapita culture represents the first immigrants into the Polynesian triangle, by 1300 B.C. into Tonga and 1000 B.C. into Sāmoa, and from here it was transmitted to the many other Polynesian island groups lying to the east. *See also* POLYNESIAN CULTURE, ANCIENT.

LATASI, NAAMA. The first (and only) woman to be elected to **Tuvalu's** national Parliament (1989), and subsequently appointed minister for health, education, and community service (1989–1993). Born on the island of Nanumea, she spent most of her childhood in Kiribati (formerly the Gilbert Islands). She returned to **Tuvalu** in 1978 with her husband, **Kamuta Latasi**, who served as prime minister between 1993 and 1996. Prior to her election to Parliament, Naama was a prominent worker in **women's** affairs and former commissioner of girl guides.

LAUAKI, NAMULAU'ULU MAMOE (?–1915). A famous **Sāmoan** chief and orator during the 19th and early 20th centuries. In the 1860s and 1870s, Lauaki (a title given to him by King George I of **Tonga**) supported the cause of high chief **Mālietoa** Laupepa as ruler of Sāmoa through his exceptional oratorial persuasion and military prowess. He criticized the **German** government when it gained control of the islands in 1889, and he subsequently became embroiled in disputes with the new German governor**, Wilhelm Solf**. Lauaki organized an opposition to the government called the ***Mau* of Pule**, but the more powerful German force was too much for the weaker Sāmoan dissidents. As a result, Lauaki and nine followers with their families were exiled to Saipan (Micronesia) in April 1909. When **New Zealand** seized Sāmoa from the Germans in 1914, Lauaki and his fellow exiles were given political amnesty. But unfortunately, Lauaki died on 15 November 1915, of dysentery, before he reached his native home of Sāmoa.

LAUTI, TOARIPI (1928–). Prime minister of **Tuvalu** from 1978 to 1981. Born on 18 November 1928 in Papua New Guinea, Lauti was educated at Queen Victoria School in Fiji, the Wesley College in Paerata, **New Zealand**, and Christchurch's Teachers' College. He became a secondary school teacher in the former Gilbert and Ellice Islands from 1953 to 1962 and labor relations and training officer for the Nauru and Ocean Island Phosphate Commission from 1962 to 1974. Lauti was then appointed chief minister and minister of home affairs from 1975 to 1978, later elected prime minister from October 1978 to 1981, and became the leader of the opposition from 1981 to 1990. He served as governor-general until 1993. He was later appointed prime ministerial special envoy on climate change to the **United Nations** conference on climate in Kyoto, **Japan**, in December of 1997.

LAVELUA, AMÉLIE (?–1895). Queen of **Wallis Island** from 1869 to 1895. Her conversion to Christianity provided the way for the missionaries to convert the majority of her subjects. Her rule (1869–1895) saw the islands come more and more under the control of **France**, and she herself was regarded as a Francophile. In 1887, the French government annexed the islands as a protectorate. Queen Amélie was affectionately regarded by her subjects. She knew everyone by name, their family genealogies, traditional rights and privileges, and quietly intervened in district or clan quarrels to prevent widespread dissension among her subjects.

LAWRY, WALTER (1793–1859). An early Methodist missionary to the Pacific. Born in Cornwall, England, Lawry came to **Australia** in 1817; shortly thereafter he was appointed one of the first missionaries to **Tonga**. He and his wife spent 14 agonizing months in the islands (1822–1823) without much success. After spending the next 18 years in England (1825–1843), he returned to the Pacific again as general superintendent of the Wesleyan missions in **New Zealand** where he became embroiled in disputes over money, policy, personalities, and his "secular pursuits." Although exonerated of all charges, his ill health forced him to retire in 1854. He died at Parramatta in 1859.

LEALOFI IV, TUPUA TAMASESE (1922–). Political leader and former prime minister of **Sāmoa**. Born on 8 May 1922, he was educated at the Marist Brothers School in Āpia, attended the Fiji School of Medicine, and became a medical practitioner with the Sāmoa health department between 1940 and 1969. He succeeded as paramount chief (Tama-a-'aiga) of Tupua Tamasese in 1965, became a member of the council of deputies from 1968 to 1969, a member of Parliament from 1970, and prime minister from 1970 to 1973, and again from May 1975 to March 1976 to complete the term of office of Prime Minister Fiame Mata'afa Mulinuu who died in office. He was one of the founding members of the **South Pacific Commission** (now the **Pacific Community**).

LEE, H. REX (1910–2001). Lee spent over four decades in U.S. government service among which was his appointment as governor of **American Sāmoa** from 1961 to 1967. Lee was a native of Rigby, Idaho, and a graduate in agricultural economics from the University of Idaho. In 1936, he entered government service as an economist with the Department of Agriculture. During World War II, he served with the War Relocation Authority and was assigned to relocate **Japanese**-Americans. Later Lee worked with the Bureau of Indian Affairs before being appointed the governor of an undeveloped American Sāmoa. His administration saw the establishment of a new airport, roads, schools, a luxury hotel in Pago Pago to cultivate the tourist industry, two fisheries canneries, new harbor facilities, an impressive education television system, and numerous other innovations. In 1962, when American Sāmoa had the opportunity of reunifying with Western **Sāmoa**, its citizens chose to remain a territory of the United States. After his six-year tenure in American Sāmoa, Lee received the Award for Distinguished Federal Civil Service and was appointed to the Federal Communications Commission where he worked until his retirement in 1973. He moved to California and became a founding chairman of the Public Service Satellite Consortium and helped establish educational television in several South American countries. He died 26 July 2001 at his home in La Jolla, California, leaving a wife, Lillian, and three of four children who survived him.

LEE, JOHN ALEXANDER (1892–1982). A **New Zealand** politician and writer, best known for his **Labour Party** activities until his expulsion in May 1940. Lee served in World War I and was awarded the Distinguished Conduct Medal. After the war, he entered politics and was elected as a member of Parliament for the Labour Party from 1922 to

1928 and again from 1931 to 1940. When **Michael Joseph Savage** became prime minister between 1935 and 1940, Lee was one of the influential members of his cabinet. In an effort to gain succession to the position of prime minister, Lee attacked Savage in a publication that was designed to destroy the prime minister's reputation. Dying from cancer, Savage had a relapse, and the party expelled Lee from its membership. Subsequently, Lee founded the Democratic Labour Party, but lost the election in 1943. He became a successful writer, printer, and publisher. His most famous works are *Children of the Poor* (1934) and *Simple on a Soapbox* (1963).

LÉONTIEFF, ALEXANDRE (1948–). President of **French Polynesia** from December 1987 to March 1991. Born at Teahupo'o (Tahiti) on 20 October 1948, Léontieff received his doctorate in economic sciences from the University of Paris. He headed the department of economic affairs from 1971 to 1973 and he was first elected to the territorial government in May 1977, and again reelected in 1982, 1986, and 1991. He became vice president of the territory under **Gaston Flosse** in 1984 and was elected deputy from French Polynesia to the French National Assembly in 1986. Léontieff was elected president of French Polynesia in December 1987 and was reelected deputy in June 1988. He formed a new party, **Te Ti'arama (The Flame)**, in January 1988. He lost his position as president of the government to Gaston Flosse in the elections held in March 1991 although he retained his position as assembly member. Charged for bribery and corruption in 1992, a court convicted him in November of 1997 and sentenced him to three years in prison (one-half suspended) and loss of some civil rights. He was con victed again in 1998 for corruption but was given a suspended sentence. Léontieff remains head of the **Haere I Mua** political party.

LEVI, NOEL (1942–). Secretary-general of the **Pacific Islands Forum** from 1998 to 2001. Born on 6 February 1942, at Nonapai Village, New Ireland Province of Papua New Guinea, Levi was educated in **Australia** and in 1973 received his bachelor's degree from the University of Papua New Guinea. He entered public service and was elected to Parliament (1977–1987) during which time he served as minister for foreign affairs (1980–1982). He was ambassador to China (1987–1995), high commissioner to the United Kingdom (1991–1995), and secretary for the prime minister's department and cabinet (1995–1997). At the September 1997 meeting of the Pacific Islands Forum, he was selected its new secretary-general, replacing Ieremia T. Tabai who had served for six years. Levi's administration focused on environmental problems, especially for the smaller island nations, and on improving trade and investment potential for all Forum member countries. He was awarded the Commander of the British Empire (CBE) in 1982. He is married with four children.

LIBERAL PARTY. A political party of **New Zealand** noted for its progressive reforms between 1890 and 1908. Its noted leaders were Prime Ministers **John Ballance** (1891–1893) and **Richard Seddon** (1893–1906). The party introduced one of the world's first old-age pensions, low-interest housing, food and drug standards, and numerous other welfare services. The party became defunct in 1927 when it was succeeded by the United Party.

LILI'UOKALANI (1838–1917). The last reigning monarch of the independent kingdom of **Hawai'i**. She succeeded her brother, **King Kalākaua**, to the throne in 1891, but her rule was to last for only two years. Dignified, educated, talented, and strong-willed, the queen was determined to regain some of the power lost by the crown in the previous constitutions. Opposition from businessmen in the **United States** as well as from the more democratic sector of the population created protracted and often heated legislative sessions. The end came on 17 January 1893 when the opposition, having gained support from John Stevens, the U.S. minister to Hawai'i, took over the government buildings and announced the establishment of a provisional government. A counterrevolution to put the queen back on the throne failed, and the queen was arrested on 16 January 1895. On 24 January, she renounced all claims to the throne and the Hawaiian monarchy came to an end. She died on 11 November 1917 as Lydia K. Dominis.

LONDON MISSIONARY SOCIETY (LMS), 1795–1901. A Protestant organization in **Great Britain** that sought to bring Christianity to the Polynesian islands. Organized in 1795 as a result of the reforming spirit of the age, the organization, under the direction of the Reverend Thomas Haweis, designated **Tahiti** as the first destination for its work. *The Dove*, captained by James Wilson, set sail in 1796 carrying 30 missionaries with their wives and children. Their destinations were Tahiti, Tongatapu, and the **Marquesas Islands**. The missions on Tongatapu and the Marquesas proved to be failures, but the one in Tahiti eventually flourished, although it took over 15 years before any great headway could be made.

Subsequent LMS missions were established in the **Cook Islands** (1821), in **Sāmoa** (1830), in **Niue** (1830 and 1842), in **Tokelau** (1861), and in **Tuvalu** (1861). Their efforts in **Tonga** (1822) were thwarted by the advancement of the Wesleyan mission, and the LMS attempts in Melanesia proved to be tragic with the murder of LMS missionary **John Williams** there in 1839. Besides bringing Christianity to the Pacific islands, the LMS missionaries were responsible for the establishment of educational systems, the transcription of indigenous languages into the Roman alphabet, the publication of numerous religious and educational texts in the local languages, and the bringing of Western "civilization" to the island people. Lack of LMS funds to the islands led many of the missionaries, however, to seek their fortunes elsewhere, and as a result, many became entrepreneurs and traders, while others became political leaders who advised the island chiefs in their rise to power. The LMS also vehemently opposed **Roman Catholic** intrusion (usually French) in its attempts to establish its own missions in the islands. International competition and rivalry ensued, in some cases only ending after long diplomatic negotiations among the capitals of Europe.

A good number of LMS missionaries left accounts of their sojourns in the islands, many of which provide some of the best descriptions of island life that are extant. (Refer to the bibliography.) The archives of the LMS (now known as the United Church of Christ Board of World Ministries) are currently housed in the School of Oriental and African Studies, University of London, and can be obtained via microfilm or microfiche. *See also* CHURCH MISSIONARY SOCIETY; EDUCATION IN THE PACIFIC; MORMON CHURCH IN POLYNESIA.

LONG, OREN E. (1889–1965). Appointed governor of the Territory of **Hawai'i** from 1951 to 1953. Long advocated immediate statehood and devoted his energies to that end. His interests also included the advancement of public welfare, the promotion of the Punchbowl Memorial (National Cemetery of the Pacific), and the settlement of major labor strikes in the islands. He died on 6 May 1965.

LOTI, PIERRE (1850–1923). Pen name of Louis-Marie-Julien Viaud, a French writer who popularized the South Seas and especially **Tahiti** more than anyone else through his romantic novel *Le Mariage de Loti* (1890). The novel describes a warm love affair between Harry Grant, an Englishman, and Rarahu, a beautiful Polynesian maiden who served at the court of **Queen Pomare IV**. Loti died on 10 June 1923. *See also* FRENCH POLYNESIA.

LUI, FRANK FAKAOTIMANAVA (1935–). Prime minister of **Niue** from April 1993 to March 1999. Born on 19 November 1935, Lui was educated at the Wellington Technical school (1942–1950) in **New Zealand**. He held numerous jobs including seaman (1951–1954), transport officer (1951–1954), clerk in the health department (1956–1959), private businessman (1961), and assemblyman (1963–1966). He became a member of the Niue cabinet in 1974 and held numerous ministerial positions before being elected prime minister in April of 1993. His objectives were to expand **tourism** in the island and to press Niueans living in New Zealand to return home. Lui was reelected again as prime minister in 1996, defeating Robert Rex, Jr., son of Niue's first premier, by 11 votes to nine. In the general elections in March of 1999, Lui lost his seat and retired from government.

LUNALILO, WILLIAM CHARLES (1835–1874). King of **Hawai'i** from 1873 until his death in 1874. A descendant of the brother of King Kamehameha I (founder of the Hawaiian monarchy). Lunalilo was elected by the Hawaiian legislature upon the death of King Kamehameha V. His popularity diminished as a result of his extravagance, the islands' economic depression, and his indecisive nature in dealing with **United States** interests in the islands. His death on 3 February 1874 forced the legislative assembly once again to select a successor to the throne. **Prince David Kalākaua** was selected over his rival, the popular Queen Emma. *See also* KAMEHAMEHA.

LUTALI, AIFILI P. (1919–). Popularly elected governor of **American Sāmoa** from 1985 to 1989 and from 1993 to 1997, speaker of the house of representatives (American Sāmoa) from 1965 to 1975, and American Sāmoa's delegate to Washington, D.C., from 1975 to 1979. His administration as governor was noted for his clean-up campaign, development of a youth fitness program and several private self-help business programs, and his opposition to nuclear testing in the Pacific. After his defeat by **Peter Coleman** in 1988, he served as vice president of the local senate. He won reelection as governor in November 1992. After his defeat to **Tauese Sunia** in 1996, Lutali returned to the American Sāmoa senate. He spearheaded the construction of the new Senior Citizen Center that now bears his name and received an Outstanding Achievement Award in 1997 from the government.

- M -

MĀHŪ. *See* HOMOSEXUALITY.

MAKEA TAKAU (?–1911). A high-ranking chiefess (*ariki*) of Rarotonga, **Cook Islands**, whose family members had been ruling chiefs in the early 19th century when the first Europeans began to arrive in the islands. Until 1874, there was no centralized government for Rarotonga or the Cook Islands, although Makea Takau, as paramount *ariki*, assumed the responsibility of enforcing the laws through her council of *ariki* (by 1882 four of the five *ariki* were women). Her position was enhanced by her marriage to Ngamaru, paramount chief of three other islands—Atiu, Mauke, and Mitiaro. When Makea Takau and a group of Cook Islanders visited **New Zealand** in 1885, she was greeted as "Queen of Rarotonga." Upon her return, she adopted Western trappings of royalty (copying Victorian England, for example) and began exercising dominant control over the other *ariki*.

In July 1888, Makea petitioned **Great Britain** for a protectorate over the islands because of her fear of French encroachment. Makea was chosen head of the new executive council, composed of all of the paramount chiefs, and was given a stipend to live on. She and her husband were influential in having the islands eventually annexed to New Zealand in 1900. She gradually lost control of the executive branch of the government to the resident commissioner, and she and the other *ariki* soon became an advisory group.

In 1908, Makea's council was abolished in favor of democratically elected ones, and by 1910, her authority had been reduced to only matters relating to land and *atinga* (obligations). She died in 1911 having lived through a tumultuous period of Pacific history. *See also* DAVIS, PA TEPAERU ARIKI; WOMEN.

MĀLIETOA. One of the two highest-ranking family titles in **Sāmoa**, having its origin about A.D. 1200 when the two victorious Sāmoan chiefs, Tanu and Fata, defeated their **Tongan** overlords and bestowed the title upon their eldest brother Savea. Not as significant as the two other Sāmoan titles, the **Tui A'ana** and the Tui Atua, the holder of the Mālietoa title, became prominent in the 1830s when Mālietoa Vai'inupō gained all five of the major Sāmoan titles and reigned as **Tupu'o Sāmoa**, king-ruler of Sāmoa. The current title holder is **Mālietoa Tanumafili II**, currently the head of state of Sāmoa.

MĀLIETOA TANUMAFILI II (1913–). Sāmoan politician and sole head of state since 1963. Born on 4 January 1913, the son of Mālietoa Tanumafili I (d. 1939), and descendant of one of the highest chiefly families in **Sāmoa**. He was educated at St. Stephen's College and the Wesley College in Auckland, **New Zealand**. In 1940, he was elected to the position of Mālietoa and thus became ***fautua***, one of the two leading high chiefs in Sāmoa. He represented Sāmoa as a member of the New Zealand delegation to the **United Nations** in 1958 to discuss independence. In 1962, he became the joint head of state of the newly independent state of Sāmoa with the late Tupua Tamasese Mea'ole. Upon Tupua's death in 1963, Mālietoa became the sole head of state (the *O le Ao o le Malo*) until his death, after which the legislative assembly (*fono*) will select his successor, a position to be held for only five years.

MALO, DAVID (1793?–1853). A Hawaiian scholar and author of an important ethnographic work entitled *Hawaiian Antiquities*, written about 1840. Born about 1793 on the Big Island, Malo learned the traditions of his ancestors, and when he became a Christian in 1831, he learned to read and write, entered the newly established Lahainaluna

High School to study for the ministry, and then set his traditions down in writing. He later worked as a pastor of a congregation in Ke'oke'a, Maui, became a friend and personal advisor to **King Kamehameha II**, served as first superintendent of all Hawaiian schools between 1841 and 1845, and spent his last years as pastor of the Congregational church in Lakepolepo, Maui, until his death on 21 October 1853. *See also* HAWAI'I.

MAOATE, TEREPAI (1934–). Prime minister of the **Cook Islands** since 1999. Born on 1 September 1934 at Ngatangiia, Rarotonga, he received his medical degree (1954) at the Fiji Medical School in Suva and an MA (1976) in public health at Amsterdam University in Holland. He was elected to the Cook Islands Parliament in 1983 and was appointed minister of health and agriculture. He became deputy prime minister from 1985 to 1989, at which time he assumed the position of deputy leader of the opposition (Cook Islands Democratic Party), and then leader at the party's national conference in 1991. When the Cook Islands Party leader, **Dr. Joe Williams**, resigned as prime minister on 18 November 1999, Maoate become prime minister and formed a coalition government. Maoate's concerns are jobs, the stagnant economy, and foreign debt. He proposes to bring the economy back from near bankruptcy due to what he claims is a 10-year, one-man control of government.

MĀ'OHI. A **Tahitian** word currently used to indicate a person of Polynesian (Tahitian) ancestry as versus ***demi*** to indicate one of mixed ancestry, or ***popa'ā*** to indicate a foreigner of Caucasian descent. *Mā'ohi* is related to the **New Zealand** and **Cook Island** word ***Māori*** and the Hawaiian *Maoli*. *See also HAOLE*; *PĀKEHĀ*; *PALAGI*.

MĀORI. A Polynesian word to indicate the indigenous peoples of **New Zealand** and the **Cook Islands** as opposed to the word ***pākehā***, which is used to designate the white immigrants to the islands. *See also HAOLE*; *MĀ'OHI*; NEW ZEALAND; *PALAGI*; *POPA'Ā*.

MĀORI KING MOVEMENT. A national movement that had its origins in the 1850s when several **New Zealand Māori** tribes met together to form an opposition against the continued white (*pākehā*) settlement of their lands. In 1858, **Potatau I** was proclaimed king, and the loose federation of tribes united to oppose the selling of their lands to the *pākehā*. Not all Māoris recognized the election, and as a result, the division weakened the movement, and it was unsuccessful in its attempts to resist the *pākehā*. Today, the title is still respected by numerous tribes who see it as a focus of Māori nationalism among its members. The current leader is **"Queen" Te-Ata-i-rangikaahu**, sixth in direct descent from Potatau I. Its primary focus today is to uphold the spiritual power, dignity, and integrity of the Māori people in New Zealand society. *See also* TE WHEROWHERO.

MĀORI LAND WARS. *See* LAND WARS IN NEW ZEALAND.

MĀORI LANGUAGE COMMISSION. Established as an official arm of the **New Zealand** government through the Māori Language Act of 1987, this organization contributes to the growth and maintenance of the **Māori** language by working through three main groups—the Māori people, the government sector, and the general population. Its main functions are to initiate, develop, coordinate, review, advise upon, and assist in the implementation of policies and practices designed to promote the Māori language as an official language of New Zealand; to promote the Māori language as a living language and as an ordinary means of communication with a legal status equal to that of English; and to issue certificates of competency in the language. It hopes to revitalize the Māori language by undertaking research, by creating new terms in the Māori language (for example, terms for "fax," "computer," "**Internet**," and so forth), and by supporting education programs that raise the standards of spoken and written Māori. Its current director is Professor Patu Hohepa and its Internet address is http://www.nzgovtdirectory.com/directory/section2/maori_lan.htm.

MĀORITANGA. A **New Zealand Māori** word meaning Māori culture or native ways, or a pride in being Māori. *See also* FA'A SĀMOA.

MARAU, JOANNA (1860–1934). Generally regarded as the last "queen" of **Tahiti**. Born on 24 April 1860 to Alexander Salmon, a prosperous merchant, and his Tahitian wife, **Ari'i Ta'ima'i**, Marau married Teri'i Tari'a, son and heir apparent to **Queen Pomare IV**. The couple separated in 1875, and when the old queen died in 1877, there was an English Protestant movement to have Marau named queen rather than naming her husband king. Not only was her genealogy impeccable, but she was Protestant and talented. The French governor, however, blocked the attempt at changing the succession to the throne, and as a result, her husband became King Pomare V.

Marau befriended the American historian Henry Adams during his visit to the islands, and she and her mother imparted their extensive knowledge of Tahitian lore to him. Upon his return to the **United States**, Adams wrote his famous book, *Tahiti: Memoirs of Arii Taimai* (1901). She left three children (although disowned by their father), was honored by the French Legion of Honor, and was beloved by her subjects, long after her husband died in 1891. She finally passed away on 2 February 1934. *See also* FRENCH POLYNESIA.

MARERE, HENRI (1930–). Political leader in **French Polynesia**, regularly elected to the territorial assembly since 1962 from the **Tuamotu-Gambier** district. A member of the **Tāhō'ēra'a Huira'atira party**, he sought the establishment of electricity in his home islands and the promotion of **tourism** and the pearl culture industry. He became vice president of the territorial assembly in 1991.

MARINER, WILLIAM (1791–1853). A young English seaman who was kidnapped and "adopted" by Tongan chief **Fīnau 'Ulukālala II**. Mariner lived four years (1806–1810) in the chief's household where he learned the language and customs of the islanders. After his return to England, he related his experiences to John Martin who published them as *An Account of the Natives of the Tongan Islands* (2 vols. 1817), an invaluable record of the customs, language, and culture of early **Tonga**.

MARSDEN, SAMUEL (1765–1838). Anglican chaplain to New South Wales, Australia, and pioneering missionary to **New Zealand**. In 1794, Marsden left his studies in England to become chaplain to the convict colony being established in Australia. For many years, he was a prosperous businessman and magistrate besides directing the religious activities in the South Pacific. The **Tahitian** mission of the **London**

Missionary Society (LMS) looked to Marsden for financial and spiritual guidance when it was forced out of the islands, and Marsden became the foreign director of the LMS operations in the Pacific. Several New Zealand **Māori** chiefs urged Marsden to open a mission to their islands, and as a result, Marsden immigrated with the first missionaries of the **Church Missionary Society** to the Bay of Islands and held the first Christian services there on Christmas Day, 1814.

Although Marsden returned to Australia, he continued to direct the affairs of the mission and to visit the islands whenever he could. Although Marsden insisted that the islanders should adopt Western civilization before conversion, he was adamant regarding their being protected against the barbarisms of the **whalers** who visited the islands.

MARQUESAS ISLANDS. One of the five island groups which make up **French Polynesia**. They consist of six large and six small volcanic islands located 760 km (475 mi) northeast of Pape'ete, **Tahiti**. These islands were the first to be settled in eastern **Polynesia** sometime around the second century B.C. presumably by explorers from **Sāmoa** or **Tonga**, and from here, Polynesian navigators sailed on to the **Society Islands**, the Austral Islands, Mangareva, the **Tuamotus**, **Hawai'i** to the north, and then on to the **Cook Islands** and to **New Zealand** to the southwest.

Their numerous population was decimated by Alvaro de Mendaña's massacre in 1595, by tribal warfare in the 19th century, and by Western diseases that reduced their population to 1,500 by 1920. Early Protestant missionaries, William P. Crook and John Harris, spent only a short time on the islands. French **Roman Catholics** arrived in 1833, and their work paved the way for French political authorities to take the islands in 1842. They became part of the French empire in the Pacific called the ***Établissements Français de l'Océanie*** **(EFO)** with its capital in Pape'ete, Tahiti. Its current population is 8,064 (1996 census). In 1999, the Marquesan representatives to the French Polynesia territorial assembly announced that should French Polynesia move to become independent from **France**, the **Marqueses** would secede and remain part of France.

MASSEY, WILLIAM FERGUSON (1856–1925). Prime minister of **New Zealand** from 1912 until his death in May 1925, representing the conservative Reform Party and the second to **Richard Seddon** as having served the longest term in office as prime minister. In 1909, Massey formed the conservative Reform Party as opposition against the long domination of the **Liberal Party**. Massey lost out to the **Labour Party** after World War I as the urban vote became more important and the farm/land interests of the Reform Party became less important to an expanding urban class. Massey University (originally called Massey Agricultural College) in Palmerston North, founded in 1928, is named after the prime minister and still maintains agriculture and food research centers.

MATĀ'AFA, FIAMĀ FAUMUNIA MULINU'U II (1921–1975). The highly respected first prime minister of the independent state of **Sāmoa** from 1959 to 1969 and then again from 1972 to 1975. Matā'afa was descended from one of the four royal families of Sāmoa, and he first appeared in politics as a member of the 1954 constitutional convention, then as minister for agriculture (1957), and in 1959 was elected prime minister at the age of 38. During his administration, Sāmoa became an independent state (1962) and made significant progress at home in its social and economic programs while at the same time becoming more involved in international affairs. He died in 1975 leaving his wife **La'ulu Fetauimalemau Matā'afa**.

MATĀ'AFA, LA'ULU FETAUIMALEMAU (1938–). Sāmoa's first female diplomat being appointed consul general to **New Zealand** in 1989. She is the widow of Sāmoa's first prime minister, **Fiamē Matā'afa Faumuina**, a respected former member of Parliament, and a voice for **women's** equality in a conservative, male-dominated Pacific island nation. She was president of the Sāmoa National Council of Women (NCW) for 20 years. Her wide interests range from nuclear protest and abuse seminars to consumer awareness workshops and women's employment issues. As consul general to New Zealand, she is nominal head of Auckland's large Polynesian community (some 90,000), most of whom are Sāmoans. Emigration to New Zealand has been a major source of contention between the two countries for a number of years. Matā'afa hopes to resolve many of their differences and to educate New Zealanders regarding the Sāmoan way of life and her compatriots on how to cope and get ahead in a modernized Western culture.

***MAU* OF PULE.** An organized rebellion of **Sāmoans** against their **German** overlords between 1908 and 1909. The chief figure of the movement was **Lauaki** Namualu'ulu Mamoe, a prominent chief from the districts of Tumua and Pule on the islands of 'Upolu and Savai'i, who opposed the newly established German administration of the islands (1909). **Wilhelm Solf**, the first German governor of the islands (1900–1911), had imposed a strong centralized government, while the traditional system of the Sāmoans had given more recognition to district chiefs. Sāmoan opposition to the new government increased, and finally Solf disbanded the Sāmoan Parliament (the *'Imua* and *Faipule*) and created the *fono* of *Faipule.*

In January 1905, Lauaki circumvented the governor and petitioned directly to the emperor in Berlin for changes in the administration. Solf was furious. Lauaki began organizing local support, and in January 1909, Solf invited the leader to Mulinu'u where he was arrested with nine other families and deported to Saipan in April 1909. The *Mau* of Pule was ended. Lauaki never returned to Sāmoa; he died of dysentery in November 1915 on his way home. The importance of the *Mau* of Pule was that it provided an example of local opposition to foreign administration that was to rise again in the 1920s and 1930s. *See also* SĀMOA.

MAURI PACIFIC PARTY. A **New Zealand** political party that had its beginnings in the breakup of the New Zealand First Party in August of 1998. One faction of the New Zealand First Party, consisting of **Māori** members of Parliament, joined together under Tau Henare, the minister of Māori affairs, to form the Mauri Pacific Party. The party calls for the country to adopt a new cultural identity based upon Māori culture, advocating, for example, the introduction of compulsory Māori language instruction to children up to Form 2 (age 12) and the installation of bilingual signposts and billboards throughout the country. Mauri Pacific means "spirit of the Pacific," and in the 1999 elections it won no seats in Parliament.

McCARTHY, CHARLES J. (1861–1929). Appointed governor of the Territory of **Hawai'i** from 1918 to 1921. His long political career included being U.S. senator, treasurer of the city and county of Honolulu, and then governor of the territory. His Waikīkī reclamation project and his promotion of Hawai'i's economy are his major contributions. He died on 26 November 1929.

McCOMBS, ELIZABETH REID (1873–1935). New Zealand's first woman member of Parliament (1933–1935). She was born at Kaiapoi, married James McCombs, and became president of the Canterbury section of the Women's Temperance Union. When her husband died in 1933, she stood for election in his place as a member of the **Labour Party** and won. She was succeeded by her son Terence Henderson McCombs.

MEAD, MARGARET (1901–1978). A famous American anthropologist whose fieldwork in eastern **Sāmoa** (1925–1926) produced one of her most famous books, *Coming of Age in Samoa* (1928), a work that won her fame during her lifetime, but one that came under criticism during the early 1980s. Mead's vast research extended throughout much of the Pacific—Sāmoa, Admiralty Islands, New Guinea, and Bali. For most of her career, she held a position as curator of Pacific ethnology at the American Museum of Natural History in New York City.

Her writings are voluminous. She was an effective and direct speaker, a warm and generous friend to many, and extremely sensitive to the indigenous peoples with whom she worked. In 1983, Derek Freeman's book, *Margaret Mead and Samoa: The Making and Unmaking of an Anthropological Myth*, attacked Mead's thesis that Sāmoan adolescents were without stress and worry because of the easy and permissive nature of their society. He claims that Mead's research is faulted. She spent too short of a time in the islands to make such sweeping generalities regarding Sāmoan society, she was duped by her teenage informants, and she ignored evidence that did not support her thesis. Since then, three camps have emerged in this intellectual debate—those that accept Freeman's position, those that criticize Freeman's own research, and those realists who attempt to mediate between the two. Without question, however, Mead's book became a widely read work that influenced hundreds of young anthropologists to turn their attention to the South Pacific. *See also* SĀMOA.

MELVILLE, HERMAN (1819–1891). A famous American novelist whose sojourn in the South Pacific (the **Marquesas**, **Tahiti**, and

Hawai'i) provided background for his numerous books: *Typee* (1846), *Omoo* (1847), *Encantadas* (*Enchanted Islands*), and of course his most famous work, *Moby Dick* (1851). It was only after his death that he obtained recognition as one of America's greatest authors.

MÉTRAUX, ALFRED (1902–1963). A Swiss anthropologist who, in 1934, joined a scientific expedition team to visit **Easter Island** to investigate the old religion and customs of the islanders. He later became a visiting professor at Yale University (1941–1945), and a staff member at the Smithsonian Institution, Washington, D.C. His work, *Easter Island: A Stone Age Civilization of the Pacific* (1940), remains the single best book on the "mystery of Easter Island."

MOA. An extinct **New Zealand** bird that inhabited the islands from about 15 million years ago until A.D. 1500. The early Polynesians of New Zealand (sometimes called Moa-hunters) trapped these large wingless birds for food, clothing, and decoration. Several species existed, the largest of which stood as tall as a man.

MOERENHAUT, JACQUES-ANTOINE (1796–1879). A Belgian/French merchant who during the 1840s became embroiled in the international conflict between **France** and **Great Britain** over the control of **Tahiti** and the neighboring islands—now **French Polynesia**. Moerenhaut first arrived in Tahiti in 1828 where for the next 20 years he became an important political figure in island affairs. When the French **Catholic** missionaries arrived in 1836, Moerenhaut gave them protection from the Protestant missionaries of the **London Missionary Society** and the English-dominated royal family. His chief adversary was **George Pritchard**, chief advisor to **Queen Pomare IV**, who maintained that only the English missionaries had the right to proselytize the islands. Determined to get British backing, Pritchard sailed to England to petition the government to annex the islands.

While Pritchard was away, French Admiral **Abel Dupetit-Thouars** arrived in Tahiti and declared a French protectorate, and Moerenhaut was appointed temporary administrator general of the island until a permanent one could be sent from France. When Pritchard returned, he attempted to undermine the French position, and as a result of "The Pritchard Affair," he was expelled from the country and Moerenhaut was reassigned to California. The ultimate result, of course, was that Tahiti and the surrounding islands fell to the French. Moerenhaut's book, *Voyages aux îles du grand océan* (1837), provides a first hand account of the affair as well as valuable data on early Tahitian society, government, and culture.

MONTPEZAT, JEAN (1937–). High commissioner of **French Polynesia** (1987–1992). After a successful career in government administration in his native home of **France**, Montpezat was selected in 1986 as high commissioner of France's overseas territory of New Caledonia. Political leaders in that country forced his exit because of his support of indigenous (Melanesian) rights, and as a result, he was appointed high commissioner to French Polynesia on 12 November 1987. He was replaced by Michel Jau in January 1992 at the end of his term of duty.

MORIORIS. Indigenous Polynesian inhabitants of the **Chatham Islands** lying approximately 800 km (500 mi) due east of **New Zealand** possibly having originally come from the South Island of New Zealand. The few thousand Morioris in the 19th century were drastically reduced through a **Māori** invasion from the mainland in 1835 and the introduction of Western diseases. Tommy Solomon, the last Moriori, died in 1933.

MORMON CHURCH IN POLYNESIA. Since its founding in 1830 in New York State, the Mormon Church (more correctly the Church of Jesus Christ of Latter-day Saints) has had a romantic tie with **Polynesia**. One of its stated goals is to attempt to convert the world (including the islands of the seas) to its religious beliefs.

In 1843, its President Joseph Smith commissioned a group to visit the **Sandwich Islands** (Hawai'i) for conversion purposes. The missionaries (Noa Rogers, Addison Pratt, and Benjamin F. Grouard) wound up in Tubuai (400 miles south of **Tahiti**) where they first established their mission. Rogers remained on Tubuai while Pratt moved on to Tahiti and Grouard settled in the **Tuamotus**. Most of the Mormon missionary work in **French Polynesia**, however, was closed down by the new, Catholic-dominated government in 1852. Many of the Mormon members were converted to the Reorganized Church of Jesus Christ of Latter-day Saints, or *kanitos* (saints) as they are called. The Mormon church was not to be revived there until 1892.

Meanwhile a mission to **Hawai'i** was opened in December 1850 with the arrival of 10 missionaries. By 1856, 4,500 converts were counted, and the *Book of Mormon* published in the Hawaiian language. Two years later, however, the mission was closed because of the political situation at the church's center in Utah. In the interim, **Walter Murray Gibson** arrived, settled its members on the island of Lāna'i, and dominated church affairs in the islands. When officials of the church arrived from Utah three years later, Gibson was excommunicated and the center of the church in Hawai'i moved to Lā'ie (O'ahu) where a sugar plantation provided for their everyday needs.

When the church returned to the South Pacific (1888), **Sāmoa** became its chief administrative center from which missionaries spread out to the other Polynesian island states. **Tonga** was first visited in 1891, but the going was slow because of the inroads of the Protestant church there. In 1904, the church established itself in Sāmoa in the village of Sauniatu (later in Pasega). **New Zealand** was first visited by Mormon missionaries in 1854, but it was not until the 1880s that active missionary work was firmly established there.

It is currently estimated (1997 figures) that the church's population in the islands is as follows: **American Sāmoa** 12,000, Sāmoa 56,000, Tonga 43,000, New Zealand 86,000, French Polynesia 15,000, Hawai'i 54,000, **Cook Islands** 9,000, **Niue** 3,000, and a handful in the other island states. In percentage of population, Tonga ranks the highest with 43 percent, followed by Sāmoa (33 percent), American Sāmoa (19 percent), Niue (16 percent), French Polynesia (6 percent), Cook Islands (5 percent), Hawai'i (4 percent), and New Zealand (2.2 percent). Sacred temples (not their regular meeting chapels) have been erected in Hawai'i (1919 and 2000), New Zealand (1958), Tonga (1981), Tahiti (1981), and Āpia, Sāmoa (1983). *See also* AMERICAN BOARD OF COMMISSIONERS FOR FOREIGN MISSION; ROMAN CATHOLIC CHURCH IN OCEANIA; CHURCH MISSIONARY SOCIETY; LONDON MISSIONARY SOCIETY.

MORUROA ATOLL. An atoll (sometimes erroneously spelled Mururoa) located 1,247 km (775 mi) southeast of Pape'ete, **Tahiti**, **French**

Polynesia, used by the French government for nuclear tests from 3 July 1966 until 27 January 1996. The tests were carried out 600 to 800 meters (2,000 to 2,600 feet) underground, and the French government officials have maintained that there is no risk of radioactivity from the tests. The actual underground testing site was moved to the island of Fangataufa, south of Moruroa, in 1975, because of apparent fractures of the rock at Moruroa.

After years of continual protest from various nations, environmental groups, and individuals, the French prime minister announced in November 1990 that **France** would not stop its tests. Its position was reversed, however, on 8 April 1992, when Prime Minister Pierre Beregovoy announced that France would suspend nuclear testing in French Polynesia for 1992 to see if other nations (the **United States** and China, for example) would follow suit. They did. The United States conducted its last test on 23 September. Three years later on 13 June 1995 President Jacques Chirac announced France's plans for a new series of tests at Moruroa. Eight tests were conducted—the last one on 27 January 1996. Since France's moritorium on its testing, restoration and decontamination work has been carried out, the facilities dismantled (July 1998), and a surveillance crew of 30 French Legionnaires left in the area to monitor the environment and to prevent any unauthorized landings. *See also* FRENCH POLYNESIA; NUCLEAR FREE ZONE TREATY; *RAINBOW WARRIOR*.

MULDOON, SIR ROBERT DAVID, GCMG (1921–1992). Prime minister of **New Zealand** from 1975 to 1984 representing the **National Party**. Born in Auckland on 25 September 1921, Muldoon was educated at Mt. Albert Grammar School and elected a member of Parliament for Tamaki in 1960. He served as under secretary to the minister of finance (1964–1966), as minister of **tourism** (1967), as minister of finance (1967–1972), as deputy prime minister (1972), and as leader of the opposition (1974–1975). He became prime minister in the elections of 1975 and served in that capacity until 1984. He was one of New Zealand's first television politicians, a master of the media, and a dominant leader of the National Party. In 1984, he lost out to **David Lange** and the **Labour Party**. He retired from politics in December 1991 and died of heart complications on 5 August 1992. His three books, *Muldoon* (1977), *My Way* (1981), and *New Zealand Economy: A Personal View* (1985), offer an insight into his political views and economic philosophy.

MURUROA. *See* MORUROA ATOLL.

- N -

NATIONAL CENTRE FOR DEVELOPMENT STUDIES (NCDS). Located within the Asia Pacific School of Economics and Management at the Australian National University (ANU), Canberra, **Australia**, the NCDS trains international students at a postgraduate level in areas critical to economic development and monitors social and economic influences on the growth and development of the island states in the Pacific. Research results—working papers, Pacific research monographs, and Pacific policy papers—are published through its own Asia Pacific Press. A biannual *Bulletin* reviews economic trends and includes articles and statistical data of relevance to policy makers and the business community. Its director is Ron Duncan, professor of economics at ANU. Further information can be found on the **Internet** at http://ncdsnet.anu.edu.au/. (*See also* CENTRE FOR SOUTH PACIFIC STUDIES.)

NATIONAL PARTY. One of the two primary parties that have dominated **New Zealand** politics for the past half a century. It adheres to a center political position and supports private enterprise, competitive business, and maximum personal freedom. It emerged in 1936 as a combination of several defeated anti-**Labour** groups and has dominated national politics since 1949 with the exceptions of Labour's governments (1947–1960, 1972–1978, and 1984–1990). In the 1990 elections, the National Party won a significant victory—68 seats to Labour Party's 28. **Jim Bolger** came to power for the next seven years, winning in 1993 and again in 1996. When Bolger retired in December of 1977, **Jenny Shipley** replaced him as head of the party and as prime minister, New Zealand's first female prime minister. An attempt at reforms during a sharp recession led to National's defeat in the 1999 elections. Labour won 49 seats versus National's 39. **Helen Clark**, head of the Labour Party, became prime minister. Its **Internet** Website is located at http://www.national.org.nz.

NATIONAL UNIVERSITY OF SĀMOA. The concept for a national university for **Sāmoa** began soon after its independence in 1962. When the **University of the South Pacific** opened in Fiji in 1968, many Sāmoan students attended that university. Cabinet discussions regarding a local university began seriously in 1983 and by 1984 the National University of Sāmoa was approved by Parliament. The first class that year included only 45 students. Its first bachelor's degree was in education, then in the arts (1988), commerce, and science. A faculty of nursing was established in 1993 and the Institute of Sāmoan Studies in 1999. The university moved into its new Lepapaigalgala campus at Vaivase (east of Āpia, island of 'Upolu) in 1997. Currently (2001), it has 1,480 students, 1,045 of which are full-time. Its most popular degree continues to be in education with 19 percent enrolled in that program. The chancellor of the university is Sāmoa's head of state Mālietoa Tanumafili II; the pro-chancellor is Minister of Education Fiamē Naomi Matā'afa; and the vice-chancellor is Magele Mauiliu Magele. The university's Website is located at http://www.nus.edu.ws. *See also* 'ATENISI INSTITUTE; UNIVERSITÉ DE LA POLYNÉSIE FRANÇAISE; UNIVERSITY OF THE SOUTH PACIFIC.

NAURU. A small oval-shaped island lying in the western Pacific Ocean 67 km (42 mi) south of the equator at 160° 56' east longitude, approximately 4,000 km (2,480 mi) northeast of Sydney, **Australia**. Nauru is considered the smallest independent republic in the world and is an associate member of the **Commonwealth**. The island has a total landmass of only 21.3 sq km (8.2 sq mi) and is surrounded by a coral reef. The highest point of land is 65 meters (213 ft) above sea level. The climate is tropical with northeast trade winds that blow from March to October. The rainy season is from November to February. The Nauruans (60 percent of the 11,346 inhabitants) are primarily of Polynesian origin with mixtures of other Pacific island groups, specifically Micronesian and Melanesian. Nauruan is the official language, but English is also widely used. Local agriculture is difficult, and almost all produce and manufactured goods are imported from foreign countries. The only export is phosphate and that industry—the Nauru Phosphate Corporation—provides a substantial income for all residents on the island. Australian currency is used.

History: The exact origin of the Nauruans is not known. The island has been inhabited for centuries, and it was probably first settled by castaways who drifted there from neighboring islands. Prior to Western contact, the Nauruans were divided into 12 clans or tribes, spoke several dialects, and traced their descent matrilineally. They made offerings to a female deity named Eijebong, and in the 1840s they acknowledged a queen of Nauru. British Captain John Fearn was the first Westerner to sight the island. Landing there in 1798, he named it "Pleasant Island," a designation that continued for almost a century. Very little contact was made after Fearn's visit until the 1830s. Similar to many of the other Polynesian islands, **beachcombers** were the first Caucasians to settle permanently on Nauru. The most notable were John Jones, an Irishman, who settled there in 1841; William Harris in 1842; and 13-year-old Ernest M. H. Stephen later in 1881. These individuals provided a valuable liaison between visiting ships and the Nauruans, who numbered approximately 1,400 at mid-century. The resultant trade in firearms and alcohol took its toll, and civil war became incessant.

Several German traders settled on the island, and when **Germany** announced its Marshall Islands Protectorate in 1888, a German gunboat landed on Nauru and the German imperial commissioner took possession. He forced the islanders to hand in their weapons, placed a local German trader in command, and left. The island thus remained under German administration until World War I. Meanwhile, Protestant missionaries arrived in 1899 (Rev. P. A. Delaporte) and Roman Catholics (Father Grundl) in 1902 and converted the islanders to Christianity.

In 1898, enormous deposits of phosphate were discovered on the island by the Sydney-based Pacific Islands Company (PIC). (Phosphate is a chemical compound used as fertilizer.) Not having direct intervention in Nauru, the PIC moved to Nauru's nearest neighbor, Ocean Island, found it too contained huge deposits of phosphate, signed an agreement with the local chiefs, and began mining. An agreement was eventually reached between the British company and the German Jaluit Gesellschaft to mine Nauru with a percentage of the royalty going to the Gesellschaft. By 1914, hundreds of thousands of tons of phosphate were mined by imported Caroline Islanders (Micronesians) and Chinese and shipped to Australia.

When World War I broke out (1914), Japan seized Germany's Micronesian possession in the North Pacific, and Australia seized Nauru and continued the phosphate mining. After the war, the League of Nations placed Nauru under a mandate of **Great Britain**, Australia, and New Zealand with Australia as prime administrator. The British Phosphate Commissioners (BPC) bought out the old Pacific Phosphate Company with royalties going to Great Britain (42 percent), Australia (42 percent), and New Zealand (16 percent). The Nauruans themselves were paid a paltry sum for the export of their island.

When World War II broke out in the Pacific, **Japanese** planes bombed the island on 9 December 1941, and Japanese soldiers invaded on 26 August 1942. The Japanese deported the Nauruans to Truk in Micronesia and used the islands for a strategic airstrip. U.S. bombers attacked the island repeatedly during 1943, and on 13 September 1945, Australia again reoccupied the island. The surviving Nauruans on Truk were returned to their homeland. Five hundred of the 1,200 had died of starvation, disease, and Japanese cruelty. Nauru was once more made a trust territory of Great Britain, Australia, and New Zealand, and the BPC began its phosphate mining again.

Similar to many of the other Pacific islands after World War II, Nauru moved toward self-government. In December 1951 a local government council was organized, and its leaders voiced their desire for independence to the United Nations, which sent them advisors to negotiate with their mandate rulers. A larger percent of royalties for the Nauruans was gained in 1965 and 1966 when a local legislative council was established. On 31 January 1968, the Republic of Nauru was created and **Chief Hammer DeRoburt** chosen its first president. Transfer of the ownership of the phosphate industry was also made to Nauru, and thus the Nauru Phosphate Corporation was created by an act of the Nauruan Parliament.

Government: The Nauruan constitution provides for an 18-member Parliament elected every three years from eight constituencies. Voting is compulsory for all over the age of 20. The president, elected by Parliament, appoints a cabinet of four or five other ministers from Parliament members.

Except for a few short interruptions, DeRoburt held the office of president from 1968 until 1989 when he was defeated by Bernard Dowiyogo, who held the position (with several short interruptions) until elections in November 1995. Nauru politics are complicated by constant jockeying for power by the 18 members of Parliament. Between 1995 and 2001, the presidency changed hands 10 times. The current president (and for the second time) is René Harris, elected on 30 March 2001. He toppled President Bernard Dowiyogo who had been elected (for the sixth time) on 20 April 2000. (See Appendix B for the dates and names of the presidents.) On 14 September 1999, Nauru became the 187th nation to join the United Nations.

Economy: As indicated above, Nauru's existence depends upon the status of its phosphate. By the mid-1990s, the per capita income of Nauruans, at $32,857, was the highest in the world. But in a nationwide speech, in April of 1999, President Dowiyogo warned the citizens that the island republic faced massive debts and that its citizens would have to rein in their excessive lifestyles because the phosphate is expected to run out within the next eight to 12 years. Royalties for the exported phosphate have been shared among the government (50 percent), the Nauruan landowners, and the Nauru Phosphate Royalties Trust. Various and sundry investments have been made in Australia, London, New Zealand, the Philippines, Fiji, **Sāmoa**, Guam, **Hawai'i**, and the U.S. mainland; however, not all have been profitable or successful—some have been labeled disastrous. The trust has also had its share of mismanagement, larceny, and fraud.

A century of mining has also created massive ecological damage to the island. Eighty percent of Nauru's landmass is currently unusable. In 1993, Nauru filed a $72 million lawsuit against Australia for its part in this damage. An out-of-court settlement was reached in 1994 with compensation set at a $37 million lump-sum payment plus $1.6 million a year over the next 20 years. It is estimated that it will cost Nauruans at least $210 million to restore the land.

To assist its diminishing phosphate returns, Nauru has diversified and developed an offshore banking industry. That too has been plagued with accusations of being a facility for the Russian mafia for laundering its money. As a result, the Organization of Economic Cooperation and

Development (OECD) has threatened to cut Nauru out of the world monetary system. In 1999, Nauru applied to the **Asian Development Bank (ADB)** for a $5 million loan to help reform its economy. The national budget has been drastically cut by 60 percent and the public sector has been reduced. It is expected that Nauru's economy will undergo even more extreme readjustments over the next few years.

NELSON, OLAF FREDERICK (1883–1944). Sāmoan businessman, patriot, and political leader. Nelson was born on 24 February 1883 on Savai'i, **Sāmoa**, to a high-ranking Sāmoan mother and a Swedish father whose business (O. F. Nelson and Company) he took over at the age of 17. An affluent member of both the Sāmoan and European communities, Nelson strenuously objected to the League of Nations' mandate after World War I that placed Sāmoa under **New Zealand** administration. He became a leader of the *Mau* movement and fought the new colonial government for 15 years. He was banished twice from Sāmoa, once in 1927 and again in 1933. In 1934, the newly elected **Labour** government in New Zealand allowed him to return to Sāmoa honorably where he died on 24 February 1944. He authored the book *Legends of Samoa* and was elected a life member of the **Polynesian Society** located in New Zealand. *See also MAU* OF PULE.

NEW LABOUR PARTY. Founded in **New Zealand** in 1989 by Jim Anderton, former president of the **Labour Party**, and others who opposed Labour's continued advocacy of privatization under Prime Minister David Lange's administration (1984–1987). In the 1990 elections, the New Labour Party gained one parliamentary seat (out of 97).

NEW ZEALAND (*Aotearoa* in New Zealand Māori). An independent nation and member of the **Commonwealth**, it lies 2,012 km (1,250 mi) east of **Australia**, and consists of two main islands, North Island (114,500 sq km/44,200 sq mi) and South Island (150,700 sq km/48,170 sq mi), and the smaller islands of Antipodes Islands, Auckland Islands, Bounty Islands, Campbell Island, Chatham Islands, and Kermadec Islands. The total landmass equals 270,534 sq km (104,454 sq mi) or about the size of the state of California and represents the largest land area of any island group in **Polynesia**. South Island's topography is characterized by a massive chain of mountains commonly referred to as the "Southern Alps," that extends the entire length of the island while North Island has proportionately fewer of these mountains. Natural resources are limited but generally consist of natural gas, iron ore, sand, coal, timber, limestone, and gold. New Zealand's current population of 3,811,000 (2000 estimate) includes 72 percent Europeans, 15.6 percent **Māori**, 6.3 percent other Pacific islanders, and 6.3 percent Asian (one of the fastest growing minorities). English is the primary language, however, since 1974, New Zealand Māori has been recognized as one of the two official languages. New Zealand's economy is primarily based upon exportation of wool, lamb, mutton, beef, fruit, fish, and cheese to Australia (25 percent), to **Japan** (14 percent), and to the **United States** (12 percent). Urbanization is high with 80 percent of the population residing in centers with populations greater than 1,000. Wellington, New Zealand's capital, has a population of 335,468 while the largest city is Auckland with a population of approximately 997,940.

Pre-European History: The Polynesians who first discovered and settled these islands came from the east—from the **Society Islands** (**French Polynesia**), the **Cook Islands**, or the **Marquesas**—possibly by A.D. 800. **Māori** oral traditions tell of numerous voyages from **Hawaiki**, and archaeological studies indicate that the islands were fairly well inhabited by the 12th century. Tribal kinship groups dominated Māori social life while their subsistence lifestyle and culture changed to accommodate the cooler climate they experienced in the islands. Classic Māori culture became unique to New Zealand (*Aotearoa*, "long white cloud," as it was called by these early inhabitants) but it still remained close to the ancient **Polynesian culture** developed in the other eastern island groups. Unique to the Māoris were their **tattoo** designs, their tools and ornaments carved from greenstone, their canoes and houses elaborately decorated, and their sophisticated flax clothing. At European contact (1769), the indigenous Māori population was estimated to be approximately 120,000 inhabitants.

Historical Period: Although the Dutch explorer Abel Tasman first sighted the islands in 1642, it was **Captain James Cook** in 1769, 1773, and 1774 who first charted the islands, took possession of them for **Great Britain**, and extensively recorded his impressions of the Māori material culture. Subsequent visits by other explorers added not only to the ethnographic understanding of the islands but also to the exploitation of the islands' resources. Sealers (1792) destroyed settlements along the southern coast, while **whaling** (1791–1792), timber, and flax (1793) provided the basis of trade before 1840, primarily with New South Wales (Australia).

Christian missionaries from the Church Missionary Society arrived in 1814 under the supervision of the **Reverend Samuel Marsden**, but their success only became apparent in the 1820s with the arrival of **William Williams** who contributed much through his knowledge of the Māori language. The Wesleyan mission was established at Whangaroa between 1823 and 1827, but then had to be reestablished in the 1830s. The **Roman Catholic** Marist mission under the direction of **Bishop Pompallier** began in 1838 and by 1841 had baptized about a thousand Māoris.

As elsewhere in the Pacific, Europeans brought a drastic change in the lifestyles of the indigenous peoples. One serious consequence was the introduction of firearms around the turn of the century. Intertribal warfare in the 1820s led to massive depopulation of areas either as a result of killings or voluntary migration to safer areas. British immigration from New South Wales soared in the 1830s as economic conditions in Australia worsened because of drought and labor shortage and a threat of French or American intervention into the affairs of the islands.

The **New Zealand Company**, supervised by **Edward Gibbon Wakefield**, promoted British intervention, and it and other organizations founded settlements in Wellington, Nelson, Wanganui, New Plymouth, Christchurch, and Dunedin. Captain William Hobson, a representative of the British government, arrived in the Bay of Islands on 29 January 1840 and assumed authority over the islands. He summoned the Māori chiefs to a meeting, and on 6 February, an ambiguous and contradictory treaty was signed—the **Treaty of Waitangi**. In 1841, the islands were declared a separate Crown Colony with Auckland as its administrative center.

In 1845, **Sir George Grey** arrived as the colony's new governor and initiated a more responsible form of government and economy. A steady stream of immigrants from Australia brought with it thousands of sheep (predominantly Merino) and as a result, large areas of tussock land were leased from the Māoris. Self-government was attained in

1852, and the government consisted of a governor appointed by London, a legislative council (chosen by the governor), and a house of representatives (elected by the people). Wellington was designated the capital in 1865.

The discovery of gold in the Otago district (South Island) in 1861 provided a new incentive for immigrants from the gold fields of Australia and California to pour into the islands as Hokitia on the west coast became a busy port. The boom lasted less than 10 years, but it established the south as a strong commercial and industrial center. By 1871, the ***pākehā*** population had soared to 256,393; a good number were working-class who found life in the growing urban cities pitifully difficult. This coupled with the economic depression of the 1880s caused many to emigrate to Australia.

The growing hardships accentuated the need for some form of social welfare assistance, especially among the elderly who had left families behind when they had emigrated to the new land. Politicians quickly capitalized on the growing dissatisfaction, especially among the unions. A Liberal government came to power in January 1891, and under the dominant leadership of **"King Dick" Seddon** from 1893 to 1896, a wide range of social legislation was passed that provided for better factory conditions, shorter hours, old-age pensions, accident compensation, and even gave **women** the right to vote (in 1893, and New Zealand was the first country in the world to do so).

World War I (1914–1918) taxed New Zealand in her support of the mother country, **Great Britain**. Out of the 100,000 troops who served, 16,000 were killed and 45,000 were wounded. An era of general prosperity followed the war, and New Zealand became a member of the League of Nations. Immigration was encouraged and by 1930, New Zealand's population numbered approximately 1.65 million.

The Great Depression caused widespread labor unrest and riots occurred in the major urban centers. In 1935, the **Labour Party**, under the direction of **Michael Joseph Savage**, **Peter Fraser**, and **Walter Nash**, was returned to power to continue the social reforms that it had begun earlier in the century. The government established fixed prices for essential commodities (milk, butter, cheese); began public works programs to build roads, railroads, and public housing; established fixed wages and shorter work weeks; introduced compulsory unionism; initiated free medical assistance; and increased old-age pensions. The **New Zealand National Party** emerged in the late 1930s as anti-Labour and as an attempt to halt socialism.

When World War II broke out in 1939, New Zealand rallied again to the cause of Great Britain in the Middle East, Europe, and the Pacific—(11,600 killed, 15,700 wounded)—while the Labour government mobilized for the war effort by introducing further controls over the economy. The straight-jacket controls for many years undermined the Labour Party, and in 1949, the antisocialist National Party won a decisive victory at the polls. **Sir Sidney Holland** became prime minister and his government attempted the relaxation of numerous government controls and ownership of mines. Holland's use of troops to end a dock workers' strike in February 1951, though criticized, was successful. Since then, the National Party has dominated politics and has returned to power between 1949–1957, 1960–1972, 1978–1984, and 1990–1999. (See Appendix B for a chronological list of New Zealand's prime ministers.) It presided over the economic boom that began during the Korean War and that lasted until about 1973.

The 1970s and 1980s, however, saw a drastic reduction in the country's economic well–being. Recession in the 1970s was brought about by an international oil crisis (1973–1974), a skyrocketing of energy costs, and Great Britain's entrance into the European Economic Community. As a result, inflation was rampant, unemployment rose, the standard of living dropped, and consequently many New Zealanders emigrated to Australia.

In response, **Robert Muldoon's** National Party began a policy of unparalleled intervention in the economy that resulted in massive budgetary deficits. The elections of 1984 brought David Lange's Labour Party to power (1984–1990), and it adopted a policy of deregulation, easing of restrictions on free enterprise, and the lifting of wage and price controls. Labour's success in easing the economic problems and stabilizing inflation and its antinuclear stance in international affairs returned Labour to power once again in 1987. Subsequent dissension within the Labour Party over privatization of state-owned enterprises, however, weakened the party. That plus high unemployment and the unsolved social and economic problems of the 1980s turned against the party, and as a result, the 1990 elections brought National back to power with

Jim Bolger as prime minister. (National gained 68 seats, Labour 28, and the New Labour Party one.) Serious national issues that National faced were unemployment (7.5 to 10 percent), deregulation, national social security (pensions over 60), national health care program, and compulsory trade union membership; National set about to correct all these by continuing many of the policies begun by Labour. The legislature passed the Employment Contracts Act which greatly reduced the power of workers to bargain collectively and to strike. Many of the state's assets were sold off and thus reduced the national debt. Social welfare programs were reduced, medical prescription fees increased, and the cost of tertiary education expanded.

These drastic actions by National, however, caused a division within the party. In 1991, several dissidents broke away and formed a New Liberal Party, and National's strength was greatly reduced in the 1993 elections when it narrowly won reelection. Although economic conditions in the country had improved, many electorates believed they had been betrayed by both National and Labour. Radical changes had brought only slight improvement in the standard of living. In the 1993 elections, National gained 50 seats, Labour 45, Alliance two, and New Zealand First two. Bolger's government held only a slim majority. In the 1996 elections, Bolger's slim majority slipped even further away. National gained 44 seats, Labour 37, New Zealand First 17, and the Alliance 13. After several weeks, Bolger formed a coalition government with New Zealand First whose chair, Winston Peters, was appointed deputy prime minister and treasurer.

Many of the new members of Parliament were dissatisfied with the coalition while other members of the electorate believed it was only an arrangement of political convenience for National. Dissatisfaction grew, and in 1997, National replaced Bolger with **Jenny Shipley**, who became New Zealand's first woman prime minister. She lost the support of New Zealand First and consequently had to rely upon a strange coalition of various members of other parties. During 1999, Shipley's government was criticized on several counts and for its handling of numerous controversies. As a result, Shipley's National Party gained only 30.5 percent of the votes and 39 seats (out of 120) in Parliament in the 1999 elections and ended the 10-year rule of National Labour, however, gained 49 seats, Alliance 10, ACT New Zealand 9

New Zealand First 7, Christian Heritage Party 5, and United New Zealand 1. The head of the Labour Party since 1993, **Helen Clark**, formed a new coalition government with New Zealand First.

Economy: With the exception of **Hawai‘i**, New Zealand enjoys the highest standard of living of any of the other Polynesian states with a per capita income of $17,000. Since 1984, the government has accomplished a major restructuring of its economy. New Zealand's leading section, however, continues to be its agricultural exports which account for approximately 44 percent of total export earnings (down from 60 percent in the early 1990s). Its second largest section is the export of natural elements such as gas, timber, and chemicals. New Zealand's major export trading partners are Australia (25 percent), the United States (17 percent), Japan (11 percent), the United Kingdom (5 percent), and China (5 percent). The tourist industry has also grown from 867,500 visitors in 1989 to over 1.5 million in 1999, approximately one-third coming from Australia. Because of its geographical location, however, the country remains vulnerable to economic forces beyond its control. The Asian financial crises of 1996–1997, for example, was particularly damaging to its export and **tourism** industries, both of which have rebounded. Unemployment has been reduced to 7.5 percent, and for the past three years, the government has announced annual budget surpluses

Māori Affairs: Resurgence of interest in their own indigenous culture during the last two decades has resulted in a more politically active Māori population. Unemployment among them continues to be much higher than the national average, almost 40 percent of them drop out of school, and half of the prison population consists of Māoris. Controversy over the interpretation of thc 1840 **Treaty of Waitangi** continues, and Māoris have filed land claims that encompass large tracts of New Zealand territory. The Māori population, as well as that of the other Pacific islanders residing in the country, continues to expand much faster than the white population, and their economic and social problems will continue to demand attention from subsequent governments in the next several decades.

For further details on New Zealand, refer to Keith Jackson and Alan McRobie's 1996 *Historical Dictionary of New Zealand* published by Scarecrow Press.

NEW ZEALAND COMPANY. A joint stock company formed in 1838 in England to aid in the colonization of **New Zealand**. An earlier attempt at colonization in 1826 was unsuccessful, but with the backing of more influential voices, it finally received government sanction in 1841. **Colonel Arthur Wakefield** headed the expedition that established the city of Wellington. Wakefield's insistence on claiming lands from the local **Māori** tribes around the Wairau region led to his expedition party of 22 settlers being slain. The company eventually relinquished its charter to the Crown and was dissolved in 1858.

NGATA, ĀPIRANA TURUPA (1874–1950). The first **New Zealand Māori** to graduate from a university in New Zealand (B.A., Canterbury 1893) and to receive a law degree (1897). A member of the **Young Māori Party**, he was elected to Parliament between 1905 and 1943 where he became an influential force as a member of the government's cabinet heading the native affairs office. He also published several volumes of Māori ethnography and culture, most important of which is his *Nga Moteatea* (1929).

NIUE. A self-governing island in free association with **New Zealand** since October 1974, Niue is approximately 58 km (36 mi) in circumference with a landmass of 262.7 sq km (101 sq mi), located 480 km (300 mi) east of **Tonga**. Niue (nicknamed "The Rock") is one of the world's largest raised coral islands with crevices and extraordinary cliffs of limestone on its eastern coast. Niueans (1,857 in 2001) are British subjects with New Zealand citizenship (approximately 18,000 Niueans live in New Zealand). Fourteen percent of the population is ethnically Tongan, **Tuvaluan**, or New Zealander. The two official languages are Niuean—a Polynesian language closely related to **Sāmoan** and Tongan—and English. (One primary school is bilingual, while English is the language of the secondary school.) Radio and television broadcasts are in both languages. Economically, Niue is one of the most dependent countries in the world, having a high standard of living where housing, health, and education are virtually free. Attempts to develop agriculture (bananas, kūmara, and **copra**) have all failed. No significant agriculture or industry exists. There is a limited export trade of **taro**, limes, and honey primarily to New Zealand. Niue's administrative center is the village of Alofi located on the west coast of the island.

History: The island was first settled by Sāmoans and Tongans perhaps a thousand years ago. Their social structure became more egalitarian than either Sāmoa or **Tonga**, however, and this characteristic continues well into modern times.

Captain James Cook was the first known European to visit the island (24 June 1774). He called it Savage Island because of the hostile character of the islanders. Missionaries from the **London Missionary Society** unsuccessfully attempted to land there in 1830 and 1842. It was only through the influence of Peniamina, a Niuean who had been trained in the mission school in Sāmoa, that Christianity was introduced into the island. Until 1861, the successful conversion of the people resulted only from the work of the Sāmoan missionaries—Paulo, Moose, and Halefa—who were protected by chief Togia at Alofi. Accompanying the conversion came the trappings of a "civilized" society and the destruction of the old.

The Reverend George Lawes (there from 1861 to 1872) and his brother Frank Lawes (from 1868 to 1910) were the most prominent missionaries in the 19th century. They are credited with establishing a central government (an assembly called a *fono* and an elected king), a legal system, medical clinics, vocational training, and with exerting a great deal of influence over the Niueans. Emigration to work in Sāmoa became common during the 1860s. Especially devastating was the **blackbirding** by slave traders in 1863 when some 109 Niuean men were captured to work in the guano mines in Peru.

Early commercial companies, Godeffroy and Son, for example, established trading centers on the island where cotton, fungus, arrowroot, and copra were the cash crops. Accompanying the introduction of a money economy were vices that shocked the Christian community and, by 1896, church membership had dropped considerably. In 1876, the island *fono* elected Mataio Tuitogia, a chief from Alofi, as king over the island. When he died on 12 July 1887, it chose as his successor Tataaiki who in 1889 (presumably backed by Frank Lawes) petitioned Queen Victoria to take the island under her protection. Tataaiki died on 15 January 1896, succeeded by Togia (already age 70) who continued his petitions for British protection.

The **Anglo-German Agreement of 1899** placed Niue (and other South Pacific islands) under the protection of **Great Britain**. On

21 April 1900, Britain annexed the island and placed it under New Zealand administration. King Togia and his *fono* objected to being administered from New Zealand and being considered part of the **Cook Islands**. As a result, a separate New Zealand administrative unit was established for Niue in 1903. Percy Smith, a highly respected **Māori** scholar, effected the transition of the rule of the island to the resident commissioner which included reorganization of the traditional *fono*. In 1904, a clash of views over salaries essentially established the resident commissioner as the most powerful individual on the island, who came to control most of the island's politics and economy.

During World War I, 150 Niueans saw military service in the trenches of Europe where a good number died from disease. World War II, however, had little effect on the island since Niueans were not encouraged to enlist for service. C. H. W. Larsen, resident commissioner from 1944 to 1953, modernized Niue by providing better medical facilities and education. But his attempts to change the blue laws which forbade working on Sunday and more specifically loading and unloading ships in the harbor, antagonized a good number of islanders. His tolerance of allowing other religious groups entrance into the island (**Mormons** in 1952 and **Roman Catholics** in 1955) further antagonized the established church, the Ekalesia. On the night of 14 August 1953, Larsen and his wife were murdered by three escaped convicts. Headlines in the New Zealand papers regarding the murder and the death sentence of the plaintiffs brought Niue to the forefront for many months.

The two violent hurricanes in 1959 and 1960 destroyed most of the islanders' homes. New Zealand responded with grants and loans that greatly enhanced the lifestyle of the island and virtually destroyed the old subsistence way of living.

Growing world opposition to imperial colonialism forced New Zealand to be more considerate in the administration of its overseas territories—the Cook Islands, Sāmoa, and of course Niue. A highly respected resident commissioner, J. M. McEwen, was appointed to succeed Larsen. He effected numerous changes. In 1960, the island council was replaced by an elected legislative assembly, and then in 1962, New Zealand announced that it would grant Niue self-government by 1965, a decision denounced by the legislative assembly because Niue had not been part of the decision-making process. Concern also was expressed been part of the decision-making process. Concern also was expressed over Niue's possible loss of New Zealand economic aid, education, and citizenship.

The Niue Act of 1966 provided for the election of an island (national) leader, a position won by **Robert Richmond Rex**, who led the country until his death in 1992, and a legislative assembly consisting of 20 members. During the 1970s, the resident commissioners delegated more and more responsibility to the legislative assembly. In 1972, a **United Nations** commission visited Niue and was impressed with its pace of development. Discussions between the island government and New Zealand ultimately ended in an agreement (the Niue Constitution Act of 1974) of "independence in free association with New Zealand." New Zealand would provide economic and administrative assistance and would continue to supervise Niue's foreign affairs, while all other internal affairs would be administered by the island government. Traditional laws regarding land tenure and usage were incorporated into the new constitution. Niueans would also continue to hold New Zealand citizenship. The first elections for the new government occurred on 26 April 1975, and the new assembly elected Robert Rex its first premier.

A driving force in Niuean politics since the 1980s has been its economy. Without mineral and agricultural resources, a small island like Niue must find ways in which to support itself. Having little incentives to keep young people on the island, many individuals emigrated to New Zealand. By 1989, the population had drastically shrunk from 5,111 in 1970 to 2,019, and the island leaders debated on what could be done. The legislative assembly proposed to loosen some of the ties with New Zealand to stop the population drain, and the New Zealand foreign affairs officers then criticized the Niuean government in its administration of the $10 million being sent to the island each year. In 1991, New Zealand announced it was reducing the annual subsidy to Niue by 10 percent, not only because of what it perceived as mismanagement of funds but because New Zealand's economy was experiencing a recession as well. By 1993, that annual aid had been reduced 30 percent. This fragile economic relationship between New Zealand and Niue continues to the present day.

In the elections of May 1990, Niue's first political party, the **Niue People's Action Party (NPAP)**, gained 12 seats and opposed Rex's government, although Rex remained in office through a successful maneuver in the legislative assembly. In July 1992, Rex announced he would not stand for reelection and on 13 December he died. Young Vivian, acting premier, was unanimously elected premier, but when legislative elections took place in February, the assembly elected Frank Lui, a former cabinet minister, as premier. Lui served until March of 1999.

The continual need for secure financial support from outside highlighted Lui's term of office. **Tourism** was encouraged. In 1990, Niue Air Lines, Ltd., had begun weekly flights to Auckland in an attempt to promote tourism for the islands. One thousand tourists visited the island that year. By 1997, there were 1,820, but by June of 1998, the tourist industry was still struggling. Possible Internet revenues were also investigated. The government proposed to rent its **Internet** connection to a Canadian company for Internet gambling. Millions of dollars, they felt, could be earned annually from this arrangement; however, the New Zealand government vetoed the idea. Another Internet idea emerged in 1997, when the state investigated the possibility of selling rights to its domain name "*.nu*" for a percentage of the annual rentals. By 1999, this arrangement has earned the government approximately $540,000 annually.

In the March 1999 elections, Lui lost his seat in the assembly and as a result lost the premiership. His opposition claimed that the economy was stagnant and tourism needed attention. The assembly elected Sani Lakatani as premier and Young Vivian as deputy premier. A new cabinet was formed. Lakatani promised to boost tourism, investigate the possibility of a new airline service, and review Niue's constitution. By April, the New Zealand government announced that it was ending Niue's aid by the year 2003. As a result, Lakatani announced a 40 percent reduction in salary of cabinet members and called for Niueans in New Zealand to return home. In October Niue celebrated its 25th anniversary of self-rule; the government freed its prisoners (all four of them) and closed its jails. Political pressures against Lakatani mounted, and a no-confidence motion was initiated by his opposition. It was put off until a December meeting of the assembly.

In the meantime, however, worldwide news broke that Niue and **Nauru** were being accused of helping the Russian mafia, the South American drug cartel, and a Panamanian drug related operation in laundering their money. Lakatani angrily denied all allegations. The no-confidence vote taken on 20 December resulted in a hung Parliament. The vote was 10-10. A high court ruled in January in favor of Lakatani, but the issue was not over. Lakatani then came under fire because of personal bankruptcy charges in New Zealand and for mismanagement of government funds. Another no-confidence vote came on 8 June, which ended in a 9-9 vote. Lakatani said he would not step down, and the tie vote prevented any further discussion. A loan from his brothers to pay off the debts ended Lakatani's legal battles.

Relations between New Zealand and Niue improved when the **Labour Party** came to power in New Zealand (November 1999). In early 2000, the New Zealand government announced that it would not reduce Niue's annual subsidy and suggested that it might even reimburse Niue for previous annual reductions. By mid-June, Niue announced an end to its issuing offshore banking licenses in compliance with the international request to clean up its banking procedures. A new budget was passed ($8.6 million), but immediately the government announced a deficit of $625,000. In August/September, a long teachers' strike crippled the schools, and by late November, another no-confidence vote was filed by the government's opposition.

NIUE PEOPLE'S PARTY (NPP). The first and only political party in **Niue**, formed in 1987 as the Niue People's Action Party to oppose **Prime Minister Sir Robert Rex**. The party is currently headed by Premier Sani Lakatani, and one aim of the party is to persuade Niueans living in **New Zealand** to support economic projects in their home state.

NORDHOFF, CHARLES BERNARD (1887–1947). A famous U.S. writer who collaborated with **James Norman Hall** in writing numerous novels regarding the South Pacific—*Faery Lands of the South Seas* (1921), *Mutiny on the Bounty* (1932), *Men Against the Sea* (1933), *Pitcairn Island* (1934), *The Hurricane* (1936), *Dark River* (1938), and *No More Gas* (1940), several of which have been made into motion pictures. After spending many years in the South Pacific, Nordhoff returned to the **United States** where he died in Santa Barbara, California, on 11 April 1947.

NORFOLK ISLAND. Officially known as the Territory of Norfolk Island, it is an external territory of **Australia** whose population of 1,772 inhabitants (1996 census) is 39 percent Polynesian extract. The small island lies 1,400 km (868 mi) east of Brisbane, Australia, and about 640 km (400 mi) north of **New Zealand** and consists of a landmass area of 34.6 sq km (13.4 sq mi). The climate is mild and subtropical, and the island is a favorite tourist destination for Aussies and New Zealanders. English is the official language, however, a local **Pidgin** dialect of English and Tahitian is also spoken. Its administrative center is the town of Kingston, located on the southern coast of the island. **Tourism** is its main industry, although farming, fishing, and philatelic sales provide additional income.

History: The island was uninhabited when **Captain James Cook** visited it in 1774, claimed it as a British possession, and named it after the Duke of Norfolk. The island was used as a British penal colony between 1788 and 1814 and then again from 1825 to 1855, and then abandoned. On 8 June 1856, 194 Pitcairn islanders arrived on Norfolk from **Tahiti**. They were descendants of the mutineers of the **Bounty** and their Polynesian wives. They had first been settled on Tahiti in 1831 by the British government because of overpopulation on **Pitcairn**. Because of disputes between them and the Tahitians, they were now relocated to Norfolk Island. For the next 40 years, the Pitcairners maintained their traditional culture, ways of life, and semi-independence. In 1897, the island became a dependency of New South Wales, and in 1913 its control was transferred to the Australian government. In 1979, Australia passed the Norfolk Island Act that provides the framework of Norfolk's current political and administrative structure. Subsequent amendments have provided the islanders with more control over internal autonomy, and on several occasions they have voiced their objection to Australia's proposals to bring them within its federal electorate.

Government: The administrator of the island is appointed by the governor-general of Australia. Since August 1997, that position has been held by Anthony J. Messner. The administrator approves all bills passed by the legislative assembly which consists of nine members elected for three-year terms. It may pass no legislation dealing with security, immigration, education, fishing, money, and so forth. An executive council consisting of four ministers chosen from the nine members of the legislative assembly advises the administrator on governance. A chief minister is chosen by the administrator after consulting with the legislative assembly. Currently, Ronald Coane Nobbs, elected on 22 February 2000, is the chief minister.

NOTT, HENRY (1774–1844). A prominent English missionary of the **London Missionary Society**, responsible for the first Protestant mission to the Pacific islands. Nott arrived with his colleagues in **Tahiti** in 1797 and preached the first Christian sermon in Tahitian in August 1801. He was the first to translate the Christian scriptures into the Tahitian language and personally presented a printed copy (1836) of them to Queen Victoria. Nott became a personal advisor to high chief **Pomare I** during the civil wars that ensued on the islands. The first real converts, however, were only made in 1815 when Pomare was baptized. Nott advised Pomare on the establishment of the first Christian laws for the islands—the **Pomare Law Code of 1819**—and exercised great influence over the royal family. He died on 2 May 1844, at Papara (Tahiti). Currently, a stone marks his grave outside of Pape'ete in Matavai, a short distance from the burial grounds of the Pomare family. *See also* FRENCH POLYNESIA.

NUCLEAR FREE ZONE (NFZ) TREATY. An agreement signed in August 1985 by the governments of **Australia**, **New Zealand**, **Cook Islands**, Fiji, Kiribati, **Niue**, **Tuvalu**, and **Sāmoa** to establish a zone free from the manufacture, possession, control, or testing of nuclear weapons. It maintains total opposition to French underground nuclear testing at **Moruroa atoll**. The treaty has also been used against U.S. warships docking in NFZ harbors, although the treaty does allow such ships to pass through NFZ's territorial waters. The treaty and subsequent relations between New Zealand and the **United States** have essentially rendered a previous defense alliance, the **ANZUS Pact** defunct. *See also* NUCLEAR TESTING IN POLYNESIA; RAROTONGA DECLARATION.

NUCLEAR TESTING IN POLYNESIA. The **United States** exploded the world's first nuclear bomb on 16 July 1945 at Almagordo, New Mexico. **France** became the fourth country to develop and explode a bomb with an actual explosion in the Sahara Desert on 13 February 1960. While the United States moved its testing to the North Pacific Micronesian atolls of Bikini and Enewetak, the French moved its from the Sahara to the Polynesian atolls of **Moruroa** and Fangataufa. France performed approximately 200 tests in the atolls between 3 July 1966 and 27 January 1996. The effort was extremely costly. At its peak in 1967, approximately 26.4 of France's defense budget went toward nuclear testing. In the view of the French, the expenditure was the price of independence. The program allowed France to deploy a mini-superpower arsenal with nuclear bombers, ground-to-ground ballistic intermediate range missiles, and nuclear submarines carrying sea-to-ground ballistic missiles; by 1991, 540 warheads had been deployed.

Over the years, France's nuclear effort has had broad public support at home. History showed France that it must not be vulnerable to invasion and occupation again as it had on two separate occasions within the 20th century. Its security and world influence have depended upon its successful competition in an arms race that France has always maintained was for its own security rather than for aggression. During the 1980s, opposition to France's testing in **French Polynesia** mounted in the Pacific, and on 10 July 1985, a Greenpeace flagship was blown up in Auckland harbor while on its way to protest French nuclear testing. Investigations revealed that the attack had been planned by French intelligence agents. A month later, the South Pacific countries of **Australia**, **New Zealand**, **Cook Islands**, Fiji, Kiribati, **Niue**, **Tuvalu**, and **Samoa** signed a **Nuclear Free Zone** (NFZ) Treaty that prohibited any nuclear substances within the area. The opposition against France's testing kept mounting even more, and in 1992, France responded by placing a moratorium on its tests. On 13 June 1995, however, French President Jacques Chirac surprisingly announced a new series to tests that finally ended on 27 January 1996. The site at Moruroa has since been closed and clean-up begun. *See also RAINBOW WARRIOR.*

- O -

OBOOKIAH, HENRY (1792?–1818). A Hawaiian, orphaned at the age of 12, who sailed (1809) to New Haven, Connecticut, where he was taught to read and write. He was befriended by numerous prominent clergymen of the day including Edwin W. Dwight, president of Yale University. Obookiah became active in the Foreign Mission Society (Cornwall, Connecticut) where he began the translation of the Bible into Hawaiian. He died of typhus fever on 17 February 1818, and it was his posthumous book, *Memoirs of Henry Obookiah* (1818), that inspired the first Christian missionaries to sail to Hawai'i (1819–1820). *See also* HAWAI'I.

OFFICE OF HAWAIIAN AFFAIRS (OHA). A **Hawai'i** state agency formed in 1978 and managed by nine trustees elected during state elections, it serves as an advocate for Hawaiians, receives and spends moneys for the benefit of native Hawaiians from income from leases of Ceded Lands, and works to obtain reparations for damages suffered as a result of the 1893 revolution. It also administers the Hawaiian Home Lands, and more recently it has advocated the move toward self-government. Some Hawaiians feel that OHA is too much under the control of the current government to act sympathetically in behalf of the Hawaiian people, and therefore they have created agencies in competition to that office—the **Ka Lāhui Hawai'i**, Nā 'Ōiwi o Hawai'i, and Ka Pākaukau, for example.

OCEANIA NATIONAL OLYMPIC COMMITTEE (NOC). An organization that coordinates and promotes the International Olympic activities in Oceania. The organization was conceived by International Olympic President Juan Antonio Samaranch while the Olympics were being held in **Germany** in 1981. The founding member nations at the initial meeting were **Australia**, **New Zealand**, Fiji, and Papua New Guinea. Since then, National Olympic Committees of **American Sāmoa**, **Cook Islands**, Federated States of Micronesia, Guam, **Nauru**, Palau, **Sāmoa**, Solomon Islands, **Tonga**, and Vanuatu have joined the organization. Meetings are held annually; the one in 2000 was held in Nuku'alofa, Tonga. Its current officers are Kevan Gosper (Australia), president, Ric Blas (Guam), vice president, and Robin Mitchell (Fiji), secretary-general. The highlight of the committee's activities during the last decade has been the Summer Olympic Games held in Sydney, Australia, in 2000, and which marked the biggest torch relay in the history of the games. The torch was carried by 12,000 runners across 60,000 km (37,200 mi) and through 14 countries of the Pacific Ocean. Fifty athletes (30 male and 20 female) from the 12 Pacific island NOCs competed in the Sydney games in archery, athletics, boxing, cycling, judo, sailing, swimming, weightlifting, and wrestling. Preparations are now under way for the next summer games to be held in Athens, Greece, in August 2004. The NOC's Website is located at http://www.oceania-olympic.org.

OLYMPICS. *See* OCEANIA NATIONAL OLYMPIC COMMITTEE.

OMAI (ca. 1753–1784). One of the first Polynesians to have visited any Western country. From the island of Rā'iatea (**French Polynesia**), Omai joined **Captain James Cook's** crew as an interpreter and guide. He spent two years in England where he was hosted by King George III and painted by Sir Joshua Reynolds. Cook returned Omai to his home in 1777 with numerous artifacts he had collected through his journey. He died in 1784 before the first Christian missionaries arrived in the islands in 1797. *See also* FRENCH POLYNESIA.

ORSMOND, JOHN M. (1788–1856). A Protestant minister for the **London Missionary Society (LMS)** in **Tahiti** from 1817 until his death on 23 April 1856. Orsmond headed the Christian school in Tahiti and then the entire Protestant church in Pape'ete after the French took control of the islands. Orsmond became interested in the culture, language, and history of Tahiti, and during most of his life compiled an extensive manuscript that he hoped would be published. He turned the finished manuscript over to French Commander Lavaud, but it appears that the manuscript became lost once it arrived in Paris. Fortunately, his granddaughter, **Teuira Henry**, resurrected the manuscript from his extant notes and edited the whole work for publication. It appeared as *Ancient Tahiti*, published by the Bernice P. Bishop Museum Press in 1928. Orsmond's influence is also seen in the *Tahitian Dictionary*, published in 1851 by the LMS. Orsmond died at sea on his way to retire in **New Zealand**. *See also* FRENCH POLYNESIA.

OUTLIERS, POLYNESIAN. These consist of 19 small islands or atolls lying in southern Micronesia and in Melanesia east of the Solomons-Vanuatu-New Caledonia chain. They are Nukuoro and Kapingamarangi (in Micronesia); Nukuria, Taku'u, Nukumanu, Ontong Java Atoll, Sikaiana, Rennell and Bellona (Solomon Islands); Tikopia and **Anuta** (eastern Solomons); Pileni and Taumako (Santa Cruz Islands); Mae, Aniwa, Mele, Fila, and West Futuna (Vanuatu); and West 'Uvea (Loyalty Islands). Archaeology and linguistic studies indicate that these islands were settled from established Polynesian settlements in the west by Sāmoic-speaking peoples. **Lapita** pottery reveals settlements dating from the middle to the last part of the first millennium B.C. Histories of the modern period are intrinsically tied to the larger island nations in Micronesia and Melanesia. *See also* CHATHAM ISLANDS; NORFOLK ISLAND; ROTUMA.

- P -

***PĀ*.** A **New Zealand Māori** word used frequently to refer to one's village or settlement. Traditionally, it referred to a fortified village with its houses (*kainga*) and open, communal assembly area (*marae*).

PACIFIC ARTS ASSOCIATION. An international organization devoted to the study of arts in Oceania. Specifically, it encourages understanding of Oceanic arts, supports high standards of research and writing about the arts, stimulates the teaching of Oceanic arts courses, encourages cooperation among institutions and individuals, and encourages high standards of conservation and preservation of the material cultures of the region. Organized first in 1974 in Hamilton, Ontario, Canada, the association holds annual symposia and publishes various books, a *Pacific Arts Newsletter* (1978–), and a journal, *Pacific Arts* (1990–). Its executive committee consists of prominent individuals currently serving on other international art boards—for example, the Metropolitan Museum of Art (New York), the Musée National des Arts d'Afrique (Paris), and the Tjibaou Cultural Center (New Caledonia). Its current president is Soroi Eoe, director of the National Museum of Papua New Guinea. Its Website is located at http://www.pacificarts.org.

PACIFIC-ASIAN CONGRESS OF MUNICIPALITIES (PACOM). Formed in December 1971 by **Mayor Frank Fasi** of Honolulu to provide an international gathering of Pacific-Asian mayors for "international research and information for the development and exchange of ideas, technical assistance and practical experience in municipal government." The general session of the meetings includes speeches, panels, and workshops on various timely topics as decided upon by the executive committee whose permanent offices are located in Honolulu. The number of participants and members has varied over the years, and the meetings have included **New Zealand** and **French Polynesia** among the 20 some countries which have attended.

PACIFIC COMMUNITY. Originally called the South Pacific Commission (SPC), it was established by the governments of **Australia**, **France**, the Netherlands, **New Zealand, Great Britain**, and the **United States**, in February 1947 (effective July 1948) primarily as an association for the peoples of the region to assist in their economic, social, and cultural development. Its permanent headquarters was established in Anse Vata, a suburb of Nouméa, capital of New Caledonia. Current members of the SPC include **American Sāmoa**, Australia, **Cook Islands**, Federated States of Micronesia, Fiji, **France**, **French Polynesia**, Guam, Kiribati, Marshall Islands, **Nauru**, New Caledonia, New Zealand, **Niue**, Northern Mariana Islands, Palau, Papua New Guinea, **Pitcairn Islands**, Solomon Islands, **Tokelau**, **Tonga**, **Tuvalu**, United Kingdom (absent 1996–1998), United States, Vanuatu, **Wallis and Futuna Islands**, and **Sāmoa**. It changed its name to the Pacific Community on 6 February 1998 to better reflect its pan-Pacific organization and interests.

The Conference of the Pacific Community, an auxiliary body composed of a representative and one alternative from each of the members, meets annually to discuss matters relating to its jurisdiction. It is the decision-making body of the commission, and each member has the right to cast one vote in behalf of his/her government or territorial administration (27 in all).

The secretariat is the administrative arm of the organization and is headed by a director-general, currently **Lourdes Pangelinan** (elected December 1999, the first woman to head the regional oganization) and two deputy directors-general.

The annual budget comes from participating members based on per capita income: Australia 33.3 percent, United States 16.8 percent, New Zealand 16.1 percent, France 13.9 percent, United Kingdom 12.2 percent, others 7.7 percent. The 1998 budget included $2.7 million for administration and $16 million for supporting its numerous programs.

The community has been influential in promoting a South Pacific regionalism while at the same time undertaking numerous projects spanning such diverse areas as atoll sanitation, boat building, crop disease, nutrition, and vocational training. It has also been instrumental in the development of the South Pacific Games, the Festival of South Pacific Arts, the **University of the South Pacific** in Suva, and its Pacific Women's Resource Center. Its publications include, among others, the *Annual Report, Monthly News of Activities, Fisheries Newsletter, Women's Newsletter, Cultural Newsletter,* technical publications, and statistical bulletins. Detailed information can be located at its Website at http://www.spc.org.nc.

PACIFIC CONFERENCE OF CHURCHES (PCC). An ecumenical council of almost all Christian church denominations in the island nations of the **Pacific Community**, excluding **Australia** and **New Zealand**, created at a Pacific-wide Conference of Churches held in New Caledonia in 1966, the purpose of which is to promote cooperation and ecumenism among the Christian churches (both Protestant and Catholic) within the region. It holds leadership seminars to develop and encourage potential church leaders and workers throughout the area. Its current general secretary is the Rev. Valamotu Palu, a **Tongan** who was known for her work in Conference **women's** affairs before she was selected secretary-general in 1997.

PACIFIC FORUM LINE (PFL). Established by the South Pacific Forum (now called the Secretariat of the **Pacific Community**) countries in 1977 to provide reliable shipping and transportation services within the region. The line mainly operates between Fiji, **New Zea-**

land, **Sāmoa**, and Tokelau (1997). By the mid-1990s, competition from other shipping lines cut into its profits, and several links (**Tuvalu** and Kiribati, for example) had to be eliminated. It currently operates three container vessels and one general cargo vessel.

PACIFIC ISLANDS ASSOCIATION. Established in 1982 by the **Foundation for the Peoples of the South Pacific** in the **United States** to provide a forum for discussion of U.S. governmental issues that affect Pacific island peoples.

PACIFIC ISLANDS CONFERENCE OF LEADERS (PICL). A gathering of government heads of the various Pacific island nations who meet informally to "identify priority areas where governmental, regional, and/or international action and research and training programs are required to establish national and regional strategies for meeting both immediate and long-term goals." The first such meeting was held in Honolulu in March 1980, out of which emerged the Center's **Pacific Island Development Program**; the second meeting was held in 1985 (**Cook Islands**), the third in 1990 (**Hawai'i**), the fourth in 1993 (**French Polynesia**), and the fifth in Fiji (1996). The sixth (January 2001) was held in Honolulu in celebration of the 20th anniversary of the Pacific Islands Development Program. Twenty-three representatives attended the first meeting, and since, the numbers have grown to include representatives not only from the Pacific island nations, but from **Japan** and Chile as well.

PACIFIC ISLANDS DEVELOPMENT PROGRAM (PIDP). Housed within the **East-West Center** in Honolulu, **Hawai'i**, the PIDP conducts a broad range of activities to enhance the quality of life in the Pacific islands. As secretariat to the **Pacific Islands Conference of Leaders** and its standing committee, PIDP provides professional services and research information to island governments. Since its establishment in 1980 as a forum through which island leaders could discuss critical issues of development with a wide spectrum of interested countries, donors, non-governmental organizations, and the private sector, PIDP's role as a regional organization has expanded. Today, PIDP's five major activity areas include the following: Secretariat of the Pacific Islands Conference of Leaders; research; education and training; Pacific islands news; and United States/Pacific Islands Nations Joint Commercial Commission Secretariat. The standing committee, composed of 12 island leaders, annually reviews PIDP's work in the foregoing areas to ensure that it is responsive to the issues and challenges facing the Pacific islands region. Further information regarding the program can be located on the **Internet** at http://pidp.ewc.hawaii.edu/pidp0001.htm.

PACIFIC ISLANDS FORUM (PIF). Formerly known as the South Pacific Forum, the PIF is an intergovernmental organization established on 5 August 1971 in Wellington, **New Zealand**, to provide a setting where the heads of the island governments could consult with each other and with **Australia** and New Zealand on economic policy and related matters. Its name was formally changed in October of 1999 to reflect more accurately its organization. Members states currently include Fiji, **Sāmoa**, **Tonga**, the **Cook Islands**, **Nauru**, Papua New Guinea (1974), **Niue**, the Solomon Islands, **Tuvalu**, Kiribati, the Federated States of Micronesia, the Republic of the Marshall Islands, Palau, and Vanuatu. Its dialogue partners are Canada, **Great Britain**, the People's Republic of China, **France**, **Japan**, Malaysia, the **United States**, the Republic of Korea, the **European Union**, and the Philippines.

The forum has no written constitution or rules governing its activities and actions. Its meetings are held annually, and all decisions of the forum have been made by consensus rather than formal voting. The administrative arm of the forum is the Pacific Islands Forum Secretariat (first formed in 1988), located in Suva, Fiji, and its current administrative officer is **Secretary-General Noel Levi** from Papua New Guinea. Its funding comes primarily from Australia and New Zealand, which provide 37 percent of the annual budget, from its member nations, and from other donors. The Forum's budget for the year 2000 was $5.985 million ($F 11.9 million).

Some of its major achievements have been the adoption of the **Convention on the Law of the Sea** and the 200-mile fishing **exclusive economic zones (EEZ)**; the establishment of a **South Pacific Forum Fisheries Agency** and a regional shipping venture—the **Pacific Forum Line**; its opposition to the use of the Pacific as a dumping ground for nuclear wastes; the **South Pacific Nuclear Free Zone Treaty**—the **Treaty of Rarotonga**; its stand on emission of gases by industrial nations that contribute to the greenhouse effect which greatly affects the environment; and more recently, economic reforms leading to the establishment of **a Pacific Free Trade Area**.

PACIFIC ISLANDS LAW OFFICERS MEETING (PILOM). An informal organization of law ministers and attorneys general of commonwealth countries in the South Pacific which had its beginning at Port Vila, Vanuatu, in 1981. The PILOM provides an annual forum in which law officers can discuss ways of improving the administration of justice throughout the area through presentation of papers and seminars. Member countries consist of **Australia**, the **Cook Islands**, Fiji, Kiribati, **Nauru**, **Niue**, **New Zealand**, Papua New Guinea, **Sāmoa**, Solomon Islands, **Tonga**, **Tuvalu** and Vanuatu. A result of the 1985 meeting was the establishment by the **University of the South Pacific** of a Pacific Law Unit at Port Vila, Vanuatu. In more recent years, it has recommended adopting greater security measures, drug control, extradition laws, customs and border control measures, and it has offered assistance to member nations in adopting needed legislation for their countries.

PACIFIC ISLANDS MONTHLY (PIM). The Pacific's oldest news magazine, having served the Pacific island nations from 1930 until its demise in June 2000. The magazine was founded by Robert William Robson (1885–1994), a **New Zealande**r who moved to Sydney during World War I. After the war, he recognized the fact that the Pacific islands had no printed communication to keep in touch with each other. The magazine's first edition in 1930 announced that the *PIM* "was the only journal circulating throughout the island territories and groups of the Central and South Pacific." Robson gave the journal a unique editorial flavor until his retirement in 1980. A close associate, Judy Tudor (1910–1997), joined his team in 1942 and remained as assistant editor until she became sole editor from 1955 to 1962. She was joined by Stuart Inder who edited the journal for 11 more years during an extremely important time in the history of the Pacific islands. The magazine continued to be the principal publication in the area. The *PIM* was part of the Fiji Times Publishing Ltd., located in Suva, Fiji, and Sophie Foster Hildebrand was its last editor. The political upheavals in

Fiji and the failure to attract advertising revenue regretfully finally led to its demise, and its last issue appeared in June 2000.

PACIFIC ISLANDS NEWS ASSOCIATION (PINA). A professional association of news media of the Pacific islands region, including radio, television, newspapers, magazines, and national media organizations from 21 Pacific islands countries and territories. Its objectives are to promote and defend freedom of information and expression; promote and develop professional standards by means of training, education, and the development of resource material; and to promote and develop professional fellowship and cooperation. Its headquarters are located in Suva, Fiji, and its current president is William Parkinson, founder of the Communications Fiji Limited group of radio stations. The organization holds annual conventions: **Tahiti** in 1998, Fiji in 1999, the **Cook Islands** in 2000, and Papua New Guinea in 2001. PINA is also a member of the International Freedom of Expression Exchange, the global network of leading freedom of expression and media freedom organizations. PINA sends out regular IFEX alerts and updates on Pacific islands issues. Its Website can be located at http://www.pinanius.org/pina.

PACIFIC MANUSCRIPTS BUREAU (PAMBU). A non-profit organization established in 1968, currently based at the Australian National University, whose purpose is to locate archives, manuscripts, and rare publications relating to the Pacific and to copy them for preservation purposes on to microfilm. It is sponsored by seven regional libraries in the Pacific—National Library of Australia, Australian National University Library, State Library of New South Wales (Mitchell Library), National Library of New Zealand (Alexander Turnbull Library), University of Auckland Library, University of Hawai'i at Mānoa Library, and the University of California at San Diego Library. Personal and organizational archives and manuscripts of all kinds are sought and copied. Its twice yearly newsletter, *Pambu*, keeps readers up-to-date on current projects and activities. Further information can be located on the **Internet** at http://rspas.anu.edu.au/pambu/.

PACIFIC PEOPLE'S PARTNERSHIP (PPP). A Canadian organization founded in 1975 and devoted to international education and advocacy on issues of concern for the South Pacific. It has grown into the principal organization in Canada (located at 1921 Fernwood Road, Victoria, British Columbia V8T 2Y6) working with Pacific island peoples. Its interests include sovereignty and decolonization, nuclear testing and militarization, environmental issues, community development, indigenous science and indigenous knowledge, sustainable development, and **women's** issues. Its Website is http://www.sppf.org/frames.html.

PACIFIC REGIONAL TRADE AGREEMENT (PARTA). A concept adopted by the **Pacific Islands Forum** at its meeting in Palau (Micronesia) in October 1999. Trade ministers from the 16 member nations endorsed the concept at a meeting earlier in June, and it was approved in principle at the full meeting in October. The idea of a free trade zone dates back to 1973, and attention was drawn again to the concept more recently as a result of other economic unions coming into existence—the **European Union (EU)** and the North America Free Trade Agreement (NAFTA), for example.

Several rounds of negotiations occurred in 2001, and it is anticipated that a draft text of an agreement can be discussed at the October 2001 forum meeting. It is envisaged that development forum members will have an eight-year timetable to eliminate import duties, while the nine forum members which are smaller island states will have 10 years to do so. Many of the small island states are reluctant to allow **New Zealand** and **Australia** to become founding members of the proposed agreement, however; and, at this point, some of the islands have expressed unwillingness to join themselves.

PACIFIC WOMEN'S RESOURCE BUREAU (PWRB). A department of the Secretariat of the **Pacific Community**, located in New Caledonia, established in 1982 to assist women's offices in SPC countries in upgrading their skills to deal with **women's** problems at local, national, and regional levels; to act as an information network among Pacific women as a means of exchanging ideas and views; to develop national and regional programs on issues and problems facing women; and to assist governments on request in bringing about the active participation of women in national development efforts. A quarterly *Women Today* magazine was begun in March 2000, and the bureau participates in the triennial conferences on women (held recently in 1997 and 2000). Its current director is Amelia Kinahoi Siamomua, and its **Internet** Website is located at http://www.spc.org.nc/ En/women.htm.

PAENIU, BIKENIBEU (1956–). Prime minister of **Tuvalu** from October 1990 until April 1999. Born on 10 May 1956 at Bikenibeu, Tarawa, Paeniu was educated in the King George V school (Tarawa), and after obtaining his degree in agriculture from the **University of the South Pacific** in Suva, he returned to Tuvalu where he worked for two years as head of the agriculture division. He obtained a master's degree in agriculture and resource economics at the University of Hawai'i, afterwards worked with the South Pacific Commission, currently called the **Pacific Community**, in Nouméa, New Caledonia, and then in October 1988 returned to Tuvalu to pursue a political career. He was appointed to a vacant position in Parliament and in the 1989 elections ran unopposed.

As a young leader, Paeniu hoped to generate more revenues for his tiny nation specifically through international subsidies and donations from more industrialized countries, to bring more equity to the outer islands in the chain, to promote a greater sense of national identity among Tuvaluans, and to make his nation more self-reliant. A vote of no confidence in April of 1999 was supported by members of his own cabinet who accused him of misconduct in his personal life and for failing to complete the programs that had brought him into office. Paeniu and his wife, Foketi, have four children—two sons and two daughters.

PĀKEHĀ. A **New Zealand Māori** word to designate foreigners and especially Caucasians; it is similar in use to the word ***haole*** in **Hawai'i**, ***palagi*** in **Sāmoa**, or ***popa'ā*** in Tahitian.

PALAGI. A Sāmoan word to designate foreigners and especially Caucasians; it is similar in use to the word ***haole*** in **Hawai'i**, ***pākehā*** in **New Zealand Māori**, or ***popa'ā*** in Tahitian.

PANGELINAN, LOURDES (1954–). Elected director-general of the Secretariat of the **Pacific Community** in December 1999. Born on 19 October 1954 on Guam, Pangelinan attended school in **France**, and then returned to the **United States** where she received her bachelor's degree in international relations from the University of California–Davis in 1976. She is fluent in Chamorro, English, and French. She served in several positions in California and Guam before starting to work for the government of Guam in 1984. She served as chief of staff to the governor (1987–1994), deputy director of communications in the superior court in Agaña, Guam (1995–1996), after which she became deputy director general of the Secretariat of the Pacific Community in Nouméa, New Caledonia. She was elected director general on 6 January 2000, the first women ever elected to a Pacific regional organization. Her predecessor, Dr. Bob Dun, left a legacy of important achievements and goals, all of which she says she will continue to enhance and carry through.

PAN-PACIFIC AND SOUTH-EAST ASIA WOMEN'S ASSOCIATION INTERNATIONAL. Formed in 1928 in Honolulu by a group of women with international concerns, hoping to promote peace through understanding and friendship. Since its inception, the organization has met approximately every three years bringing women together in meetings, lectures, workshops, and cultural programs concerned with **women** and families. Recent meetings were held in **Japan** (1984), **Australia** (1988), Thailand (1990), **Tonga** (1994), Honolulu (1999), and the **Cook Islands** (2000). The association is considered to be the first women's group founded upon transcultural values, having, at that time, representation from 11 Pacific nations and territories. Honorary president of the association is Thanpuying Sumalee Chartikavanij of Thailand, and its **Internet** Website can be located at http://www.ppseawa.org.

PAULET, GEORGE (1803–1867). An English naval officer who temporarily seized the islands of **Hawai'i** for **Great Britain** in 1843. In 1833, Paulet had been appointed captain of the *Carysfort* and assigned duties in the Pacific. In February 1843 when reports of mistreatment of certain British subjects in Hawai'i reached him, he set sail for Honolulu where he demanded not only retribution by the Hawaiian government but outright annexation to Great Britain. **King Kamehameha** could do nothing but acquiesce. On 25 February, the Hawaiian flag was lowered and the British Union flag raised, and Paulet began his reorganization of the government.

Meanwhile a Hawaiian delegation made its way to London where it laid its petition before the British government which responded in favor of restoring the independence of the kingdom. British admiral Richard Thomas set sail from Valparaiso to Honolulu and returned the control of the kingdom to the king. In a thanksgiving address, the king spoke the words that became the motto of the state of Hawai'i—*Ua mau ke ea o ka 'āina i ka pono* [The life of the land is preserved in righteousness]. *See also* RICHARDS, WILLIAM.

PIDGIN. A language widely spoken throughout **Polynesia** as an "unofficial" second or third language of the indigenous population. It was developed locally in the 19th century by islanders after contact with foreign-speaking immigrants to their islands—both Westerners and Asians. Throughout Polynesia, pidgin is regarded by educators and the upper class as corrupt and restrictive, but it is not regarded as such in other parts of the Pacific (Melanesia, for example) where it has become the official language in Papua New Guinea, the Solomon Islands, and Vanuatu. Today, one can read parts of Shakespeare written in Melanesian pidgin. In 1999, British actor Ken Campbell toured Papua New Guinea, **Australia**, **New Zealand**, Vanuatu, and the Solomon Islands with an acting troupe presenting Macbeth spoken in pidgin!

U.S. tourists first encounter the language when visiting **Hawai'i**, where they hear such expressions as "Whassamatta you?" for "What's the matter with you?" or "When you pau hana koma mai." for "When you get done (*pau*) work (*hana*) come over to my house." Nonessential words are eliminated whenever possible, and the vocabulary consists of primarily English, interspersed with local and other foreign words. Heavily criticized, it still remains the lingua franca of most island nations. An English-Pidgin dictionary, as spoken in Port Moresby, Papua New Guinea, can be found on the **Internet** at http://www.june29.com/HLP/lang/pidgin.html.

PINKHAM, LUCIUS EUGENE (1850–1922). Governor of the Territory of **Hawai'i** from 1913 to 1918. Born and educated in Massachusetts, Pinkham came to Hawai'i as a businessman in 1892. He was appointed director of the board of health in 1904 and then governor in 1913. His five-year administration is noted for numerous social improvements in the islands that included several homestead bills as well as upgrading of the islands' transportation and water systems. After several years of illness, he died in San Francisco on 2 November 1922.

PITCAIRN ISLANDS. A British dependency that includes Pitcairn Island and three uninhabited islands—Henderson, Ducie, and Oeno—located about 2,160 km (1,350 mi) southeast of **Tahiti**, with a total landmass of approximately 47 sq km (18 sq mi). The only settlement, Adamstown, consisting of 13 homes, is located on the northeast side of Pitcairn, a volcanic island which is only 3-km (2-mi) long and 1.5-km (1-mi) wide. Most of Pitcairn's population of 57 (1999) are descendants of the ***Bounty*** mutineers and their Polynesian (Tahitian) wives who settled there in 1790. English (official) and Pitcairnese (a Tahitian dialect) are both spoken. In 1989, UNESCO placed Henderson Island on the World Heritage List as a bird sanctuary. Henderson is home to 10 plants and four land birds endemic to the island.

Economy: Most of the Pitcairners exist on subsistence fishing and agriculture, the principal crops being citrus, melons, bananas, yams, **taro**, sugar cane, and **coconuts**. Artists sell their carvings to **tourists** on passing ships or through mail order. (See additional information below in this entry under "Government.") The **New Zealand** monetary system is the standard currency used on the island.

History:Archaeological evidence indicates that the island was inhabited by Polynesians possibly by A.D. 1100. It was deserted, however, by European contact (Captain Philip Carteret in 1767). Carteret named the island after the midshipman, Robert Pitcairn, who first sighted it. In January 1790, the mutineers of the *Bounty* (*see* **Bligh, William**), fleeing possible British criminal charges, anchored in what is now called Bounty Bay where they burned the ship and where they planned to remain forever. The small community consisted of Fletcher Christian (organizer of the mutiny), eight mutineers (William Brown, Isaac Martin, William McCoy, John Mills, Matthew Quintal, Alexander Smith alias John Adams, John Williams, and Edward Young), six Polynesian men, 12 Polynesian women, and a small girl (William McCoy's daughter).

The next several years witnessed violence, murder, and massacre between the various families until by 1800, John Adams was the only man remaining on the island with nine women and 19 children. He attempted to bring some semblance of moral order to the group by educating the children from books taken from the *Bounty*. The islanders' first visiting foreign ship was the American *Topaz* under Captain Mayhew Folger (February 1808) who sent reports of his findings to both the American and British authorities. By the time of Adams' death in 1829, numerous other sailing ships had stopped by the island, and their captains' reports stirred the interest and concern of benevolent societies who sent supplies, books, and Bibles to the island.

By 1831, the group had grown to 77, and in March the British government attempted to alleviate their subsistence survival by transporting them to **Tahiti** where it was thought they could best feel at home. Unfortunately, 12 Pitcairners died from Western diseases, and by September, the group decided to return to their home island. For the next six years (1832–1838), the island fell under the dictatorial power of a new arrival—Joshua Hill. When the British ejected him in 1838, Captain Russell Eliott of the HMS *Fly* assisted the islanders in drawing up a constitution and code of laws. It provided for universal suffrage (the first people ever to give **women** the right to vote!) for an island magistrate assisted by a council of two, as well as compulsory education for the children. In 1856, the entire community of 193 was resettled on **Norfolk Island** over a disagreement with Sir William Denison, the governor-general of New South Wales, but by 1864, five of the families (43 persons) had returned (surnames of Christian, Young, McCoy, Buffett, and Warren).

In 1886, the islanders adopted the Seventh-Day Adventist faith through the influence of a sailor named John I. Tay. In 1898, administration of the island came under the jurisdiction of the British High Commissioner for the Western Pacific (formerly located in Fiji, but since 1970 in **New Zealand**). The population reached its all time high of 233 persons in 1937. Even though developments since World War II have brought electricity, telecommunications, roads, and a school, the population continues to decline. During the 1990s, the population fluctuated from 30 to 57, and most of the young people who travel for school in New Zealand never return.

Between 1987 and 1990, fishing leases in Pitcairn's **exclusive economic zone (EEZ)** to the Japan Tuna Fisheries Cooperative Association brought some additional funds to the island budget. Harbor improvements hopefully will encourage passing ships to stop more frequently at the island. (No scheduled passenger ship's have stopped at the island since 1968.) Currently, ships must anchor away from the island and passengers and cargo are transferred via small motorized boats. In 1988, Island Magistrate Brian Young announced the formation of the Bounty Adventure Ltd. to provide passenger and cargo services to the **Cook Islands** and **French Polynesia** and the possibility of the construction of a small airstrip on the island. As of 2001, these have not occurred.

During the early 1990s, the Pitcairners filed official grievances with the governor that expressed their dissatisfaction of British policy toward them. They even suggested that they might relinquish their ties with **Great Britain** and approach **France** for a transfer of sovereignty. Those talks halted, however, when France resumed its nuclear testing at **Moruroa atoll**, dangerously close to Pitcairn.

Discussion of the building of an airstrip continues through the 1990s and into the new millennium, and in 1998 an engineering study was financed by Dick Smith, an Australian millionaire and philanthropist. The small airstrip, some believe, would bring additional tourists to the island resulting in more income to the islanders. At the same time, the new source of income would be an incentive to keep the young people from emigrating to New Zealand to find employment. Another recent source of income for the island is the **Internet**. Not that the island has an Internet connection, but the fact that the island has been granted exclusive rights to its own domain name "*.pn*," and as a result of advertising, the island has been selling domain Websites worldwide. The "*.pn*" is an international abbreviation for "phone." In 2000, income from this new venture amounted to approximately $78,900.

An archeological team from James Cook University, Townsville, Queensland, reached the island in October of 1998 and by January 1999 began raising artifacts, cannon, and other items from the HMS *Bounty*.

Government: Internal affairs are controlled by an island council consisting of 10 members (five of whom are elected annually on Christmas Day) and by an island magistrate (elected every three years). The British High Commissioner in **New Zealand**, who also retains the title of governor (Martin Williams since 1998), may revoke the island's legislative decisions, but that rarely occurs. The island magistrate is currently Jay Warren, elected since 1990. He also convenes and presides over the island court. Two-thirds of the current government revenues come from the sale of local postage stamps and currency (amounting to about $197,000 in 2000) and other financial assistance from the United Kingdom. Personal income amounts to approximately $6,000 annually, one-third of which comes from government work. There are no taxes on the island. A small mimeographed newspaper, the *Pitcairn Miscellany*, appears monthly since April 1959 (circulation is about 1,600). An **Internet** Website dedicated to Pitcairn Island is found at http://www.lareau.org/pitc.html.

POHIVA, SAMUELA 'AKALISI (1941–). Founding member of **Tonga's** pro-democracy political party, the Human Rights and Democracy Movement. Born on 7 April 1941 at Fakakakai, Ha'apai, Tonga, Pohiva earned a teaching certificate from Tupou College (1961) and then graduated from the **University of the South Pacific** in 1978 with a bachelor's degree in education. He taught in Tonga for 15 years (1967–1982) before beginning work with the National Office for Disaster, Relief, and Reconstruction (NODRR) organization for two years. Pohiva was first elected as a people's representative to Tonga's legislative assembly in 1987 and is currently serving his fifth term in that assembly. His crusades against government corruption and lawbreaking have caused him to be labeled a "terrorist" by the Minister of Police 'Akau'ola and a "Marxist" by **King Tāufa'āhau Tupou IV**. In 1988, Pohiva won a censorship battle with the government and obtained $T29,000 in damages; in 1990, he brought suit against the government for selling Tongan passports to foreigners; and then in 1991, he headed a popular demonstration and petition against the government's legalizing the sale. In 1996, he and the editor of the *Tonga Times* were arrested and imprisoned over an issue of freedom of the press. Pohiva represents a vocal minority that calls not only for more democratic reforms of the conservative monarchy but for a better accountability system within the government. He is a popular figure and garners a large percentage of votes in Tonga's elections.

POINDEXTER, JOSEPH BOYD (1869–1951). Appointed governor of the Territory of **Hawai'i** from 1934 to 1942. Poindexter came to Hawai'i in 1917 as United States District Judge. During his eight years as governor, Poindexter promoted social and educational rights for the Hawaiians and made major advances in the defense of Hawai'i against the growing threat of Japanese expansion in Asia. When **Japan** bombed Pearl Harbor on 7 December 1941, Poindexter declared martial law and prepared the islands for possible invasion. After 1942, he returned to practicing law until his death on 3 December 1951.

POLYNESIA. A term derived from two Greek words, *πολης* (many) and *νησος* (islands), to refer to the culture of the islanders living in the eastern Pacific between the three geographical points of **Hawai'i** in the north, **New Zealand** in the southwest, and **Easter Island** in the southeast as opposed to the island groups of Melanesia ("black islands") and Micronesia ("small islands") located further to the west. (Refer to frontispiece map.) These terms were first coined by the French navigator Dumont d'Urville in 1832. When British navigator **Captain James Cook** reached Easter Island in March 1774, he exclaimed: "It is extraordinary that the same Nation should have spread themselves over all the isles in this vast Ocean from New Zealand to this Island which is almost a fourth part of the circumference of the Globe."

POLYNESIAN CULTURE, ANCIENT. Although many similarities existed among the ancient cultures (pre-European) found in the various Polynesian islands, one should not assume that all island groups had identical social organizations or cultural characteristics. A description of the culture of one village should not be taken to represent the culture within its entire chain or for all of **Polynesia**. Detailed research in the last decade has graphically shown that a diversity existed among islands far more often than what earlier scholars would have us believe. Books and articles listed in the bibliography should be consulted for precise accounts of each island society.

In general, ancient Polynesians were collectivists, that is, they saw themselves as belonging to certain descent groups, they carried out most of their activities in groups, and they generally regarded property as belonging to their community. An individual with the highest genealogical rank was regarded as the group's secular and religious leader—their chief. Islands were normally divided into districts, each occupied by related kin groups and administered by a hierarchy of powerful chiefs. Seldom if ever did one chief exercise domination over a whole island much less over a whole chain. Frequently, the highest genealogical title was not always the most powerful secular ruler on an island.

Social and political conduct was based on kinship ties as well as on the concepts of *mana* and *tabu*. *Mana* was a supernatural power gained through inheritance and daring exploits. *Tabu* was the prohibition of using certain articles or property belonging to a person of higher rank. Certain high chiefs were so *tabu* that they had to be carried on a dais to prevent their feet from touching land and property not belonging to them. Rivalry between district chiefs and their followers was common, the result of which was almost constant warfare.

The stratified social order included the numerous chiefly and priestly classes with subordinate commoners and slaves. **Women** were subservient to men, but occasionally certain chiefly women inherited powerful social and political status. Population was kept stable as a result of general marauding as well as infanticide practiced by parents of unwanted children.

Elaborate ceremonies in open air temples and detailed mythologies characterized their religious beliefs and dominated their everyday life. Subsistence agriculture and fishing was the workaday norm of most Polynesians whose diet consisted of **breadfruit**, **taro**, **coconut**, sweet potatoes, fish, and less frequently pig and chicken. Polynesian navigational techniques were unsurpassed among all Neolithic peoples. They constructed large double-hulled, ocean-going vessels on which they frequently would travel hundreds or even thousands of miles. Art forms included elaborate **tattooing** with intricate designs; stone adzes and other tools of excellent craftsmanship; carvings in bone, wood, and stone; geometric motifs and other imaginative decorations on **tapa** cloth; large stone *marae* (open-air temples) and tribal assembly houses; and woven baskets and mats of extraordinary quality. Amusements were provided by songs (chants accompanied by drums and flutes), dances (frequently religious in nature), games (string figures, checkers, bowls, javelin throwing, sledding, and surfing), and listening to storytellers.

Complex, living, and vibrant, ancient Polynesian culture succumbed to a superior technology when Western intruders arrived in the islands. The simple introduction of iron nails and tools by the early navigators caused an immediate and drastic transformation in almost every aspect of this ancient culture.

POLYNESIAN SOCIETY. Founded in Wellington, **New Zealand**, on 8 January 1892, it was one of the first scholarly organizations solely dedicated to the study of Pacific peoples and more specifically Polynesians. Its inaugural meeting was called by the renowned S. Percy Smith (1840–1922), who essentially remained its motivational force until his death. The society's aims were to afford a means of "communication, cooperation and mutual criticism between scholars of anthropology, philology, history, manners and customs of the Oceanic races, and the preservation of all that relates to such subjects in a permanent form." Best and Edward Tregear (1846–1931) were elected joint-secretaries and joint-editors of its new journal, the *Journal of the Polynesian Society* (*JPS*). The journal continues to be the premier vehicle for publications of academic articles by scholars around the world. Approximately one-third of its articles deal with the New Zealand **Māori**, one-third with other Polynesian peoples, and one-third with the rest of the Pacific. Its current editor is Professor Judith Huntsman. The society, now located at the University of Auckland, also publishes memoirs, Māori texts, monographs, and other Polynesian source materials. Its **Internet** address is http://www.arts.auckland.ac.nz/ant/ JPS/polsoc.html.

POLYNESIAN VOYAGING SOCIETY (PVS). An organization founded in **Hawai'i** in 1973 to research and teach the ship building and sailing techniques used by ancient Polynesian seafarers before Western intrusion. Founded by anthropologist Dr. Ben Finney, Hawaiian artist Herb Kane, and Tommy Holmes, the society's first project was to construct a replica of an ancient voyaging canoe. The result was the ***Hōkūle'a***, launched on 8 March 1975. The voyages of the *Hōkūle'a* are now legendary. A second canoe, the *Hawai'iloa*, was launched in 1993. Over the past 25 years, more than 525,000 men, women, and children have participated in PVS programs of education, training, research, and dialogue. Both PVS ships have renewed pride of all Polynesian peoples in their traditional culture and heritage. For further information, explore the PVS Website at http://leahi.kcc.hawaii.edu/ org/pvs/.

POMARE FAMILY. The royal family that ruled the **Society Islands** and the **Tuamotus**, currently part of **French Polynesia**, from approximately 1780 until 1880. Holding important genealogical titles on the island of **Tahiti**, Pomare I (ca. 1751–1803) extended his political influence through the use of European firearms and social connections with the arriving foreigners. The first Christian missionaries of the **London Missionary Society** (1797) regarded him as "king" over the island although such a position had not been known in pre-European Tahitian society. When he died in 1803, his son Pomare II finally accepted Christianity and introduced many reforms into the islands, including the first written law code in Oceania (1819). He died in December 1821 from alcoholism, and his young son, Pomare III, was ceremoniously crowned by the missionaries. The young king died in 1824, leaving as heir his sister who took the title Queen Pomare IV (1813–1877). It was during her reign that the greatest changes came about in the islands. Conflict between British Protestants and French **Catholics** (1843) resulted in a French Protectorate by 1845. Little by little, the queen lost control over her islands. When she died in 1877, her son Pomare V negotiated with the French to cede Tahiti to them (1880) in return for the cancellation of his heavy debts and for a pension for the rest of his life. He retained the title of king, but the position died with him in 1891.

POMARE LAW CODE OF 1819. The first written law code to be set down in Oceania. Promulgated by King Pomare II of **Tahiti** after his having been converted to Christianity by the missionaries of the **London Missionary Society**, the document was printed and distributed throughout the South Pacific where it became the model upon which the early law codes of the other Pacific island nations were based. Its 19 points were related primarily to Christian principles found in the Old and New Testaments—murder, theft, adultery, false witness, divorce, not keeping the Sabbath day holy, and so on. *See also* FRENCH POLYNESIA; POMARE FAMILY.

POMARE, MAUI WIREMU PITA NAERA (1876–1930). A **New Zealand Māori** leader who became the first Māori health officer in 1900 and who greatly remedied the deplorable living conditions of the Māoris at the turn of the century. Born on 13 January 1876, Pahou

Pa, New Zealand, he was elected a member of Parliament between 1911 to 1930 and advocated the acceptance of ***pākehā*** (white) ways in order to survive in their society, a policy adopted by many other members of the newly formed **Young Māori Party** and one which was opposed by other Māori leaders. Pomare was knighted in 1922. He served as minister of health (1923–1926) and as minister for the **Cook Islands** (1916–1928). He collaborated with James Cowan in writing *The Legends of the Māori*. He died 27 June 1930 in Los Angeles.

POMPALLIER, JEAN-BAPTISTE FRANÇOIS (1801–1871). A French Catholic bishop who headed the first **Catholic** mission to the southwest Pacific. In 1837, he left Le Havre with a group of Marist (Society of Mary) missionaries. After landing them on several island groups, he finally established himself in **New Zealand** where he eventually was appointed Bishop of Auckland. Despite Protestant opposition, Catholic Christianity was established in most of the Polynesian islands before he retired and returned to Europe in 1869. He died near Paris on 21 December 1871.

POPA'Ā**.** A **Tahitian** word meaning "foreigner" used in everyday speech to refer to individuals of Caucasian ancestry versus the word *demi* to indicate an individual of mixed ancestry, or ***mā'ohi*** for Tahitian (Polynesian) ancestry. *See also HAOLE*; *PĀKEHĀ*; *PALAGI.*

POUVANA'A A OOPA, MARCEL (1895–1977). A popular Tahitian leader whose leadership helped pave the way for more internal autonomy for **French Polynesia**. Born on 10 May 1895 on the island of Huahine, Pouvana'a served **France** during World War I. Afterwards, he returned to **Tahiti** where he became head of a Tahitian nationalist movement, and because of his actions was exiled back to Huahine by the French government.

In 1947, he and his followers formed a political party called the Comité Pouvana'a, later renamed the **Rassemblement Démocratique des Populations Tahitiennes (RDPT)**. He was elected in 1949 as deputy of French Oceania to the French Parliament in Paris, reelected again in 1951 and 1956, while his party gained a majority of the seats in the local territorial assembly in 1953 and 1957. After vigorously campaigning for independence from **France** in the 1958 elections, his party gained only 36 percent of the votes. Shortly thereafter he and several of his followers were arrested on criminal charges of attempting to burn down the capital city of Pape'ete. He was exiled for 15 years and imprisoned for eight until he was pardoned and allowed to return to Tahiti in 1968.

In 1971 and with his popularity as high as ever, he was elected to the French senate for a nine-year term. By then, however, he was too old to effect any further changes. He died on 10 January 1977 in Pape'ete. A statue of him, sculpted by George Oudot, now stands in front of the territorial assembly building in Pape'ete.

POWLES, SIR GUY RICHARDSON (1905–1994). New Zealand high commissioner of **Sāmoa** who prepared the country for political independence after World War II. After serving in World War II as a brigadier-major and then in Washington, D.C. (1946–1948), Powles was appointed high commissioner of Sāmoa charged with preparing the country for self-government. He gradually divorced himself from internal Sāmoan politics while at the same time helping guide the various factions of Sāmoan politicians to a mutual compromise. Powles relinquished his position of high commissioner in April 1960 as the country prepared for independence (1962). Powles later served as New Zealand high commissioner to India (1960–1962) and then ombudsman to the New Zealand government in 1962. He died on 24 October 1994.

PRITCHARD, GEORGE (1796–1883). A missionary of the **London Missionary Society (LMS)** and later a British consul to **Tahiti** and **Samoa**. In 1824, Pritchard sailed to the South Pacific as a missionary to Tahiti. By 1832, he had become the most influential counselor to **Queen Pomare IV**. When French **Catholic** missionaries attempted to land in 1836, Pritchard forced their expulsion. When the French government intervened, Pritchard began a lengthy correspondence with the British government on the subject of annexation. In 1842, he sailed to London to try to convince the government to take action.

Unsuccessfully, he returned to find that the French had established a protectorate over the islands. The ensuing verbal attacks and counterattacks ("The Pritchard Affair") resulted in Pritchard's arrest and expulsion from Tahiti (1844). Being appointed British consul in Sāmoa,

Pritchard dreamed of establishing a British colony with its accompanying garrison of soldiers to protect the British citizens who would immigrate and develop the unoccupied lands. His clashes with the **French** and other European communities in Sāmoa eventually forced his resignation in 1856.

His son, William Pritchard (1829–1909), succeeded him as consul of Sāmoa for nine months, but then was appointed the first British consul to Fiji. George Pritchard returned to England in 1857 as director of the LMS for Scotland and Ireland. He died on 6 May 1883, at Hove near Brighton. *See also* ROMAN CATHOLIC CHURCH IN OCEANIA; FRENCH POLYNESIA.

PUPU TAINA, or by the French designation "Rassemblement des Libéraux." A contemporary conservative political party in **French Polynesia**, founded in 1976, that seeks to maintain close ties with **France**. Its leader, Michel Law, maintains close relationship with the Union pour la Démocratie Française (UDF) and gains most of his support from the Chinese population.

- Q -

QUINN, WILLIAM F. (1919–). Appointed governor of the Territory of **Hawai'i** from 1957 to 1959 and then elected Hawai'i's first governor (1959–1962) after statehood. Although Quinn was born in Rochester, New York, on 13 July 1919, he grew up in St. Louis, Missouri. During World War II, he served in naval intelligence in the Pacific, and after graduating from Harvard (1947) he and his family moved to Honolulu where he entered law, served on the statehood commission, and in 1957 was appointed territorial governor by President Dwight Eisenhower. When Hawai'i became a state in 1959, Quinn (a Republican) won the elections against rival Democrat **John A. Burns** to become Hawai'i's first elected governor. Unsolved economic and labor problems brought about his defeat for a second term, losing to Burns in the 1962 elections. Afterwards, Quinn became an executive for the Dole Pineapple Company (1965–1972) and unsuccessfully attempted to gain a seat in the U.S. Senate (1976). He currently resides in Honolulu.

- R -

RAINBOW WARRIOR**.** A Greenpeace flagship, sunk in Auckland harbor, **New Zealand**, on 10 July 1985, while on its way to protest French nuclear testing in the Pacific. Greenpeace, an international anti-nuclear and environmental organization, proposed to send its flagship to **France's** testing site, **Moruroa atoll**, to oppose the underground tests being conducted there.

While berthed in Auckland harbor, it was blown up, and a Greenpeace photographer, Fernando Pereira, was killed. New Zealand investigations revealed that the attack had been planned by French intelligence agents of the General Directorate for External Security (DGSE). The event caused a furor in France, and as a result, its minister of defense, Charles Hernu, eventually resigned because of the allegations brought against his organization, Admiral Pierre Lacoste (director of the DGSE) was dismissed, and François Mitterand's government politically damaged. In November, the two French agents arrested for the incident, Alain Mafart and Dominique Prieur, pleaded guilty, and charges against them were reduced to manslaughter. France agreed to pay New Zealand $7 million in indemnity.

The net result, however, was more international attention being brought upon Greenpeace's protests and France's unpopular nuclear testing program in the Pacific than had France simply ignored the flagship altogether. *See also* NUCLEAR FREE ZONE TREATY.

RAPANUI. Indigenous name for **Easter Island** and the Polynesian dialect spoken by its inhabitants.

RAPU, SERGIO (1950–). Governor of **Easter Island** from 1984 to 1989. Having been educated in Chile and completing graduate work in the **United States** at the Universities of Wyoming (BA) and Hawai'i (MA), Rapu returned to his native island where he become involved in the restoration process of the island's statuary and where he became head of the archaeological museum. In January 1984, he was appointed governor of Easter Island, its first indigenous governor since it was annexed to Chile in 1888. As governor, Rapu supported the building of a NASA emergency landing site on the island and successfully lobbied the Chilean government for subsidized housing and the establishment of new schools and roads. In 1989, Rapu left Easter Island for **Hawai'i** where he worked for the **Polynesian Cultural Center** and for a while was director of the **Institute for Polynesian Studies**.

RAROTONGA DECLARATION. A paper adopted at an environmental conference held at Rarotonga (**Cook Islands**) in March 1982 which provides guidelines for the suitable management of land, sea, and air resources in the region. The conference was organized by the United Nations Environment Program and several agencies of the South Pacific Commission, now called the **Pacific Community**, and was attended by over 20 countries. The declaration took a firm stand against the testing of nuclear devices or the storing of nuclear wastes in the Pacific basin, a position later made official when in 1985 the South Pacific nations signed the **Nuclear Free Zone Treaty**.

RAROTONGA, TREATY OF. A **South Pacific Forum** agreement signed in August 1985 in Rarotonga, **Cook Islands**, by eight of the Forum countries—**Australia**, **Cook Islands**, Fiji, Kiribati, **New Zealand**, **Niue**, **Sāmoa**, and **Tuvalu**—to create a **nuclear-free zone** in the South Pacific. The articles of the treaty prohibit nuclear testing, storing, or dumping within the designated zone as delineated in Annex 1 of the treaty. Member nations that have signed since the original agreement are Papua New Guinea (1985), **Nauru** (1986), and the Solomon Islands (1987). The Soviet Union signed Protocols 2 and 3 of the agreement in December 1986 and the People's Republic of China followed in February 1987. It was only a decade later that on 25 March 1996 at the headquarters of the **South Pacific Forum** in Suva, Fiji, that **France**, **Great Britain**, and the **United States** finally signed the document. This signing means that all five nuclear weapon states are henceforth committed not to use or threaten to use nuclear explosive devices against any South Pacific Forum member, not to test nuclear explosive devices within the treaty area, and to apply the provisions of the treaty to their nonself-governing territories within the zone.

RASSEMBLEMENT POUR LA RÉPUBLIQUE (RPR). A political party in **French Polynesia**. *See also* TĀHŌ'ĒRA'A HUIRA'ATIRA.

RATANA MOVEMENT. A religious/political movement in **New Zealand** in the 1920s and 1930s, headed by its founder, Tahupotiki Wiremu "Bill" Ratana (1873–1939). Ratana claimed to have received a vision from God in 1918 that demanded that he unite the downtrodden **Māori** people as a chosen race similar to the ancient Hebrew prophets. As *Mangai* (the mouthpiece of God), his preaching and healing practices appealed to what he called the *morehu*, the common people, the working class and farmers. In 1928, the movement became political and enjoyed widespread success in the 1930s as a result of the Great Depression and its alliance with the **Labour Party**, an alliance that continued into the 1940s and 1950s to the benefit of the Māori people. The movement did much to develop a nationwide consciousness of being Maori rather than of tribal identity. The religion claimed 36,456 adherents in the 1996 census.

REFORM PARTY of **New Zealand**. A powerful political party from 1912 until 1935. Formed in 1905 from conservative groups which opposed the **Liberal** government of Prime Minister **Richard Seddon (1893–1906)** and Joseph Ward (1906–1912), **William Massey** organized the opposition forces and the new Reform Party gained 15 Parliament seats in the 1905 election. By 1912, Reform gained enough seats to form a new government under Massey. After Massey's death, the party gained the majority in the 1925 election, but lost to a coalition of the United Party and the **Labour Party** in 1928. The party became defunct by 1935, losing out to Labour.

REGIONAL COMMITTEE ON TRADE (RCT). A subsidiary body of the **Pacific Islands Forum**, formed in 1981 and consisting of trade ministers from the Pacific island states of **Australia**, **Cook Islands**, Fiji, **New Zealand**, Papua New Guinea, Solomon Islands, **Tonga**, **Tuvalu**, **Sāmoa**, Kiribati, **Niue**, **Nauru**, and Vanuatu, who meet annually to discuss mutual cooperation in a type of economic union in which certain products move between the islands duty-free.

REX, ROBERT RICHMOND (1909–1992). Premier of **Niue Island** from October 1974 until December 1992. Born on 25 January 1909 at Hamula, Alofi, Niue Island, Rex was educated at the Tufukia government school in Niue and later established his own business. He married Patricia Tagaloa Vatolo and had two sons and two daughters. Rex became Niue's first national leader after Niue gained internal autonomy in 1966 and as such worked toward establishing a satisfactory relationship with **New Zealand**, resulting in the Niue Constitution Act of 1974. He retained the position of premier for 18 years. He announced in July 1992 that he would not run for another term. He died on 13 December 1992.

RICHARDS, WILLIAM (1793–1847). A missionary for the **American Board of Commissioners for Foreign Missions (ABCFM)** who became chief advisor to **King Kamehameha III**. Born in Massachusetts on 22 August 1793, Richards was ordained a minister and set sail to **Hawai'i** where he arrived on 27 April 1823. Richards was responsible for the construction of the high school at Lahainaluna where he taught young Hawaiians for many years. He became chaplain, teacher, and translator for King Kamehameha III, and in 1838 he resigned his missionary post to become chief advisor to the king. Richards' democratic influence can be seen in the 1840 constitution. When British admiral **George Paulet** unilaterally seized the islands for **Great Britain** in 1843, Richards made his way to England to obtain British recognition of the independence of the Hawaiian kingdom. Afterwards, Richards continued as an important minister in the government, primarily as minister of public instruction and charged with the task of organizing an educational system for the kingdom of Hawai'i. Highly respected and revered, he died in Honolulu on 7 November 1847.

ROBARTS, EDWARD (ca. 1771–1832). A **beachcomber** in the **Marquesas Islands** between 1798 and 1806. Deserting the whaling ship *Euphrates*, Robarts lived with chief Keattonnue and became a self-appointed mediator between the local rulers and visiting foreigners—for example, the Russian explorers Adam Johann Krusenstern and Yuri Lisiansky in 1804. Robarts left in 1806 because of a pending civil war, finally making his way to India where he lived out the rest of his life in general obscurity. His autobiography edited by Greg Dening, *The Marquesan Journal of Edward Robarts,* represents the principal source on Marquesan culture at Western contact. *See also* FRENCH POLYNESIA.

ROMAN CATHOLIC CHURCH IN OCEANIA. Catholic missionary work first began in the Pacific in 1668 when Father Diego Luis de Sanvitores landed on Guam in Micronesia. It took almost two centuries, however, before the Catholic missionaries made any headway in the area of **Polynesia**—only after 1836 when Protestantism had already been firmly established.

In that year, western Polynesia was incorporated into the Apostolic Vicariate of Western Oceania and entrusted to the French Society of Mary (Marist Fathers) to proselytize. Bishop **Jean-Baptiste François Pompallier** headed the first mission to the islands in 1837, landing missionaries on **Wallis and Futuna** and establishing his headquarters in **New Zealand**. Catholics made their first incursions into **Tonga** in 1842, into **Sāmoa** in 1845, and into **Rotuma** in 1846; but because of Protestant strongholds, it was several years before any secure foothold could be established. This was accomplished only with great difficulty and accompanied with international conflicts in **Tahiti** in 1838, **Hawai'i** in 1839, and Tonga in 1855.

Evangelization of Polynesia was complete by 1900, but in almost all geographical areas, Catholicism remains the minority religion with the exception of Wallis and Futuna and **Easter Island**. Current membership by country is listed below:

*Country	Membership	Parishes
American Sāmoa	9,000	10
Cook Islands	3,000	15
French Polynesia	89,000	85
Hawai'i	220,000	69
Nauru	4,000	1
New Zealand	505,000	283
Niue	200	1
Sāmoa	37,000	6
Tokelau	1,000	2
Tonga	14,000	13
Tuvalu	100	1
Wallis and Futuna	14,000	5
Totals	896,300	491

*All are members of the *Conferentia Episcopalis Pacifici* (1974) except New Zealand and Hawai'i.

By the 1970s, most positions within the Catholic church hierarchy had been taken over by indigenous bishops and clergy, and one should not be alarmed in some areas at seeing **breadfruit** being used as the bread and **coconut** juice as the wine in the Holy Eucharist. The Catholic Church is a member of the **Pacific Council of Churches** and is committed to promoting the protection of both the culture and the enviroment of the islands. *See also* AMERICAN BOARD OF COMMISSIONERS FOR FOREIGN MISSIONS; CHURCH MISSIONARY SOCIETY; LONDON MISSIONARY SOCIETY; MORMON CHURCH IN POLYNESIA.

ROTUMA. A volcanic island of approximately 44 sq km (17 sq mi), located 400 km (248 mi) north of Fiji's main islands. The island currently belongs to the political boundaries of Fiji, a Melanesian state, although its culture and ethnic background are **Polynesian**. Its traditional legends indicate both **Sāmoan** and **Tongan** settlements, and the first European to visit the island was Captain Edwards in the HMS *Pandora* during his attempts to locate the ***Bounty*** mutineers in 1791. Protestants and **Catholics**, **whalers**, and labor recruiters all made their way to the island for conversion, refueling, and capitalistic enterprises. The resultant conflicts among them and the island leaders led the seven paramount chiefs to petition **Great Britain** for annexation (1881), and the island was placed under the administration of the nearest British commissioner located in Suva, Fiji, hence its Fijian relationship.

Currently, there are approximately 2,800 Rotumans living on the island while another 4,600 or more live in Fiji. After the Fijian coup of 1987 that established an independent republic, Rotumans announced that they did not recognize the new state and affirmed their loyalty to the **Commonwealth**, whereupon the new Fijian government sent in troops and squelched the movement. In the subsequent constitution and government organization, Rotuma is represented in the upper house of the Fiji legislature by a senator, and is represented in the lower house by part of a larger regional division. A secessionist movement occurred once again in January 2000 when an American by the name of David

Korem also known as Mark Pedley visited the island and attempted to get the island leaders to sign a new constitution that provided secession from Fiji. He declared himself Head of the House of Elders of the Dominion of Melchizedek (DOM) and established a Website announcing his plan. The Fijian government sent a delegation to the islands in February to investigate. It returned saying that the Rotumans had rejected Korem's plans and that Korem was no longer on the island. It did, however, recognize that the Rotumans had grievances that needed to be addressed—unfinished government projects and unsatisfactory medical and educational services. The old issue does not look like it will be settled soon. *See also* OUTLIERS, POLYNESIAN.

ROUTLEDGE, KATHERINE PEASE (1866–1935). An **Australian** who in 1914 undertook the first archaeological expedition to **Easter Island** where she made a detailed study of the large Easter Island statues, petroglyphs, and ancient scripts and tablets. From 1921 to 1923, she led an expedition to **French Polynesia**. She had planned a massive scientific volume on Easter Island but died before it was completed.

- S -

SALAZAR, HELENA KALOKUOKAMAILE 'ELUA (1917–1988). Claimant to the **Hawaiian** monarchy and elected (1987) Ali'i Nui (high chief) of the **Ka Lāhui Hawai'i** organization that promotes an independent sovereign nation of indigenous Hawaiians within the federal U.S. governmental structure. Salazar claimed direct descent from **King Kamehameha I** and his favorite wife **Ka'ahumanu**, and upon her death on 19 September 1988, the position of Ali'i Nui was bestowed upon her grandson Noa (1982–) with Helena's daughter Owana Salazar as regent. *See also* HAWAI'I; KAWĀNANAKOA, ABIGAIL KEKAULIKE.

SĀLOTE, MAFILI'O PILOLEVU (1900–1965). Queen of **Tonga**. Born on 13 March 1900 to King George (Siaosi) Tupou II and his wife Lavina Veiongo, the young princess was educated in Auckland, **New Zealand**. At the age of 15, she married Prince William Tupoulahi Tungi from whom she had three sons—Tungi (Tāufa'āhu), Tuku‘aho, and Tu‘ipelehake. Upon her father's death in 1918, she was crowned Queen Sālote Tupou III and ruled until her death on 16 December 1965.

Her long personal reign brought significant social and economic changes to Tonga, changes that endeared her to the Tongan people. Her visit to England for the coronation of Queen Elizabeth II brought international interest to the small island state. She was created a Commander of the Order of the British Empire (CBE) in 1945 from King George VI, a Dame Grand Cross Commander of the Order of the British Empire (DBE) in 1952, a Dame Grand Cross of the Royal Victorian Order (GCVO) in 1953, and Dame Grand Cross of the Order of Saint Michael and Saint George (GCMG), the first woman in history to be so honored by a British monarch.

SĀMOA (*Malo Sa‘oloto Tuto‘atasi o Sāmoa i Sisifo*), also known as Western Sāmoa until 4 July 1997. An independent nation (since 1962) and member of the **Commonwealth**, Sāmoa consists of the two major islands of Savai‘i and ‘Upolu and seven small islands, five of which are uninhabited. They are located in the southwest Pacific Ocean between 168° to 178° west longitude and 13° to 14° south latitude. The total land area of these high volcanic islands is 2934 sq km (1,133 sq mi), but only 45 percent of the land is arable, the rest is rocky or mountainous. There are no significant mineral resources on the islands. The population, 167,988 (1999 estimate), is primarily of Polynesian extraction (over 90 percent) and approximately 72 percent of all the people live on the island of ‘Upolu where the capital of Āpia is located. Most of the 90,000 Pacific islanders living in the Auckland, **New Zealand**, metropolis are emigrants from Sāmoa. Sāmoan (Polynesian) and English are both spoken, although Sāmoan is more widely used. The climate is tropical with little or no variation from season to season. The average mean temperature is 26°C (78.8°F), and the rainy season lasts from November to April. Although Sāmoa has a high quality of life, it is economically poor. Its developing economy is dependent largely on subsistence farming and fishing. Its principal crops are **coconuts**, cocoa, **taro**, and bananas. **Tourism** provides an important source of earnings for a number of Sāmoans although they have generally maintained a cautious attitude toward development because of their fear of disrupting the Sāmoan way of life (*fa'a Sāmoa*), a way of life dominated by many characteristics of their traditional culture before European contact.

Matai Titles: Sāmoan traditions maintain that their islands were created by the great god Tagaloa and that his offspring became the ruling chiefs of Sāmoa. Ordinary mortals, however, sprang as worms from a rotting vine. Primacy was given to the first islands created—Ta'ū in Manu'a—and subsequently its rulers (the *tui Manu'a*). Sāmoan governmental structure was and continues to be feudal in nature with a hierarchy of chiefly titles (*matai*). The two prominent families were Tupua and **Mālietoa**, rulers of the islands (excluding Manu'a). The three important titles of the Tupua family—the Mata'afa, Tamasese, and Tuimaleali'ifano—and the Mālietoa title are collectively known as the *Tama'a-'aiga* and have been the object of political intrigue for hundreds of years.

The *matai* presides over his *'aiga* (extended family), owns all the land and its resources, and parcels it out according to need. The *matai* also holds an important position in each village *fono*, a sovereign, governing council that generally meets weekly to discuss village affairs, to resolve disputes, and to award judgments. The Village Fono Act of 1990 gives the village *matai* absolute control over village affairs. *Matai* titles are not necessarily passed down from father to son. They change hands when the *matai* becomes too old to function effectively. Titles often are split with several individuals sharing the position.

Disputes over titles are resolved in the Lands and Titles Court, headed by a chief justice, and resolutions subsequently registered. Approximately 15 percent of the adult population are *matais*, and until 1991 only they could vote in general elections.

Modern History: The first Europeans to visit the Sāmoan islands were **Jacob Roggeveen** in 1721 and 1722 and **Louis de Bougainville** in May 1768, but neither landed. In 1787 **Jean-François Lapérouse** lost 12 men in a scuffle with the Sāmoans at Tutuila (**American Sāmoa**). Missionaries from the **London Missionary Society** landed at Sapapali'i on Savai'i in July 1830 under the leadership of **John Williams** who had been invited to the islands by the Sāmoan chief Fauea. A written language was established (1834), and within a short period of time, numerous Sāmoans had been converted.

By 1838, a reciprocal commercial treaty had been concluded between Captain Bethune of the HMS *Conway* and the Sāmoan chiefs regarding the payment of harbor dues in exchange for protection of foreign interests in the islands. **United States** interests began with the expedition of **Captain Charles Wilkes** to the South Pacific (1838–1842). Wilkes surveyed the islands and, similar to Bethune, extracted an agreement with the Sāmoan chiefs regarding the excellent harbor at Pago Pago (American Sāmoa). Mālietoa Vai'inupo's attempts at possession of the Tafa'ifā and to create a centralized kingdom as had emerged in some of the other Polynesian states (**Hawai'i** and **Tonga**, for example) failed. Upon his death in 1841, his titles were scattered, and internal civil war ensued for over 20 years. Guns and ammunition introduced by Westerners gave a new dimension to the internal wars.

Meanwhile, Europeans continued to visit the islands in increasing numbers, apparently little threatened by the ensuing civil wars and profiting from the sale of such weapons to the Sāmoans. Godeffroy & Son (a German commercial firm) and the Central Polynesian Land and Commercial Company (a U.S. firm) both claimed to have purchased vast stretches of territory amounting to about one-half of Sāmoa. Āpia became an important **whaling** town similar to Honolulu and Pape'ete, and by 1860, there were over one hundred European residents, most of whom demanded rights and protection under Western legal codes.

British, United States, and German interests in the islands led to such competitive international rivalry that in March 1889, warships of all three nations were anchored in Āpia harbor glowering at one another. The famous hurricane of 16 March 1889, sank six ships, and 92 German sailors and 54 American sailors lost their lives. The 1889 **Berlin Act** in June, provided for a tripartite condominium rule for the islands, but it failed to settle their major differences. As a result, a final agreement in December 1899 provided that **Germany** and the United States would divide Sāmoa between them—the eastern islands (Tutuila and the Manu'a group) going to the United States, and Germany receiving the western islands (Savai'i and 'Upolu). Britain withdrew her demands when she was granted concessions elsewhere in the Pacific—Tonga, **Niue**, and the Solomon Islands.

German Administration (1890–1914): By a formal treaty in 1873, Mālietoa Laupepa was recognized as king with a constitution and state based upon the European model, but shortly thereafter, the monarchy was challenged again. When Germany gained control of the islands, Mālietoa was recognized sovereign again, but within five years Matā'afa was challenging his position and war resumed. Opposition, the ***Mau* of Pule**, to German high-handed rule broke out in 1908, but it was squashed by the German governor **Wilhelm Solf**, who exiled its leaders to the Mariana Islands in Micronesia and then took punitive measures against their supporters. When World War I commenced in August 1914, the New Zealand government was swift to move troops into the islands and to seize them from Germany.

New Zealand Administration (1914–1962): Sāmoans, who had never been party to the 1889 agreement nor to the 1899 division of their islands, opposed their New Zealand overlords as they had the Germans. In 1918, they blamed the inept government of Colonel Robert Logan for the death of 22 percent of the population from the Spanish influenza, and they claimed that arrogant military officers from colonial New Zealand cared little about the Sāmoan culture and way of life. Anti–New Zealand sentiment found expression in the *Mau* movement that lasted from 1926 to 1936. They refused to assist the government and to pay their taxes. In December 1929, members of the *Mau* marched through Āpia, and in an affray between them and the armed police, 11 Sāmoans, mostly of high rank, were killed including Tamasese Lealofi II. Tensions eased slowly between the two factions after the **New Zealand Labour Party** came to power in 1936 and made peace with the Sāmoan dissidents.

Similar to most Pacific islands, World War II brought the 20th century directly to their doorsteps. U.S. Marines stationed on 'Upolu built roads and an airport and generally introduced the islanders to an advanced industrialized society. Developing world sentiment against colonialism after the war led the New Zealand government to begin to prepare the islands for some type of self-government and independence. In 1947, 1953, and 1957 specific acts were passed that brought the islands closer to independence.

By the end of 1960, the Sāmoan Constitutional Convention had drafted a constitution, and in January 1961, Prime Minister Fiamē Matā'afa took the proposal before the **United Nations**. A U.N. supervised plebiscite, held on 9 May 1961, overwhelmingly confirmed the wish to become independent, and as a result, Sāmoa became the first Pacific island nation to gain independence (1 January 1962). The 1960 constitution, which incorporates traditional systems of government and social control, provides for an executive head of state and a parliamentary-type government.

Government: The constitution made Mālietoa Tanumafili II and Tupua Tamasese Mae'ole joint heads of state until their deaths. Tamasese died in 1963, and upon the death of Mālietoa, the legislative assembly will elect his successor. Future heads of state, however, will be elected and will serve for only a five-year term. That position in the government remains primarily ceremonial. The government consists of a single-house legislature (*fono*) with 49 members, two of whom are non-Sāmoan and represent the European community. Elections are held every five years. Until 1990, only *matai* could vote in elections, however, a referendum in October 1990 introduced universal suffrage (over 21), but still only *matai* can stand for election. The prime minister, the effective head of state, is elected by the majority of the members of the legislative assembly and presides over a cabinet of eight appointed members. Local government continues to reside in the hands of the chiefs of the villages.

Contemporary History: Since independence, Sāmoan politics have reflected the tensions of modernizing and Westernizing while at the same time trying to maintain the strong traditional culture that dominates society. Two major concerns have required state attention—the poor economy and the demand for more democratic reforms by elements within the population.

In 1969, a National Women's Committee was formed under the leadership of Masiofo Fetaui Matā'afa and other wives of government officials to promote the causes of Sāmoan **women**. By 1970, no changes had been made to the constitution to provide further suffrage or democratic reforms. The elections that year brought to power a new prime minister, Tupua Tamasese Lealofi IV, referred to as a "liberal" by the newspapers. He remained in office for only one term. The elections of 1972 brought back into office Matā'afa Fiamē Faumuinā Mulinu'u II, but his death on 23 May 1975 returned Tupua Tamasese Lealofi IV to power.

In 1976, a new prime minister, **Tupuola Efi**, was chosen by a solid majority of 15 votes, and this new government undertook numerous rural development projects sponsored primarily through international aid organizations. However, these were not successful because outside influences seriously affected Sāmoa's economy—world inflation, recession, and so forth.

In 1979, Sāmoa's first political party, the **Human Rights Protection Party (HRPP)**, was organized under the leadership of Va'ai Kolone, Tofilau Eti Alesana, La'ulu Fetauimalemau, and other well-known Sāmoans. During the next three years, relations between the opposition leaders and the government were tense. The elections of 1982 resulted in a win for the new HRPP party, and Va'ai Kolone was elected prime minister. That year—the year of confrontation—saw the government change hands three times because of the slim majority each group held in Parliament. Tupuola Efi (head of the Christian Democratic Party) began the year as prime minister. Va'ai Kolone (HRPP party) won the February elections, but by September, he had lost an appeal case over his election, and Tupuola Efi was appointed interim prime minister. He resigned in December when Parliament refused to approve his budget, whereupon Tofilau Eti Alesana (the new leader of the HRPP) was appointed prime minister.

Although Alesana won the elections three years later in 1985, he resigned in December of that year because Parliament again rejected his budget. Va'ai Kolone was again appointed prime minister with Tupuola Efi as his deputy prime minister. The elections of 1988 saw the return of Alesana as prime minister.

To indicate the growing concern for the status of women in Sāmoa, a new holiday was also declared—Women's Day—the last Thursday of every May, a women's affairs ministry was established, and the government promised $WS 1 million every year to assist community women's projects in the villages. Maternity leave entitlement for women in the work place was also extended from zero to eight weeks. (All this indicates that attitudes toward women in Sāmoa are changing, but as of 2001, only three women sit in the legislature and one woman is a member of the cabinet. Only 5 percent of the 25,000 *matai* are women, and only *matai* can be elected to the assembly. Thus the traditional subordinate role of women has not yet ceased. The Ministry of Women's Affairs in the cabinet oversees and helps ensure the rights of women.)

The interim government, headed by Alesana, also busied itself with squeezing other new legislation in before the April election. The government introduced an old age pension of $WS50 for those 65 and over, promised to develop more youth programs, and increased the minimum wage to $WS1.00 an hour.

In the 5 April 1991 general elections, the new electoral policy of universal suffrage progressed peacefully and apparently caused no great changes in the projected political outcome. The ruling Human Rights Protection Party, headed by Alesana, gained 26 of the 47 seats in Parliament against the opposition Sāmoan National Development Party. This marked the fourth election won by the prime minister since he first entered Parliament in 1957. Alesana continued to rule as prime minister until his retirement in November of 1998. He died of cancer on 19 March 1999, having been the longest serving head of state in the Pacific. He was replaced by Deputy Prime Minister Tuilaepa Sailele Malielegaoi, the current prime minister.

The political history of Sāmoa during the past decade has been anything but tranquil. The seemingly autocratic character of the HRPP succeeded in creating an atmosphere in which its opponents, both public and the media, exposed scandals and corruption in the government, the net result of which culminated in the political assassination of a cabinet member in 1999. Inversely, the government initiated numerous economic reforms that transformed Sāmoa's struggling, poor economy at the beginning of the decade into one that is now exceptional among other Pacific island countries.

The allegations of government corruption were not new in Sāmoa, but they seemed to have gained momentum during the 1990s. Between 1994 and 1998, there were six public demonstrations against the government, most of which were organized by the Tumua ma Pule, a group that protested against the high cost of living, the political scandals and corruption in government, and the new taxes (VAT). It pointed out the government's numerous shady political dealings—the electoral malpractice in the 1996 elections, the 1997 passport scandal involving the chief immigration officers, and the corruption in the various government departments (Public Works and Revenues, for example). Added to these was the media conflict with the *Sāmoa Observer* newspaper in 1997. The *Observer's* editor, Savea Sano Malifa, published numerous articles revealing damaging evidence against various individuals high in the government. Intolerant of dissent, the prime minister and cabinet attempted to shut down the press. Several lawsuits resulted in which the editor was found guilt and heavily fined. Other government actions during the 1990s appeared equally arbitrary, and in February of 2000, a U.S. Department of State Report on Human Rights was critical of the Sāmoan government on several points. Some references in the report were made to the Sāmoan policy of ostracism by village councils, references most likely leveled at the expulsion of a Bible study group from its village simply because it refused to disband. A few of the 200 members served prison sentences, and eventually a police force had to be used to expel the group from the village.

The culminating scandal was the 1999 assassination of the Minister of Public Works Luagalau Levaula Kamu by the son of another cabinet minister. The son testified that he acted upon his father's instigation, and it is assumed that the minister was murdered to try to prevent him from revealing widespread corruption and misuse of public funds. Another cabinet member was implicated in the murder as well. After a long-running murder trial, the son was found guilty and sentenced to death, however, his sentence was commuted to life imprisonment by the head of state. The two cabinet members were found guilty and sentenced to life in prison.

The elections of 3 March 2001 returned the HRPP back to power, but it lost its absolute majority in Parliament (wth a loss of 10 seats). As a result, negotiations with the independents was required before the outcome was certain. Eventually, Tuiaepa Malielegaoi was returned as prime minister; but in a surprise move, Tuiatua Tupua Tamasese Efi stepped down from his position as opposition leader. That office was filled by the new SNDP leader Le Mamea Ropati. Five former cabinet members also lost their seats in the general election, and three women were elected to Parliament, the same as in 1996.

Economy: Despite the demonstrations, government scandals, and assassinations, Sāmoa's economy during the past decade showed remarkable improvement; but the early 1990s were not kind to Sāmoa. In one year (1990–1991), its national debt soared from $92 million to $140 million. Two cyclones (Val and Ofa) devastated the **copra** and coconut industry, a **taro** blight in 1993 almost wiped out that crop, and a heavily debt-ridden Polynesian Air Lines provided a financial crisis in 1994. The government took the initiative and abandoned its planned economic program and embraced a broader agenda based mainly on markets and market principles. It prepared a proposal—a *Development Plan, 1992–2001*—in which it encouraged the growth of **tourism**, the diversification of agriculture, and increased privatization. The government initiated a subsidy to aid coconut growers replant, a value-added tax (VAT) was passed, and other financial reforms were passed to facilitate the public sector. The dynamic mover behind these reforms was Deputy Prime Minister Malielegaoi who proposed various fiscal reforms, deregulation, and improvement of state-owned enterprises. By 1995, the economy began a rebound with a strong increase in tourism and the recovery in agriculture. In 1996, fish became Sāmoa's biggest export, and by 1999 exports of fish, coconut, and **kava** had made positive developments. For four fiscal years in succession (1995–1999), the government ran an overall budget surplus, an indication that the government's reform and firm fiscal management policies have produced substantial results.

Tourism, which was a minor contributor to the economy in 1990, has now become one of the Sāmoa's major contributors. Nineteen percent of the gross domestic product (GDP) comes from tourism. The number of tourists grew from 48,000 in 1990 to 85,122 in 1999. The political crises in Fiji and the Solomon Islands in 2000 contributed to an even larger influx of tourists during that year. There continues to be an acute hotel shortage, however, and currently there appears to be no plans to build any more hotels.

Large-scale emigration continues to be both a curse and a blessing to Sāmoa. For various reasons, intellectuals and skilled workers opt to emigrate, thus depriving Sāmoa of competent individuals who could provide the needed talent to improve its economy and society. On the other hand, this emigration allows dissidents to leave which usually provides a more stable society at home, and emigration has also slowed down Sāmoa's rapid population growth. Another positive consequence is the high level of monetary remittances from overseas relatives (primarily in New Zealand) sent to their families in Sāmoa. These remittances amount to approximately $10 million a month.

According to UN criteria, Sāmoa still remains one of the world's least developed nations despite the fact that it has received foreign aid from several international organizations and nations (primarily New Zealand). Its annual GDP is approximately $394 million with a per capita income of only $1,755. Sāmoa ranks 174th out of 191 countries in terms of its GDP. The word "poor" to describe Sāmoa's economy can be deceiving, however. "Poor" often connotes words like "dirty, squalid, and slums." This is not the case in Sāmoa. The traditionally built homes in the villages are kept clean, neat, and orderly, and the dignity and pride the Sāmoans show in their country and culture are enviable among many other Pacific islanders.

SĀMOA NATIONAL DEVELOPMENT PARTY (SNDP). One of the two major political parties in **Sāmoa**, it was founded in 1985 as the Christian Democratic Party (CDP). In the 1988 elections, the CDP won 25 of the 47 seats in the legislative assembly (*fono*) but only with support of its independent voices. As a result of the coalition of opposition forces, the party was renamed the Sāmoa National Development Party (SNDP), gained 21 seats in the 1991 elections, 11 seats in the 1996 elections, and continues to be headed by the former **Prime Ministers Tupua Tamasese**, **Tupuola Taisi Efi**, and Va'ai Kolone. *See also* HUMAN RIGHTS PROTECTION PARTY.

SANDALWOOD TRADE. During the 19th century, sandalwood trees (of the genus *Santalum*) were cut in the Pacific islands to satisfy the profitable trade with China where the trees were used in incense for burnt offerings in Buddhist temples and in the production of inlaid boxes, perfume, and other products. In 1789, an American sea captain, John Kendrick, discovered the source in **Hawai'i**, and a mad dash for sandalwood profit caused numerous foreigners to visit the islands. The boom in Hawai'i came between 1811 to 1828 and in the **Marquesas**—currently part of **French Polynesia**—from 1813 to 1817. The islands were stripped of their trees while the Western entrepreneurs brought foreign diseases that decimated much of the population in the Marquesas. After the sources in the Polynesian islands dried up, India again became the main supplier of sandalwood.

SANDWICH ISLANDS. Named by Britsh explorer **Captain James Cook** and are now known as the islands of **Hawai‘i**.

SANFORD, FRANCIS ARIIOEHAU (1912–1996). Political leader of **French Polynesia**, born on 11 May 1912 in Pape‘ete, and educated at the Pape‘ete Central School. Sanford was a schoolteacher from 1929 to 1932, then held several civil government positions in the **Tuamotu and Gambier islands**, and became liaison officer with the American forces stationed on Bora Bora between 1942 and 1946, a duty that earned him many distinguished citations (U.S. Medal of Freedom, for example). He served as director of education from 1950 to 1965, and later entered politics and was elected mayor of Fa‘a‘a, **Tahiti**, in 1965 and deputy to **France** in 1967 for four consecutive terms.

When French Polynesia gained internal autonomy on 14 July 1977, Sanford's party, ‘Ē‘a Āpi (New Way), gained a clear majority of seats, and he became the first head (vice president) of French Polynesia's government, a position he held until 1985. He worked strenuously to bring about internal autonomy for French Polynesia, work that often brought him into conflict with Paris as well as the opposition party, the **Tāhō‘ēra‘a Huira‘atira** of **Gaston Flosse**, his successor. In the territorial elections of 1982, he won the only seat obtained by his party. Without a strong political base and because of advancing age, Sanford retired on 17 October 1985. He died at his home in Fa‘a‘a on 21 December 1996.

SAVAGE, MICHAEL JOSEPH (1872–1940). Prime minister of **New Zealand** from 1935 until his death in 1940. An immigrant from **Australia** in the early 1900s, Savage brought with him his radical ideas of introducing socialist reforms. His experience in his new homeland and his associations within the **New Zealand Labour Party**, however, tempered his attitudes. He became deputy chairman of the Labour Party in 1923 and then chairman in 1933. His associates, **Peter Fraser** and **John A. Lee**, contributed to the successful election campaign of 1935 that brought their party to power. Until his death in 1940, Savage and his party initiated an onslaught of legislation that essentially set out to alleviate the problems the Great Depression had inflicted upon jobs, housing, and education. The party was returned to power in 1938 with an even larger majority, and Parliament continued to pass social legislation that essentially created a welfare state. Dissension in the party developed, however, in 1939 as Savage was suffering from a bout with cancer. Lee struck out verbally against the prime minister and in March 1940 left the party. Two days later Savage died, mourned as deeply as any in New Zealand history. Peter Fraser succeeded him as prime minister.

SECURITY TREATY BETWEEN AUSTRALIA, NEW ZEALAND, AND THE UNITED STATES. *See* ANZUS PACT.

SEDDON, RICHARD JOHN (1845–1906). Prime minister of **New Zealand** from 1893 to 1906 during New Zealand's sweeping social legislative reform period. Born at School Brow, Eccleston, Lancashire, England, Seddon immigrated to **Australia** in 1863 and then to New Zealand three years later. He entered public service as a member of the Westland Provincial council in 1874, then as mayor of Kumara in 1877. In 1879, he was elected a member of Parliament for Hokitika (1881–1890) and then for Westland the rest of his life. He served as minister of public works, defense, and marine under Prime Minister John Ballance, and when Ballance died in 1893, Seddon was chosen his successor.

Seddon's character resembled the rustic pioneer spirit of the late 19th century—brash, supporter of the working class, and imperialist. As prime minister, Seddon spearheaded the introduction of numerous labor reform movements to New Zealand—labor arbitration acts, better working conditions in the factories, shorter hours, old-age pensions, accident compensation, the right to vote for **women** (the first country in the world to do so), all of which marked New Zealand as a progressive, liberal, and far-sighted country. Seddon's abrasive character and his domineering personality earned him the title "King Dick."

SELWYN, GEORGE AUGUSTUS (1809–1878). The first Anglican bishop of **New Zealand**, between 1841 and 1868, and a prominent influence in the early development of not only the history of New Zealand but of Christianity in the Pacific (primarily in Melanesia). Arriving in 1841 as the first missionary bishop to the new diocese of New Zealand, Selwyn energetically set out to visit each of the mission settlements. His first synod was convened in 1844, and by 1858 the constitution of the Anglican Church was adopted by the New Zealand government. Selwyn gave opinions on government actions and offered political advice when called upon. His interest in Melanesian mission, although criticized by some New Zealanders, led to the introduction of the Anglican religion to the New Hebrides (Vanuatu), New Caledonia, and the Loyalty Islands. (His son, John Richardson Selwyn, was ordained and later became bishop of Melanesia.) In 1867 Selwyn returned to England as Bishop of Lichfield where he died in 1878. Several geographical sites in New Zealand as well as a college at Cambridge University are named after him.

SHAW, ELAINE (?–1990). An activist for indigenous rights in the Pacific and director of the Greenpeace organization in **New Zealand**. Elaine Shaw devoted most of her life to the Greenpeace organization and to its antinuclear stance against French tests in the Pacific. Several months after the ***Rainbow Warrior*** affair in 1985, she left the organization, but remained a valuable source for advice and contacts. Her position as Pacific campaign coordinator was assumed by Bunny McDiarmid. Shaw died of cancer at age 48 in October 1990.

SHIPLEY, JENNIFER (JENNY) (1952–). Prime minister **of New Zealand** from 8 December 1997 to 5 December 1999. Born on 4 February 1952, at Gore, New Zealand, Shipley grew up in Wellington and Blenheim. She graduated from Christchurch Teachers College in 1971 and worked as a primary teacher in Christchurch for several years. She became interested in local politics before winning as the **National Party** candidate from the Ashburton electorate (1987), a position she has retained ever since. When National swept into office in 1990, Shipley led the dismantling of what was left of New Zealand's welfare state. National's policy was unpopular, and Shipley, labeled "the perfumed bulldozer," saw protesters burn her effigy in the streets. She was appointed minister of women's affairs (1990–1996), minister of health in 1993, and minister of state services, transport, state-owned enterprises, ACC, and Radio New Zealand after the 1996 elections. She assumed leadership of the National Party when **Prime Minister Jim Bolger** retired in December 1997, and as such she became New Zealand's first **woman** prime minister. In 1999, she hosted the Asia-Pacific Economic Cooperation (APEC) which attracted some of the world's top political leaders. Late in 1999, she failed to capture the voter's support and, on 27 November 1999, she lost her position as prime minister to **Helen Clark**, leader of the **Labour Party**. Shipley currently maintains her position as leader of the opposition.

SHORT, SIR APENERA (1916–). Queen Elizabeth II's representative and the head of state in the **Cook Islands** since 1991. Born on 4 February 1916, in Rarotonga, Short was educated at the Loughborough Cooperative College in England. He was an educator (teacher and then registrar) from 1937 to 1965, when he became minister of the crown and deputy premier (1965–1978). Highly respected, he holds offices in numerous Cook Islands associations, including as a member of the Cook Islands Party (1965–1990). Short holds the traditional title of Takau Rangatira and was knighted Knight, Order of the British Empire, by Queen Elizabeth II in 1997. He is married to Maui Timata i te Rui Cowan and has 14 children.

SMALLER ISLAND STATES (SIS). An organization formed in 1985 as part of the Secretariat of the **Pacific Community** and consisting of the small island states of **Nauru**, **Niue**, **Tuvalu**, **Cook Islands**, and Kiribati (in Micronesia). These five island states have particularly acute characteristics of smallness, isolation, shortages of natural resources, little manufacturing potential, and weak bargaining power. Together they have a combined population of 120,000 people living on just 1,332 sq km (512 sq mi) of land, which in most cases is sitting a few vulnerable yards above sea level. The organization, consisting of the individual heads of state, meets annually to discuss mutual problems and solutions.

SOCIAL CREDIT PARTY of **New Zealand.** Originally founded in 1953 as the Social Credit Political League. Based upon the monetary doctrines of Major C. H. Douglas of the 1930s, it maintained that the government should stop the profiteering of banks charging excessive interest by offering free or cheap credit. The party gained its first seat in Parliament in the 1966 elections, one seat in 1978, and two seats in 1981 with 20 percent of the total votes cast. In 1985, in order to broaden its electoral appeal and to lessen its traditional monetary emphasis, the party changed its name to the Democratic Party.

SOCIETY ISLANDS. One of the five island groups that make up **French Polynesia**, it includes the high windward islands of **Tahiti**, Mo‘orea, Mehitia (Maitea), Tubuai Manu, and Tetiaroa (a small atoll) and the northwest leeward islands of Huahine, Rā‘iatea, Taha‘a, Bora Bora, Tupai, Mophia‘a (Mopelia), and Maupiti.

SOLF, WILHELM HEINRICH (1862–1936). German governor of **Sāmoa** from 1900 to 1911. Highly educated and trained, Solf entered the German diplomatic service in 1885, and after a stint in India and East Africa, he was appointed to Sāmoa where he became the governor of the newly acquired islands. He served effectively over the islands for more than 10 years. Despite the organized resistance by the ***Mau* of Pule** during his administration, his toleration of Sāmoan customs, his firm but fair treatment of the warring factions, and his encouragement of the development of the islands' economy all contributed to his successful and highly respected administration. In December 1911, he was promoted to the colonial office in Berlin, a post he held until 1918. *See also* ANGLO-GERMAN AGREEMENT OF 1899; BERLIN ACT OF 1889; BISMARCK AGREEMENT OF 1879; GERMANY; LACKAWANA AGREEMENT; WEBER, THEODOR.

SOUTH PACIFIC APPLIED GEOSCIENCE COMMISSION (SOPAC). An independent, intergovernmental, regional organization established by several South Pacific nations in 1972, as the Committee for Coordination of Joint Prospecting for Mineral Resources in South Pacific Offshore Areas. Its mission is to improve the well-being of the peoples of the Pacific island member countries through the application of geosciences to the management and sustainable development of their nonliving resources. Annual sessions are held in member countries with technical advisors attending from the numerous industrial countries of the world—the **United States**, **Germany**, Canada, China, **France**, **Japan**, and Norway, among others. Its name was changed in 1989, and in 1990 a new constitution allows Pacific island territories to participate as associate members. Its Polynesian member countries include **Cook Islands**, **French Polynesia**, **Nauru**, **New Zealand**, **Niue**, **Sāmoa**, **Tonga**, and **Tuvalu**. (Other Pacific members are **Australia**, Micronesia, Fiji, Guam, Kiribati, Marshall Islands, New Caledonia, Papua New Guinea, Solomon Islands, and Vanuatu.) Successful projects have included locating cobalt, manganese, petroleum, and other minerals in various island nations as well as the training sessions in annual workshops that offer a Certificate in Earth Science and Marine Geology. SOPAC's office is located in Suva, Fiji. Its annual funding ($2.8 million) comes from member countries and grants from donor governments and international agencies. Its Website can be located at http://www.sopac.org.fj.

SOUTH PACIFIC ARTS FESTIVAL. *See* FESTIVAL OF SOUTH PACIFIC ARTS.

SOUTH PACIFIC BOARD FOR EDUCATIONAL ASSESSMENT (SPBEA). An organization of Pacific island nations—**Cook Islands**, Fiji, Kiribati, Solomon Islands, **Tonga**, **Tuvalu**, **Sāmoa**, and **Tokelau**—whose purpose is "to assist each country to develop its assessment procedures towards national educational certificates" so that standardized tests can be developed to evaluate students' progress from their primary to tertiary educational levels. The SPBEA secretariat is located outside of Suva, Fiji, where the **University of the South Pacific** gives it professional guidance and support. *See also* EDUCATION IN THE PACIFIC.

SOUTH PACIFIC BUREAU FOR ECONOMIC COOPERATION (SPEC). Predecessor of the South Pacific Forum Secretariat (SPC). *See* PACIFIC ISLANDS FORUM.

SOUTH PACIFIC COMMISSION (SPC). *See* PACIFIC COMMUNITY.

SOUTH PACIFIC CONFERENCE. An annual meeting of the **Pacific Community** members who collectively represent the governing body of the Pacific Community.

SOUTH PACIFIC FORUM (SPF). *See* PACIFIC ISLANDS FORUM.

SOUTH PACIFIC FORUM FISHERIES AGENCY (FFA). Established in 1978 by the **South Pacific Forum** to provide coordination among its member nations (currently 16) in promoting cooperation and mutual assistance in fishing matters within the region. The FAA has its headquarters in Honiara, Solomon Islands, and the governing body of the agency, the Forum Fisheries Committee (FFC), meets annually to approve the budget and work programs. Funding for the agency ($4.8 million in 1999) comes from member countries (12 percent) and the rest from grants and donations from AusAID, the European Union, the Canadian International Development Agency, the **Commonwealth** Secretariat, and the New Zealand Development Assistance Programme.

The functions of the FCC include accumulating detailed information on all aspects of living marine resources in the region; providing accurate, clear, and timely advice to member countries; and developing and maintaining communications networks for the dissemination of this information. Tuna fishing in the central and western Pacific, for example, is an important industry worth $1.7 billion annually of which $60 to $70 million is earned by the 16 FFA members. Some of the achievements of the FFA consist of establishing a two-hundred mile (370-km) **exclusive economic zone (EEZ)** and negotiating a five-year multilateral agreement with the **United States** in 1987 to allow U.S. fishing fleets rights to fish within the area in exchange for $60 million.

SOUTH PACIFIC GAMES. International amateur athletic competitions between the South Pacific island nations. The concept of the games was first introduced by Dr. Sahu Kahn of Fiji in 1959 to the South Pacific Commission, now called the **Pacific Community**, and the first games were held in Suva, Fiji, in 1963. The games are currently being held every four years, generally hosted by one of the member island nations. Some 2,000 athletes from 22 different Pacific territories meet together to compete for gold, silver, or bronze medals. The current games have been held in Papua New Guinea (1991), **Tahiti** (1995), Guam (1999), and the ones for 2003 will be held in Suva, Fiji. Since 1981, mini-games have been scheduled and hosted by countries not capable of hosting full-scale Games—**Cook Islands** (1985), **Tonga** (1989), Vanuatu (1993), and **American Sāmoa** (1997), for example. A regionwide representative South Pacific Games Council supervises its activities.

SOUTH PACIFIC JUDICIAL CONFERENCE (SPJC). An organization founded in January 1972 by the chief justices, attorney generals, and judicial experts from the independent South Pacific island nations (some 16 are represented) to discuss law and law enforcement. Subjects of their biennial meetings have included narcotics control, land and land titles, treatment of criminals and juvenile delinquents, and numerous other subjects common to this area of the Pacific. A subsequent offshoot of the SPJC was the **Pacific Islands Law Officers Meeting (PILOM)** in 1981.

SOUTH PACIFIC LABOR MINISTERS CONFERENCE (SPLMC). First organized by Australian Prime Minister Gough Whitlam in 1973, in which South Pacific labor ministers meet to exchange views on employment problems, industrial relations, and world economic conditions and to provide liaison with the International Labour Organization (ILO). Participating countries have been **American Sāmoa**, **Australia**, **Cook Islands**, Fiji, Guam, Kiribati, **Nauru**, **New Zealand**, Papua New Guinea, Solomon Islands, **Tonga**, Trust Territories of the Pacific islands, **Tuvalu**, Vanuatu, and **Sāmoa**. The SPLMC, however, has not met since 1983.

SOUTH PACIFIC REGIONAL CIVIL AVIATION COUNCIL (SPRCAC). A consultative body on civil aviation first convened by the **South Pacific Forum** in 1976, currently consisting of the aviation ministers from the countries of **Australia, Cook Islands**, the Federated States of Micronesia, Fiji, Kiribati, **Nauru**, **New Zealand**, **Niue**, Papua New Guinea, **Sāmoa**, Solomon Islands, **Tonga**, **Tuvalu**, and Vanuatu. The SPRCAC discusses regional air services, routes, schedules, providing better service in the region, training, airport security, tariff reductions, departure taxes, and so forth.

SOUTH PACIFIC REGIONAL ENVIRONMENT PROGRAMME. A regional organization, founded in 1982 by the South Pacific Commission, currently called the **Pacific Community**, responsible for environmental matters. Its mission is to promote cooperation in the South Pacific and to provide assistance in order to protect and improve its environment and to ensure sustainable development for present and future generations. Its activities include environmental education, waste management, coastal management, wetland and mangrove protection, links between **tourism** and the environment, and support to governments at international environment negotiations. In 1991, it became an autonomous regional organization and moved its headquarters to Āpia, **Sāmoa**. Its staff has grown from 10 to almost 60, and it has expanded its international network. New facilities were completed in August of 2000. Its membership consists of the 22 Pacific island countries and territories, and four development countries with interest in the area—**Australia**, **France**, **New Zealand**, and the **United States**. Its Website at http://www.sprep.org.ws provides a wealth of information on its organization. *See also* SOUTH PACIFIC REGIONAL ENVIRONMENTAL PROTECTION CONVENTION.

SOUTH PACIFIC REGIONAL ENVIRONMENTAL PROTECTION CONVENTION. A joint communiqué approved in Nouméa, New Caledonia, on 25 November 1986 by delegates from 16 countries, including the **United States**, **France**, **Australia**, **New Zealand** and a dozen other South Pacific island states, which aims at preventing the disposal of hazardous wastes in the Pacific. The treaty establishes a blacklist of substances—oil, mercury, and nuclear wastes—that would be absolutely barred from being put into the South Pacific Ocean, other substances such as lead and arsenic could be dumped with special permission. The treaty ended five-years negotiation sponsored by the United Nations Environment Program. The area affected is roughly an area bounded by Papua New Guinea in the west to **Pitcairn Island** in the east. *See also* SOUTH PACIFIC REGIONAL ENVIRONMENT PROGRAMME.

SOUTH PACIFIC REGIONAL SHIPPING COUNCIL (SPRSC). An organization first convened in 1975 upon request of the **South Pacific Forum** to "make proposals regarding general policy on regional shipping arrangements and services." One of its first tasks was to create the **Pacific Forum Line** to provide shipping and transportation within the region as well as to draft a South Pacific Maritime Code and a South Pacific Seafarers Wage Rates Agreement. Member countries consist of **Australia**, **Cook Islands**, the Federated States of Micronesia, Fiji, Kiribati, **Nauru**, **New Zealand**, **Niue**, Papua

New Guinea, **Sāmoa**, Solomon Islands, **Tonga**, **Tuvalu**, and Vanuatu.

SOUTH PACIFIC REGIONAL TELECOMMUNICATIONS MEETING (SPECTEL). Formed at the request of the **South Pacific Forum** in 1983 to upgrade and provide better telecommunications services to its member nations—**Australia, Cook Islands**, Federated States of Micronesia, Fiji, Kiribati, the Marshall Islands, **Nauru**, **Niue**, **New Zealand**, Papua New Guinea, **Sāmoa**, Solomon Islands, **Tonga**, **Tokelau**, **Tuvalu**, and Vanuatu. Ministers of telecommunications of the various islands meet together annually to discuss mutual problems, technical assistance, personnel, and construction of new hardware, and so forth.

SOUTH PACIFIC TOURISM ORGANIZATION (SPTO). A council formed on 21 March 1983, at a session of the **South Pacific Bureau for Economic Cooperation (SPEC)** held in Suva, Fiji, with a goal to "develop through cooperation, the tourism industries of the South Pacific and by doing so, seek to foster travel in the region." The SPTO currently consists of four divisions—marketing and member services, human resources development, research and development, and finance and administration. The principal office, the secretariat, is located on the grounds of the SPEC in Suva. Its original name was the Tourism Council of the South Pacific until October of 1999.

The original member countries in 1983 were **American Sāmoa**, the **Cook Islands**, Fiji, **Niue**, **French Polynesia**, New Caledonia, **Tonga**, and **Sāmoa**, with Papua New Guinea, the Solomon Islands, and Vanuatu joining in 1984, and Kiribati and **Tuvalu** in 1986. Annual meetings are held in alternating island groups with the ministers of tourism from each of the member nations attending. Assessment funds from members along with other outside assistance—primarily from **Australia**, **New Zealand** and the European Union—provide for **tourism** research, information, and training. Among other things, the SPTO has developed information packets to assist tourism employees, designed curriculum materials for marketing and promotional purposes, and produced documentary films and slides for marketing campaigns. Its current chief executive is Lisiate 'Aialoa from Tonga. Update information on tourism in the South Pacific can be found on its Website http://www.tcsp.com.

SOUTH PACIFIC TRADE COMMISSION. An agency of the **South Pacific Forum Secretariat**, based in Suva, Fiji. established by the Australian government in 1979 to aid and assist the 16 Pacific Forum Island nations in their trade with **Australia**. The commission provides a wide variety of services such as investment promotion, trade and export development, and public relations. It has offices in Auckland, **New Zealand** and Tokyo, **Japan**. Its **Internet** Website, http://www.sptc.gov.au/home/home.htm, offers assistance, reports, and other data to Pacific island entrepreneurs. *See also* SOUTH PACIFIC BUREAU FOR ECONOMIC COOPERATION; SOUTH PACIFIC FORUM.

SPRECKELS, CLAUS (1828–1908). A German businessman who helped establish the sugar industry in **Hawai'i** and California during the 1860s and 1870s. Born in Lamstedt, Hanover, Germany, Spreckels immigrated to the **United States** in 1846 and made his fortune in the grocery business on the east coast. During the U.S. Civil War when sugar prices soared on the world market, Spreckels founded the Bay Sugar Refining Company in San Francisco. After returning to Germany to learn more about sugar processing, he returned to the United States in 1867 and established the California Sugar Refinery Company. Becoming interested in the Hawai'i sugar business, especially after the Reciprocity Treaty of 1875, Spreckels established the Hawaiian Commercial Company which became the largest sugar producer in the islands. In 1883, he founded his own steamship line that transported most of the cane to California for processing, and as a result, he controlled the price of most of the sugar industry in Hawai'i and California. He died in San Francisco on 26 December 1908.

STAINBACK, INGRAM MACKLIN (1883–1961). Appointed governor of the Territory of **Hawai'i** from 1942 until 1951, the longest term of any of Hawai'i's governors. Appointed in wartime, Stainback's major concerns were the defenses of the territory, promotion of its economy, and planning for its postwar normalcy. His "Work to

Win" campaign won popular support among the islands' citizens. Stainback died on 12 April 1961.

STAMPS. A lucrative source of income for smaller Pacific island nations, and the **Polynesian** islands contain a great diversity of stamps and postal history. The romance of the South Pacific draws thousands of individuals into collecting stamps from the region, and most of the Polynesian states have realized the potential of the philately business and the potential marketability of their stamps among collectors. **Pitcairn Island**, an island of 47 inhabitants, for example, earns $500,000 annually from its sale of stamps, and with the introduction of the **Internet**, several of the islands are advertising worldwide and benefiting from this new medium. **Tongan** stamps are the most unusual and sought after, but almost all of the other Polynesian states print colorful stamps each year. Several released special millennium stamps late in December 1999.

STEINBERGER, ALBERT BARNES (1840–1894). A **United States** "special agent" to **Sāmoa** from 1873 to 1876. Charged by President Ulysses S. Grant to collect information on the islands of Sāmoa for the government, Steinberger was sent to Sāmoa in 1873 where for several months he involved himself in the internal political disputes of the day. He returned to the United States with requests that the United States establish a protectorate over the islands and that he be appointed its governor. Steinberger then sailed to **Germany** where he negotiated with the Godeffroy and Son commercial enterprise regarding the exploitation of Sāmoan lands and labor to his own financial and political profit. Upon returning to Sāmoa, he immediately immersed himself in politics, rewrote the constitutions, and after having been appointed premier on 4 July 1875, he assumed almost absolute power in the islands. As such, he antagonized every important element of the foreign community—the **London Missionary Society** and both the American consul (S. S. Foster) and the British consul (S. F. Williams)—all of whom conspired to have him deported. Steinberger was arrested (1876) and two months later sent to Fiji. He continued to write letters back to Sāmoa in an attempt to influence politics. His petition for an indemnity from the British government failed. (Both the British and American consuls, however, were dismissed over the affair.) Steinberger never saw Sāmoa again. He died on 1 May 1894 in Massachusetts. *See also* AMERICAN SĀMOA.

STEVENSON, ROBERT LOUIS (1850–1894). A Scottish author, essayist, and writer, whose last years were spent in **Sāmoa** where he hoped to recover from his long bout with tuberculosis. After visiting the **Marquesas**, **Tahiti**, **Hawai'i**, and **Australia**, he finally settled permanently in Sāmoa where in 1899 he built a home at Vailima ("five waters") about three miles outside Āpia. His last years in Sāmoa were among his happiest and most productive. His *The Beach of Faleia* (1892), one of the best South Seas stories ever written, and his *Weir of Hermiston* (1896) were both written here. Stevenson died on 3 December 1894 and was buried on Mount Vaea, overlooking Āpia Bay.

STEWART, WILLIAM (1829–1873). An Irish entrepreneur who settled on **Tahiti** in 1864 to establish a cotton plantation at Atimaono. Local permission was granted to import nearly 3,000 Chinese laborers. At first the company was profitable because of the effects of the U.S. Civil War upon cotton prices. His company eventually went bankrupt in 1873. The Chinese settlement no longer stands, but Stewart's legacy is the industrious Chinese population that dominates the economic life of Tahiti today. *See also* FRENCH POLYNESIA.

SUNIA, TAUESE PITA, (1941–). Democratic governor of **American Sāmoa** as of 1997. Sunia was born on 29 August 1941 in the village of Fagatogo, American Sāmoa. His parents were ministers in the Congregational Christian Church. He graduated from Samoana High School (1960) and attended York College (Nebraska) and Ottawa College (Kansas) before receiving his bachelor's degree in political science with a teacher's certificate from the University of Nebraska. His graduate work later took him to the University of Hawai'i where he obtained a master's degree. He served in several administrative positions in the department of education and then as its deputy director (1972–1974). In 1974, he was appointed as the first vice president of the newly established American Sāmoa Community College and then as director of the department of education (1984–1988).

Sunia's political career began in 1992 when he ran successfully as lieutenant governor on the Democratic ticket with **A. P. Lutali**. He successfully ran for governor in November of 1996 and was sworn in on 3 January 1997. He received an honorary doctorate of humane letters from the Golden Gate University (San Francisco) during graduation ceremonies at American Sāmoa Community College in July of 1997. In the 2000 elections, the results were close, Sunia having received 50.7 percent of the votes. The election results were immediately contested by his opponent, Peter Reid, but the results were later upheld in court. Sunia is married to Fagaoali'i Satele, and they are the parents of 10 children.

SWAINS ISLAND. Also called Olosenga or Olohega, it is a privately owned coral atoll currently under the political administration of **American Sāmoa**. Swains Island comprises a landmass of only 2.6 sq km (1 sq mi) 338 km (210 mi) northwest of Tutuila, American Sāmoa. Geographically a part of **Tokelau**, the island was first inhabited by eastern Polynesians hundreds of years ago. The island was first visited by Pedro Fernandez de Quiros, a Spanish explorer, on 1 March 1606. It was not visited again until 1840 when Captain W. C. Swains, a **whaling** captain from New Bedford, Massachusetts, visited the island and believing he was the first outsider to visit, named the island after himself. In 1856, an American trader by the name of Eli Jennings claimed the island after having been "given" rights to it by the British naval administrator in **Sāmoa**. It has remained in the Jennings family ever since. From 1916 to 1925, Swains was part of the Gilbert and Ellice Islands group under British administration.

A dispute over inheritance in the early 1920s threw the case into both the courts in Sāmoa and American Sāmoa and then to the U.S. government in Washington D.C. On 4 March 1925, Secretary of State Charles Evan Hughes succeeded in having Congress adopt legislation which formally extended U.S. control to Swains Island and made it an administrative part of American Sāmoa which it has retained ever since. A formal treaty between **New Zealand** (administrator of Tokelau) and the **United States** was concluded in June of 1983 that recognized U.S. control over the island in return for the United States giving up claims to the atolls in Tokelau (Atafu, Nukunonu, and Fakaofu).

Some Tokelauans continue to maintain that the island belongs to them. In 1999, local leader Aliki Faipule Falimateao addressed the

United Nations decolonization committee regarding Tokelau's progress. During his speech, he caused some embarrassment when he pressed Tokelau's claims to the islands. He said that the island was theirs historically and that it was annexed unfairly by the United States in 1925.

SZASZY, MIRAKA RATARUHI PETRECEVICH (1921–). Teacher and long-time activist for **Māori women's** rights in **New Zealand**, honored in 1990 with the title "Dame." Dame Mira was one of the first Māori university graduates. After some postgraduate work in **Hawai'i**, she returned to New Zealand to begin her career working for the Māori Affairs Department. In 1951, she was a founding member of the Māori Women's Welfare League, an organization of which she later became secretary and president (1973–1977). Szaszy's active life includes being a social worker, a member of the Māori Education Foundation and the Race Relations Committee, senior lecturer in Māori Studies at the Auckland Teachers College, in the first women's delegation to Parliament seeking equal pay for equal work, and active in establishing Māori fishing rights and a Māori fishing industry. More recently her "radical views" included allowing women speaking rights on the traditional *marae*, and setting up the Māori women's secretariat of the Ministry of Women's Affairs. After the death of her husband, Albert Szaszy, she retired to Ngataki, but continues her outspoken views regarding her people's traditional rights.

- T -

TA'ATIRA POLYNESIA or **TA'ATIRA PORINETIA (*Union pour la Polynésie*).** A political party founded in 1977 in **French Polynesia**, currently headed by Arthur Chung and whose support comes chiefly from the Chinese population in the islands. The party usually aligns itself with the **Here 'Ai'ā party**.

TAHITI. An island located in the **Society Islands**, **French Polynesia**, currently administered as an overseas territory of **France**.

TAHITIAN ACADEMY. *See* FARE VANA'A.

TĀHŌ'ĒRA'A HUIRA'ATIRA ("Rally for the People") or its French designation—the *Rassemblement pour la République* (RPR). A moderately conservative political party in **French Polynesia**, founded in 1971, but with antecedents going back to the 1950s. It is currently the most popular political party, having gained 18 out of the 41 seats in the territorial assembly in the March 1991 elections. This proved to be a major comeback after having been ousted from power in December 1987. It gained even more in popularity in the 1996 elections, having won 22 assembly seats, and again 28 out of 49 seats in the May 2001 elections. Its platform advocates internal autonomy but with close ties to **France**, more economic independence for the islands, and the preservation and cultural identity of the Polynesians. Its current leader is **Gaston Flosse**, president of French Polynesia since 1991. *See also* 'ĀI'A 'ĀPI; FETIA 'ĀPI.

TAPA. A Polynesian cloth made from the inner bark of certain trees, anciently used for everyday wear, but today worn only for special occasions or used for decorative purposes. Each Polynesian island applied designs unique to its own culture and thus it is possible to recognize the country of origin of most tapa.

Tapa production is traditionally a time-consuming job done by the **women**. Strips of the inner bark of the mulberry, hibiscus, or **breadfruit** trees are soaked in water and then pounded with a grooved ironwood beater over a smooth wooden anvil until the strip widens to almost nine times the width it was when started. Next, the smooth side of the pounder is used to flatten out the cloth, and then it is hung up to dry. A glue is prepared (usually from the tapioca plant) and various pieces are glued cross-grained to add stability to the cloth. It is then decorated by using either a stencil, a wooden block, or by free hand with paints made from roots, berries, leaves, bark, or flowers. Because of the labor involved, tapa production has almost died out in the islands. Today, **Sāmoa** and **Tonga** are the only two major Polynesian producers of tapa.

TARINGA, RAUTUTI (1922–). Speaker of Parliament, **Cook Islands** government (1989–1996), he was born on 15 February 1922 on Rarotonga (Cook Islands), where he received (1937) the Pomare Medal for his meritorious work in school. He became a schoolteacher and then headmaster. After extensive travels in Europe, he returned to his former positions. Since 1967, Taringa has held numerous positions in the government including the chief community development officer and more recently the speaker of Parliament. His expert knowledge of the Cook Islands **Māori** language aided in the publication of a valuable *Cook Islands Māori Dictionary,* published by Cook Islands government and Australia National University in 1995. He is married to Tepaeru Tuaineiti, and they have seven children.

TARO (*Alocasia macrorrhiza, Colocasia esculenta*). A major food source among the Polynesians, one that comes in over 20 varieties. The plant originated in the Indo-Malayan peninsula, and the roots were carried to all the islands of the Pacific. Taro is cultivated from cuttings after which it is planted in various garden sites—from wet to dry—depending on the variety being grown. The tuberous plant usually matures in seven to 12 months, and its elongated, heart-shaped leaves average one to two feet in height while the underground tuber may be from a few inches to a few feet in length. Both the tuberous root (starch) and the tender young leaves (vegetable) are eaten in a variety of ways. The roots are usually baked, toasted over embers, or boiled; the leaves are oven-baked usually with pork (resembling cooked spinach) and seasoned with coconut milk. In **Hawai'i** and a few other islands, the boiled tubers are also pounded into a paste substance called *poi* and eaten with almost every meal. Anciently in some island groups, *poi* was stored underground where it fermented and was thus preserved in case of an impending famine. *See also* BREADFRUIT; COCONUT PALM.

TATI (ca. 1770–1854). A high chief from Papara, **Tahiti**, currently **French Polynesia**, whose authority rivaled that of the ruling **Pomare** family. When Pomare II died in 1824, custom would have transferred the ruling power to Tati, however, the Christian missionaries insisted that the young Pomare III be crowned king. During the religious crisis between the Protestants and **Catholics**, Tati supported **France's** intervention in the islands to prevent anarchy, and he signed the protectorate document in 1842. He later became president of the legislative assembly under Queen Pomare IV from 1848 to 1852. He was a brilliant orator, handsome in demeanor, and highly respected among his countrymen. When he died on 16 July 1854, his title of chief passed to his famous granddaughter **Ari'i Ta'ima'i**.

TATTOO. A highly sophisticated art form that had its origins in **ancient Polynesia** and was disseminated throughout the world. Tattoo (from the Tahitian *tatau*) had its origins in the ancient **Lapita** culture of Melanesia and Southeast Asia. An archeological find in 1998 shows a pottery figure of a human head decorated with tattoo. The figure is dated 1500 B.C. and is the oldest evidence of tattoo in the Pacific. These ancient Lapita explorers settled **Tonga** and **Samoa**, bringing the art form with them, and from here it spread to the rest of the Polynesian islands. Tattooing instruments consisted of a 12-to-18 inch tapper or baton and a six inch rod with several sharp toothed blades (whale bone) attached to its end. The tattooer held the blades over the skin and tapped lightly or as hard as needed to puncture the skin and deposit the prepared inks. The original designs were similar to those found in Lapita culture, but as the island groups separated themselves from one another, each developed its own forms and legends. Of all the Polynesians, the **Marquesans** tattooed their bodies more extensively than the others. The Christian missionaries forbade tattooing when they arrived in the islands in the 19th century, but not before the early European sailors saw the art form, and spread its popularity throughout the world. A renaissance of the art form began in Polynesia in the 1980s, and today many young people are imitating their ancestors and having the ancient forms stamped upon their bodies once again.

TĀUFA'ĀHAU, GEORGE (SIAOSI) TUPOU I (ca. 1797–1893). Considered the first king of modern **Tonga**, generally referred to simply as Tupou I. Originally chief of Lifuka and the 19th **Tu'i Kanokupolu**, Tupou became ruler of Ha'api and was one of the first Tongans to accept Christianity (1830). He allied with his friend, chief **'Ulukālala**, in expanding Christian influence and domination, and when 'Ulukālala died in 1833, he willed his territory to Tupou. By 1850, Tupou had through conquest become paramount ruler in all of the islands.

Tupou set about making Tonga a modern nation with the assistance of **Shirley Baker** who arrived in Tonga in 1860 and who had become Tupou's chief advisor. A revised law code of 1862 abolished the ancient customs of feudalism, land was forbidden to be sold to foreigners, an assembly of chiefs (*fakataha*) was established in 1862, and a modern constitution (modeled after the one in **Hawai'i**) promulgated in 1875. Finances were systematized, land laws implemented, and surprisingly Tonga was able to remain fairly independent despite attempts to make it part of a European empire.

When Tupou I died in February 1893, he was mourned for six months. He continues to be regarded as one of the greatest Tongans who ever lived. He had outlived his son and grandson, and it was his great-grandson who became King Tupou II.

TĀUFA'ĀHAU, TUPOU IV (1918–). King of **Tonga** since 1965, and the direct descendant of **King George Tupou I**, the founder of modern Tonga. Born on 4 July 1918, the eldest son of Queen Sālote Tupou III and her husband, Viliami Tungi, premier of Tonga, three of Tonga's ancient kingly lines became united in one upon his birth—the **Tu'i Tonga**, Tu'i Ha'atakalaua, and **Tu'i Kanokupolu**.

Tupou IV was educated at the Tupou College in Tonga (1927) and Sydney University in **Australia** where he gained his BA (1939) and LLB (1942) degrees and became the first Tongan to receive a university degree. He married the princess Mata'aho in 1947 in a double marriage ceremony with his brother. He was named premier of Tonga from 1949 to 1965 (until his mother's death), and then king. He was appointed first chancellor of the **University of the South Pacific** in Fiji (1970–1973) and honored with numerous citations and awards.

Modernization of Tonga has been his major concern since becoming king. Land scarcity, burgeoning of population, unemployment, inflation, dependence on foreign aid, and democratic movements within his kingdom are only a few of the problems facing him in his small island kingdom.

TAVINI HUIRA'ATIRA ("Serving the People"). A political party also known in French as the *Front de Libération de la Polynésie* (FLP). Founded in 1977, it is considered a radical political party in **French Polynesia**, currently headed by **Oscar Temaru**, the mayor of Fa'a'a (town west of Pape'ete), that advocates immediate independence from **France**, stopping of all future nuclear tests by France at the **Moruroa atoll**, the protection of traditional **Polynesian** culture, the use of **Tahitian** as the official language, moderation of **tourist** development, and the return of alienated land to the indigenous population (*mā'ohi*). Its rising popularity is indicated by the results of the recent elections. It gained two territorial assembly seats in the 1986 elections, four in the March 1991 elections, 11 in the 1996 elections, and 13 in the 2001 elections.

TE ATA-I-RANGIKAAHU (1931–). Current leader ("queen") of the **New Zealand Māori King Movement**. Born at Huntly, the daughter of **Koroki Te Wherowhero** and sixth in line of direct descent from Potatau I, she was educated at the Waikato Diocesan School in Hamilton and was crowned on 23 May 1966 to succeed her father. During her 35-year reign, she has been active in numerous political, social, and cultural organizations. A collection of speeches given during her reign was published in 1991. Respected and greatly loved, she continues to be active and currently lives at Turangawaewae, Ngaruawahia.

TE AU O TONGA*.** A 72-foot, double-hulled voyaging canoe, similar in design and purpose as the ***Hōkūle'a in **Hawai'i**, designed and built by Sir Tom Davis (former prime minister of the **Cook Islands**). The traditional design was taken from drawings of the canoe *Tepa'irua* in **Tahiti** as documented by **Captain James Cook** in his travels two hundred years ago. Since its construction in 1993, the *Te Au O Tonga* has sailed to Rā'iatea, Hawai'i, the **Marquesas**, the Society Islands (Tahiti), the **Tuamotus**, **Sāmoa**, **Tonga**, and **New Zealand**, covering some 35,000 nautical miles. The canoe is currently owned by the Cook Islands Voyaging Society. It played a prominent role in the America's Cup regatta on 15 October 1999 in Auckland, New Zealand.

TE 'AVEI'A MAU ("True Path or Guide"). A political party in **French Polynesia**, it broke off from **Jean Juventin's Here 'Āi'a party** in late 1994, and is currently headed by Tinomana Milou Ebb. The party favors a type of semi-independence from **France**, similar to the relationship between the **Cook Islands** and **New Zealand**, but it frequently allies with **Gaston Flosse**, the current president of French Polynesia. The party gains its support from the indigenous population (the *mā'ohi*), and in the 1996 elections, it gained one seat having won 5.3 percent of the votes cast.

TE ʻĒʻA NO MĀʻOHI NUI ("Voice of the Great Polynesian People"). Formerly known as Te ʻĒʻa ʻĀpi ("New Way"), it is a current political party in **French Polynesia** which advocates increased autonomy for the islands in an "associated state" with **France**. Its former leader, **Francis Sanford**, was the first vice president (essentially prime minister) of French Polynesia in 1977. The Te ʻĒʻa ʻĀpi gained only one seat in the May 1982 elections, and Sanford lost his position in the government. In August of 1985 the split came, headed by Daniel Millaud and Marius Raʻapoto, who continues to head the party. It won one seat in the 1986 elections and no seats in either the 1991 or 1996 elections.

TEMARU, OSCAR (1944–). Founder and president of the Tavini Huiraʻatira, a political party in **French Polynesia** that proposes independence from **France** and that vigorously opposed France's **nuclear testing** during the 1990s. Born on 1 November 1944 and reared in Faʻaʻa, **Tahiti**, Temaru has been the charismatic mayor of Faʻaʻa, a working class suburb just west of Papeʻete, since his first election in 1983. He also has been elected to the territorial assembly since 1986. In 1991, his party (known also by the French title *Front de Libération de la Polynésie*) gained 17 percent of the votes and four seats in the assembly. In the next elections in 1996, Tavini Huiraʻatira won 24.8 percent of the votes and garnered 11 seats in the assembly. He competed with his long-time opponent **Gaston Flosse** in the territorial assembly for the presidency but lost 28 to 11. A **Catholic**, Temaru is received well though by the Protestant majority in the islands. He has chosen the cross to symbolize his party, and "The Lord is My Master" as its motto. In adopting religious symbolism and values in his campaigns, Temaru follows closely in the footsteps of an earlier leader of French Polynesia, **Povanaʻa A Oʻopa**.

TE MOANA, CHARLES (ca. 1821–1863). High chief of the island of Nuku Hiva, **Marquesas**, currently in **French Polynesia**, who signed the annexation document on 31 May 1842 that transferred the islands to **France**. In his youth, he signed on as cook on an English **whaling** ship, and in each port the sailors would show him off for a few pennies a head. Herman Melville called him "Mowanna" and said that his **tattoos** resembled the sculpture around Trajan's columns in

Rome. He died in the great smallpox epidemic that raged through the islands and that carried off half of its population. His wife, **Queen Elisabeth Vahekehu**, survived him and was extremely influential among the islanders until her death in 1901.

TE PUEA HERANGI (1883–1952). One of the most influential **Māori** tribal leaders in contemporary **New Zealand** history. Born of chiefly status, she possessed a sharp intellect, remarkable fluency in her native language, and a determination to raise not only the quality of life among her people but also the pride in their Māori heritage. She established a model traditional village (the Turangawaewae Marae at Ngaruawahia) that gained national recognition. She sponsored better health programs in the 1930s and 1940s, and gained government funds for doing so by speaking out in public and by appealing to the traditions of her people. She made certain aspects of Western education acceptable to her people and as a result strengthened Māori values and institutions. In 1949, she proclaimed, "The language, history, crafts, and traditions of the Māoris should be an essential part of the curriculum throughout the country. . . . Unity of Māori and ***pākehā*** can only grow from each sharing the worthwhile elements in the other's culture."

TERAUPO'O, WAR OF (1880–1897). A war between chief Teraupo'o of the island Rā'iatea, **Society Islands**, **French Polynesia**, and **France** which resulted in the island's losing its independence and becoming part of France's overseas territory. In 1880, Teraupo'o and his followers refused to accept annexation by the French of **Tahiti** and its dependencies and refused to pay their taxes. Finally, in 1897, the French organized a military expedition under the leadership of Captain Boyle and forced the rebels into submission. Many were sent to a penal colony in New Caledonia or to the **Marquesas**. Teraupo'o eventually returned to Rā'iatea (1905) where he spent his last years.

TE TI'ARAMA ("The Torch"). A political party in **French Polynesia** which represented the center-right and which split from the *Rassemblement pour la République* (RPR) or the **Tāhō'ēra'a Huira'atira** party in 1987. It was headed by **Alexandre Léontieff**, former economic minister under **Gaston Flosse**, and president of French Polynesia from December of 1987 to March of 1991. The party, however, lost its control of the government in the March 1991 elections and ended its identity when Léontieff became the head of a new party, the Haere I Mua.

TE WHEROWHERO. Family name of the **Māori** "kings" of **New Zealand** and so designated by the **Māori King Movement** in the 1850s. The first designated with this title was Potatau Te Wherowhero (ca. 1800–1860) whose military prowess and prestige led to his selection in 1858 in ceremonies held at Ngaruawahia. Upon his death in 1860, his son Matutaera Te Pukepuke Te Paue Te Karato Te-a-Potatau Te Wherowhero (1825–1894) succeeded him and continued his father's policy of opposing further British encroachment upon their lands until peace was established in 1881. His second son Mahuta Tawhiao Putatau Te Wherowhero (1855–1912) was selected by the Kauhanganui (king Parliament) and became a member of **Prime Minister Richard Seddon's** Legislative Council in exchange for one million acres of land. Mahuta's eldest son, Te Rata Mahuta Tawhiao Putatau Te Wherowhero (1880–1933) succeeded him, traveled to England in 1914, and was generally in ill health, but well respected throughout the rest of his life. He was succeeded by his only son Koroki Mahuta Te Wherowhero (1909–1966) but with opposition from the popular **Princess Te Puea Herangi** (1884–1952), the eldest daughter of the second Māori king Tawhiao. The current leader of the movement is **Dame Te Ata-i-Rangikaahu** (1931–).

THOMAS, JOHN (1795–1881). Founder of the first permanent Wesleyan mission to **Tonga**. It was through his work (1826–1850 and 1855–1859) that most of Tonga became Christian. Thomas and his companion, John Hutchinson, arrived in Tonga in 1826. After three unsuccessful years of proselytizing and Hutchinson's departure because of ill health, Thomas moved to Nuku'alofa where he was instrumental in converting high chief **Tāufa'āhau** who soon united all of the Tongan islands and became its first king as George Tupou I. Conversion spread rapidly after this. Thomas left for England in 1850 only to return to Tonga for a four-year stay. Suffering from ill health, he and his wife returned to England in 1859. He died in Stourbridge on 29 January 1881.

THOMSON, BASIL HOME (1861–1939). British colonial administrator in Fiji, **Tonga**, and New Guinea between 1883 and 1893. In 1890, Thomson was sent to Tonga to reestablish peace and order after the dismissal of its illustrious prime minister, **Shirley Baker**. Thomson returned again to Tonga in 1900 to settle chaotic problems and to pressure King George Tupou I (see **Tāufa'āhau**) to sign a treaty that effectively established a British protectorate over the islands. His personal accounts of his work in the Pacific were published as *Diversions of a Prime Minister* (1894), *South Sea Yarns* (1894), and *The Fijians* (1908). After leaving the Pacific, he worked in London where he died on 26 March 1939.

THOMSON, ROBERT (1816–1851). Sent as a missionary of the **London Missionary Society (LMS)** to the South Pacific in 1839. At first he worked in the **Marquesas Islands**—currently part of **French Polynesia**—without success and then in **Tahiti** where he headed the French Protestant Mission after the establishment of the French protectorate in 1842. Illness forced his early retirement, and he died at sea on 1 January 1851. Thomson's two journals, *History of the Marquesas* and *History of Tahiti*, are both important historical documents.

THURSTON, LORRIN ANDREWS (1858–1931). A leading force in the overthrow of the **Hawaiian** monarchy in 1893 and in the annexation of the islands to the **United States**. Born in Honolulu in 1858 of a New England immigrant family, Thurston was educated at Punahou College (Honolulu) and Columbia University School of Law. He practiced law in the islands, owned the Halakala Ranch Company, and was elected to the Hawaiian legislature in 1886 and 1892. In 1887, Thurston joined a group of U.S. businessmen in their bloodless revolution against the king, a revolution that brought about a reduction in the king's power and the adoption of a new constitution.

When **Queen Lili'uokalani** succeeded to the throne in 1891, Thurston and the group were convinced that only through revolution and annexation to the United States could their economic interests, and subsequently Hawaiian interests, best be served. The revolution came when the queen attempted to replace the current constitution with one that would return more royal power to the throne.

Annexation to the United States did not come as expected, and as a result, a republican government under **President Sanford B. Dole** was established with Thurston as Hawaiian envoy to Washington. For the next several years, Thurston spent his energies convincing the U.S. government in Washington to annex the islands. After annexation in 1898, Thurston retired from office, became part owner of the *Honolulu Advertiser*, and assisted in writing and editing numerous Hawaiian legal documents. His book, *A Handbook on the Annexation of Hawaii* (1897) and his *Memoirs of the Hawaiian Revolution* (1936) provide first-hand accounts of the turbulent years of the transition from kingdom to republic to territory.

TOKELAU. An island territory of **New Zealand**, it comprises three atolls—Atafu, Nukunonu, and Fakaofo—with a total land area of 12.2 sq km (4.7 sq mi), lying 480 km (300 mi) north of Āpia, **Sāmoa**. The 1996 population of 1,507 (Atafu 449, Nukunonu 430, Fakaofo 578) consists of Polynesians, who speak Tokelauan (the official language) and English, and who are British subjects and New Zealand citizens. It is also estimated that 2,316 Tokelauans live in New Zealand, having emigrated there for employment. The majority (67 percent) of the islanders belong to the Congregational Christian Church, introduced by the **London Missionary Society** in the 19th century, while approximately 30 percent are **Roman Catholic**. (Atafu is primarily Congregational, Nukunonu Roman Catholic, and Fakaofo mixed.)

Economy: Because of limited topsoil on these small atolls, agriculture remains subsistence based. Food crops include coconuts, **breadfruit**, bananas, pulaka, and papaya. **Copra** was its main export crop until most of its trees were destroyed by cyclone Ofa in February 1990. A tuna cannery, opened in October 1990, generates some employment for the local workers. Sales of postage stamps and souvenir coins provide other income. New Zealand grants annual subsidies ($2.5 million in 1998) to balance Tokelau's annual deficits, and remittances from Tokelauans living in New Zealand provide additional revenues. There are no roads, vehicles, or harbor facilities on the atolls, and an inter-island ferry (begun late in 1991 and subsidized by New Zealand) is the only source of transport among the islands. (The islands have no airstrip.) A **United Nations** report in October 1989 listed Tokelau as one of the atoll groups that is threatened with being submerged under the ocean in the 21st century because of the rising sea level due to the greenhouse effect.

Ancient History: According to one tradition, the first two mortals on Tokelau were Kava and Pi'o who immigrated from Sāmoa, while many others maintain that both originated from the atoll itself—the first man from stone and the woman from earth or that both originated from maggots (similar to the Sāmoan creation stories). Tokelauan legends (*tala*) describe the wars among the atolls until Fakaofo subjected Nukunonu and exiled the inhabitants of Atafu. Having possession of the stone god Tui Tokelau, Fakaofo demanded tribute from the others, a political domination that lasted until 1918.

Modern history: In 1765, the British navigator John Byron of HMS *Dolphin* was the first known European to visit the atolls (Atafu) in his round-the-world voyage. Edward Edwards landed in 1791 while searching for the ***Bounty*** mutineers; he sighted Nukunonu a few days later. Fakaofo, the most populated atoll, was first sighted by U.S. Captain Smith of the whaler *General Jackson* in February 1835. Five years later when the U.S. Scientific Exploring Expedition visited the group, its ethnologist, Horatio Hale, was the first to make detailed notes regarding the atolls and their inhabitants. He recorded that between 500 and 600 people lived on Fakaofo, and approximately 120 on Atafu. By the 1850s, the Tokelauans had come into direct contact with Western civilization, and several of them had traveled abroad and returned with remarkable tales of exotic civilizations and religions from across the waters.

Protestantism was introduced into Atafu by Sāmoan teachers in 1861; Catholicism made its way into Nukunonu through contact with Catholics in 'Uvea (**Wallis Island**). Both groups saw their conversion in part as an escape from Fakaofoan domination. Fakaofo held out against the Christian religion until 1863 when its inhabitants allowed the Protestants onto the island.

Double tragedy struck that same year. **Blackbirders** from Peru visited the atoll and made off with approximately half of the population. Later that year, a dysentery epidemic broke out and carried away another quarter of the population—only 200 people survived. The political result was that Fakaofo never regained its political prominence over the other two atolls, although all three were linked by genealogical ties and cultural bonds that could not be forgotten. As **whalers**, **beachcombers**, and other Pacific islands people moved into the atolls, a racial mixture of the population resulted.

In 1877, **Great Britain** assumed a protectorate over her citizens in the group, and in 1889 Commander Oldham of the *Egeria* sailed through the atolls and declared a formal British protectorate. Called the Union Islands, they became part of the Gilbert and Ellice Islands Colony when Britain annexed them in 1916. The office of high chief (*aliki*) on each of the atolls (a position elected on Fakaofo and inherited on Nukunonu and Atafu) was abolished in the same year. Most significant during the Gilbert and Ellice Islands period was the establishment of effective medical services that greatly improved the health of the islanders.

Because of the vast distances between the administrative center of the Gilbert and Ellice group and the Tokelaus, administration of the atolls was transferred to the **New Zealand** government in 1925 which administered them from its office in Sāmoa. In 1948, with the Tokelau Act, full sovereignty was assumed by New Zealand. After Sāmoa became independent, supervision of the group was transferred to the Foreign Affairs Office in New Zealand but administered through its Office for Tokelau Affairs in Āpia, Sāmoa. On several separate occasions (1976, 1981, 1987, 1992, and again in 1994), Tokelau has reiterated its approval of the relationship between it and New Zealand. A visiting UN delegation to the islands in July and August of 1994 found that the islands were willing to assume more responsibility and to move toward greater internal self-government. As a result, a National Strategic Plan was adopted, the year 1995 was declared Tokelau's "Year of the Constitution," and an amendment bill was introduced into New Zealand's Parliament (19 December 1995, passed in May 1996) that acknowledged Tokelau's move to greater internal autonomy, an act that will eventually remove Tokelau from the UN's list of non-self-governing territories. The amendment gave the general *fono* (assembly) power to make laws, to impose taxes, and to declare public holidays, but it also gave veto power to the New Zealand administrator over the *fono's* decisions. The elections in January 1996 marked the beginning of a new era for the Tokelauans. Their island governments began to view themselves as a national state, and the *faipule* as not merely the elected head of an atoll, but representatives to a national government.

Telephone service was introduced in Tokelau in April 1997, and New Zealand purchased a Polish-built freighter to augment the island's irregular inter-island shipping service. In May, the MV *Forum Tokelau* made its first voyage to Tokelau from Āpia. The nation-building momentum continued into 1997 as a committee presented a draft constitution, written in Tokelauan, to the *fono.* But the movement toward any changes in Tokelau's future has been conservative with an aim to unite traditional culture and to stress continuity with the past rather than to be revolutionary. In fact, by the end of 1997, little local interest was being shown in a constitution when "there were money problems to deal with." Constitution discussions continue, however, in an attempt to create a state that wishes to keep its traditional values while at the same time introduces modern and Western democratic ideals to a small community of Pacific islanders.

Government: Executive, political, and judicial powers over the territory are held by three elected officials called *faipule*, one from each atoll. The three *faipule* chair sessions of the territorial assembly, an advisory body called the general *fono*, that consists of 15 delegates from each of the three atolls, elected every three years. Each atoll is an autonomous atoll community governed by the *faipule*, a *pulenuku* (atoll mayor), and a *taupulega* (an atoll council on Atafu, consisting of heads of every family group, or a council of elders on Nokunonu and Fakaofo). The current *faipules* (elected January 1999) are Kolouei O'Brien for Fakaofo, Pio Tuia for Nokunonu, and Kuresa Nasau for Atafu. New Zealand continues to be responsible for the territory's external relations. Changes in the exact make-up and relationship of these government bodies are expected over the next few years.

TOMA, MAIAVA IULAI (1940–). Political leader of **Sāmoa**, born on 5 July 1940, educated at the Marist Brothers School in Āpia, and at Victoria University in Wellington, **New Zealand**. Toma entered Sāmoan public service as a member of the prime minister's office in 1964. He was later appointed senior commissioner to the South Pacific Commission, now called the **Pacific Community** from 1973 to 1974, secretary to the government of Sāmoa from 1975 to 1977, and permanent representative to the **United Nations** and ambassador to the **United States** in 1977.

TONGA (*Pule'anga Fakatu'i 'o Tonga*, Kingdom of Tonga). A small independent kingdom located between 15° and 23° south latitude and 173° and 175° west longitude, consisting of 172 islands, totaling 748 sq km (289 sq mi), 36 of which are inhabited. The islands are divided into three main groups: Tongatapu, Vava'u, and Ha'apai, made up of both volcanic and coral islands. The population of 100,200 (2001 estimate; 97,784 in the 1996 census) is predominantly Polynesian, and the indigenous islanders are bilingual speaking Tongan and English (the language of administration and education). Tonga has a high literacy rate (99 percent) and the government plans to build its first national university by 2002. Over half of the population lives on the island of Tongatapu where the capital, Nuku'alofa (28,899 population), is situated. On 14 September 1999, Tonga was admitted as the 188th member of the **United Nations**.

Climate, Fauna, Flora: Due to its distance from the equator, Tonga enjoys a milder, more comfortable climate than many other South Pacific island states. Temperatures average during the winter (July to September) between 17°C and 22°C and during the summer (December to April) between 25°C and 33°C. Tonga lies within the cyclone-typhoon belt and has experienced severe devastations on numerous occasions. Annual rainfall is 150 cm (59 in.) at Nuku'alofa with Vava'u the wettest with up to 250 cm (98 in.) of rainfall annually. Although the flora and fauna are not extensive, Tonga has established several marine parks and sanctuaries to protect its more important species of birds and fish. The only land mammal native to Tonga is the flying bat. **Copra** and bananas are the two principal export items; coconut oil accounts for 50 percent of all of Tonga's exports. Vanilla and vegetables, such as ginger, watermelon, **taro**, and capsicum, are primarily shipped to **Australia** and **New Zealand**. Most Tongans engage in some sort of subsistence farming including taro, yams, and bananas.

Pre-European History: As part of the western-Polynesian group, Tongan history and culture are intrinsically tied to the neighboring islands states of Fiji and **Sāmoa**. Archaeological investigations indicate that Tonga was the first of the Polynesian islands to be settled, sometime around 1300 B.C. Not having a written language until the coming of the first Europeans in the 17th and 18th centuries, most of what is known of the early history comes through detailed mythologies and genealogies. Early Tonga developed an elaborate social system based upon sacred chiefs and a paramount ruler called the Tu'i Tonga (the King of Tonga). 'Aho'eitu, the first Tu'i Tonga, founded a dynasty in the 10th century that lasted until the death of Laufilitonga in 1865. The 11th Tu'i Tonga, Tuitātui (ca. 1200), allegedly built the famous stone trilithon (the Ha'amonga a Maui), and Talakaifaiki (ca. 1250) invaded and conquered Sāmoa. The 25th Tu'i Tonga, Kau'ulufonua Fekai (ca. 1470), divided the spiritual and temporal powers of the office. He retained the sacred part of the office and bestowed the temporal powers (*hau*) upon his brother Takalaua who became the Tu'i Ha'atakalaua. A third collateral line of kings was founded about 1610 when the sixth Tu'i Ha'atakalaua bestowed upon his younger brother Ngata the title of **Tu'i Kanokupolu**. Although inferior in rank, it was to become the most powerful. Civil war (1799–1852) ensued with the murder of the despotic Tu'i Kanokupolu, Tuku'aho, in 1799.

Modern History: The first Europeans to arrive in Tonga were the Dutch explorers Jacques Le Maire and W. C. Schouten (1616) and Abel Tasman (1643). **Captain James Cook** visited Tonga in the 1770s and recorded extensive information regarding Tongan society. **William Mariner**, a captive seaman, spent four years (1806–1810) in the islands as the adopted son of chief **Fīnau 'Ulukālala II** and left an excellent account as well (see bibliography). Numerous other European explorers visited the islands—Francisco Antonio Mourelle, a Spaniard in 1781; Jean-François Lapérouse, a Frenchman, in 1787; **William Bligh** and his abandoned crew in 1789; Edward Edwards, an Englishman, in 1791; and Alesandro Malaspina, a Spaniard in 1799.

The first Christian missionaries from the **London Missionary Society** arrived in 1797 in the midst of the raging civil wars, and the mission had to be abandoned in 1800. It was only with the coming of Wesleyan minister **William Lawry** in 1822 (for 16 months) and **John Thomas** and John Hutchinson in 1826 that Christianity gained a foothold among the Tongans.

Their success came with the conversion of the brilliant warrior-chief **Tāufa'āhau** in 1831. When his uncle died in 1845, he succeeded to the title of Tu'i Kanokupolu, and as a result, Christianity spread more rapidly. By 1852, Tāufa'āhau had successfully defeated his rivals and unified all of the islands under his authority. He ruled as King Siaosi (George) Tupou I until his death in 1893 at the age of 96.

His accomplishments in bringing Tonga into the modern world earned him the appellation, "The Maker of Modern Tonga." He established a law code (1850 and 1852), a constitution (1875), built schools, roads, and buildings, and signed treaties of friendship with **France** (1855), **Germany** (1876), **Great Britain** (1879), and the **United States** (1888) that guaranteed Tongan protection against aggressive European powers in the Pacific. Influential in the modernization of Tonga was Tupou's famous advisor and premier, the **Reverend Shirley Baker**, a Wesleyan missionary who arrived in the islands in 1860 and who was eventually deported in 1890 by the British because of the opposition to his interference in the Tongan courts.

A British official, **Basil Thomson**, was sent from Fiji to assist in straightening out Tongan affairs. In 1900, the king signed a Treaty of Friendship with Great Britain that gave the British consul in Tonga control over all of Tonga's external affairs. A modified treaty in 1905 gave the British consul in Tonga the right to approve or dismiss government officials, essentially bringing Tonga within the realm of the growing British empire.

King George II's turbulent reign (1893–1918) was followed by that of a remarkable woman, **Queen Sālote Tupou III**. If George Tupou I had united Tonga and created a powerful monarchy, it was Queen Sālote who made it beloved. Her 47 years of reign saw significant contributions made in education, health, agriculture, literature, and religion. An Education Act of 1927 and 1929 made education mandatory, and a teacher training college was established in 1944. A Central Medical School was established in Suva in 1929 to assist Tongan practitioners. She encouraged diversification of the economy which up to that time had depended primarily upon the production of copra. Her ability as a poet and her Tongan nationalism endeared her to the hearts of her subjects. Her pious determination led to the union of the Free Church of Tonga (proclaimed by George I in 1885) and the Wesleyan church in 1924.

In 1953, Queen Sālote attended the coronation of Queen Elizabeth II in London, and during her two months' visit charmed all those who saw and met her. In December of that year, Queen Elizabeth and her husband, the Duke of Edinburgh, paid a royal visit to the tiny kingdom in the Pacific. Sālote's able administration and insight contributed to the lessening of British control over the island's government. A new treaty was ratified between the two governments in 1959, and within five years after the death of the queen, in 1970, Tonga's protectorate status was lifted altogether by the British government. Since then, Tonga has been an independent kingdom within the **Commonwealth.**

When Queen Sālote died in December 1965, her son, Prince Tungi, acceded to the throne as **King Tāufa'āhau Tupou IV**, and his brother **Prince Tu'ipelekake** became premier. Many of the achievements of Tonga since then have been a result of the progressive nature of its king. He became the first Tongan to receive a university degree (BA 1939 and LLB 1942, Sydney University). Upon returning to Tonga, he established the Tonga High School, provided scholarships for Tongans to study abroad, opened a Teachers Training College (1944), and in 1969, became the first chancellor of the newly established **University of the South Pacific** in Suva, Fiji. To provide stability and prosperity to a small island nation thrust into 20th century technology, he established the Tonga Electric Power Board, the Tonga Water Board, the Tonga Construction Company, and the Tonga Shipping Company. He built the Dateline Hotel, a new wharf, a new hospital, and the Friendly Islands Airways to promote **tourism** within his country. In 1976, Tonga attracted the attention of her neighbors as well as the United States by establishing diplomatic relations with the Soviet Union. In October 1986, Tonga signed a five-year fishing agreement with the United States that allowed the U.S. tuna fleet license to fish within Tonga's exclusive fishing zone. Then, in July 1988, a friendship treaty between Tonga and the United States provided for the safe transit of U.S. nuclear-capable ships within Tongan waters, making Tonga one of the few members of the **South Pacific Forum** not to agree to the **South Pacific Nuclear Free Zone Treaty**.

The most significant political development in Tonga over the past decade has been the rise of the pro-democracy movement. The Tongan constitution provides for a government consisting of the sovereign, a privy council (the sovereign and cabinet members), a cabinet (the prime minister, deputy prime minister, and eight other ministers plus the governors of Ha'apai and Vava'u), and a legislative assembly (the king, cabinet members, nine hereditary nobles elected by the 33 nobles of Tonga, and nine commoner representatives elected by universal adult suffrage).

In the late 1980s, many Tongans began to express criticism of this conservative governmental structure and the absolute authority of its king. In September 1989, the nine commoner representatives boycotted the legislative assembly meeting, and a motion was tabled that would have involved increasing commoner representation from nine to 15 and reducing nobility representation from nine to three. The king opposed such democratic moves, having argued that his royal-dominated government could react more quickly to the needs of Tonga and its people than a democratically controlled one.

In 1991, a controversy between the new movement and the government arose over the sale of Tongan passports to foreigners (primarily to Chinese). In March, members of the group protested against the government and petitioned the king to invalidate the 426 passports in question (including those of the Marcos family of the Philippines). Tonga's outspoken pro-democracy member of the legislative assembly, **'Akilisi Pohiva**, initiated court action that began the controversy. He claimed to have positive evidence of further misuse of public funds, gross incompetence, and stark corruption. (The government only stopped the sales of passports in December 1998 after having made $40 million.)

By August of 1992, enough interest in changing the government had been generated that a group met to form Tonga's first political party—the Tonga Democratic Party (then called the People's Party). Its principal founders were 'Akilisi Pohiva, Viliami Fukofuka, Father Seluini 'Akau'ola, and Futa Helu, and its broad aims were to establish a constitutional monarchy and to educate the public as to what democracy was. A general convention on the constitution was held in November, but the government boycotted the sessions and forbade foreign visitors' entrance into the kingdom to participate. Despite government opposition, the pro-democracy party won six of the nine commoner seats in the legislative assembly in the February 1993 elections.

Disagreements among the leaders of the fledgling pro-democracy movement between 1993 and 1996 prevented a united front in its opposition to the government. Nevertheless, the party retained its six seats in the 1996 election, and Pohiva was elected for his fifth consecutive term, winning 64 percent of the popular vote in his district.

In 1996, the *Tonga Times* editor and staff clashed with the government in two legal battles over freedom of the press. In March, the *Times* criticized the minister of police, whereupon he arrested and imprisoned its editor and three journalists. Later that year, the *Times* released a notice of the impending impeachment by the legislative assembly of the minister of justice for misuse of per diem funds. Again the editor, deputy editor, and Pohiva were arrested and imprisoned for contempt of Parliament. They spent 26 of the 30 days in prison until a judge declared the arrest unconstitutional and illegal and ordered their immediate release. Fearing further possible embarrassment to the government in the pending impeachment investigations, the king ordered an early closure of Parliament. The issue continued through 1997 while the international media brought world attention to the government-newspaper battle. (As late as March 2000, the U.S. State Department's annual human rights report criticized Tonga for its censure of speech and the press.)

In April 1998 a conflict broke out in the assembly between the Minister of Lands Fakafanua and the Minister of Police Clive Edwards over Edwards' disregard for Tonga's environmental laws. Enraged, Edwards arrested the minister along with his secretary and other personnel on corruption charges. Tongans were dismayed and shocked over the incident, and the minister resigned his position in the government.

In September of 1998, a petition signed by more than a thousand people called for the removal of the Speaker of the Assembly Eseta Fusiu'a for misuse of public funds. In this case, the king supported the petition and initiated an investigation that found Fusiu'a guilty. As a result, a bill was passed that required cabinet member appointments to be approved by the assembly, an action heretofore reserved for the king and an action that now makes cabinet members' behavior subject to legislative scrutiny.

In the March 1999 elections, the pro-democracy party (since April of 1998 called the Human Rights and Democracy Movement) garnered only five of the nine peoples seats in the legislature. Pohiva retained his seat but with less of a margin than in 1996. The four other people's candidates are active businessmen, highly respected by the community, and who hold varying opinions regarding Tonga's future. The conservatives believe in making no changes to the existing political structure; others believe that if changes come about they must be initiated by the king; and yet others say that no changes are likely during the lifetime of the current king.

A major readjustment of duties among the royal family was required twice—once in 1998 and again in 2000. On 4 May 1998, Crown Prince Tupouto'a (age 50) resigned as minister of foreign affairs and defense in order to pursue his personal business affairs. He has often been heard to express his disinterest in becoming king, and his disparaging comments regarding Tongan customs are well known. In January 2001, for example, he remarked that Tongans were "heathens who leave their pig trappings everywhere." Another high-ranking readjustment was needed when Baron Vaea resigned as prime minister. The king accepted his resignation on 3 January 2000, although Vaea had submitted it in 1995. The king appointed his youngest son, **'Ulukalala Lavaka Ata**, 41 years old, as prime minister, and by tradition the appointment is for life. Ata had had only one year experience in government as minister of foreign affairs, having replaced his brother in 1998. His opposition to the pro-democracy movement is predictable, and it is expected that future clashes between these conflicting forces will most likely bring about major changes in the governmental structure of Tonga.

Economy: An annual per capita income of $1,574 (1999) ranks Tonga as one of the poorer nations of the world (placing it 128 out of 191), but at the same time, the quality of life is high, which includes a strong sense of community and national identity. Agriculture, forestry, and fishing accounts for 36 percent of Tonga's gross national product, and these industries employ 39 percent of the workforce. Squash pumpkin, Tonga's major export (primarily to **Japan**), earns between $10 and $15 million a year. Other exports are **coconuts**, bananas, vanilla, vegetables, manufactured goods (handicrafts), and machinery. New Zealand and Australia are Tonga's two principal trading partners. Tonga's fishing exports declined over the last half of the decade because of the ban against harvesting sea cucumbers. In March 2000, however, Tonga opened its **exclusive economic zone** for the first time to foreign fishing, and its licenses to Korean vessels will net approximately $64,000 per year. **Tourism** has been slow in developing (approximately 27,000 tourists annually), but it does provide from 8 to 10 percent of Tonga's gross national product. The trade deficit (imports running 10 times more than exports) is high, but it is offset by income from remittances (estimated to be about $2 million annually) from Tongans working overseas in Australia, New Zealand, and the United States. Tonga's economy is also augmented by grants from foreign Pacific nations—Australia, New Zealand, and Japan. Tonga's recognition of China in 1998 may lead to a substantial increase in trade between those two countries. Tonga continues to seek alternative money-making opportunities and to diversify its economy—for example, selling of Tongan passports to foreigners, building and renting a six-story office building in New York City, leasing of land in Hawai'i for growing sweet potatoes, investing in a farmers' market in **American Sāmoa**, and building an office complex and warehouse in **Sāmoa**. The national budget for the fiscal year 2000–2001 amounted to $74.9 million, 44 percent of which comes from taxes.

TOURISM. One of the major contributors to the gross domestic product of **Polynesia** and an economic activity that has more than doubled in the last part of the 20th century. Some forms of tourism date back to antiquity when islanders traveled from one island group to another for adventure and curiosity—and many stayed as immigrants to the new islands. In the 18th and 19th centuries, European explorers, **beachcombers**, and missionaries all contributed to the romantic myth of the South Seas. The modern tourist, however, came only with the 20th century and the development of a larger number of affluent foreigners who were interested in the exotic and far away. As a result, the last half of the 20th century witnessed an unprecedented record of world travelers as shown in the following chart:

Selected States	1980	1990	1999
American Samoa	n/a	26,000	21,000
Cook Islands	476,660	933,400	1,620,000
Easter Island	n/a	4,961	21,434
French Polynesia	114,000	132,000	210,800
Hawai'i	4,300,000	6,900,000	6,800,000
Niue	n/a	1,668	1,778
Sāmoa	32,000	55,000	85,124
Tonga	15,000	24,400	30,883
Tuvalu	n/a	862	770

The top four countries that provide tourism to Polynesia are **Australia** (23 percent), the **United States** (16 percent), **New Zealand** (15 percent), and **Japan** (9 percent).

All of the islands have tourist potential, but several constraints hinder major developments in some. The cost of air transportation, poor tourist infrastructure (accommodations and recreational facilities), and the high cost of promotion hinder further development in the less accessible island groups.

Many island governments wrestle with the pros and cons of tourism development primarily because they do not want their islands and cultures to become bastardized as so often happens when droves of foreigners come to the islands and destroy what they have come to see. Waikīkī and **Hawai'i** are frequently cited as examples of what they do not want to happen to their islands. But tourism is an inevitable fact in Polynesia, and the tourist will continue to seek that exotic South Sea paradise so often written about in tour and guide books.

TOURISM COUNCIL OF THE SOUTH PACIFIC (TCSP). Changed its name to the **South Pacific Tourism Organization** in October 1999.

TRASK, MILILANI. Lawyer and activist for Hawaiian rights, was educated at the Kamehameha (school for Hawaiians only) in Honolulu, **Hawai'i**, and then received a degree in political science from San Jose State University (California) and a law degree from the University of Santa Clara (California). Returning to Hawai'i in 1978, she became an activist in Hawaiian affairs being responsible for the establishment and growth of the **Ka Lāhui Hawai'i**, a Hawaiian native organization formed in 1987 to bring about self-governance for the native Hawaiian people. She currently holds the elected position of *Kia 'Aina* (governor) in that organization. In 1998, she was popularly elected as trustee at large on the state board of the Office of Hawaiian Affairs, but narrowly lost in 2000. *See also* SALAZAR, HELENA KALOKUKAMAILE 'ELUA.

TUAMOTU-GAMBIER ARCHIPELAGO. Also called the Paumotu Archipelago, it is one of the five island groups that make up **French Polynesia**. The Tuamotus consist of one large coral island Makatea and 75 smaller atolls or low islands scattered 240 km (92 mi) east and southeast of **Tahiti**, and the Gambiers include Mangareva and 22 outlying atolls. The total landmass measures 922 sq km (356 sq mi). Because of the treacherous nature of their reefs, they were nicknamed "the Dangerous Islands." The limited arable land cannot support a wide range of plant life but does grow **coconut palms**, pandanus, and **breadfruit** trees. The 1996 census lists 15,370 individuals living in the islands or 7 percent of all of French Polynesia. The history of the Tuamotus is closely connected with that of its neighbor island, Tahiti, since the ruling **Pomare family** claimed both island chains.

Resources and Economy: Pearls and pearl shells used for buttons and ornaments still remain a major economic resource for the islands, but recently commercial fishing and **tourism** have surpassed that industry. The phosphate deposits on Makatea were exhausted by 1966. Rangiroa has become the vacation paradise for many Tahitians and foreigners alike who seek the solitude of a South Pacific vacation. **France's** nuclear test site is located on **Mururoa atoll** in the southeastern end of the chain. During the last decade, the French military and government organizations have provided a major income for service personnel in this area.

TUI A'ANA AND TUI ATUA. The two highest ranking political titles in **Sāmoa**. Tradition maintains that they were anciently awarded by the demigod Pili to his two sons, the first of whom inherited west 'Upolu (*Tui Atua*, king of Atua) while the second inherited east 'Upolu (*Tui A'ana*, king of A'ana). The central part fell to *Tuamasaga*, the third major title on 'Upolu. The titles carried with them the traditional rights and privileges including sacredness of person, food, and belongings. The titles were not hereditary, but were conferred on candidates by senior talking-chiefs from members of the royal family of Tupua (with the titles *Tamasese*, *Matā'afa*, or *Tuimaleali'ifano*).

The incessant civil wars of the late 19th century were primarily over the ownership of these titles. During German control of the islands (1900–1914), many of the titles were declared defunct, but upon independence (1962) the two titles *Tui A'ana* and *Tui Atua* were revived once again. **Tupuola Efi**, eldest son of Tupua Tamasese Mea'ole and prime minister from 1976 to 1982, was elected to the title *Tui A'ana*, and **Tupa Tamasese Lealofi IV** was elected *Tui Atua*. *See also* MĀLIETOA; TUI MANU'A.

TU'I KANOKUPOLU. Tongan title that had its origins perhaps in the late 15th century, when it became necessary to send a representative of the ruler in eastern Tongatapu, the Tu'i Ha'atakalaua, to Hihifo in the west to quiet factious groups there. Because of the difficult area and the exploits rendered by the various rulers, the title grew in prestige and power. The 19th holder of the title, **Tāfa'āhau Tupou**, succeeded to the title in 1845, extended his sovereignty over all of **Tonga**, and crowned himself king. As a result, the power and prestige of the title became greater than ever before. Since then, all rulers of Tonga have held the title. *See also* TĀUFA'ĀHAU, GEORGE SIAOSI TUPOU I.

TUI MANU'A. Anciently the highest ranking chiefly title in all of **Sāmoa**, having been first established by the god Tagaloa on the islet of Ta'ū in the Manu'a group (eastern Sāmoa). During subsequent years, the Tui Manu'a lost its political influence primarily because the rest of the islands were separated through **Tongan** conquest (ca. A.D. 1200) and because of the rivalries on the island of 'Upolu for control of the three political titles there. In 1905, the Tui Manu'a Eliasara signed the act of cession that brought the eastern islands of Sāmoa under **United States** control. Since the "royal" title does not harmonize with the United States constitution, the title currently remains vacant. *See also* AMERICAN SĀMOA; TUI A'ANA AND TUI ATUA.

TUILA'EPA, MALILELEGAOI SA'ILELE (1945–). Prime minister of **Samoa** since 1998. Born on 14 April 1945, Tuila'epa was educated by the Marist brothers at Mulivai and later at St. Joseph's College at Lotopa. He studied in **New Zealand** under a scholarship at Auckland University and was the first Sāmoan to graduate with a master's degree in accounting and economics. He returned to Sāmoa in 1970 where he worked with the treasury department, becoming director of the economics department, then deputy financial secretary from 1973 to 1977. He and his family moved to Brussels (Belgium) in 1978 where he worked in the general secretariat of the European Economic Community until 1980. He entered the Sāmoan Parliament in 1981 and held the portfolios of minister of economic affairs (1982–1983) and of finance (1984–). Following the resignation of Prime Minister **Tofilau Eti Alesana** (due to illness), Tuila'epa, being deputy prime minister, became prime minister as well as head of his party, the **Human Rights Protection Party**.

TU'IPELEHAKE, FATAFEHI (1922–1999). Prime minister of **Tonga** from 1965 to 1991 and a member of the royal family. Born second son of **Queen Sālote Tupou III** on 7 January 1922 and the only brother to the current king, **Tāufa'āhau Tupou IV**, he was educated at Newington College in Sydney and Gatton Agricultural College in Queensland, **Australia**. He married Princess Melenaite Tupoumoheofo in 1947 in a dual marriage ceremony with his brother. He was appointed governor of Vava'u between 1952 and 1965, later held numerous ministerial posts as governor of Ha'apai and minister of lands, and became prime minister in 1965, a position he held until his retirement in August 1991. He was succeeded by his cousin, **Baron Vaea of Houma**. He died on 10 April 1999 in Auckland, New Zealand, after a long illness.

TUITA, SIOSAIA ALEAMOTU'A LAUFILITONGA (1920–). Political leader in **Tonga**. Born on 29 August 1920 at Lapaha, Tongatapu, he was educated at Tupou College, Wesley College in Auckland, **New Zealand**, and Oxford in England. He held numerous positions in the government—governor of Vava'u, assumed the title of Tuita in 1972, became deputy prime minister in 1974, acting prime minister in 1981, a member of the king's cabinet and Privy Council, and member of Parliament. Tuita is married to Fatafehi Lapala Tupou, and they have four children.

TU'I TONGA, "ruler of Tonga." A title believed to have descended from the god Tagaloa 'Eitumatupu'a through his son, 'Aho'eitu, and a mortal woman about A.D. 950. In early times, the holder of the title was sacred and whatever he touched or ate became *tapu* (taboo) to all others. 'Aho'eitu established several other chiefly lines to wait upon the Tu'i Tonga, and all Tongan chiefly lines today claim descent from the three that have survived (the Tu'i Tonga, Tu'i Palehake, and Kauhala'uta).

TUKI, LUCIA (1940–). First female elected mayor of Hangaroa, **Easter Island**. An Easter Islander by birth, Lucia Tuki comes from a large family of noble (*ariki*) descent. In 1961, she became the first **Rapanui** schoolteacher on the island with professional training, a position she held until her election in 1988 as Hangaroa's first female mayor, and the seventh mayor (all Rapanui) since elections began for the position in 1966. She ran unsuccessfully for mayor again in November 2000 losing to the incumbent mayor Petero Edmunds. She currently serves as librarian at the local school.

TUKINO, HEPI TE HEUHEU (1919–1997). The seventh paramount **Māori** chief of the Ngāti Tūwharetoa tribe and one of the most revered leaders in modern **New Zealand**. Born in Wellington, he worked as a farmer until his father's death in 1944. At that time he succeeded him, and gave over a half century of firm and successful economic leadership to his tribe. He supported Māori autonomy, was instrumental in forming the Federation of Māori Authorities, led discussions with the government regarding Māori affairs, and helped form the National Māori Congress in 1989. He was knighted in 1979. He died on 31 July 1997.

TULAFONO, TOGIOLA T. A. Lieutenant governor **of American Sāmoa** since 1996. Born on 28 February 1947 on Aunu'u Island, American Sāmoa, Tulafono graduated from American Samoana High School in 1966 and received a bachelor's degree from Chadron State College (Nebraska) in 1970. He served as a legal assistant in the attorney general's office (1970) and as an administrative assistant to the secretary of Sāmoan affairs (1970–1972). He received his law degree from Washburn University (Topeka, Kansas) in 1975 after which he returned to American Sāmoa where he practiced law (1975–1977). Tulafono was appointed a district court judge from 1980 to 1996 when he successfully ran for lieutenant governor of American Sāmoa on the Democratic ticket with Tauese P. Sunia as governor. He and Governor Sunia were both reelected in November 2000. Tulafono is married to Mary Mauga, and they have six children.

TUNGI, WILLIAM TUPOULAHI (1887–1941). High chief of **Tonga**. A direct descendant of the chiefly title Tu'i Ha'atakalaua, second to the royal throne, and father of the current king **Tāufa'āhau Tupou IV**. Born on 1 November 1887, Tungi was educated at Tupou College and Newington College in Sydney. He married **Sālote Mafile'o**, heir to the Tongan throne on 19 September 1917, and was her consort throughout her reign until his death. He was premier of Tonga and in later years minister of foreign affairs, public works, education, health, and agriculture. He died on 20 July 1941, highly beloved by his subjects, who referred to him as *koe tangata alafua*—"a man of many parts."

TUPAI'A (?–1770). A high priest from the island of Rā'iatea, currently **French Polynesia**, who met **Captain James Cook** in **Tahiti** in 1769 and who, because of his linguistic and extensive seafaring expertise, accompanied Cook in his explorations. He acted as Cook's navigator and named over 130 islands, many of which found their way onto the maps of the Pacific which Cook brought back. In **New Zealand**, the **Māoris** especially reverenced him because of his extensive knowledge of island mythology. He died in November 1770 in Batavia (Jakarta) where Cook's ships were undergoing repair.

TUPU'O SĀMOA, "Ruler of Sāmoa." Traditionally referred to the individual (king or queen) who gained the four royal titles of **Sāmoa** (collectively called the *Tafa'ifā*—the *Tui A'ana, Tui Atua, Ngatoaitele*, and *Tamasoali'i*). The first to hold the title of *Tupu'o Sāmoa* was Queen Salamasina (ca. A.D. 1500). Control over this and other titles in Sāmoa led to the wars of the 19th century that subsequently resulted in the islands being partitioned between **Germany** and the **United States**. When Germany gained control over Sāmoa in 1900, the title *Tupu'o Sāmoa* was conferred upon the German emperor in Berlin and has never been used in Sāmoa since. *See also* AMERICAN SĀMOA; TUI A'ANA AND TUI ATUA; TUI MANU'A.

TUVALU. Formerly known as the Ellice Islands (1916–1975) but since 1978 an independent state within the **Commonwealth**, Tuvalu consists of nine small islands and atolls—Funafuti, Nanumaga, Nanumea, Niulakita, Niutao, Nui, Nukufetau, Nukulaelae, and Vaitupu—extending some 560 km (350 mi) from north to south with a total land area of only 26 sq km (10 sq mi). It ranks second to Vatican City as the world's smallest nation in population and the fourth smallest in area (after Vatican City, Monaco, and Nauru). Tuvalu is located between 5° and 10° south latitude and 176° and 179° east longitude in the Pacific Ocean. Its nearest neighbors are Fiji to the south, Kiribati to the north, and Solomon Islands to the west. Tuvalu's 10,114 inhabitants (est. 1999) speak Tuvaluan, a Polynesian language related to Sāmoan, and English. Ninety-eight percent belong to the Protestant Church of Tuvalu (Ekalesia Tuvalu), a congregational descendent of the **London Missionary Society's** activities in the 19th century. The capital and administrative center, Fongafale, is located on Funafuti atoll. Nearly half of the population lives on Funafuti, making it one of the most densely populated atolls in the Pacific. Ninety-five percent of the population is literate, but with only 6 percent having a secondary school (age 12–18) education.

Pre-European History: Traditions claim that these small coral atolls were first settled by Polynesians from **Sāmoa**. The inhabitants of Nanumea maintain that their first inhabitant, Tefaola'a, first landed alone on the island, but he then returned to Sāmoa to obtain a wife and to bring back others with him. From time to time, Tongans and Micronesians may also have drifted to the islands and intermingled with the inhabitants.

Modern History: Nui and Niulakita were first sighted by the Spanish explorer Alvaro de Mendaña in 1568 and 1595, but like many of the other Polynesian outliers, they were not visited again for over two centuries. The name Ellice comes from Edward Ellice, owner of the British ship *Rebecca* whose captain, Arent de Peyster, visited Funafuti in 1819 and named it after his patron. The name later became synonymous with the whole group through the work of the English hydrographer A. G.

Findlay. The islands were visited by **whalers** and **beachcombers** in the early 19th century, and in the early 1860s **blackbirders** carried off approximately 400 islanders to work in the plantations and mines of Peru. None ever returned home.

Christianity was first introduced in 1861 from **London Missionary Society** missionaries adrift from the **Cook Islands**. Serious conversion began in 1865 through the efforts of the Reverend A. W. Murray and his Sāmoan missionaries. They established churches and schools while simultaneously suppressing all aspects of traditional culture. During the last half of the 19th century, the islands remained somewhat isolated from the mainstream of capitalistic exploitation that dominated the rest of the Pacific basin. Small amounts of **copra** were produced, however, and a few Europeans settled on the islands to supervise the activity.

In September 1892, British Captain H. W. S. Gibson of HMS *Curaçoa* arrived and declared a British protectorate over all nine of the Ellice Islands primarily to prevent **France** from doing the same. They were administratively joined with the Gilbert Islands which **Great Britain** had annexed the previous month. In 1916, the British government annexed the protectorate and renamed it the Gilbert and Ellice Islands Colony (GEIC).

Beginning in 1956, several advisory and legislative bodies worked to prepare the GEIC for self-government and division between the two island groups. In 1963 an advisory council was established, and in 1967, a written constitution provided for elections for a 23-member house of representatives (seven were appointed) now advisory to a governing council consisting of five elected and five appointed delegates. Friction soon became apparent when Ellice Islanders wished more representation in the government than they had been allotted.

A new constitution in 1974 provided for a ministerial government and later that year (August/September) a referendum (92 percent) showed that the Ellice Islanders wished separation. On 1 October 1975, the Ellice Islands declared their separation from the GEIC, adopted a new name—Tuvalu ("eight standing alone")—and became a British dependency. (The remaining Gilbert Islands became independent in July 1979 under the name Kiribati.)

Elections were held for a new legislative assembly, and Toaripi Lauti, an important official in the Burns Philip Corporation on **Nauru**, became Tuvalu's first chief minister with Taui Finikaso and Tomu Sione as the two other ministers. Disagreements between the islands and the British government regarding budgetary funds plagued the new relationship, but internal self-government (April 1978) led to independence (but retaining a special membership in the **Commonwealth**) on 1 October 1978. Lauti became Tuvalu's first prime minister until 1981 (later in 1990, he was appointed Tuvalu's governor-general). Lauti lost in the September 1981 parliamentary election for prime minister to Dr. Tomasi Puapua, a medical doctor who had retired from medical service to take up a political career. Lauti's defeat resulted from a bad investment in 1979 to a California real estate dealer, Sidney Gross. The purchased parcels were found to be only barren desert land, but by 1984 the money had been returned to the lenders in Tuvalu.

The 10-year anniversary of Tuvalu's independence was held in 1988 amid jubilant celebrations and speeches in which the growth and progress of Tuvalu were extolled. Tuvalu was now an integral part of the **South Pacific Forum** and its **Forum Fisheries Agency**. It has admirably sponsored dance and singing groups to the **Festival of South Pacific Arts** in 1985 and 1988, and could also boast (because of its improved private ventures and the established government trust fund) of an improved economy and standard of living.

The 1989 elections brought a change in the government when **Bikenibeu Paeniu**, a relative newcomer to politics, entered the race, won his seat in Parliament, and was subsequently elected Tuvalu's new prime minister. The same elections in 1989, saw Tuvalu elect its first woman representative to Parliament, **Naama Latasi** of Nanumea. She was subsequently appointed minister for health, education, and community service.

Politics during the decade of the 1990s was dominated by two prime ministers—Bikenibeu Paeniu (1989–1993 and 1996–1999) and Kamuta Latasi (1993–1996). During the early 1990s, the relationship with Great Britain became strained. First, Tuvalu maintained that Great Britain had not properly prepared the country economically for independence in 1978 and that it had not compensated Tuvalu for the damage done to the island during World War II. A motion to establish Tuvalu as a republic in 1992, however, failed with only one member of Parliament voting to support the motion. That strained relationship continued to be precarious, however, and in 1995 the government voted to remove the British Union flag from the Tuvaluan flag. A new flag was designed and raised over the islands. It is reported, however, that when the new flag was first raised on Niutao atoll, the people promptly chopped down the flagpole. In late 1996, Paeniu became prime minister again, restored the original flag, and halted all efforts to move the country to a republic. Paeniu also proposed new constitutional reform bills—a code of conduct for political leaders and the establishment of an ombudsman's office. The 1998 elections became heated. Sexual misconduct was levied at Paeniu while at the same time former prime minister Latasi was accused of taking bribes from an Italian businessman. Paeniu was forced to resign on 13 April 1999, and **Ionatana Ionatana**, former minister of health, education, culture, and **women's** affairs, became the new prime minister and selected a new cabinet.

Ionatana's government assisted in transferring needed funds to Tuvalu's outer islands, in expanding health facilities, and in increasing funds to education, new housing upgrades, and new government buildings. On 11 January 2000, Tuvalu applied for membership to the **United Nations**. It became the 189th member on 18 February. On 1 September 2000, Tuvalu became a full member of the **Commonwealth**. Ionatana died unexpectedly from a cardiac arrest after having given a speech at an Air Fiji Christmas party in Funafuti on 8 December 2000. His deputy prime minister Lagitupu Tuilimua became acting head of the government. On 22 February 2001, Faimalaga Luka, a former civil servant from Nukufetau atoll, was elected Tuvalu's new prime minister.

Government: Tuvalu's 1978 Independence Constitution provides for a Westminster-style parliamentary democracy with the British monarch as head of state and represented locally by a governor-general who must be a Tuvaluan citizen, through a 12-member unicameral Parliament elected directly by its citizens (over age 18) for a four-year term. The cabinet consists of the prime minister, the head of the government, and up to four other ministers. Tuvalu has no political parties. The constitution provides protection of all fundamental rights and freedoms and for the determination of citizenship.

Economy: In 1987, Tuvalu was placed on the United Nations' list of least developed countries (at its own request) in order to be eligible for special export tariff and international loan rates. By 2000, however, Tuvalu's economic structure had changed—its gross domestic product had doubled and the government budget improved enough to initiate numerous infrastructure expansions. In the first half of the last decade, loans from various nations were obtained to assist in the establishment of a small tourist industry—a 16-room hotel was built on Funafuti and an airport upgraded with a loan ($A30 million) from the **European Union**. Subsistence farming on the soil-poor atolls is augmented by fishing and by the production of **copra** (Tuvalu's only real export), by Tuvaluans working abroad (estimated to be 2,000, primarily in Nauru and New Zealand) who send remittances back to their families and by a trust fund established in 1987 by **New Zealand**, **Australia**, and the United Kingdom to generate government budgetary income. The value of the fund in 1998 stood at approximately $60 million, and the interest supplies some 11 percent of the government's budgetary income. Other government income consists of fishing licenses (40 percent) and taxation (17 percent). The value of imports ($6.1 million in 1997), generally in the form of food and manufactured articles, far outstrips the value of exports ($280,000).

In order to stabilize its economy during the last decade, Tuvalu has attempted to diversify its internal economic infrastructure and to find other resources to curb the ever increased dependency upon foreign countries. Philatelic revenues have proven to be an excellent source of income. Despite criticism from all sides, in 1996 the government rented its "688" phone line out to Asia Pacific Telecommunications who used it for international "phone sex" lines. By 1997, approximately 10 percent of Tuvalu's national income came from this source. Then in 1997 and 1998, Tuvalu negotiated the lease of its **Internet** domain "*.tv*" to a Canadian firm with high anticipation of making millions. That particular negotiation fell through, but a year later, it negotiated a 10-year deal with a California company, Idealab, for $50 million. The first check for $19 million went toward the improvement of roads, education, Internet access, the expansion of the airport and runway, and other miscellaneous projects. The government also announced in late 2000 that it was not renegotiating its phone sex contract.

- U -

'ULUKĀLALA II, FĪNAU (?–1809). A Tongan chief who aggressively set out to gain control over the Tongan islands. His planned assassination of the high ranking title Tu'i Kanokupolu in 1799 precipitated a long and bloody civil war (1799–1810). In the same year, he attacked the British ship *Port-au-Prince*, massacred most of its crew, and took the others prisoner. One of them, **Will Mariner**, lived among the Tongan royal family, survived, and recorded his memoirs in an account that includes extensive data on the culture of **Tonga** at the time of European contact.

***UNION POUR LA DÉFENSE DE L'OCÉANIE* (UDO).** A conservative political party that emerged in **French Polynesia** during the 1952 elections, organized by Alfred Poroi, a strong supporter of **France's** presence in the Pacific. The UDO was an outgrowth of Poroi's earlier party, the *Union Populaire Océanienne* (UPO), which he had organized against the popular Tahitian politician **Marcel Pouvana'a a Oopa**. In 1956, the UDO changed names to the *Union Tahitienne* (the UT) and then in 1958 to the *Union Tahitienne Démocratique* (UTD), and finally in 1977 to its Tahitian name, the **Tāhō'ēra'a Huira'atira**, currently in power.

UNITED NATIONS (UN). A world organization founded on 24 October 1945 to maintain international peace and security, to develop friendly relations among nations based on equal rights and self-determination, to achieve international economic, social, cultural, and humanitarian cooperation, and to promote human rights as well as to encourage economic and social development. It is composed of the General Assembly, a Security Council, a Secretariat, an Economic and Social Council, a Trusteeship Council, and an International Court of Justice. Although the Security Council was given the most important functions of the new organization (maintenance of peace and security), it is its Economic and Social Council (ECOSOC) that contributes most to the development and advancement of the South Pacific nations but more specifically through its **Economic and Social Commission for Asia and the Pacific** (ESCAP). A considerable role is also played in the region by other UN agencies such as the Food and Agriculture Organization (FAO), the World Bank, International Fund for Agriculture Development (IFAD), the International Monetary Fund (IMF), and the World Health Organization (WHO). **New Zealand** (1945), **Sāmoa** (1976), **Nauru** (1999), **Tonga** (1999), and **Tuvalu** (2000) are the only Polynesian nations who are currently members of the UN.

UNITED NATIONS CONVENTION ON THE LAW OF THE SEA. A **United Nations** document that includes a comprehensive regime of law and order that govern all uses of the oceans and their resources. After 14 years of work involving 150 countries, the initial document was opened for signature on 10 December 1982 in Montego Bay, Jamaica. It entered into force on 16 November 1994. At its inception, the **United States** and other industrialized nations demanded clarification of deep sea resources before they would ratify the document. Later supplements led to most of the other countries doing so. The United States still has not determined whether it is in its best interest to remain outside the treaty or to join it. the **Pacific Islands Forum** countries have all signed the agreement since the ocean and its recourses are of vital concern to them. The UN Website on the convention is located at http://www.un.org/Depts/los/index.htm.

UNITED STATES. A colonial power whose Pacific empire in the late 19th and 20th centuries included not only Guam, the Philippines, and the Micronesian islands in the North Pacific but the Polynesian islands of **Hawai'i** and **American Sāmoa**.

U.S. interest in the Pacific began in the late 18th century as U.S. trading ships plied the Pacific in search of goods to trade in China. Pacific **whaling** added to that interest, and by the 1830s, U.S. ships were visiting every major island group within the Pacific basin in search of whales, **sandalwood**, bêche-de-mer, tortoise shell, and **copra**. Protestant missionaries from New England pushed into Hawai'i (1820) which they later used as a base for promoting missionary work into Micronesia further west in the North Pacific. The South Pacific was left to the Europeans to proselytize, except for the **Mormons**, the Seventh-Day Adventists, who made their advances into the South Pacific in the last half of the century.

The government-sponsored Wilkes expedition (1838–1842) (See **United States Exploring Expedition**) stirred further interest in the Pacific, but most U.S. activity in the Pacific came from private rather than government initiatives. The 1893 overthrow of the Hawaiian monarchy by U.S. businessmen, for example, was at first disavowed by Congress, and it was only in 1899 that it was persuaded to annex the islands. At the same time, the United States, opposing English and German annexation of **Sāmoa**, entered into several agreements (1879–1899) that resulted in partitioning the islands between **Germany** and the United States.

The reason for the change in U.S. policy was the acquisition of Guam and the Philippines after the Spanish-American War (1898). Hawai'i and American Sāmoa provided stepping stones across the wide Pacific basin. The U.S. government, however, never subsequently established a federal office or agency that would develop a consistent and efficient policy to administer its foreign possessions. As a result, Guam and the Philippines were placed under the Department of War, and American Sāmoa was placed under the Department of the Navy, both of which, inexperienced in such matters, neglected the islands' development.

World War II and the acquisition of hundreds of Micronesian islands as **United Nations** trust territories brought world attention to U.S. colonial policy in the Pacific. As a result, administration of the islands was turned over to the Department of the Interior in 1951, and by the 1960s, still little had been done toward their development. (The Philippines, however, gained independence in 1946, and Hawai'i became a state in 1959.) Criticisms in the late 1950s and early 1960s brought positive congressional action, and millions of dollars were awarded (and still are) to their annual budgets. Ironically, the critics that once complained of U.S. neglect now complain that its liberal economic generosity has tied the islands' economies so closely to that of the United States that they (American Sāmoa and Guam) will cease striving for self-sufficiency and independence.

U.S. policy toward the Pacific islands continues to be ambiguous, naïve, contradictory, and, as a result, is criticized on all levels. The Pacific basin countries remain secondary in importance to the more lucrative trade routes between the United States and its Asian-rim partners—**Japan**, Taiwan, and China. Excluding the subsidies to the governments of American Sāmoa and Guam, the United States contributes only a fraction of what **Australia**, **New Zealand**, and Japan individually contribute to the region. In 1999, for example, Australia contributed $84.7 million, New Zealand $52.5 million, and the United States a mere $12.4 million. A bipartisan congressional delegation, consisting of Congressmen Steve Solarz (Democrat, New York), **Eni F. H. Faleomavaega** (Democrat, American Sāmoa), and Robert K. Kornan (Republican, California), visited the area in 1989, and its subsequent report, *Problems in Paradise: United States Interests in the South Pacific*, suggested that the United States should give far more political attention and financial assistance to the region.

UNITED STATES EXPLORING EXPEDITION. The first **United States** government sponsored scientific and trade expedition to the Pacific, led by Charles Wilkes from August 1838 to June 1842, sometimes referred to as "The Wilkes Expedition." The expedition set out from Norfolk, Virginia, with six vessels and a crew of civilian scholars including James Dana, a geologist; William Rich, a botanist; William Brackenridge, a horticulturist; Titian Peale and Charles Pickering, naturalists; Horatio Hale, ethnologist and philologist; and Joseph Couthouy, a conchologist.

The expedition surveyed and mapped coastlines of continents and islands from the northwest coast of America to the Antarctic in the southern hemisphere. Thousands of specimens of flora and fauna were brought back to augment the U.S. Botanic Garden in Washington, D.C. Numerous volumes of valuable data were eventually published, including five volumes of Wilkes's own narrative account (1844). Despite the rancor between Wilkes and his colleagues during and after the expedition, the net result was that the expedition greatly improved U.S. prestige abroad and opened U.S. interests for expansion in the Pacific. *See also* AMERICAN SĀMOA.

UNIVERSITÉ DE LA POLYNÉSIE FRANÇAISE (University of French Polynesia). Originally created on 29 May 1987 as part of the French University of the Pacific (Université Française du Pacifique) with two centers—one in New Caledonia and the other in **Tahiti**, each headed by a director. The concept of a Pacific university had first been proposed by President Charles de Gaulle in his visit to the islands in 1956. The demise of the Université Française du Pacifique came in 1999 with the creation of two independent universities; the one in Tahiti was renamed the Université de la Polynésie Française, whose beautiful campus is located southwest of Pape‘ete between Outumaoro and Puna‘auia. Its offerings include preparations in law, sciences, letters, foreign languages, tropical agriculture, and aquaculture. The university has increased enrollment from approximately 112 students in 1988 to over 2,000 students today. There are approximately 170 full-time and part-time instructors. A small library supplies the print and nonprint materials for the campus, and the university boasts having several research centers whose interests are **Polynesia** in general and French Polynesian in particular. The university president is Dr. Sylvie André, who has been the executive director for over 10 years. The university Website is located at http://www.upf.pf. *See also* ‘ATENISI INSTITUTE; UNIVERSITY OF THE SOUTH PACIFIC.

UNIVERSITY OF THE SOUTH PACIFIC (USP). A four-year, bachelor-degree-granting institution, established in 1968 at Laucala Bay, Fiji, to provide advanced education for the young people of the Pacific Basin countries. The university is owned and operated by 12 Pacific island countries. Dr. Colin C. Aikman, professor of law in Wellington, was appointed its first vice-chancellor, and Queen Elizabeth visited and formally opened the institution on 5 March 1970. **King Tāufa‘āhau Tupou IV** of **Tonga** became its first chancellor, a titular position usually held by prominent leaders in the South Pacific. Its current chancellor, appointed in August 2000, is **Sani Lakatani**, premier of **Niue**, and its vice-chancellor is Savenaca Siwatibau. The university‘s three main campuses are locatd at Laucala, Fiji; Port Vila, Vanuatu; and Āpia, **Sāmoa**; however, it has satellite centers with small staffs located in 11 of the 12 Pacific island countries it serves.

Currently, there are approximately 9,200 students (5,300 full-time) enrolled on its three main campuses with over 16,000 enrolled in its distance education classes. Sixty-eight percent of the students come from Fiji. The university graduated 1,346 students in 1999. The approved annual budget for the fiscal year 2000 was $24.5 million, an 8 percent increase over the 1999 budget. During the 2000 political coup in Fiji, many education ministers from member countries called their students back home, and there was talk about moving the university out of Fiji for the safety of faculty, staff, and students. By the end of the year, however, it was evident that the worst was over, and most of the students returned to the Laucala campus for the February 2001 semester. *See also* ʻATENISI INSTITUTE; NATIONAL UNIVERSITY OF SĀMOA; UNIVERSITÉ DE LA POLYNÉSIE FRANÇAISE.

ʻUVEA ISLAND. *See* WALLIS AND FUTUNA

- V -

VAEA OF HOUMA, BARON (1921–). Prime minister of **Tonga** from August 1991 until 3 January 2000. Born on 15 May 1921 in Tonga, Vaea was educated at Wesley College in Auckland, **New Zealand**. He became a member of the New Zealand air force (1942–1944), entered Tonga's civil service (1942–1953), and served as governor of Haʻapi (1959–1967), acting minister of police (1968–1969), high commissioner (1970–1972), member of the privy council of Tonga since 1959, and minister of commerce, labor, and industry. When **Prime Minister Tuʻipelehake** retired in August 1991, Vaea succeeded him. Vaea asked the king for retirement in 1995, but the king refused to accept it. Finally on 3 Januay 2000, the king announced his decision to name his youngest son, **ʻUlukalala Lavaka Ata**, prime minister.

VAHEKEHU, ELISABETH (1823?–1901). Regardedd as "queen" of Nuku Hiva in the **Marquesas Islands**, currently **French Polynesia**, during the last half of the 19th century. Her husband, **Charles Te Moana**, was chief of the Bay of Taiohae where most European ships made their landing, and when French Admiral **Abel Dupetit-**

Thouars took possession of the islands in 1842, Te Moana was recognized as "king." Both became Christians in 1853, and Te Moana died in 1863 leaving her as his heir. She generally supported French and **Catholic** causes and was awarded a pension and a small European-built house at Taiohae. French writer Eugène Caillot met her just before her death and wrote in glowing terms of her dignity and exemplary life. He also included a photograph of her in his work *Histoire de la Polynésie Orientale* (1910), plates 60 and 61.

VASON, GEORGE (1772–1838). One of the first Christian missionaries sent to **Tonga** in 1796 to convert the islanders. Vason lived with chief Mulikiha'amea, the Tu'i Ha'atakalaua, and eventually abandoned his missionary work to become a Tongan nobleman. He became involved in the Tongan civil wars (1799–1810) and narrowly escaped a violent death. He left Tonga in 1801, and returned to England where he died in 1838. His 234-page memoirs, *An Authentic Narrative of Four Years' Residence at Tongataboo*, were published in London (1810).

VERNAUDON, ÉMILE (1944–). Political leader of **French Polynesia**. Born in Pape'ete on 8 December 1944, Vernaudon was elected mayor of Mahina in 1977 as a member of the 'Ē'a 'Āpi Party. He founded his own party, the 'Āi'a Āpi, in 1982 and rallied his support to the leadership of **Gaston Flosse**, president of French Polynesia. The coalition was short-lived, however, and then under a coalition government of **Alexandre Léontieff**, Vernaudon became president of the territorial assembly (1982–1983). Another coalition with Flosse in early 1991 ended suddenly in September, and the resultant enmity between the two leaders is apparent. Vernaudon publically refers to Flosse as the "local despot." He currently allies himself with **Oscar Temarau**, head of the pro-indepence party, and serves as deputy of French Polynesia to the French National Assembly, a position he held first from 1988 to 1993 and then again since the elections in 1998.

- W -

WAIHE'E, JOHN (1946–). Governor of the state of **Hawai'i** for two consecutive terms (1986–1990 and 1990–1994), the first elected governor of the state of Hawaiian descent. Born on 19 May 1946 at Honoka'a, Hawai'i (the Big Island), Waihe'e received his bachelor's degree in history and business from Andrews University in Michigan (1968). After obtaining his law degree from the University of Hawai'i (1976), he became a lawyer in Honolulu, where he organized his own law firm. He entered politics as the Democratic party's delegate to the State Constitutional Convention in 1978, and was elected to the State House between 1980 and 1982. He became lieutenant governor in 1982 under **Governor George Ariyoshi**, and then in 1986 was elected governor of the state.

Wahie'e's achievements include tax reforms, the development of affordable housing, a school reform program that includes new school facilities, repairs, and extra funds for O'ahu's leeward school districts, and a unique universal health care insurance (the first state in the United States to offer such a program). His popularity plummeted, however, from 65 percent in 1989 to 27 percent in 1994 due to a great extent by Hawai'i's economic recession. He and his wife Lynne Kobashigawa Wahie'e have two children.

WAIKATO RAUPATU CLAIMS SETTLEMENT ACT. Signed in November 1995 by Queen Elizabeth II in Wellington, **New Zealand**, it provides for the return to the Tainui people of a substantial amount of land (the whole of the Onewhero forest land) and an apology from the crown for the loss of **Māori** lives during the 19th century. The signed document, part of the **Waitangi Treaty** negotiations, became effective on 28 August 1997. The full text can be found on the **Internet** at http://nativenet.uthscsa.edu/archive/nl/9511/ 0077.html.

WAITANGI, TREATY OF. A document hastily drawn up in February 1840 by Captain William Hobson, representing the British Crown in **New Zealand**, and numerous **Māori** chiefs regarding the relationship between the immigrating British settlers and the indigenous Māori people. Various versions of the treaty were drawn up both in English and Māori, the interpretations and versions of which continue to be a center of confusion even today. The three articles in the English version say that the chiefs ceded their sovereignty to the English queen, that the chiefs had "full and exclusive and undisturbed possession of their Lands and Estates Forests Fisheries and other properties," and that the Māoris had the rights and privileges of British subjects. The Māori text, translated by Henry Williams and his son Edward, differs in several points, and it appears that they were rewriting the treaty to make it acceptable to the Māori chiefs.

In 1986, **Prime Minister David Lange** established a Waitangi tribunal to consider Māori grievances dating back to 1840. The tribunal's rulings regarding land rights have generally favored the Māori (representing about 9 percent of the population) over the New Zealand ***pākehā*** (whites). In 1998, the Waitangi Tribunal ordered the government to return $NZ6.1 million of confiscated land to Māoris. For further information, an **Internet** Website can be found at http://www.nzhistory.net.nz/Links/treaty.htm.

WAKEFIELD, EDWARD GIBBON (1796–1862). A prominent Englishman who shaped colonization policies not only for **New Zealand** but Canada and **Australia** as well. He organized the **New Zealand Company** in 1838 and later helped to settle Wellington, Wanganui, New Plymouth, and Nelson. He maintained that the settlements should be systematically colonized, self-governing, and self-sufficient. Wakefield finally arrived in New Zealand (Wellington) in 1853 where he spent the remaining years of his life. His four brothers—Daniel (1798–1858), Arthur (1799–1843), William (1803–1848), and Felix (1807–1875)—all contributed to the early settlement and organization of the new colony.

WALLIS AND FUTUNA. A self-governing overseas territory of **France**, it comprises two island groups lying west of **Sāmoa** and approximately 230 km (144 mi) northeast of Fiji. Wallis Island, whose native name is 'Uvea, consists of a volcanic island (60 sq km, 23 sq mi) with 19 uninhabited islets (99 sq km, 38 sq mi); Futuna (64 sq km, 24.6 sq mi) includes the island of Futuna and its smaller, uninhabited neighbor Alofi (51 sq km, 19 sq mi) with a total land area of 275 sq km (106 sq mi). The climate is tropical with high humidity and temperatures but moderated by trade winds coming predominantly from the southeast. The capital is Mata Utu on Wallis Island. Its rapidly growing population (1996 census) consists of 14,166 of which 97 percent are Polynesians. It is estimated that more Wallisians reside overseas in New Caledonia, emigrating there because of lack of employment opportunities in their own island nation. All are French citizens.

The economy is primarily subsistence agriculture consisting of yams, **taro**, **coconuts**, bananas, **breadfruit**, with a few individuals (70 percent of the workforce, however) earning a salary income from government service or teaching. French subsidies provide for the major social and economic developments planned for the island. Wallis and Futuna remains one of the most staunchly Catholic places in the world. Its people are almost 100 percent Roman **Catholic**, and 85 percent of them are regular churchgoers. It has had its own diocese (Wallis and Futuna) since 1935 and its own native bishop, Monsignor Lolesio Fuahea. Two Polyncsian dialects (Wallisian is similar to Tongan and Futunian is similar to Sāmoan) are spoken although French is the language of the schools and administration.

History: Tradition maintains that the original Wallisians came from **Tonga** about A.D. 1450–1550 and that rivalry between the various chiefs caused constant warfare until the 19th century. The two islands of Futuna and Alofi were settled from Sāmoa only in the 17th century. The first Europeans to visit the islands were the Dutch explorers W. C. Schouten and Jacques Le Maire (1616) who landed on Futuna. British Captain Samuel Wallis was the first European to visit Wallis Island (1767) and hence its name. Very few Europeans visited or settled there until the 1820s.

Roman Catholicism was introduced by Marist priests both on Wallis and Futuna on their way from **Tahiti** to Sydney in November 1837. Chief Tungahala persuaded **Bishop Jean-Baptiste François Pompallier** to allow at least one of the priests to stay on the island. Father (later Bishop) **Pierre Bataillon** converted the king, and all his subjects followed his example and adopted Roman Catholic Christianity. **Father Pierre Chanel** was landed on Futuna where he was murdered by the islanders in 1841 (canonized in 1954). In November 1842, French Captain Mallet sailed to the islands where king Lavelua and his chiefs Malahama and Maulisio signed a "protectorate" agreement that was ratified in Paris only on 5 April 1887, upon the insistence of **Queen Amélie**. In 1888, the French ministry of colonies formally proclaimed a protectorate over the islands and placed their jurisdiction under an administrator in New Caledonia.

In 1909, Wallis and Futuna were separated from the other overseas French possessions and, in 1913, were declared an overseas colony.

During World War II (1942–1944), between 4,000 and 6,000 American troops were stationed on Wallis Island. They not only boosted the cash economy to the highest level the islands have ever known but to a great extent introduced the islanders to the 20th century. A referendum in the islands was held on 22 December 1959, and the two island groups voted (94 percent Yes, 6 percent No) to become "an integral part of the French Republic as an overseas territory of France," an act ratified by the French Parliament on 29 July 1961.

Government: Under the 1961 statute, the territory is administered by a chief French administrator (*administrateur supérieur*), responsible to the French high commissioner in New Caledonia. He is assisted by a Territorial Council consisting of the three traditional kings—Lavelua (king of Wallis), Tuiagaifao (king of Alo, Futuna), and Tuisigave (king of Sigave, Futuna) and three members appointed by the administrator with the approval of the territorial assembly. Each king controls the internal affairs of his own political domain—issuing its own passports, receiving tribute, and so forth. (The kings are elected and can be deposed.)

The legislature consists of the 20-member territorial assembly (13 from Wallis and seven from Futuna), elected for five-year terms by universal suffrage. The territory also elects one deputy to the French National Assembly in Paris (by general suffrage for a five-year term) and one representative to the French Senate in Paris (elected by the territorial assembly for a term of nine years). The chief administrator has veto power over legislative decisions except those concerning internal social and economic programs, customs, and excise duties.

The major political parties consist of the *Rassemblement Pour la République* (RPR), a right wing conservative party which supports the monarchy and the traditional way of life, currently headed by Clovis Logologofolau, and the *Union Pour la Démocratie Française* (UDF), or known locally as the *Lua Kae Tahi*, a center right party which emphasizes local issues and social and economic changes. Other minor parties include the *Union Populaire Locale* (UPL), headed by Falakiko Gata, and the *Mouvement des Radicaux de Gauche* (MRG), a socialist party.

The elections on 6 March 1997 were extremely popular with 87.2 percent of the constituents voting. The RPR party secured 14 seats while the socialist and other parties gained only six. Victor Brial was elected president of the assembly. Allegations regarding election fraud resulted in new elections being called on 28 September 1998. As a result, the RPR lost three seats to the opposition, now holding only 11 seats in the assembly, while the opposition holds nine. These elections also saw for the first time traditional chiefs running as candidates for public office.

A three-day celebration in March of 1999, commemorated the 40th anniversary of the rule of King Lavelua Tomasi Kulimoetoke, then 81 years of age. Lavelua came to power two years before Wallis and Futuna acquired its French overseas territorial status. His appointment restored stability to a difficult post-war period in the island's history. The capital, Matu Uta, was all spruced up and the government buildings freshly painted in anticipation of the numerous foreign dignitaries who arrived to celebrate the event.

Currently (2000), the chief French administrator is Christian Dors, the president of the territorial assembly is Soane Muni Uhila (RPR), the deputy to the French national assembly is Victor Brial (RPR), and the representative to the French senate is Fr. Robert Laufoaulu. The current king of Wallis (Lavelua) is Tomasi Kulimoetoke (serving since 1959), the king of Alo (Tuiagaifo) is Sagato Alofi, and the king of Sigave (Sau) is Pasilio Keletaona. Party lines and loyalties are fluid, and politics generally remain conservative. However, popular demonstrations against the French administration broke out on several occasions, but these incidents remain trivial when compared to the violence in **France's** other Pacific territories—New Caledonia, for example. The islanders are not unafraid to forcibly show their disapproval of unpopular policies. In 1998, for example, 50 villagers demonstrated against a local TV station and held its directors hostage because the station had not given them sufficient air time during a local dance competition. A more dramatic demonstration occurred in 1999 when local teachers closed the schools for 35 days in protest against their French colleagues who were being paid more than they. It was only through the intervention of the traditional chiefs and the king that normality was restored.

During 2000, representatives from Wallis and Futuna met with leaders in New Caledonia to discuss their relationship to each other in light of the Nouméa Agreement (1998) in which France granted the government of New Caledonia more internal autonomy. Wallis and Futuna, which has a sizeable population living in New Caledonia, is afraid that employment might be cut off for their overseas citizens. A bilateral agreement between the two island governments will outline the relationship between the two French overseas territories. Negotiations continued into the year 2001.

Economy: Subsistence fishing and agriculture remain the way of life for most of the islanders. The islands remain relatively isolated from the outside world, thus, **tourism** and foreign economic development are minimal. High population growth has resulted in high outmigration, mostly to New Caledonia. These expatriates send remittances back to their relatives on Wallis and Futuna. In a 1995 agreement, the French government provides substantial subsidies to the islands' economy; in 1998, it provided resources amounting to 6.5 billion Pacific francs ($56.6 million), half of which went to public education. The 1999 territorial budget amounted to more than 2 billion Pacific francs ($17.4 million). Since 1995, these funds have contributed to the construction of roads, school buildings, a technical college in 'Uvea, a wharf in Futuna, and moneys to develop a small tourist industry (currently only 400 tourists a year). Imports, consisting primarily of food and building materials, come from France, New Caledonia, **Australia**, and **New Zealand**, and average some $13.5 million a year while exports (copra, trochus shells, and handicrafts) average only $370,000.

Wallisians exhibit a strong pride in their **Polynesian** traditions and customs and have some reserves about the French intrusion into their way of life, but Wallis and Futuna will most likely remain loyal to France because of the disproportionate amount of subsidies provided to them by the mother country.

WEBB, WILLIAM HENRY (1816–1899). A shipbuilder and Pacific entrepreneur and influential in U.S. involvement in **Sāmoa**. Webb was born in New York City and had a long career in shipbuilding and Pacific transportation. When the transcontinental railroad was completed in 1869, the distance from New York to Pacific countries became drastically shorter. As a result, representatives of the Webb Steamship Lines from California set out to find adequate harbors for coaling and refueling stations in the Pacific. In 1871, Webb's agent, Captain E. Wakeman, made a survey of the Sāmoan islands that described the excellent conditions of the deep harbor at Pago Pago. Webb's findings were made known to the U.S. government, and in 1872 Commander Meade of the *Narragansett* set out to investigate the conditions. Meade negotiated a treaty with the local chiefs that granted the **United States** a naval station at Pago Pago. Webb continued to make recommendations to the executive branch of the government, recommendations that were economically beneficial to his business interests in Sāmoa. Webb died in New York City on 30 October 1899. *See also* AMERICAN SĀMOA.

WEBER, THEODORE (1844–1889). First German consul in Āpia, **Sāmoa**, and head of the famous J. C. Godeffroy and Son Company (after 1878 called the Deutsche Handels und Plantagen Gesellschaft, DHPG), a company that had an extensive network of commercial branches throughout the Pacific islands. Webb arrived in Sāmoa in 1862 and shortly became head of the Godeffroy Company as well as consul general for **Germany**. Through his skillful entrepreneurship and sometimes unscrupulous dealings, the Godeffroy Company extended its vast trading network from Chile to China. He played an active role in the civil wars that were raging throughout the islands by supplying his Sāmoan allies with firearms and munitions. Throughout the 1870s and 1880s, Weber worked for eventual German annexation of the islands, an act that occurred only after his death in 1889. *See also* ANGLO-GERMAN AGREEMENT OF 1899; SOLF, WILHELM.

WENDT, ALBERT (1939–). Sāmoan novelist, scholar, critic, and considered the Pacific's most talented writer. Born on 27 October 1939 in Āpia, **Sāmoa**, Wendt received his BA and MA at Victoria University, Wellington, **New Zealand**, and then returned to Sāmoa where he became a high school principal (1970–1973), lecturer at the University of the South Pacific (1974–1975), director of the University of the South Pacific extension division in Āpia (1976), and ultimately a professor of English at Auckland University in New Zealand (1988). He was chair of the English department from 1993 to 1995. Wendt is the author of numerous novels, the most famous of which is *Flying Fox in a Freedom Tree* (1975), a story of a displaced Sāmoan who unsuccessfully tries to live by traditional and modern-day existentialist teachings.

The novel was made into a movie which had its premiere in California and **Hawai'i** in December 1991. A previous novel, *Sons for the Return Home* (1973), was turned into the first film ever based on a literary source by a native Pacific islander. He received the Arthur Lynn Andrews Distinguished Visiting Professor Award from the University of Hawai'i to lecture on its campus during the 1999–2000 school year.

WESTERN SĀMOA. *See* SĀMOA.

WHALING IN THE PACIFIC. An economic activity, primarily during the 19th century (especially between 1835 and 1860), when hundreds of Yankee, English, and French ships made their way through Pacific waters in search of the sperm whale.

The heads of these large mammals provided spermaceti oil that lit the lamps and candles of the world as well as supplying a fine lubricant for machinery until it was replaced by cheaper oil products later in the century. Whalebone stays also provided Victorian women with supports for their multishaped corsets.

The New England cities of Nantucket and New Bedford were especially important, but almost every New England port sent expeditions to the Pacific. By mid-century, the U.S. whaling fleet numbered some 736 vessels, and it is not unusual to read **Polynesian** accounts of dozens of ships lying anchor in the harbors of Pape'ete, Āpia, Pago Pago, or Honolulu at any one time. Polynesian ports provided refreshing and refueling stops for the whaling fleets, while the ships and their crews usually brought news from the outside as well as vices and disease.

Although whaling declined drastically after 1860, it never really died. In the 20th century, more effective hunting procedures and the rise in the demand for whale meat, oil, and blubber in the 1960s has resulted in the drastic decline in the number of whales, and as a result, they have been placed on the endangered-species list.

WILKES EXPEDITION. *See* UNITED STATES EXPLORING EXPEDITION.

WILLIAMS, HENRY (1782–1867). Head of the Anglican Church missionary work in **New Zealand** as of 1823. An ex-naval officer, Williams was ordained a minister and sailed for Sydney in 1822. He was appointed head of the New Zealand missionary work among the **Māoris** by **Samuel Marsden**, and he became a staunch supporter and protector of Māori land rights. He encouraged the signing of the **Treaty of Waitangi** (1840) in order to protect Māori lands from further encroachments of the New Zealand whites (***pākehā***). Dismissed from the **Church Missionary Society's** services in the 1850s because of his own refusal to give up acquired lands, he was reinstated in 1855.

WILLIAMS, JOHN (1796–1839). One of the most effective of the early **London Missionary Society (LMS)** missionaries to the South Pacific. Williams and his wife arrived in **Tahiti** in 1817 where he spent most of his life on Mo'orea and Rā'iatea, from where he supervised the introduction of Christianity into many of the surrounding islands—the **Cook Islands** (1823) and **Sāmoa** (1832), for example. He translated the New Testament into Rarotongan (1834) and his biographical *Narrative of Missionary Enterprises in the South Sea Islands* (1837) became a bestseller. After spending seven years in England on LMS business (1832–1839), Williams returned to the Pacific to continue his missionary work. He was killed in the New Hebrides (Vanuatu) on 20 November 1839 by Erromango islanders. His interest and enthusiasm in their languages and culture endeared him to the islanders with whom he labored. *See also* AMERICAN SĀMOA; FRENCH POLYNESIA; SĀMOA.

WILLIAMS, JOSEPH (1934–). Prime minister of the **Cook Islands** between July and November 1999. Born 4 on October 1934, Aitutaki, Cook Islands, Williams received his medical training at Northland College (1950–1960) and the University of Hawai'i (1969). He served as surgeon at the Dannevirke Hospital and the Napier Hospital (both in **New Zealand**) and at the Rarotonga Hospital before becoming a legislative assemblyman (Cook Islands Party) and director of health in 1968. He served as a member of Parliament for overseas constituencies 12 years before 1999. In a flurry of political maneuverings after the June elections of 1999, Prime Minister Sir Geoffrey Henry of the Cook Islands Party resigned, and his position was taken by Williams who then was confirmed as the new prime minister. He headed a minority government until October when he dismissed two of his own party who then joined the opposition. When a new session of Parliament convened on 18 November, Williams offered his resignation, ending 10 years of his party's control of government. In July of 2000, Williams announced that he would become an independent member of Parliament.

WILLIAMS, WILLIAM (1800–1878). Anglican missionary to **New Zealand** (1826), brother to **Henry Williams**, first bishop appointed to Waiapu (1859–1876), and a philologist responsible for publishing the ever-popular *Dictionary of the New Zealand Language and Concise Grammar* (1844) and for translating the New Testament into **Māori** (1837). His son, William Leonard Williams, and grandson, Herbert William Williams, both held the position of Bishop of Waiapu.

WOMEN. The general patriarchal character of traditional **Polynesian** societies coupled with the introduction of 19th-century Western culture resulted in the secondary role allocated to Pacific women in the 20th century. Women form the backbone of most island societies. They rear the children, provide labor for most of the subsistence agriculture, and donate time and energies to welfare and health agencies. But in most island nations, they are not socially or politically equal with their male counterparts. A paradox does exist, however, because **Pitcairn Island** and **New Zealand** were the first countries in the world to award women the right to vote (in 1838 and 1893 respectively), and most islanders can name women in their traditional societies or in the 19th century that held powerful political or social positions.

The current worldwide movement for women's rights has brought changes into even the most conservative of Polynesian societies. In 1990, for example, **Sāmoa** finally granted women the right to vote, allocated funds for women's projects, and created a women's affairs ministry in the government. During the 1990s, women were appointed or elected to high positions. Sereima Lomaloma, a **Tongan** but living in Fiji, became the first indigenous woman to be ordained an Anglican priest (1996); the House of Ariki in the **Cook Islands** is predominantly women, and all the chiefs on Rarotonga are women; Carol Moseley-Braun was appointed U.S. ambassador to Sāmoa and New Zealand by President Bill Clinton in 1999; Lourdes Pangelinan from Guam is currently the director-general of the Secretariat of the Pacific Community; Sāmoa's Archdeacon Faga Matalavea was appointed Anglican representative to the **United Nations** by the archbishop of Canterbury in 2001; and on 18 May 2001, Lucette Taero was elected president of the territorial assembly in **French Polynesia**, the first woman ever to hold that position. New Zealand again takes the lead regarding gender equality. All senior positions in the government are currently (2001) being staffed by women—the head of state, of course, is Queen Elizabeth, the governor-general is Dame Silvia Cartwright, Helen Clark is the current prime minister, Jenny Shipley is head of the opposition, and the chief justice is Sian Elias.

That enviable political structure is not seen elsewhere in the Pacific, but progress toward greater social and political equality in all the islands will continue if more women become interested in advancing their cause and in speaking out in their behalf. Those who wish to retain their traditional culture, however, must work to find that precarious balance between what poses to be tradition and what modern forces, if accepted, might destroy it. *See also* ARI'I TA'IMA'I, PRINCESS; BARET, JEANNE; CARTWRIGHT, SILVIA; CLARK, HELEN; DAVIS, PA TEPAERU ARIKI; GREY, AGGIE; HENRY, TEUIRA; KA'AHUMANU; KAWĀNANAKOA, ABIGAIL; LATASI, NAAMA; LAVELUA, AMÉLIE; LILI'UOKALANI; MAKEA KARIKA TAKAU MARGARET ARIKI; MAKEA TAKAU; MARAU, JOANNA; MATĀ'AFA, LA'ULU FETAUIMALEMAU; MCCOMBS, ELIZABETH; MEAD, MARGARET; POMARE (QUEEN POMARE IV); ROUTLEDGE, KATHERINE PEASE; SALAZAR, HELENA; SĀLOTE, MAFILI'O PILOVELU; SHAW, ELAINE; SHIPLEY, JENNIFER; SZASZY, MIRAKA; TE ATA-I-RANGIKAAHU; TRASK, MILILANI; TUKI, LUCIA; TUPU'O SĀMOA; VAHEKEHU, ELIZABETH.

- Y -

YOUNG, JOHN (ca. 1742–1835). A **beachcomber** in **Hawai'i** who became one of the most influential advisors and aids to **King Kamehameha I**. Young arrived in Hawai'i in 1790 aboard the *Elea-*

nor, commanded by Captain Simon Metcalfe. He was detained from leaving by King Kamehameha who wished to have a ***haole*** (white man) as an advisor. Young and **Isaac Davis** became important influences upon the rising power of the Kamehameha family. Young was made governor of O'ahu in 1796 and governor of the Big Island at various times for the king. Young married into the Kamehameha family, and his descendants became prominent in Hawaiian history. His granddaughter Emma was King Kamehameha IV's queen. Young died on 17 December 1835 and was buried with ceremonies befitting a high chief of Hawai'i.

YOUNG MĀORI PARTY. An informal group of **New Zealand Māoris** from the 1890s to 1914 who hoped to revitalize Māori culture and lifestyle among their race by adopting Western skills and ideas. Prominent among them were Peter Buck, **Āpirana Ngata**, and **Maui Pomare**. They organized themselves as a political party in 1909 but disbanded by World War I.

APPENDIX A

NAMES OF POLYNESIAN ISLANDS

The following is a listing of the major islands and atolls (*) within Polynesia. Names in parentheses are variants for which the island was known at different times since its first European discovery.

AGAKAUITAI; Gambier Islands, French Polynesia

AHE* (Peacock); Tuamotu Islands, French Polynesia

AHUNUI* (Byam Martin); Tuamotu Islands, French Polynesia

AITUTAKI; Lower Cook Islands

AKAMARU; Gambier Islands, French Polynesia

AKIAKI (Lancier, Thrum Cap); Tuamotu Islands, French Polynesia

ALOFI; Wallis and Futuna, French territory.

AMANU* (Moller); Tuamotu Islands, French Polynesia

ANA'A* (Chain); Tuamotu Islands, French Polynesia

ANIWA; Polynesian Outlier, Vanuatu

ANUANURARO* (Archangel); Tuamotu Islands, French Polynesia

ANUANURUNGA* (Four Crowns); Tuamotu Islands, French Polynesia

ANUTA; Polynesian Outlier, Eastern Solomon Islands

APATAKI* (Hegemeister); Tuamotu Islands, French Polynesia

APOLIMA; Sāmoa

ARATIKA* (Karlshoff); Tuamotu Islands, French Polynesia

ARUTUA* (Rurick); Tuamotu Islands, French Polynesia

ATA; Tongatapu Group, Tonga

'ATA; Tongan Outlier

ATAFU*; Tokelau

ATATA; Tongatapu Group, Tonga

ATIU; Lower Cook Islands

AUKENA; Gambier Islands, French Polynesia

'AUNU'U; American Sāmoa

BELLONA; Polynesian Outlier, Solomon Islands

BORA-BORA; Society Islands, French Polynesia
CHATHAM ISLAND; Chatham Group, New Zealand
CHATHAM ISLANDS; New Zealand
CURTIS; Kermadec Islands, New Zealand
DUCIE*; Pitcairn Islands
EASTER ISLAND (Rapa Nui, Isla de Pascuq)
EIAO; Marquesas, French Polynesia
EUA; Tongatapu Group, Tonga
'EUAKIKI; Tongatapu Group, Tonga
FA'AITE* (Miloradovitch); Tuamotu Islands, French Polynesia
FAFA; Tongatapu Group, Tonga
FAIOA; Wallis and Futuna, French territory
FAKAHINA* (Enterprise); Tuamotu Islands, French Polynesia
FAKAOFO*; Tokelau
FAKARAVA* (Wittgenstein); Tuamotu Islands, French Polynesia
FANGATAU* (Arakchev); Tuamotu Islands, French Polynesia
FANGATAUFA* (Cockburn); Tuamotu Islands, French Polynesia
FATU HIVA; Marquesas, French Polynesia
FATU HUKU; Marquesas, French Polynesia
FETOA; Kotu Group, Ha'apai, Tonga
FETOKOPUNGA; Otu Tolu Group, Ha'apai, Tonga
FILA; Polynesian Outlier, Vanuatu
FOA; Ha'apai Group, Tonga
FONOIFUA; Nomuka Group, Ha'apai, Tonga
FONUAFO'OU (Falcon); Ha'apai Group, Tonga
FONUAIKA; Kotu Group, Ha'apai, Tonga
FONUALEI; Tongan Outlier
FOTUHA'A; Ha'apai Group, Tonga
FUKAVE; Tongatapu Group, Tonga
FUNAFUTI*; Tuvalu
FUTUNA (Horne, Hoorn); Wallis and Futuna
GREAT BARRIER ISLAND; New Zealand
HA'AFEVA; Kotu Group, Ha'apai, Tonga
HA'ANO; Ha'apai Group, Tonga
HAO* (Bow, Harp); Tuamotu Islands, French Polynesia
HARAIKI* (Croker, San Quentin); Tuamotu Islands, French Polynesia
HATUTA'A; Marquesas, French Polynesia
HAWAI'I (Sandwich Islands); Hawai'i
HENDERSON ISLAND; Pitcairn Islands
HERALD ISLETS; Kermadec Islands, New Zealand
HEREHERETUE* (St. Paul); Tuamotu Islands, French

Polynesia
HIKUERU* (Melville); Tuamotu Islands, French Polynesia
HITI* (Ohiti, Clute); Tuamotu Islands, French Polynesia
HIVA OA; Marquesas, French Polynesia
HUAHINE; Society Islands, French Polynesia
HUNGA; Vava'u Group, Tonga
HUNGA HAAPAI; Ha'apai Group, Tonga
HUNGA TONGA; Ha'apai Group, Tonga
KAHO'OLAWE; Hawai'i
KALAU; Tongatapu Group, Tonga
KAMAKA; Gambier Islands, French Polynesia
KAO; Ha'apai Group, Tonga
KAPA; Vava'u Group, Tonga
KAPINGAMARANGI; Polynesian Outlier, Micronesia
KATIU* (Saken); Tuamotu Islands, French Polynesia
KAUA'I; Hawai'i
KAUEHI* (Vincennes); Tuamotu Islands, French Polynesia
KAUKURA* (Auura, Oura); Tuamotu Islands, French Polynesia
KA'ULA; Hawai'i
KELEFESIA; Nomuka Group, Ha'apai, Tonga
KERMADEC ISLANDS; New Zealand
KOLOA; Vava'u Group, Tonga
KOTU; Kotu Group, Ha'apai, Tonga
LALONA; Otu Tolu Group, Ha'apai, Tonga
LATE; Vava'u Group, Tonga
LĀNA'I; Hawai'i
LEHUA; Hawai'i
LEKELEKA; Kotu Group, Ha'apai, Tonga
LIFUKA; Ha'apai Group, Tonga
LIMU; Ha'apai Group, Tonga
LOFANGA; Ha'apai Group, Tonga
LUAHOKO; Ha'apai Group, Tonga
MACAULEY; Kermadec Islands, New Zealand
MAE; Polynesian Outlier, Vanuatu
MAIAO (Tubuai-Manu); Society Islands, French Polynesia
MAKAROA; Gambier Islands, French Polynesia
MAKATEA (Aurora); Tuamotu Islands, French Polynesia
MAKEMO* (Koutousof Smolenski); Tuamotu Islands, French Polynesia
MANGAIA; Lower Cook Islands
MANGAREVA (Magareva); Gambier Islands, French Polynesia
MANGO; Nomuka Group, Ha'apai, Tonga
MANIHI* (Wilsons); Tuamotu Islands, French Polynesia
MANIHIKI*; Northern Cook Islands
MANONO; Sāmoa
MANU'A (Islands); American Sāmoa
MANUAE* (Fenauaura, Scilly); Society Islands, French

Polynesia
MANUAE*; Lower Cook Islands
MANUHANGI* (Cumberland); Tuamotu Islands, French Polynesia
MANUI; Gambier Islands, French Polynesia
MARIA* (Moerenhout); Tuamotu Islands, French Polynesia
MARIA*; Austral Islands, French Polynesia
MAROKAU* (Manaka); Tuamotu Islands, French Polynesia
MAROTIRI ISLES (Bass Islands); Austral Islands, French Polynesia
MAROTIRI ITI; Austral Islands, French Polynesia
MAROTIRI NUI; Austral Islands, French Polynesia
MARUTEA NORTH* (Furneaux); Tuamotu Islands, French Polynesia
MARUTEA SOUTH* (Lord Hood); Tuamotu Islands, French Polynesia
MATAIVA* (Matahiva, Lazareff); Tuamotu Islands, French Polynesia
MATUKU; Kotu Group, Ha'apai, Tonga
MATUREIVAVAO* (Melbourne); Tuamotu Islands, French Polynesia
MAUI; Hawai'i
MAUKE; Lower Cook Islands
MAUPIHA'A* (Mopelia, Mopiha'a); Society Islands, French Polynesia
MAUPITI; Society Islands, French Polynesia
MEAMA; Ha'apai Group, Tonga
MEHETIA (Meetia); Society Islands, French Polynesia
MELE; Polynesian Outlier, Vanuatu
MITIARO; Lower Cook Islands
MO'OREA; Society Islands, French Polynesia
MO'UNGA'ONE; Ha'apai Group, Tonga
MOHOTANI; Marquesas, French Polynesia
MOLOKA'I; Hawai'i
MOLOKINI; Hawai'i
MORANE* (Cadmus); Tuamotu Islands, French Polynesia
MOROTIRI (Bass); Austral Islands, French Polynesia
MORUROA* (Mururoa, Matilda); Tuamotu Islands, French Polynesia
MOSES REEF; Austral Islands, French Polynesia
MOTANE; Marquesas, French Polynesia
MOTU ITI; Marquesas, French Polynesia
MOTU ONE* (Bellingshausen); Society Islands, French Polynesia
MOTU ONE; Marquesas, French Polynesia
MOTUTAPU; Tongatapu Group, Tonga
MOTUTUNGA* (Adventure); Tuamotu Islands, French Polynesia
NANUMANGA; Tuvalu
NANUMEA*; Tuvalu

NAPUKA* (Isle of Disappointment); Tuamotu Islands, French Polynesia
NASSAU; Northern Cook Islands
NEILSON REEF; Austral Islands, French Polynesia
NENGONENGO (Prince Wm. Henry); Tuamotu Islands, French Polynesia
NEW ZEALAND (Aoteroa)
NIAU* (Greig); Tuamotu Islands, French Polynesia
NIHIRU* (Nigeri); Tuamotu Islands, French Polynesia
NI'IHAU; Hawai'i
NINIVA; Ha'apai Group, Tonga
NIUAFO'OU; Tongan Outlier
NIUATOPUTAPU; Niuatoputapu Group, Tongan Outlier
NIUATOPUTAPU GROUP; Tongan Outlier
NIUE; Niue, New Zealand dependency
NIULAKITA; Tuvalu
NIUTAO; Tuvalu
NOMUKA; Nomuka Group, Ha'apai, Tonga
NOMUKA IKI; Nomuka Group, Ha'apai, Tonga
NORTH ISLAND; New Zealand
NUAPAPU; Vava'u Group, Tonga
NUI*; Tuvalu
NUKU; Tongatapu Group, Tonga
NUKU HIVA; Marquesas, French Polynesia
NUKUFETAU*; Tuvalu
NUKULAELAE*; Tuvalu
NUKUMANU; Polynesian Outlier, Ontong Java atoll,
NUKUNAMO; Ha'apai Group, Tonga
NUKUNONU*; Tokelau
NUKUORO; Polynesian Outlier, Micronesia
NUKUPULE; Ha'apai Group, Tonga
NUKURIA; Polynesian Outlier, Ontong Java atoll
NUKUTAVAKE (Queen Charlotte); Tuamotu Islands, French Polynesia
NUKUTIPIPI* (Margaret); Tuamotu Islands, French Polynesia
O'AHU; Hawai'i
OENO*; Pitcairn Islands
OFOLANGA; Ha'apai Group, Tonga
OFU; American Sāmoa
OLOSEGA; American Sāmoa
ONEVAI; Tongatapu Group, Tonga
'O'UA; Kotu Group, Ha'apai, Tonga
OVAKA; Vava'u Group, Tonga
PALMERSTON*; (Avarua) Lower Cook Islands
PANGAIMOTU; Vava'u Group, Tonga
PARAOA* (Gloucester); Tuamotu Islands, French Polynesia
PENRHYN* (Tongareva); Northern Cook Islands
PILENI; Polynesian Outlier, Santa Cruz Islands
PINAKI* (Whitsunday); Tuamotu Islands, French Polynesia
PITCAIRN ISLAND; Pitcairn Islands

PITT ISLAND; Chatham Group, New Zealand
PUKAPUKA* (Dog); Tuamotu Islands, French Polynesia
PUKAPUKA*; Northern Cook Islands
PUKARUA* (Serle); Tuamotu Islands, French Polynesia
RĀ'IATEA; Society Islands, French Polynesia
RAIVAVAE; Austral Islands, French Polynesia
RAKAHANGA*; Northern Cook Islands
RANGIROA* (Deans); Tuamotu Islands, French Polynesia
RAOUL; Kermadec Islands, New Zealand
RAPA; Austral Islands, French Polynesia
RARAKA*; Tuamotu Islands, French Polynesia
RAROIA* (Barclay de Tolley); Tuamotu Islands, French Polynesia
RAROTONGA; Lower Cook Islands
RAVAHERE* (Dawhaida); Tuamotu Islands, French Polynesia
REAO* (Clermont-Tonnere); Tuamotu Islands, French Polynesia
REITORU* (Bird's); Tuamotu Islands, French Polynesia
REKAREKA* (Tehuata, Good Hope); Tuamotu Islands, French Polynesia
RENNELL; Polynesian Outlier, Solomon Islands
RIMATARA; Austral Islands, French Polynesia
ROSE*; American Sāmoa
RURUTU; Austral Islands, French Polynesia
SAVAI'I; Sāmoa
SIKAIANA; Polynesian Outlier, Solomon Islands
SOUTH ISLAND; New Zealand
SOUTH-EAST ISLAND; Chatham Group, New Zealand
STEWART ISLAND; New Zealand
SUWARROW* (Suvarov); Northern Cook Islands
SWAINS ISLAND; American Sāmoa
TAENGA* (Holt, Yermalov); Tuamotu Islands, French Polynesia
TAFAHI; Niuatoputapu Group, Tongan Outlier
TAHA'A; Society Islands, French Polynesia
TAHANEA* (Tchitchagoff); Tuamotu Islands, French Polynesia
TAHITI; Society Islands, French Polynesia
TAHUATA; Marquesas, French Polynesia
TAIARO* (King); Tuamotu Islands, French Polynesia
TAKAPOTO* (Spiridof); Tuamotu Islands, French Polynesia
TAKAROA* (King George's Islet); Tuamotu Islands, French Polynesia
TAKUME* (Volkonsky); Tu-

amotu Islands, French Polynesia
TAKUTEA; Lower Cook Islands
TAKU'U; Polynesian Outlier, Ontong Java atoll
TANOA; Nomuka Group, Ha'apai, Tonga
TARAVAI; Gambier Islands, French Polynesia
TATAFA; Ha'apai Group, Tonga
TATAKOTO* (Clerke, Narcissus); Tuamotu Islands, French Polynesia
TAU; Tongatapu Group, Tonga
TA'Ū (Tau); American Sāmoa
TAUERE* (St. Simeon); Tuamotu Islands, French Polynesia
TAUMAKO; Polynesian Outlier, Santa Cruz Islands
TEAUPA; Kotu Group, Ha'apai, Tonga
TEKOKOTA* (Doubtful); Tuamotu Islands, French Polynesia
TELEKITONGA; Otu Tolu Group, Ha'apai, Tonga
TELEKIVAVA'U; Otu Tolu Group, Ha'apai, Tonga
TEMATANGI* (Bligh's); Tuamotu Islands, French Polynesia
TEMOE* (Timoe); Gambier Islands, French Polynesia
TENARARO* (Marokao); Tuamotu Islands, French Polynesia
TENARUNGA (Minto); Tuamotu Islands, French Polynesia
TEPOTO NORTH (Otooho); Tuamotu Islands, French Polynesia
TEPOTO SOUTH* (Eliza); Tuamotu Islands, French Polynesia
TETIAROA*; Society Islands, French Polynesia
THOMASSET ROCK; Marquesas, French Polynesia
TIKEHAU* (Krusenstern); Tuamotu Islands, French Polynesia
TIKEI (Romanzoff); Tuamotu Islands, French Polynesia
TIKOPIA; Polynesian Outlier, Eastern Solomon Islands
TOAU* (Elizabeth); Tuamotu Islands, French Polynesia
TOFANGA; Ha'apai Group, Tonga
TOFUA; Haapai Group, Tonga
TOKELAU (Union Group); Tokelau
TOKU; Tongan Outlier
TONGATAPU; Tongatapu Group, Tonga
TONUMEA; Nomuka Group, Ha'apai, Tonga
TUANAKE* (Reid); Tuamotu Islands, French Polynesia
TUBUAI; Austral Islands, French Polynesia
TUNGUA; Kotu Group, Ha'apai, Tonga
TUPAI* (Motu Iti); Society Islands, French Polynesia
TUREIA* (Carysfort); Tuamotu Islands, French Polynesia
TUTUILA; American Sāmoa
UA HUKA; Marquesas, French

Polynesia
UA POU; Marquesas, French Polynesia
‘UIHA; Ha‘apai Group, Tonga
UOLEVA; Ha‘apai Group, Tonga
UONUKUHAHAKE; Ha‘apai Group, Tonga
‘UPOLU; Sāmoa
‘UTUNGAKE; Vava‘u Group, Tonga
‘UVEA (Wallis); Wallis and Futuna (French)
VAHANGA* (Bedford); Tuamotu Islands, French Polynesia
VAHITAHI* (Cook’s Lagoon); Tuamotu Islands, French Polynesia
VAIRAATEA* (Egmont); Tuamotu Islands, French Polynesia
VAIRIAVAI (Vairivai); Austral Islands, French Polynesia
VAITUPU; Tuvalu
VANAVANA* (Barrow)
VAVA‘U; Vava‘u Group, Tonga
WALLIS (‘Uvea); Wallis and Futuna (French)
WEST FUTUNA; Polynesian Outlier, Vanuatu
WEST ‘UVEA; Polynesian Outlier, Loyalty Islands

APPENDIX B
RULERS AND ADMINISTRATORS

AMERICAN SĀMOA

(U.S. Naval Governors 1900–1951)
(Appointed Civil Governors 1951–1978)

Elected Governors

Peter Tali Coleman (1978–1984)
A. P. Lutali (1984–1988)
Peter Tali Coleman (1988–1992)
A. P. Lutali (1992–1996)
Tauese Sunia (1996–)

COOK ISLANDS

(New Zealand administration 1901–1965)

Premiers

Albert R. Henry (1965–1978)
Tom Davis (1978–1983)
Geoffrey Henry (1983)
Tom Davis (1983–1987)
Pupuke Robati (1987–1989)
Geoffrey Henry (1989–1999)
Joe Williams (1999)
Terepai Moate (1999–)

EASTER ISLAND

(Appointed civilian governors from Chile until 1964.)

Elected Magistrates—Mayors/Governors

Sergio Rapu (1984–1989)
Jacobo Hey Paoa (1989–2000)
Enrique Pakarati Ikia (2000–)

FRENCH POLYNESIA

Monarchs

King Pomare I (ca. 1743–1803)
King Pomare II (1803–1821)
King Pomare III (1821–1827)
Queen Pomare IV (1827–1877)
King Pomare V (1877–1891)

(French Naval Administrators, 1843–1881)
(Appointed French Governors, 1881–1977)
(Internal autonomy granted 1977.)

Vice President

Francis Sanford (1977–1985)

President

Gaston Flosse (1985–1987)
Alexandre Léontieff (1987–1991)
Gaston Flosse (1991–)

HAWAI'I

(Independent kingdom until 1893.)

Monarchs

Kamehameha I (1795–1819)
Kamehameha II (1819–1824)
Kamehameha III (1824–1854)
Kamehameha IV (1854–1863)
Kamehameha V (1863–1872)
Lunalilo (1873–1874)
Kalakaua (1874–1891)
Queen Lili'uokalani (1891–1893)

President of the Republic

Sanford B. Dole (1893–1898)

Appointed U.S. Territorial Governors

Sanford B. Dole (1900–1903)
George Robert Carter (1903–1907)
Walter Francis Frear (1907–1913)

Lucius Eugene Pinkham (1913–1918)
Charles James McCarthy (1918–1921)
Wallace Rider Farrington (1921–1929)
Lawrence McCully Judd (1929–1934)
Joseph Boyd Poindexter (1934–1942)
Ingram Macklin Stainback (1942–1951)
Oren Ethelbirt Long (1951–1953)
Samuel Wilder King (1953–1957)
William Francis Quinn (1957–1959)

Elected State Governors

William Francis Quinn (1959–1962)
John Anthony Burns (1962–1974)
George R. Ariyoshi (1974–1986)
John Waihe'e (1986–1994)
Benjamin J. Cayetano (1994–)

NAURU

Presidents

Hammer DeRoburt (1968–1976)
Bernard Dowiyogo (1976–1978)
Lagumot Harris (1978)
Hammer DeRoburt (1978–1986)
Kennan Adeang (1986)
Hammer DeRoburt (1986)
Kennan Adeang (1986)
Hammer DeRoburt (1986–1989)
Kenos Aroi (1989)
Bernard Dowiyogo (1989–1995)
Lagumot Harris (1995–1996)
Bernard Dowiyogo (1996)
Kennan Adeang (1996)
Rueben Kun (1996–1997)
Kinza Godfrey Clodumar (1997–1998)
Bernard Dowiyogo (1998–1999)
René Harris (1999–2000)
Bernard Dowiyogo (2000–2001)
René Harris (2001–)

NEW ZEALAND

Premiers/Prime Ministers

George Grey (1877–1879)
John Hall (1879–1882)
Frederick Whitaker (1882–1883)
Harry Albert Atkinson (1883–1884)
Robert Stout (1884)
Harry Albert Atkinson (1884)
Robert Stout (1884–1887)
Harry Albert Atkinson (1887–1891)
John Ballance (1891–1893)
Richard John Seddon (1893–1906)
William Hall–Jones (1906)
Joseph George Ward (1906–1912)
Thomas MacKenzie (1912)
William Ferguson Massey (1912–1925)
Francis Henry Dillon Bell (1925)
Joseph Gordon Coates (1925–1928)
Joseph George Ward (1928–1930)
George William Forbes (1930–1935)
Michael Joseph Savage (1935–1940)
Peter Fraser (1940–1949)
Sidney George Holland (1949–1957)
Keith Jacka Holyoake (1957)
Walter Nash (1957–1960)
Keith Jacka Holyoake (1960–1972)
John Ross Marshall (1972)
Norman Eric Kirk (1972–1974)
Wallace Edward Rowling (1974–1975)
Robert David Muldoon (1975–1984)
David Russell Lange (1984–1989)
Geoffrey Winston Russell Palmer (1989–1990)
Michael (Mike) Moore (1990)
James (Jim) Bolger (1990–1997)
Jennifer (Jenny) Shipley (1997–1999)
Helen Elizabeth Clark (1999–)

NIUE

(Internal autonomy from New Zealand 1965.)

Premiers

Robert Richmond Rex (1965–1992)
Young Vivian (1993–1993)
Frank Lui (1993–1999)
Sani Elia Lakatani (1999–)

SĀMOA

(Administered by New Zealand from 1914 until independence in 1962.)

Heads of State

Tupua Tamasese (1962–1963)
Malietoa Tanumafili II (1962–)

Prime Ministers

Fiamē Matā'afa Mulinu'u (1959–1969)
Tupua Tamasese Lealofi (1969–1972)
Fiamē Matā'afa Mulinu'u (1972–1975)
Tupua Tamasese Lealofi (1975–1976)
Tupuola Efi (1976–1982)
Va'ai Kolone (1982)
Tupuola Efi (1982)
Tofilau Eti Alesana (1982–1985)
Va'ai Kolone (1985–1988)
Tofilau Eti Alesana (1988–1998)
Tuila'epa Sailele Malielegoai (1998–)

TOKELAU

New Zealand Administrators

R. O. Gabites (1967–1971)
R. B. Taylor (1971–1973)
W. G. Thorpe (1973–1984)
Frank H. Corner (1984–1988)
Neil Walter (1988–1990)
Graham K. Ansell (1990–1993)
Lindsay Watt (1993–1994)
Brian Absolum (1994–1996)
Lindsay Watt (1996–)

TONGA

Monarchs

King Tāufa'āhau George Tupou I (1845–1893)
King George Tāufa'āhau Tupou II (1893–1918)
Queen Sālote Tupou III (1918–1965)
King Tāufa'āhau Tupou IV (1965–)

TUVALU

(Administered by a resident commissioner as the Ellice Islands from 1892 to 1977.)

Governor-Generals

Fiatao Penitala Teo (1978–1986)
Tupua Leupena (1986–1990)
Toaripi Lauti (1990–1993)
Tomu Sione (1993–1994)
Tulaga Manuella (1994–1998)
Tomasi Puapua (1998–)

Prime Ministers

Toaripi Lauti (1978–1981)
Tomasi Puapua (1981–1988)
Bikenibeu Pacniu (1989–1993)
Kamuta Latasi (1993–1996)
Bikenibeu Paeniu (1996–1999)
Ionatana Ionatana (1999–2000)
Faimalaga Luka (2001–)

APPENDIX C – SUMMARY GUIDE TO POLYNESIA

Island Group	Population	Area Sq Mi/Sq. Km	Per Capita Income*	Political Status
American Sāmoa	64,100	76.1/194.8	$2,600	U.S. territory; Tauese Sunia elected governor (1996).
Cook Islands	14,300	91.5/237	$4,000	Self-governing territory in free association with New Zealand; Prime Minister Terepai Maoate (1999).
Easter Island	2,721	60/158	N/A	Territory of Chile; Governor Enrique Pakarati Ikia (2000).
French Polynesia	233,000	1,544/4,014	$10,980	Autonomous overseas territory of France; President Gaston Flosse (1991).
Hawai'i	1,211,537	6,450/16,770	$29,029	U.S. state; Benjamin J. Cayetano elected governor (1994).
Nauru	11,346	21/54.6	$10,000	Independent republic; President René Harris elected 2nd time (2001).
New Zealand	3,862,000	103,415/ 267,844	$17,400	Independent state, member Commonwealth; Prime Minister Helen Elizabeth Clark (1999).
Niue	1,857	101/262.7	$1,200	Self-governing in free association with New Zealand; Premier Sani Elia Lakatani (1999).

(Continued on next page.)

Island Group	Population	Area Sq Mi/Sq. Km	Per Capita Income	Political Status
Pitcairn	47	18/47	N/A	British dependent territory; Governor Martin Williams (1998); Jay Warren, island magistrate (1991).
Sāmoa	169,200	1,133/2934	$2,100	Independent state, member Commonwealth; Head of State Malietoa Tanumafili II (1962); Prime Minister Tuila‘epa Sailele Malielegoai (1998).
Tokelau	1,500	4.7/12.2	$796	Island territory of New Zealand; Administrator Lindsay Watt (1996).
Tonga	100,200	289/748	$2,100	Independent kingdom, member Commonwealth; King Tāufa‘āhau Tupou IV (1965).
Tuvalu	9,900	10/26	$826	Democratic soverign state, special member Commonwealth; Prime Minister Faimalaga Luka (2001).
Wallis and Futuna	14,600	106/275	$1,939	Self-governing French overseas territory; Chief Administrator Christian Dors (1998); Tomasi Kulimoetoke, king of Wallis; Lafaele Malau, king of Sigave; Lomano Musulamu, king of Alo.

*Per capita income in U.S. dollars from *1999 CIA World Fact Book* and from local government statistics.

BIBLIOGRAPHY

Contents

Introduction

The following bibliography lists nearly 1,200 important books relating to Polynesian history, nearly 40 percent of them are newly published volumes that have appeared since the first edition of this *Historical Dictionary* in 1993. Some citations from the 1993 *Dictionary* have been dropped in favor of these new listings. This does not necessarily mean that the newer ones outrank the older works nor that they are recommended by the author, but that they are worthy of examination in the light of their newness.

The two major research languages of the Pacific continue to be primarily French and English, French because of the extensive French territories in Polynesia and Melanesia and English because of Great Britain's vast empire that once spread throughout the Pacific and whose now independent states remain members of the Commonwealth.

Research on almost any Pacific subject requires a visit to at least one of the major archival resource centers of the Pacific. They are the Mitchell Library, part of the State Library of New South Wales, located in Sydney, Australia; the Alexander Turnbull Library, housed within the National Library of New Zealand, located in Wellington; the New Zealand and Pacific Collection of the University of Auckland Library; the Australian National University Library, Canberra, which also houses the Pacific Manuscripts Bureau; the Pacific Collection at the University of Hawai'i—Mānoa Campus, Honolulu; and the Bishop Museum Library, downtown Honolulu. All these libraries have unique collections of original manuscripts, drawings, prints, photographic collections, maps, newspapers, microfilms, books, and journals for research. Their card catalogs, and in some instances databases and other digital reproductions, are available on the Internet for on-line bibliographical research.

Scholarly journals provide an avenue for much deeper insight and current discussion on specific topics far better than books and other print materials. Polynesian journals, published in the Pacific, date back to 1892 with the first publication—the *Journal of the Polynesian Society* (Auckland). It continues to provide the most current results of contemporary research on a wide variety of Pacific topics. Two important French journals devoted to the Pacific are the *Bulletin de la Société des*

Études Océaniennes (Pape'ete, founded in 1917) and the *Journal de la Société des Océanistes* (Paris, 1945). More recent English language additions are the *Journal of Pacific History* (Australian National University, founded 1966), *Pacific Studies* (Brigham Young University–Hawai'i Campus, 1977), and the *Contemporary Pacific* (University of Hawai'i, 1989).

There have been several important bibliographical and reference books that have been published since the first edition of this *Dictionary*. Two are worthy of special mention. The first is John Thawley's outstanding *Australasia and South Pacific Islands Bibliography* (Scarecrow Press, 1997), and the other is *The Pacific Islands: An Encyclopedia* (University of Hawai'i Press, 2000), edited by Brij V. Lal and Kate Fortune. The encyclopedia's superb coverage of Pacific history, politics, society, and cultural will not soon be surpassed. The inclusion of a CD-ROM makes it an ideal reference tool for the classroom or library.

Modern Polynesian historical research essentially dates from the end of World War II when the Pacific empires of Great Britain, France, and to some extent the United States began disappearing. Up until then, most of the island histories were written as appendages to the larger histories of the islands' metropolitan countries. Beginning with the independence of Sāmoa (1962) and extending over the next several decades, histories emerged that began to reflect the internal developments of these nascent states. Until then, the only one-volume survey of Pacific history was Douglas Oliver's *The Pacific Islands* (1951), and that was written by an anthropologist. It is still recommended; however, it has been superceded by newer, more complete histories of the Pacific, but they essentially can be numbered on one hand! There still exists a dearth of histories for the entire Pacific and even more so with the area of this dictionary—Polynesia. There have been no excellent one-volume histories of Polynesia that have appeared to date. Currently, the best recommendation is Kerry Howe's two volumes—*Where the Waves Fall: A New South Sea Islands History from First Settlement to Colonial Rule* (1984) and *Tides of History: The Pacific Islands in the 20th Century* (1994) (see full citations below) A thematic and interesting approach was recently used in the *Cambridge History of the Pacific Islanders* (Cambridge University Press, 1997), but because each chapter was written by a different scholar, the volume lacks a cohesiveness normally expected in area histories.

Polynesian prehistory is best detailed in Jesse D. Jenning's *The Prehistory of Polynesia* (Cambridge University Press, 1979), in Peter Bellwood's *Man's Conquest of the Pacific* (Oxford University Press, rev. ed., 1987), and in his shorter *The Polynesians: Prehistory of an Island People* (Thames and Hudson, 1978). A perennial favorite is still Robert C. Suggs's *The Island Civilizations of Polynesia* (New American Library, 1960), a more popular work that went into paperback. Recent scholarly undertakings have contributed to the study of ancient Polynesian seafaring. Recommended are David Lewis's *The Voyaging Stars: Secrets of the Pacific Island Navigators* (Norton, 1978) and Ben Finney's various volumes listed in section "D" below.

European exploration of the Pacific is well documented in J. C. Beaglehole's *The Exploration of the Pacific* (Stanford University Press, 3d ed., 1966) and in his volumes on Captain James Cook (see below) as well as in Oscar Spate's three volumes: *The Pacific Since Magellan, Volume 1: The Spanish Lake*; *Volume 2: Monopolists and Freebooters;* and *Volume 3: Paradise Found and Lost* (Australian National University, 1981–1988). Books that detail exploration by specific countries—Britain, France, Russia, and the United States, for example—are listed in the bibliography below.

Colonial history (1760–1960) is best portrayed in Deryck Scarr's *History of the Pacific Islands: Kingdoms of* the Reefs (Macmillan, 1990) and in Kerry Howe's *Where the Waves Fall* . . . (cited above). W. P. Morrell's *Britain in the Pacific Islands* (Clarendon Press, 1960) is old but still recommended. France's contributions are documented in the numerous publications of John Dunmore, but more specifically his *Visions and Reality: France in the Pacific, 1695–1995* (Heritage Press, 1997). Early U.S. activities are recorded in R. Gerard Ward's eight-volume work *American Activities in the Central Pacific, 1790–1870: A History, Geography and Ethnography Pertaining to American Involvement and Americans in the Pacific, Taken from Contemporary Newspapers, etc.* (Gregg Press, 1966–1967).

For general histories of individual Polynesian countries, refer to the specific sections below.

One cannot leave a bibliographical essay without mentioning the impact the Internet has had on Pacific research. When the first edition of this work appeared (1993), Internet activities (primarily within the universities) consisted of accessing the card catalogs of major university libraries and sending e-mail back and forth to colleagues throughout the world. Since the development of the World Wide Web, the commercial expansion of the Internet, and its resultant popularity, sources, newspapers, and databases are now on-line and within a finger click of the researcher. Almost all Pacific island governments now have their Internet Websites, numerous Pacific island news reporting agencies are currently on-line, and many statistical databases on population, health, welfare, and the like are available to the public. A few important Internet Website addresses are listed in sections "N" and "O" below. Internet addresses change frequently, so it is advisable to use an appropriate Internet search engine if the address has expired or is no longer available.

1. General References

A. Bibliographies and Reference Works

Angleviel, Frédéric, and others, eds. *Le Pacifique Sud: bibliographie des thèses et mémoires récents.* Talence, France: Centre de Recherche sur les Espaces, University of Bordeaux, 1991.

Aoki, Diane, and Norman Douglas, comps. *Moving Images of the Pacific Islands: A Guide to Films and Videos.* Honolulu, Hawai'i: Center for Pacific Island Studies, University of Hawai'i, 1994.

Australian National University. *Pacific History Bibliography.* 15 vols. Canberra, Australia: Australian National University, 1981–1996.

Buernhult, Goran, ed. *New World and Pacific Civilizations: Cultures of America, Asia, and the Pacific.* St. Lucia, Queensland, Australia: University of Queensland Press, 1994.

Craig, Robert D., and Frank P. King, eds. *Historical Dictionary of Oceania.* Westport, Conn.: Greenwood Press, 1981.

Davidson, James W., and Deryck Scarr, eds. *Pacific Island Portraits.* Canberra, Australia: Australian National University Press, 1973.

Day, A. Grove. *Pacific Islands Literature: One Hundred Basic Books.* Honolulu, Hawai'i: University Press of Hawai'i, 1971.

Douglas, Norman, and Ngaire Douglas, eds. *Pacific Islands Yearbook, 17th Edition.* Suva, Fiji: Fiji Times, 1994.

Doumenge, François. *L'Homme dans le Pacifique sud: Étude géographique.* Paris: Musée de l'Homme, 1966.

Dousset-Leenhardt, Roselene, and Étienne Taillemite. *The Great Book of the Pacific.* Translated by Edita Lausanne. Secaucus, N.J.: Chartwell Books, 1979.

Dunmore, John. *Visions and Reality: France in the Pacific, 1695–1995.* Waikanae, New Zealand: Heritage Press, 1997.

———. *Who's Who in Pacific Navigation.* Honolulu, Hawai'i: University of Hawai'i Press, 1991.

DuRitz, Rolf. *Bibliotheca Polynesiana: A Catalogue of Some of the Books in the Polynesian Collection Formed by the Late Bjarne Kropelien.* Uppsala, Sweden: Almqvist & Wiksell Boktryckeri AB, 1969.

Eldredge, Lucius G. *Bibliography of Marine Ecosystems, Pacific Islands.* Rome, Italy: Food and Agricultural Organization of the United Nations, 1987.

The Far East and Australasia, 2001. 32d ed. London: Europa Publications, 2001.

Frey, Gerald W., and Rufino Mauricio. *Pacific Basin and Oceania. World Bibliographical Series. Volume 70.* Oxford, England: Clio Press, 1987.

Furuhashi, Lynette, comp. *Pacific Islands Dissertations and Theses from the University of Hawai'i, 1923-1996.* Honolulu, Hawai'i: Center for Pacific Islands Studies, University of Hawai'i at Manoa, 1996.

Goetzfridt, Nicholas J. *Indigenous Navigation and Voyaging in the Pacific—A Reference Guide.* Westport, Conn.: Greenwood Press, 1992.

Hanson, Louise, and F. Allan Hanson. *The Art of Oceania: A Bibliography.* Boston: G. K. Hall and Company, 1984.

Ivory, Arthur E. E. *Pacific Index of Abbreviations and Acronyms in Common Use in the Pacific Basin Area.* London: Whitcoulls, 1982; reprinted Christchurch, New Zealand: Whitcoulls, 1993.

Jackson, Miles, ed. *Pacific Island Studies: A Survey of the Literature.* Westport, Conn.: Greenwood Press, 1986.

Kirtley, Bacil F. *A Motif-Index of Traditional Polynesian Narratives.* Honolulu, Hawai'i: University of Hawai'i Press, 1971.

Lal, Brij V., and Kate Fortune, eds. *The Pacific Islands: An Encyclopedia.* Honolulu, Hawai'i: University of Hawai'i Press, 2000.

Langdon, Robert. *The Pacific Manuscripts Bureau Book of Pacific Indexes.* Canberra, Australia: Australian National University, 1978.

———. *Where the Whalers Went: An Index to the Pacific Ports and Islands Visited by American Whalers in the Nineteenth Century.* Canberra, Australia: Pacific Manuscripts Bureau, 1984.

Lie, Rico. *Television in the Pacific Islands: An Annotated Bibliography, 1990.* Honolulu, Hawai'i: East West Center, 1990.

Macintyre, Michael. *The New Pacific.* London: Collins/British Broadcasting Corp., 1985.

McFadden, Clifford H. *A Bibliography of Pacific Area Maps.* San Francisco, Calif.: American Council, Institute of Pacific Relations, 1941; reprinted New York: AMS Press, 1978.

Mitchell Library. *Dictionary Catalogue of Printed Books.* 38 vols. Boston: G. K. Hall, 1968.

Moore, Clive. *Pacific History Journal Bibliography.* Canberra, Australia: Pacific Manuscripts Bureau, Australian National University, 1992.

Nunn, Godfrey R. *Asia and Oceania: A Guide to Archival and Manuscript Sources in the United States.* 5 vols. London: Mansell, 1985.

Pacific Manuscripts Bureau Book of Pacific Indexes. Canberra, Australia: Pacific Manuscripts Bureau, Australian National University, 1988.

Salvat, Bernard, and others, eds. *L'Encyclopédie de la Polynésie.* 9 vols. Pape'ete, Tahiti: Éditions de l'Alizé, 1985–89.

Scarr, Deryck, ed. *More Pacific Island Portraits.* Canberra, Australia: Australian National University Press, 1979.

Segal, Gerald, ed. *Political and Economic Encyclopedia of the Pacific.* Harlow, England: Longman, 1989.

Simmons, Donita Vasoto, and Sin Joan Yee. *Women in the South Pacific: A Bibliography.* Suva, Fiji: University of the South Pacific, 1982.

Simms, Norman. *Writers from the South Pacific.* Washington, D.C.: Three Continents Press, 1992.

South Pacific Bibliography 1989–1990. Suva, Fiji: Pacific Information Centre and the University of the South Pacific, 1991.

Sperry, Robert. *Education in the South and Central Pacific: A Bibliography.* Lawton, Okla.: Cameron University Library, 1989.

Spickard, Paul R, and others. *Pacific Islander Americans: An Annotated Bibliography in the Social Sciences.* Lāʻie, Hawaiʻi: Institute for Polynesian Studies, 1995.

Taylor, C. R. H. *A Pacific Bibliography: Printed Matter Relating to the Native Peoples of Polynesia, Melanesia, and Micronesia.* Oxford, England: Clarendon Press, 1965.

Thawley, John. *Australasia and South Pacific Islands Bibliography.* Lanham, Md.: Scarecrow Press, 1997.

Thompson, Anne-Gabrielle. *The Southwest Pacific: An Annotated Guide to Bibliographies, Indexes, and Collections in Australian Libraries.* Canberra, Australia: Research School of Pacific Studies, Australian National University, 1986.

Titcomb, Margaret. *Bibliography of the Pacific: 500 Books.* Ann Arbor, Mich.: Xerox University Microfilms, 1973.

Tudor, Judy, ed. *Pacific Islands Year Book and Who's Who.* Sydney, Australia: Pacific Publications, Ltd., 1984.

Turner, Harold W. *Bibliography of New Religious Movements in Primal Societies. Vol. 3 Oceania.* Boston: G. K. Hall, 1990.

University of the South Pacific. *Nuclear Issues in the South Pacific: A Bibliography.* Suva, Fiji: University of the South Pacific, 1987.

———. *South Pacific Bibliography, 1997.* Suva, Fiji: University of the South Pacific, 1997.

Uschtrin, Cornelia. *Südpazifik, Inselstaaten und Territorien: Eine Auswahlbibliographie.* Hamburg, Germany: Deutsches Übersee-Institut, Übersee-Dokumentation, Referat Asien und Südpazifik, 1999.

Who's Who in the South Pacific. Wellington, New Zealand: New Zealand Ministry of Foreign Affairs and Trade, 1990.

Woodbury, Susan. *Journeys through Pacific History: A Guide to the Pacific Islands Library and the Papers of H. E. and H. C. Maude.* Adelaide, Australia: University of Adelaide, 1995.

Woods, Anne Catherine. *Women in the Islands: An Annotated Bibliography of Pacific Women's Issues, 1982–1989.* Honolulu, Hawai'i: University of Hawai'i Pacific Islands Center, 1990.

Yen, Cynthia D. *A Directory of Libraries and Information Resources in Hawaii and the Pacific Islands.* 7th ed. Honolulu, Hawai'i: Hawai'i State Public Library System, 1989.

B. Atlases, Maps

Antheaume, Benoît, and J. Bonnesmaison. *Atlas des îles et états du Pacifique sud.* Paris: GIP Reclus, 1988.

Bier, James A. *Reference Map of Oceania: The Pacific Islands of Micronesia, Polynesia, and Melanesia.* Honolulu, Hawai'i: University of Hawai'i Press, 1995.

Bramwell, Martyn, ed. *Rand McNally Atlas of the Oceans.* Chicago: Rand McNally, 1987.

Frey, Gerald. *Pacific Basin and Oceania.* Santa Barbara, Calif.: Clio Press, 1989.

Hinz, Earl R. *Landfalls of Paradise: Cruising Guide to the Pacific Islands.* 4th ed. Honolulu, Hawai'i: Latitude 20, 1999.

McKnight, Tom Lee. *Oceania: The Geography of Australia, New Zealand, and the Pacific Islands.* Englewood Cliffs, N.J.: Prentice Hall, 1995.

Motteler, Lee S. *Pacific Island Names: A Map and Name Guide to the New Pacific.* Honolulu, Hawai'i: Bernice P. Bishop Museum Press, 1986.

Nile, Richard, and Christian Clerk. *Cultural Atlas of Australia, New Zealand and the South Pacific.* Surry Hills, New South Wales, Australia: RD Press, 1996.

C. History—General

Aldrich, Robert. *France, Oceania and Australia, Past and Present.* Sydney, Australia: Department of Economic History, University of Sydney, 1991.

Barclay, Glen St. John. *A History of the Pacific from the Stone Age to the Present.* New York: Taplinger Publishing Company, 1978.

Barratt, Glynn. *Russia in the South Pacific. Vol 2: Southern and Eastern Polynesia.* Vancouver: University of British Columbia Press, 1988.

Biersack, Aletta. *Clio in Oceania: Toward a Historical Anthropology.* Washington, D.C.: Smithsonian Institution Press, 1991.

Borofsky, Robert, ed. *Remembrance of Pacific Pasts: An Invitation to Remake History.* Honolulu, Hawai'i: University of Hawai'i Press, 2000.

Campbell, Ian C. *A History of the Pacific Islands.* Berkeley: University of California Press, 1989.

Crocombe, Ron, and others, eds. *Culture and Democracy in the South Pacific.* Suva, Fiji: Institute of Pacific Studies, University of the South Pacific, 1992.

Deckker, Paul de, and Pierre-Yves Toullelan, eds. *La France et la Pacifique.* Paris: Société Française d'Histoire d'Outre-Mer, 1990.

Denoon, Donald, ed. *The Cambridge History of the Pacific Islanders.* New York: Cambridge University Press, 1997.

Dorrance, John C. *The United States and the Pacific Islands.* Westport, Conn.: Praeger, 1992.

Drysdale, Peter, and Martin O'Hare, eds. *The Soviets and the Pacific Challenge.* Townsville, Queensland, Australia: Australian Institute of Marine Science, 1990.

Dunningan, James F., and Albert A. Nofi. *Victory at Sea: World War II in the Pacific.* New York: William Morrow, 1995.

Ford, Douglas. *The Pacific Islanders.* New York: Chelsea House, 1989.

Gwynn-Jones, Terry. *Wings Across the Pacific.* Sydney, Australia: Allen and Unwin, 1991.

Henningham, Stephen, and Desmond Ball, eds. *South Pacific Security: Issues and Perspectives.* Canberra, Australia: Strategic and Defence Studies Centre, Australian National University, 1991.

Johnson, Donald Dalton. *The United States in the Pacific: Private Interests and Public Policies, 1784–1899.* Westport, Conn.: Praeger, 1995.

Malcomson, Scott L. *Tuturani: A Political Journey in the Pacific Islands.* New York: Poseidon Press, 1990.

Mara, Ratu Sir Kamisese. *The Pacific Way: A Memoir.* Honolulu, Hawai'i: University of Hawai'i Press, 1997.

Maude, H. E. *Of Islands and Men: Studies in Pacific History.* Melbourne, Australia: Oxford University Press, 1968.

McDougall, Walter A. *Let the Sea Make a Noise: A History of the North Pacific from Magellan to MacArthur.* New York: Basic Books, 1993.

Rennie, Neil. *Far Fetched Facts: The Literature of Travel and the Idea of the South Seas.* Oxford, England: Oxford University Press, 1995.

Ross, Ken. *Regional Security in the South Pacific: The Quarter-Century 1970–1995.* Canberra, Australia: Strategic and Defence Studies Centre, Australian National University, 1993.

Sahlins, Marshall. *Islands of History.* Chicago: University of Chicago Press, 1985.

Scarr, Deryck. *The History of the Pacific Islands: Kingdom of the Reefs.* Melbourne, Australia: Macmillan Company of Australia, 1990.

Segal, Gerald. *Rethinking the Pacific.* London: Clarendon Press, 1990.

Theroux, Paul. *The Happy Isles of Oceania: Paddling the Pacific.* New York: G. P. Putnam's Sons, 1992.

University of the South Pacific. *Law, Government, and Politics in the Pacific Island States.* Suva, Fiji: University of the South Pacific, Institute for Pacific Studies, 1988.

D. History—Prehistory

Bellwood, Peter. *Man's Conquest of the Pacific: The Prehistory of Southeast Asia and Oceania.* London: Collins, 1978.

———. *The Polynesians: Prehistory of an Island People.* Rev. ed. London: Thames and Hudson, 1987.

Bellwood, Peter, James J. Fox, and Darrell Tryon, eds. *The Austronesians. Historical and Comparative Perspectives.* Canberra, Australia: Research School of Asian and Pacific Studies, Australian National University, 1995.

Buck, Sir Peter H. *Vikings of the Pacific.* Chicago: University of Chicago Press, 1959.

Crawford, Peter, and the British Broadcasting Corporation. *Nomads of the Wind: A Natural History of Polynesia.* London: BBC Books, 1993.

Dodd, Edward. *The Island World of Polynesia: A Survey of the Racial Family and Its Far-Flung Cultures.* Putney, Vt.: Windmill Hill Press, 1990.

Dye, Thomas S. *Social and Cultural Change in the Prehistory of the Ancestral Polynesian Homeland.* New Haven, Conn.: Yale University Press, 1987.

Ellis, William. *Polynesian Researches: Polynesia.* Rev. ed. Rutland, Vt.: Charles E. Tuttle Company, 1969.

Finney, Ben. *Pacific Navigation and Voyaging.* Wellington, New Zealand: Polynesian Society, 1976.

Firth, Stewart. *Primitive Polynesian Economy.* 2d ed. London: Routledge & Kegan Paul, 1965.

Fornander, Abraham. *An Account of the Polynesian Race: Its Origins and Migrations and the Ancient History of the Hawaiian People to the Times of Kamehameha I.* London: Trubner & Co., 1878-85; reprinted Rutland, Vt.: Charles E. Tuttle Company, 1969.

Goldman, Irving. *Ancient Polynesian Society.* Chicago: University of Chicago Press, 1970.

Graves, Michael W., and Roger Curtis Green. *The Evolution and Organization of Prehistoric Society in Polynesia.* Auckland, New Zealand: New Zealand Archaeological Association, 1993.

Heyerdahl, Thor. *American Indians in the Pacific: The Theory Behind the Kon-Tiki Expedition.* Chicago: Rand McNally, 1953.

———. *Early Man and the Ocean: A Search for the Beginnings of Navigation and Seaborne Civilization.* New York: Vintage Books, 1980.

———. *Sea Routes to Polynesia.* London: Allen & Unwin, 1968.

Hill, Adrian V. S., and Susan W. Serjeantson, eds. *Colonization of the Pacific: A Genetic Tale.* New York: Oxford University Press, 1989.

Howard, Alan, and Robert Borofsky, eds. *Developments in Polynesian Ethnology.* Honolulu, Hawai'i: University of Hawai'i Press, 1989.

Irwin, Geoffrey. *Prehistoric Exploration and Colonisation of the Pacific.* Melbourne, Australia: Oxford University Press, 1992.

Jennings, Jesse D., ed. *The Prehistory of Polynesia.* Cambridge, Mass.: Harvard University Press, 1979.

Kirch, Patrick Vinton. *On the Road of the Winds: An Archaeological History of the Pacific Islands before European Contact.* Berkeley, Calif.: University of California Press, 2000.

Kirk, Robert. *Out of Asia: Peopling the Americas and the Pacific.* Canberra, Australia: Australian National University, 1990.

Langdon, Robert. *The Lost Caravel.* Sydney, Australia: Pacific Publications, 1975.

———. *The Lost Caravel Re-Explored.* Canberra, Australia: Brolga Press, 1988.

Lewis, David. *From Maui to Cook: The Discovery and Settlement of the Pacific.* Sydney, Australia: Doubleday Australia, 1977.

———. *The Voyaging Stars: Secrets of the Pacific Island Navigators.* New York: W. W. Norton, 1978.

Nunn, Patrick D. *Environmental Change and the Early Settlement of the Pacific Islands.* Honolulu, Hawai'i: East-West Center, 1994.

Sharp, Andrew. *Ancient Voyagers in Polynesia.* Berkeley: University of California Press, 1964.

Shutler, Richard, and Mary E. Shutler. *Oceania Prehistory.* Menlow Park, Calif.: Cummings Publishing Company, 1975.

Spriggs, Matthew, ed. *A Community of Culture: The People and Prehistory of the Pacific.* Canberra, Australia: Research School of Asian and Pacific Studies, Australian National University, 1993.

Suggs, Robert C. *The Island Civilizations of Polynesia.* New York: New American Library, 1960.

Terrell, John. *Prehistory in the Pacific Islands: A Study of Variation in Language, Customs, and Human Biology.* Cambridge, Mass.: Cambridge University Press, 1986.

Thorne, Alan, and Robert Raymonde. *Man on the Rim: The Peopling of the Pacific.* Sydney, Australia: Angus & Robertson, 1989.

E. History—Exploration

Account of the Mutinous Seizure of the Bounty. Guildford, England: Genesis Publications, 1987. Reprint of 1790 publication.

Badger, G. M. *The Explorers of the Pacific.* Kenthurst, New South Wales, Australia: Kangaroo Press, 1988; 2d rev. ed., 1996.

Barratt, Glynn. *Russia and the South Pacific: 1696–1840. Vol. 2. Southern and Eastern Polynesia.* Vancouver: University of British Columbia Press, 1988.

———. *Russia in Pacific Waters, 1715–1825: A Survey of the Origins of Russia's Naval Presence in the North and South Pacific.* Vancouver: University of British Columbia Press, 1981.

Barrow, John, ed. *Voyages of Discovery.* Chicago: Academy Chicago Publishers, 1993.

Beaglehole, John C. *The Exploration of the Pacific.* 3d ed. Stanford, Calif.: Stanford University Press, 1966.

———. *The Journals of Captain James Cook on His Voyages of Discovery.* 4 vols. Cambridge, Mass.: Cambridge University Press for the Hakluyt Society, 1955, 1961, 1967, 1974.

Bligh, William. *A Voyage to the South Seas.* Adelaide, Australia: Libraries Board of South Australia, 1969. Reprint of 1790 publication.

Buck, Peter. *Explorers of the Pacific: European and American Discoveries in Polynesia.* Honolulu, Hawai'i: Bishop Museum, 1953.

Cathcart, Michael, and others. *Mission to the South Seas: The Voyage of the Duff, 1796–1799.* Parkville, Victoria, Australia: University of Melbourne History Department, 1990.

Conte, Eric. *Tereraa: Voyaging and the Colonization of the Pacific Islands.* Pape'ete, Tahiti: Polymages-Scoop, 1992.

David, Andrew, and others, eds. *The Chart and Coastal Views of Captain Cook's Voyages. Vol. 1, The Voyage of the Endeavour, 1768–1771.* London: Hakluyt Society, 1988.

Dening, Greg. *The Death of William Gooch: A History's Anthropology.* Honolulu, Hawai'i: University of Hawai'i Press, 1995.

Dodge, Ernest S. *Beyond the Capes: Pacific Exploration from Cook to the* Challenger, *1776-1877.* Boston: Little, Brown, 1971; reprinted London; Victor Gollancz, 1971.

Dunmore, John. *French Explorers of the Pacific.* 2 vols. Oxford, England: Clarendon Press, 1965.

———. *Who's Who in Pacific Navigation.* Honolulu, Hawai'i: University of Hawai'i Press, 1991.

Forster, Johann Reinhold. *Observations Made during a Voyage round the World.* Ed. by Nicholas Thomas, Harriet Guest, and Michael Dettelbach. Honolulu, Hawai'i: University of Hawai'i Press, 1996.

———. *A Voyage round the World.* Ed. by Nicholas Thomas and Oliver Berghof. Honolulu, Hawai'i: University of Hawai'i Press, 1999.

Friis, Hermen R., ed. *The Pacific Basin: A History of its Geographical Exploration.* New York: American Geographical Society, 1967.

Frost, Alan. *Convicts and Empire: A Naval Question, 1776–1811.* Melbourne, Australia: Oxford University Press, 1980.

Horner, Frank. *Looking for La Pérouse: D'Entrecasteaux in Australia and the South Pacific, 1792–1793.* Carleton, Victoria, Australia: Miegunyah Press, 1995.

Howse, Derek, ed. *Background to Discovery: Pacific Exploration from Dampier to Cook.* Berkeley: University of California Press, 1990.

Langdon, Robert. *The Lost Caravel.* Sydney, Australia: Pacific Publications, 1975.

Lewis, David. *We the Navigators: The Ancient Art of Landfinding in the Pacific 2d.* ed. Honolulu, Hawai'i: University of Hawai'i Press, 1994.

Napier, William. *Pacific Voyages: The Encyclopaedia of Discovery and Exploration.* London: Aldus Books, 1971.

Nordyke, Eleanor C. *Pacific Images: Views from Captain Cook's Third Voyage.* Honolulu, Hawai'i: University of Hawai'i Press, 1999.

Obeyesekere, Gananath. *The Apotheosis of Captain Cook: European Mythmaking in the Pacific.* Princeton, N.J.: Princeton University Press, 1992; and Honolulu, Hawai'i: Bishop Museum Press, 1992.

Rodao, Florentino, ed. *España y el Pacífico.* Madrid, Spain: Agencia Española de Cooperación Internacional, 1989.

Rosenman, Helen. *Two Voyages to the South Seas by Captain Jules S.-C. Dumont d'Urville.* 2 vols. Honolulu, Hawai'i: University of Hawai'i Press, 1992.

Sahlins, Marshall David. *How "Natives" Think: About Captain Cook, for Example.* Chicago: University of Chicago Press, 1995.

Sharp, Andrew. *The Discovery of the Pacific Islands.* Oxford, England:Clarendon Press, 1960.

Spate, O. H. K. *The Pacific Since Magellan, Volume I: The Spanish Lake; Volume 2: Monopolists and Freebooter; Volume 3: Paradise Found and Lost.* Canberra, Australia: Australian National University, 1981–1988.

F. History—Colonial

Aldrich, Robert. *The French Presence in the South Pacific, 1842–1940.* Honolulu, Hawai'i: University of Hawai'i Press, 1990.

Barratt, Glynn. *Russia and the South Pacific: 1696–1840. Vol. 2. Southern and Eastern Polynesia.* Vancouver: University of British Columbia Press, 1988.

Brookes, Jean Ingram. *International Rivalry in the Pacific Islands, 1800–1875.* London: Sidgwick & Jackson, 1978.

Calder, Alex, Jonathan Lamb, and Bidget Orr, eds. *Voyages and Beaches: Europe and the Pacific, 1769–1840.* Honolulu, Hawai'i: University of Hawai'i Press, 1999.

Howe, Kerry R. *Where the Waves Fall: A New South Seas Islands History from First Settlement to Colonial Rule.* Honolulu, Hawai'i: University of Hawai'i Press, 1984.

Lal, Brij V., and Hank Nelson, eds. *Lines acrosss the Sea: Colonial Inheritance in the Post Colonial Pacific.* Brisbane, Australia: Pacific History Association, 1995.

Maude, H. E. *Slavers in Paradise: The Peruvian Slave Trade in Polynesia, 1862–1864.* Stanford, Calif.: Stanford University Press, 1981.

Morrell, W. P. *Britain in the Pacific Islands.* Oxford, England:Clarendon Press, 1960.

Moses, John A. and Paul M. Kennedy, eds. *Germany in the Pacific and Far East 1870–1914.* St. Lucia, Queensland, Australia: University of Queensland Press, 1977.

Oliver, Douglas. *The Pacific Islands.* 3d. ed. Honolulu, Hawai'i: University Press of Hawai'i, 1989.

Scarr, Deryck. *Fragments of Empire: A History of the Western Pacific High Commission, 1877–1914.* Canberra, Australia: Australian National University Press, 1967.

Snow, Philip, and Stefanie Waine. *The People from the Horizon: An Illustrated History of the Europeans among the South Sea Islanders.* Oxford, England: Phaidon Press, 1979.

Strauss, W. Patrick. *Americans in Polynesia.* East Lansing: Michigan State University Press, 1963.

Ward, John M. *British Policy in the South Pacific, 1786–1893.* Westport, Conn.: Greenwood Press, 1976.

Ward, R. Gerard, ed. *American Activities in the Central Pacific, 1790–1870: A History, Geography and Ethnography Pertaining to American Involvement and Americans in the Pacific, Taken from Contemporary Newspapers, etc.* 8 vols. Ridgewood, N.J.: Gregg Press, 1966–1967.

G. History—Contemporary

Albinski, Henry S. *The South Pacific: Political, Economic, and Military Trends.* Washington, D.C.: Brassey's, 1989.

Aldrich, Robert. *France and the South Pacific since 1940.* Honolulu, Hawai'i: University of Hawai'i Press, 1993.

Bates, Stephen. *The South Pacific Island Countries and France: A Study in Inter-State Relations.* Canberra, Australia: Department of International Relations, Australian National University, 1990.

Bayliss-Smith, T., and others. *Islands, Islanders and the World.* Cambridge, Mass.: Cambridge University Press, 1988.

Chesneaux, Jean. *La France dans le Pacifique: De Bougainville à Moruroa.* Paris: Découvette, 1992.

Colbert, Evelyn Speyer. *The Pacific Islands: Paths to the Present.* Boulder, Colo.: Westview Press, 1997.

Connell, John, and John P. Lea. *Pacific 2010: Urbanisation in Polynesia.* Canberra, Australia: National Centre for Development Studies, Australian National University, 1995.

Crocombe, Ron, ed. *The Pacific Islands and the USA.* Rarotonga, Cook Islands: Institute of Pacific Studies, Univesity of the South Pacific, 1995.

Crocombe, Ron, and Amed Ali, eds. *Politics in Polynesia.* Suva, Fiji: Institute of Pacific Studies, 1983.

Davidson, James W. *Decolonisation of Oceania, A Survey, 1945–70.* Wellington, New Zealand: Institute of International Affairs, 1971.

Davis, Peter, ed. *Social Democracy in the Pacific.* Auckland, New Zealand: Ross Publishing, 1983.

Fairbairn, Te'o I. J., C. E. Morrison, R. W. Baker, and S. A. Groves. *The Pacific Islands: Politics, Economics, and International Relations.* Honolulu, Hawai'i: International Relations Program, East-West Center, 1992.

Ghai, Yash P., and Jill Cottrell. *Heads of State in the Pacific: A Legal and Constitutional Analysis.* Suva, Fiji: Institute of Pacific Studies, 1990.

Grattan, C. Hartley. *The Southwest Pacific since 1900: A Modern History.* Ann Arbor, Mich.: University of Michigan Press, 1963.

Hegarty, David, and Peter Polomka, eds. *The Security of Oceania in the 1990s. Vol. 1, Views from the Region.* Canberra, Australia: Strategic and Defence Studies Centre, Australian National University, 1989.

Henningham, Stephen. *France and the South Pacific: A Contemporary History.* Honolulu, Hawai'i: University of Hawai'i Press, 1992.

———. *The Pacific Island States: Security and Sovereignty in the Post-Cold War World.* New York: St. Martin's Press, 1995.

Hiery, Hermann Joseph. *The Neglected War: The German South Pacific and the Influence of World War I.* Honolulu, Hawai'i: University of Hawai'i Press, 1995.

Hinz, Earl R. *Pacific Island Battlegrounds of World War II: Then and Now.* Honolulu, Hawai'i: Bess Press, 1995.

Howe, K. R., Robert C. Kiste, and Brij V. Lal, eds. *Tides of History: The Pacific Islands in the Twentieth Century.* Honolulu, Hawai'i: University of Hawai'i Press, 1994.

Millar, T. B., and James Walter, eds. *Asian-Pacific Security After the Cold War.* 2d ed. Canberra, Australia: Allen & Unwin, 1993.

Renzi, William A., and Mark D. Roehrs. *Never Look Back: A History of World War II in the Pacific.* Armonk, N.Y.: M. E. Sharpe, 1991.

Sack, Peter, ed. *Pacific Constitutions.* Canberra, Australia: Australian National University, 1982.

Sanday, Jim. *South Pacific Culture and Politics, Notes on Current Issues.* Canberra, Australia: Australian National University, Pacific Studies, 1988.

Seward, Robert. *Radio Happy Isles: Media and Politics at Play in the Pacific.* Honolulu, Hawai'i: University of Hawai'i Press, 1998.

Smith, Roy H. *The Nuclear Free and Independent Pacific Movement: After Moruroa.* London: Tauris Academic Studies, 1997.

Tcherkezoff, Serge, and Françoise Douarie-Marsaudon. *Le pacifique sud aujourd'hui: identités et transformations culturelles.* Paris: CNRS Éditions, 1997.

Thakur, Ramesh Chandra. *The Last Bang before a Total Ban: French Nuclear Testing in the Pacific.* Canberra, Australia: Peace Research Centre, Australian National University, 1995.

Thompson, Roger C. *The Pacific Basin since 1945: A History of the Foreign Relations of the Asian, Australasian and America Rim States and the Pacific Islands.* London: Longman, 1994.

White, Geoffrey M., ed. *Remembering the Pacific War.* Honolulu, Hawai'i: Center for Pacific Islands Studies, University of Hawai'i–Mānoa, 1991.

White, Geoffrey M., and Lamont Lindstrom, eds. *The Pacific Theatre: Island Representations of World War II.* Honolulu, Hawai'i: University of Hawai'i Press, 1989.

———, eds. *Chiefs Today: Traditional Pacific Leadership and the Postcolonial State.* Stanford, Calif.: Stanford University Press, 1997.

H. History—Religion

Afeaki, Emilana, and others. *Religious Cooperation in the Pacific.* Suva, Fiji: Institute of Pacific Studies, 1983.

Barker, John, ed. *Christianity in Oceania: Ethnographic Perspectives.* Lanham, Md.: University Press of America, 1990.

Boutillier, James A., and others, eds. *Mission, Church and Sect in Oceania.* Ann Arbor, Mich.: University of Michigan Press, 1978.

Ellsworth, Samuel George. *Zion in Paradise: Early Mormons in the South Pacific.* Logan: Utah State University, 1959.

Ernst, Manfred. *Winds of Change: Rapidly Growing Religious Groups in the Pacific Islands.* Suva, Fiji: Pacific Conference of Churches, 1994.

Findlay, George G., and W. W. Holdsworth. *The History of the Wesleyan Methodist Missionary Society. Vol. 3. The Pacific.* London: Epworth Press, 1922.

Forman, Charles W. *The Island Churches of the South Pacific: Emergence in the Twentieth Century.* Maryknoll, N.Y.: Orbis Books, 1982.

Garrett, John. *Footsteps in the Sea: Christianity in Oceania to World War II.* Suva, Fiji: Institute for Pacific Studies, 1992.

———. *Where Nets Were Cast: Christianity in Oceania since World War II.* Suva, Fiji: Institute of Pacific Studies and World Council of Churches, 1997.

Gunson, W. Niel. *Messengers of Grace: Evangelical Missionaries in the South Seas 1797–1860.* Melbourne, Australia: Oxford University Press, 1978.

Handy, E. S. C. *Polynesian Religion.* Honolulu, Hawai'i: Bishop Museum Press, 1927.

James, Kerry, and Akuila Yabaki, eds. *Religious Cooperation in the Pacific Islands.* Rev. ed. Suva, Fiji: Institute of Pacific Studies, University of the South Pacific, 1989.

Lovett, Richard. *The History of the London Missionary Society, 1795–1895.* 2 vols. London: London Missionary Society, 1899.

Miller, Char, ed. *Missions and Missionaries in the Pacific.* New York: Edwin Mellen Press, 1985.

Pompallier, J. B. *Early History of the Catholic Church in Oceania.* Translated by A. Herman. Auckland, New Zealand: Brett, 1888.

Swain, Tony, and Garry Trompf. *The Religions of Oceania.* London: Routledge, 1995.

Turner, Harold W. *Bibliography of New Religious Movements in Primal Societies. Vol. 3 Oceania.* Boston: G. K. Hall, 1990.

Williamson, Robert W. *The Religious and Cosmic Beliefs of Central Polynesia.* 2 vols. Cambridge, Mass.: The University Press, 1933.

I. Cultural Arts: Language, Literature, Mythology, and so forth.

Alpers, Antony. *The World of the Polynesians: Seen through Their Myths and Legends, Poetry and Art.* Auckland, New Zealand: Oxford University Press, 1987.

Amadio, Nadine. *Pacifica: Myth, Magic, and Traditional Wisdom from the South Sea Islands.* Sydney, Australia: Angus and Roberson, 1993.

Andersen, Johannes C. *Myths and Legends of the Polynesians.* London: George G. Harrap, 1928; reprinted Rutland, Vt.: C. E. Tuttle Company, 1969.

Arbeit, Wendy (photographs by Douglas Peebles). *Baskets in Polynesia.* Honolulu, Hawai'i: University of Hawai'i Press, 1990.

Archey, Gilbert. *The Art Forms of Polynesia.* Auckland, New Zealand: Whitcombe & Tombs, 1965.

Barrow, Terence. *Art and Life in Polynesia.* Rutland, Vt.: Charles E. Tuttle, 1973.

Carell, Beth Dean. *South Pacific Dance.* Sydney, Australia: Pacific Publications, 1978.

Carr, D. J., ed. *Sydney Parkinson: Artist of Cook's* Endeavour *Voyage.* Honolulu, Hawai'i: University Press of Hawai'i, 1983.

Chapman, Murray, and Jean-François Dupon, eds. *Renaissance in the Pacific.* Paris: Survival International, 1989.

Craig, Robert D. *Dictionary of Polynesian Mythology.* Westport, Conn.: Greenwood Press, 1989.

Dark, Philip J., and Roger G. Rose, eds. *Artistic Heritage in a Changing Pacific.* Honolulu, Hawai'i: University of Hawai'i Press, 1993.

Davidson, Janet, and others, eds. *Oceanic Culture History: Essays in Honour of Roger Green.* Dunedin: New Zealand Journal of Archaeology, 1996.

Davidson, Jeremy H., ed. *Pacific Island Languages: Essays in Honour of G. B. Miller.* Honolulu, Hawai'i: University of Hawai'i Press, 1990.

Dodd, Edward. *Polynesian Art.* New York: Dodd, Mead, 1967.

Edler, John Charles, and Terence Barrow. *Art of Polynesia.* Honolulu, Hawai'i: Hemmeter Publishing, 1990.

Finnegan, Ruth H., and Margaret Rose Orbell, eds. *South Pacific Oral Tales.* Bloomington, Ind.: Indiana University Press, 1995.

Gathercole, Peter W., Adrienne L. Kaeppler, and Douglas Newton. *The Art of the Pacific Islands.* Washington, D.C.: National Gallery of Art, 1979.

Gell, Alfred. *Wrapping in Images: Tattooing in Polynesia.* Oxford, England:Clarendon Press, 1993.

Gill, William Wyatt. *Myths and Songs from the South Pacific.* London: H. S. King, 1876; reprinted New York: Arno Press, 1977.

Goetzfridt, Nicholas J. *Indigenous Literature of Oceania: A Survey of Criticism and Interpretation.* Westport, Conn.: Greenwood Press, 1995.

Hamblin, Charles L. *Languages of Asia and the Pacific.* London: Angus & Robertson, 1988.

Hanson, F. Allan, and Louise Hanson, eds. *Art and Identity in Oceania.* Honolulu, Hawai'i: University of Hawai'i Press, 1990.

Kaeppler, Adrienne L. *L'art océanien.* Paris: Citadelles & Mazenod, 1993.

Knappert, Jan. *Pacific Mythology: An Encyclopedia of Myth and Legend.* London: Aquarian/Thorsons, 1992.

Kooijman, Simon. *Tapa in Polynesia.* Honolulu, Hawai'i: Bishop Museum Press, 1972.

Lacabanne, Sonia. *Les premiers romans polynésiens: Naissance d'une littérature de la langue anglaise, 1948–1983.* Paris: Société des Océanistes, 1992.

Luomala, Katharine. *Voices on the Wind: Polynesian Myths and Chants.* Rev. ed. Honolulu, Hawai'i: Bernice P. Bishop Museum Press, 1986.

Lynch, John. *Pacific Languages: An Introduction.* Suva, Fiji: University of the South Pacific, 1993; reprinted Honolulu, Hawai'i: University of Hawai'i Press, 1998.

McLaren, John. *New Pacific Literatures: Culture and Environment in the European Pacific.* New York: Garland, 1993.

McLean, Mervyn. *An Annotated Bibliography of Oceanic Music and Dance.* Wellington, New Zealand: Polynesian Society, 1977; 2d ed. Warren, Mich.: Harmonie Park Press, 1995.

———. *Maori Music.* Auckland, New Zealand: Auckland University Press, 1996.

Mead, Sidney M., and Bernie Kernot, eds. *Art and Artists of Oceania.* Palmerston North, New Zealand: Dunmore Press, 1983.

Meyer, Anthony J. P. *Oceanic Art: Ozeanische Kunst: Art océanien.* 2 vols. Cologne, Germany: Konemann, 1995.

Moulin, Jane Freeman. *Music of the Southern Marquesas Islands.* Auckland, New Zealand: University of Auckland, Department of Anthropology, 1994.

Moyle, Richard M. *Polynesian Music and Dance.* Auckland, New Zealand: Centre for Pacific Studies, University of Auckland, 1991.

Nicholson, Bronwen. *Gauguin and Maori Art.* Auckland, New Zealand: Godwit Publisher, 1995.

Nuanua: Pacific Writing in English since 1980. Albert Wendt, ed. Auckland, New Zealand: Auckland University Press, 1995.

Oliver, Douglas L. *Native Cultures of the Pacific Islands.* Honolulu, Hawai‘i: University of Hawai‘i Press, 1989.

———. *Oceania: The Native Cultures of Australia and the Pacific Islands.* 2 vols. Honolulu, Hawai‘i: University of Hawai‘i Press, 1989.

Poort, W. A. *The Dance in the Pacific: A Comparative and Critical Survey of Dancing in Polynesia, Micronesia and Indonesia.* Katwijk, the Netherlands: Van der Lee Press, 1975.

Robie, David, ed. *Nius Bilong Pasifik: Mass Media in the Pacific.* Port Moresby: University Papua New Guinea Press, 1995.

Simmons, David. *Art of the Pacific.* Wellington, New Zealand: Oxford University Press, 1979.

Sinclair, Marjorie, comp. and ed. *The Path of the Ocean: Traditional Poetry of Polynesia.* Honolulu, Hawai‘i: University of Hawai‘i Press, 1982.

Smith, Bernard. *European Vision and the South Pacific.* 2d ed. New Haven, Conn.: Yale University Press, 1985.

———. *Imagining the Pacific: In the Wake of the Cook Voyages.* Melbourne, Australia: Melbourne University Press, 1992.

Thomas, Nicholas. *Oceanic Art.* London: Thames & Hudson, 1995.

Tryon, Darrell T., ed. *Comparative Austronesian Dictionary: An Introduction to Austronesian Studies.* Berlin, Germany: Mouton de Gruyter, 1995.

Williams, Esther W., ed. *Lisitala: A Bibliography of Pacific Writers.* Suva, Fiji: Pacific Information Centre in association with the 4th Festival of Pacific Arts Committee, 1984.

Wurm, S. A., and S. Hattori. *Language Atlas of the Pacific Area. Part I: New Guinea Area, Oceania, Australia.* Canberra, Australia: Australian Academy of the Humanities, 1981.

J. Economy

Acquaye, Ben. *Land Tenure and Rural Productivity in the Pacific Islands.* Rome, Italy: United Nations Food and Agricultural Organization, 1987.

Barrau, Jacques. *Subsistence Agriculture in Polynesia and Micronesia.* Honolulu, Hawai'i: Bernice P. Bishop Museum, 1961.

Bayliss-Smith, Timothy, and Richard Feachem. *Subsistence and Survival: Rural Ecology in the Pacific.* New York: Academic Press, 1977.

Bergerud, Eric M. *Touched with Fire: The Land War in the South Pacific.* New York: Viking, 1996.

Browne, Christopher, and Douglas A. Scott. *Economic Development in Seven Pacific Island Countries.* Washington, D.C.: International Monetary Fund, 1989.

Crocombe, Ron, ed. *Land Tenure in the Pacific.* 3d ed. Melbourne, Australia: Oxford University Press, 1987.

Crocombe, Ron, and Malama Meleisea, eds. *Land Issues in the Pacific.* Christchurch, New Zealand: Macmillan Brown Centre for Pacific Studies, 1994.

Fairbairn, Te'o I. J., C. E. Morrison, R. W. Baker, and S. A. Groves. *The Pacific Islands: Politics, Economics, and International Relations.* Honolulu, Hawai'i: International Relations Program, East-West Center, 1992.

Finney, Ben, and Karen Ann Watson, eds. *A New Kind of Sugar: Tourism in the Pacific.* Honolulu, Hawai'i: East-West Center, 1977.

Fisk, Ernest K. *Pacific Island Agriculture.* Canberra, Australia: Australian National University, 1986.

———. *The Subsistence Sector in Pacific Island Countries.* Canberra, Australia: National Centre for Development Studies, Research School of Pacific and Asian Studies, Australian National University, 1995.

Grynberg, Roman, and Matthew Powell. *Taxation in the Island Nations of the South Pacific.* 3 vols. Canberra, Australia: National Centre for Development Studies, Australian National University, 1994.

Haas, Michael. *The Pacific Way: Regional Cooperation in the South Pacific.* New York: Praeger, 1989.

Hailey, John M. *Business and Economic Development in the Pacific Islands Countries: A Select Bibliography.* Honolulu, Hawai'i: East-West Center, 1987.

Henningham, Stephen, R. J. May, and Lulu Turner, eds. *Resources, Development, and Politics in the Pacific Islands.* Bathurst, New South Wales: Crawford House Press, 1992.

Howard, Michael C. *The Political Economy of the South Pacific: An Introduction.* Townsville, Queensland, Australia: James Cook University, 1983.

———. *Mining, Politics and Development in the South Pacific.* Boulder, Colo.: Westview Press, 1991.

Larmour, Peter, and others, eds. *Land, People and Government: Public Lands Policy in the South Pacific.* Suva, Fiji: Institute of Pacific Studies, 1983.

Lieber, Michael D., ed. *Exiles and Migrants in Oceania.* Honolulu, Hawai'i: University of Hawai'i Press, 1977.

Lodewijks, John, and John Zerby, eds. *Recent Developments in the South Pacific Island Economies: Research Report.* Kensington, New South Wales: University of New South Wales, 1989.

Mamak, Alexander. *Paradise Postponed: Essays on Research and Development in the South Pacific.* Rushcutters Bay, New South Wales: Pergamon Press, 1978.

McKee, David L. *Developmental Issues in Small Island Economies.* New York: Praeger, 1990.

Minerbi, Luciano. *Impacts of Tourism Development in Pacific Islands.* San Francisco, Calif.: Greenpeace Pacific Campaign, 1992.

Picard, Michel, and Robert E. Wood. *Tourism, Ethnicity, and the State in Asian and Pacific Socities.* Honolulu, Hawai'i: University of Hawai'i Press, 1997.

Quarterly Economic Review of Pacific Islands: Papua New Guinea, Fiji, Solomon Islands, Western Samoa, Vanuatu, Tonga. London: Economist Intelligence Unit, 1985–, plus supplement.

Radvany, Janos, ed. *The Pacific in the 1990s: Economic and Strategic Change.* Lanham, Md.: University Press of America, 1990.

Rajotte, Freda, and others. *Pacific Tourism as Islanders See It.* Suva, Fiji: Institute of Pacific Studies, 1980.

Ralston, Caroline. *Grass Huts and Warehouses.* Honolulu, Hawai'i: University Press of Hawai'i, 1978.

Segal, Gerald, ed. *Political and Economic Encyclopedia of the Pacific.* Harlow, England: Longman, 1989.

Shineberg, Dorothy. *They Came for Sandalwood: A Study of the Sandalwood Trade in the Southwest Pacific, 1830–1865.* London: Cambridge University Press, 1967.

South Pacific Forum Fisheries. *The Forum Fisheries Agency: Achievements, Challenges, and Prospects.* Suva, Fiji: Institute of Pacific Studies, 1990.

Statistical Yearbook for Asia and the Pacific. Bangkok, Thailand: Economic and Social Commission for Asia and the Pacific, annual 1971–.

Steven, Margaret. *Trade, Tactics, and Territory: Britain in the Pacific, 1783–1823.* Melbourne, Australia: Melbourne University Press, 1983.

Thirlwall, A. P. *The Performance and Prospects of the Pacific Island Economies in the World Economy.* Honolulu, Hawai'i: Pacific Islands Development Program, East-West Center: 1992.

United Nations. *Economic and Social Survey of Asia and the Pacific.* New York: United Nations, annual 1974–.

Universal Business Directory: Asia-Pacific. [Variant title name.] Auckland, New Zealand: University Business Directories, annual 1986–

Ward, R. G., and A. W. Proctor. *South Pacific Agriculture: Choices and Constraints.* Canberra, Australia: Australian National University Press, 1980.

Ward, R. G., and Elizabeth Kingdon, eds. *Land Custom and Practice in the South Pacific.* Cambridge, Mass.: Cambridge University Press, 1994.

Wiktor, Christian L. *Marine Affairs Bibliography: A Comprehensive Index to Marine Law and Policy Literature.* Halifax, Canada: Dalhousie Law School, 1980– (quarterly).

World Bank. *Pacific Island Economies: Towards Higher Growth in the 1990s.* Washington, D.C.: World Bank, 1991.

K. Education

Crossley, Michael, ed. *Education in the South Pacific.* Abingdon, England: Carfax Publishing Company, 1993.

Gannicott, K. G., ed. *Education for Economic Development in the South Pacific.* Canberra, Australia: Australian National University, 1990.

"Higher Education in the Pacific." *Pacific Perspectives* 12, no. 1 (1985):1–84.

Jones, David R., ed. *Explorations in Higher Education: A South Pacific Critique.* Parkville, Australia: University of Melbourne, 1991.

Kamins, Robert, Robert E. Potter, and others. *Mālamalama: A History of the University of Hawai'i.* Honolulu, Hawai'i: University of Hawai'i Press, 1998.

Literacy and Learning in the South Pacific. Adelaide, Australia: Australian Reading Association, 1987.

Mugler, France, and John Lynch, eds. *Pacific Languages in Education.* Suva, Fiji: Institute of Pacific Studies, The University of the South Pacific, 1996.

Pacific Universities: Achievements, Problems, Prospects. Suva, Fiji: University of the South Pacific, Institute for Pacific Studies, 1988.

Siegel, Jeff. *Vernacular Education in the South Pacific.* Canberra, Australia: Australian Agency for International Development, 1996.

Sperry, Robert. *Education in the South and Central Pacific.* (A bibliography). Lawton, Okla.: Cameron University Library, 1989.

Thomas, R. Murray, and T. Neville Postlethwaite, eds. *Schooling in the Pacific Islands; Colonies in Transition.* New York: Pergamon Press, 1984.

Throsby, Charles David, and K. Gannicott. *The Quality of Education in the South Pacific.* Canberra, Australia: Research School of Pacific Studies, Australian National University, 1990.

Wedgwood, Camilla H. *Education in the Pacific Islands: A Selective Bibliography.* Nouméa, New Caledonia: South Pacific Commission, 1956.

Yount, David. *Who Runs the University? The Politics of Higher Education in Hawai'i, 1985–1992.* Honolulu, Hawai'i: University of Hawai'i Press, 1992.

L. Society: Population, Minorities, Women, Statistics

Barkan, Elliott Robert. *Asian and Pacific Islander Migration to the United States: A Model of New Global Patterns.* Westport, Conn.: Greenwood Press, 1992.

Barrow, Terence. *Women of Polynesia.* Wellington, New Zealand: Seven Seas Publishing, 1967.

Chapman, Murry, and Philip S. Morrison. *Mobility and Identity in the Island Pacific.* Wellington, New Zealand: Department of Geography, Victoria University, 1985.

Connell, John, ed. *Migration and Development in the South Pacific.* Canberra, Australia: Research School of Pacific Studies, Australian National University, 1990.

Counts, Dorothy Ayers, ed. *Domestic Violence in Oceania.* Lā'ie, Hawai'i: Institute for Polynesian Studies, 1990.

———, and David R. Counts, eds. *Aging and Its Transformations: Moving toward Death in Pacific Societies.* Lanham, Md.: University Press of America, 1985.

Dodd, Edward. *The Island World of Polynesia: A Survey of the Racial Family and its Far-flung Cultures.* Putney, Vt.: Windmaill Hill Press, 1990.

Fairbairn-Dunlop, Margaret. *Women's Status in the South Pacific.* Āpia, Sāmoa: School of Agriculture, University of the South Pacific, 1993.

Hassall, Graham. *Nationalism and Ethnic Conflict in the Pacific Islands.* London: Research Institute for the Study of Conflict and Terrorism, 1992.

Hooper, Antony, and Judith Huntsman, eds. *Transformations of Polynesian Culture.* Auckland, New Zealand: The Polynesian Society, 1985.

Howard, Alan, and Robert Borofsky, eds. *Developments in Polynesian Ethnology.* Honolulu, Hawai'i: University of Hawai'i Press, 1989.

Huntsman, Judith, ed. *Tonga and Sāmoa: Images of Gender and Polity in 1995.* Christchurch, New Zealand: Macmillan Brown Centre for Pacific Studies, University of Canterbury, 1995.

Ishtar, Zohl de. *Daughters of the Pacific.* North Melbourne, Victoria, Australia: Spinifex Press, 1994.

Kirch, Patrick V. *The Evolution of the Polynesian Chiefdoms.* Cambridge, Mass.: Cambridge University Press, 1984.

Kunitz, Stephen J. *Disease and Social Diversity: The European Impact on the Health of Non-Europeans.* New York: Oxford University Press, 1994.

Levy, Robert I. *Personality Studies in Polynesia and Micronesia: Stability and Change.* Honolulu, Hawai'i: University of Hawai'i Social Science Research Institute, 1969.

Linnekin, Jocelyn, and Lin Poyer, eds. *Cultural Identity and Ethnicity in the Pacific.* Honolulu, Hawai'i: University of Hawai'i Press, 1990.

Marksbury, Richard A., ed. *The Business of Marriage: Transformations in Oceanic Matrimony.* Pittsburgh, Pa.: University of Pittsburgh Press, 1993.

McCall, Grant, and John Connell, eds. *A World Perspective on Pacific Islander Migration: Australia, New Zealand, and the USA.* Kensington, New South Wales: Centre for South Pacific Studies, University of New South Wales, 1993.

Moss, Joyce, and George Wilson. *Peoples of the World: Asians and Pacific Islanders: The Cultures, Geographical Setting, and Historical Background of 41 Asian and Pacific Island Peoples.* Detroit, Mich.: Gale Research, 1993.

Murray, Stephen O. *Oceanic Homosexualities.* With additional contributions by Arnold R. Pilling and others. New York: Garland Publishing, 1992.

Ralston, Caroline, and Nicholas Thomas, eds. *Sanctity and Power: Gender in Polynesian History.* Canberra, Australia: Australian National University Press, 1987.

Rensel, Jan, and Margaret Rodman, eds. *Home in the Islands: Housing and Social Change in the Pacific.* Honolulu, Hawai'i: University of Hawai'i Press, 1997.

Robie, David, ed. *Tu Galala. Social Change in the Pacific.* Leichhardt, New South Wales: Pluto Press, 1991.

Robillard, Albert, ed. *Social Change in the Pacific Islands.* London: Kegan Paul, 1992.

Sahlins, Marshall D. *Social Stratification in Polynesia.* Rev. ed. Seattle, Wash.: University of Washington Press, 1967.

Scott, Gillan, comp. *Women in the Pacific: A Guide to the Records on Microfilm Written by or about Women in the Pacific, Copied by the Pacific Manuscripts Bureau.* Canberra, Australia: Pacific Manuscripts Bureau, Australian National University, 1992.

Sharp, Roslyn, ed. *Pacific Women's Directory: A Guide to 500 Women's Organisations in the South Pacific.* Nouméa, New Caledonia: South Pacific Commission, 1993.

Simmons, Donita Vasoto, and Sin Joan Yee. *Women in the South Pacific: A Bibliography.* Suva, Fiji: University of the South Pacific, 1982.

South Pacific Commission. *Pacific Island Populations: Report Prepared for the International Conference on Population and Development, 1994, Cairo.* Nouméa, New Caledonia: South Pacific Commission, 1998.

Tongamoa, Taiamonie, ed. *Pacific Women: Roles and Status of Women in Pacific Socities.* Suva, Fiji: Institute of Pacific Studies, University of the South Pacific, 1988.

United Nations. *Economic and Social Survey of Asia and the Pacific.* New York: United Nations, annual 1974–.

Woods, Anne Catherine. *Women in the Islands: An Annotated Bibliography of Pacific Women's Issues, 1982–1989.* Honolulu, Hawai'i: Pacific Islands Center, University of Hawai'i Press, 1990.

Yee, Sin Joan. *The Chinese in the Pacific.* Suva, Fiji: South Pacific Social Science Association, 1976.

M. Science: Botany, Ecology, Environment, Geography, Marine, Navigation, Ornithology, and so forth

Åkerblom, Kjell. *Astronomy and Navigation in Polynesia and Micronesia.* Stockholm, Sweden: Ethnografiska Museet, 1968.

Alexander, Ronni. *Putting the Earth First: Alternatives to Nuclear Security in Pacific Island States.* Honolulu, Hawai'i: Matsunaga Institute for Peace, University of Hawaii, 1994.

Angleviel, Frédéric, C. Jost, and P. LeBourdiec, eds. *The French-Speaking Pacific Population, Environment and Development Issues.* Mt Nebo, Queensland, Australia: Boombana Publications, 1998.

Burt, Ben, and Christian Clerks, eds. *Environment and Development in the Pacific Islands.* Canberra, Australia: Australian National University Press, 1997.

DeLuca, Charles J. *Pacific Marine Life: A Survey of Pacific Ocean Invertebrates.* Rutland, Vt.: Charles E. Tuttle Company, 1976.

DeVries, Pieter, and Han Seur. *Moruroa and US: Polynesians' Experiences During Thirty Years of Nuclear Testing in the French Pacific.* Lyon, France: Centre de Documentation et de Recherche sur la Paix et les Conflits, 1997.

Dodd, Edward. *Polynesian Seafaring.* New York: Dodd, Mead, 1972.

Eldredge, Lucius G. *Bibliography of Marine Ecosystems, Pacific Islands.* Rome, Italy: United Nations Food and Agricultural Organization, 1987.

Finney, Ben R., and Marlene Among. *Voyage of Rediscovery: A Cultural Odyssey through Polynesia.* Berkeley: University of California Press, 1994.

Frodin, D. G. *Papuasia and Oceania. Guide to the Standard Floras of the World.* Cambridge, Mass.: Cambridge University Press, 1984.

Guinness, Patrick, and Michael Young, eds. *The Power of Kava.* Canberra, Australia: Australian National University, 1995.

Huang, Paul Te-Hsien, comp. *The World Oceans: A Selected Bibliography of Social and Natural Sciences.* Halifax, Nova Scotia: The Compiler, 1985.

Kirch, Patrick V., and Terry L. Hunt, eds. *Historical Ecology in the Pacific Islands: Prehistoric Environmental and Landscape Change.* New Haven, Conn.: Yale University Press, 1997.

Mayr, Ernst. *Birds of the Southwest Pacific.* New ed. Rutland, Vt.: Charles E. Tuttle Company, 1978.

Menard, Henry W. *Marine Geology of the Pacific.* New York: McGraw-Hill, 1964.

Merrill, Elmer. *Botanical Bibliography of the Islands of the Pacific.* Washington, D.C.: Smithsonian Institution, 1947.

Morrison, John, Paul Geraghty, and Linda Crowl, eds. *Science of Pacific Island Peoples.* 4 vols. Suva, Fiji: Institute of Pacific Studies, University of the South Pacific, 1994.

Nunn, Patrick D. *Environmental Change and the Early Settlement of Pacific Islands.* Honolulu, Hawai'i: East-West Center, 1994.

Rapaport, Moshe, ed. *The Pacific Islands: Environment and Society.* Honolulu, Hawai'i: Bess Press, 1999.

Rensch, Karl Heinz M. *A Dictionary of Polynesian Fish Names.* Mawson, Australia: Archipelago Press, 1999.

Roedelberger, Franz A., and Vera I. Groschoff. *Wildlife of the South Seas.* New York: Viking Press, 1967.

Smith, Roy H. *The Nuclear Free and Independent Pacific Movement: after Moruroa.* London: Tauris Academic Studies, 1997.

van Balgooy, M. M. J. *Plant Geography of the Pacific.* Leiden, the Netherlands: J. J. Green, 1971.

Watling, Dick. *Birds of Fiji, Tonga and Samoa.* Wellington, New Zealand: Millwood Press, 1982.

Whistler, W. Arthur. *Coastal Flowers of the Tropical Pacific: A Guide to the Widespread Seashore Plants of the Pacific Islands.* Lāwai, Kaua'i, Hawai'i: Pacific Tropical Botanical Garden, 1980.

Whistler, W. Arthur. *Polynesian Herbal Medicine.* Lāwai, Kaua'i, Hawai'i: National Tropical Botanical Garden, 1992.

N. Internet Resources—Governments or Sponsored Websites

American Sāmoa—www.government.as/

Cook Islands—www.cook-islands.gov.ck/

—www.kiaorana.com/main.html

Easter Island—www.netaxs.com/~trance/rapanui.html
—www2.hawaii.edu/~ogden/piir/pacific/Rapanui.html
French Polynesia—www.presidence.pf/
Hawai'i—www.hawaii.gov/
Nauru—www.airnauru.com.au/nauru.html
New Zealand—www.govt.nz/
Niue—www.gov.nu/
Norfolk Island—www.pitcairners.org/pitcairners/
Pitcairn— www.government.pn/homepage.htm
Rotuma—www2.hawaii.edu/oceanic/rotuma/os/hanua.html
Sāmoa—none at this writing.
Tokclau—nonc at this writing.
Tonga—www.tongaonline.com/
Tuvalu—members.nbci.com/tuvaluonline/
Wallis and Futuna—www.wallis.co.nc/
—wallis-islands.com/index.gb.htm

O. Internet Resources—Newspapers, News, Magazines

Asian Times—www.atimes.com/oceania/oceania.html
Coconut Wireless—www.uq.edu.au/coconet/
Cook Islands News—www.cinews.co.ck/
Honolulu Advertiser—www.honoluluadvertiser.com/
Honolulu Star-Bulletin—starbulletin.com/
New Zealand Herald—www.nzherald.co.nz/
Niue News—www.cas.nu/niue_news.htm
Pacific Business News—pacific.bcentral.com/pacific/
Pacific Islands Reports—pidp.ewc.hawaii.edu/pireport/
Sāmoa News—www.samoanews.com/
Tahiti-Pacifique Magazine—www.tahiti-pacifique.com/
Tonga Online—www.tongaonline.com/news

2. COOK ISLANDS

Asian Development Bank. *Cook Islands: Economic Performance, Issues and Strategies.* Manila, Philippines: Asian Development Bank, 1995.

Buse, Jasper, and Rautiti Taringa. *Cook Islands Maori Dictionary.* Ed. by Bruce Biggs and Rangi Moekaa. Rarotonga, Cook Islands: Cook Islands Ministry of Education, 1995.

Bishop, Russel. *The Cook Islands: Images of Polynesia.* Rarotonga, Cook Islands: Cook Islands Topographical Services, 1987.

Buck, Peter. *The Material Culture of the Cook Islands.* New Plymouth, New Zealand: Avery, 1927; reprinted New York: AMS Press, 1976.

Campbell, Andrew R. T. *Social Relations in Ancient Tongareva.* Honolulu, Hawai'i: Bernice P. Bishop Museum, 1985.

Carpentier, Tai, and Clive Beaumont. *Kai Kōrero: A Cook Islands Maori Coursebook.* Auckland, New Zealand: Pasifika Press, 1996.

Cook Islands Government. *Cook Islands Second Development Plan, 1988–1992.* Rarotonga, Cook Islands: Cook Islands Government, 1988.

———. *Summary of the Cook Islands First Development Plan, 1982–1985.* Rarotonga, Cook Islands: Government Printer, 1983.

Cook Islands News. Rarotonga, Cook Islands: Cook Islands Broadcasting & Newspaper Corporation, 1958 –.

Coppell, William. *Bibliography of the Cook Islands.* Canberra, Australia: Australia National University, 1970.

Craig, E. W. G. *Destiny Well Sown: A Biography of Lt. Col. W. E. Gudgeon, Resident Commissioner Cook Islands, 1841–1920.* Whakatane, New Zealand: Whakatane & District Historical Society, 1985.

Crocombe, Ron, ed. *Cook Island Politics: The Inside Story.* Auckland, New Zealand: Polynesian Press, 1979.

———. *Land Tenure in the Cook Islands.* New York: Oxford University Press, 1964.

———. *Voluntary Service and Development in the Cook Islands.* Suva, Fiji: Institute of Pacific Studies, 1990.

Davis, Tom. *Island Boy: An Autobiography.* Suva, Fiji: Institute for Pacific Studies, 1992.

Davis, Tom, and others. *Cook Island Politics: The Inside Story.* Auckland, New Zealand: Polynesian Press, 1979.

Duff, Roger. *Prehistory of the Southern Cook Islands.* Ed. by Michael M. Trotter. Christchurch, New Zealand: Bascands, 1974.

Gill, William Wyatt. *Cook Islands Custom.* Reprint of 1892 edition. Suva, Fiji: Institute of Pacific Studies, 1993.

Gilson, Richard. *The Cook Islands: 1820–1950.* Ed. by Ron Crocombe. Wellington, New Zealand: Victoria University Press, 1980.

Haas, Anthony, ed. *New Zealand and the South Pacific: A Guide to Economic Development in the Cook Islands, Fiji, Niue, Tonga, and Western Samoa.* Wellington, New Zealand: Asia Pacific Research Unit, Ltd., 1977.

Hancock, Kathleen. *Sir Albert Henry: His Life and Times.* Auckland, New Zealand: Methuen, 1979.

Helm, Arthur S., and W. H. Percival. *Sisters in the Sun: The Story of Suwarrow and Palmerston Atolls.* London: Robert Hale, 1973.

Hooper, Antony, and others, eds. *Class and Culture in the South Pacific.* Auckland, New Zealand: Center for Pacific Studies, 1987.

Idiens, Dale. *Cook Islands Art.* Princes Risborough, England: Shire, 1990.

Katayama, Kazumichi, and Akira Tagaya, eds. *People of the Cook Islands, Past and Present: A Report of thc Physical Anthropological and Linguistic Research in the Cook Islands in 1985–87.* Rarotonga, Cook Islands: Cook Islands Library and Museum Society, 1988.

Kautai, Ngatupuna, and others. *Atiu: An Island Community.* Suva, Fiji: Institute of Pacific Studies, 1984.

Keller, Nancy J. *Rarotonga and the Cook Islands.* (Lonely Plant Travel Guide.) Oakland, Calif.: Lonely Planet, 1998.

Loomis, Terrence. *Remittances and Development. Cook Island Migrants in New Zealand and Their Influence on Cook Islands Development.* Auckland, New Zealand: Social Research and Development Trust, 1986.

Maretu. *Cannibals and Converts: Radical Change in the Cook Islands.* Translated and edited by Marjorie T. Crocombe. Suva, Fiji: Institute of Pacific Studies, 1983.

Moyle, Richard M. *Report on Survey of Traditional Music of Northern Cook Islands.* Auckland, New Zealand: University of Auckland Anthropology Department, 1985.

Rademaker, Cor S. M. *The Catholic Mission in the Cook Islands, 1894–1994.* Bavel, the Netherlands: Fathers of the Sacred Heart, 1994.

Savage, Stephen. *A Dictionary of the Maori Language of Rarotonga.* Reprint ed. Suva, Fiji: Institute of Pacific Studies, 1980.

Scott, David. *Years of the Pooh-Bah: A Cook Islands History.* Auckland, New Zealand: Hodder and Stoughton, 1991.

Shapiro, H. L., and Peter H. Buck. *The Physical Characters of the Cook Islanders.* Honolulu, Hawai'i: Bishop Museum, 1936; reprinted New York: Kraus Reprints, 1985.

Siikala, Jukka. *'Akatokamanåva: Myth, History and Society in the Souther Cook Islands.* Auckland, New Zealand: Polynesian Society in association with the Finnish Anthropological Society, 1991.

Williams, John. *A Narrative of Missionary Enterprises in the South Seas.* London: John Snow, 1837.

3. EASTER ISLAND

Bahn, Paul, and John Flenley. *Easter Island. Earth Island.* London: Thames & Hudson, 1992.

Barthel, Thomas S. *1500 Jahre Kultur der Osterinsel: Schätze aus dem Land des Hotu Matua.* Mainz, Germany: P. von Zabern, 1989.

———. *The Eighth Land: The Polynesian Discovery and Settlement of Easter Island.* Translated by Anneliese Martin. Honolulu, Hawai'i: University Press of Hawai'i, 1978.

Bothmer-Plates, Arno Graf von, and others. *L'Île de Pâques: Une énigme?* Brussels, Belgium: Royal Museum of Art and History, 1990.

Campbell, Ramón. *La cultura de la isla de Pascua: Mito y realidad.* 2d ed. Santiago, Chili: Editorial Andrés Bello, 1987.

Charola, A. Elena. *Easter Island: The Heritage and its Conservation.* New York: World Monuments Fund, 1994.

Du Feu, Veronica. *Rapanui.* New York: Routledge, 1996.

Englert, Sebastian. *Island at the Center of the World: New Light on Easter Island.* Translated and edited by William Mulloy. New York: Charles Scribner's, 1970.

———. *Leyendas de Isla de Pascua: Textos bilingues.* Santiago, Chili: Ediciones de la Universidad de Chile, 1980.

Fischer, Steven Roger, ed. *Easter Island Studies: Contributions to the History of Rapanui in Memory of William T. Mulloy.* Oxford, England: Oxbow Books, 1993.

Fischer, Steven Roger. *Rongorongo: The Easter Island Script, History, Traditions, Texts.* New York: Clarendon Press, 1997.

Fuentes, Jordi. *Dictionary and Grammar of the Easter Island Language.* Santiago, Chili: Editorial Universitaria, 1960.

Goetzfridt, Nicholas J., comp. *Indigenous Navigation and Voyaging in the Pacific: A Reference Guide.* New York: Greenwood Press, 1992.

Heyerdahl, Thor. *Aku-Aku: The Secret of Easter Island.* New York: Rand McNally, 1958; London: Unwin, 1989.

———. *The Art of Easter Island.* London: Allen & Unwin, 1976.

———. *Easter Island: The Mystery Solved.* New York: Random House, 1989.

Heyerdahl, Thor, and Edwin N. Ferdon, eds. *Reports of the Norwegian Archaeological Expedition to Easter Island and the East Pacific.* 2 vols. Chicago: Rand McNally, 1961, 1965.

Hughes, H. G. A. *Rapa Nui: A Select Bibliography.* Afonwen, Wales: Gwasg Gwenffrwd, 1992.

Jumeau, Michel-Alain, and Yves Pioger. *Bibliographe de l'île de Pâques.* Paris: Musée de l'Homme, 1997.

Langdon, Robert, and Darrell Tryon. *The Language of Easter Island: Its Development and Eastern Polynesian Relationships.* La'ie, Hawai'i: Institute for Polynesian Studies, 1983.

Lee, Georgia. *Rock Art of Easter Island: Symbols of Power, Prayers to the Gods.* Los Angeles: Institute of Archaeology, University of California, 1992.

———. *An Uncommon Guide to Easter Island: Exploring Archaeological Mysteries of Rapa Nui.* Arroyo Grande, Calif.: International Resources, 1990.

———. *Rapa Nui: Histoire de l'Île de Pâques.* Geneva, Switzerland: Olizane, 1995.

Martinsson-Wallin, Helene. *Ahu—The Ceremonial Stone Structures of Easter Island: Analyses of Variation and Interpretation of Meanings.* Uppsala, Sweden: Societas Archaeoloigca Upsaliensis, 1994.

McCall, Grant. *Rapanui: Tradition and Survival on Easter Island.* 2d ed. Honolulu, Hawai'i: University of Hawai'i Press, 1994.

Métraux, Alfred. *Easter Island: A Stone-Age Civilization of the Pacific.* Translated by Michael Bullock. New York: Oxford University Press, 1957.

Orliac, Catherine, and Michel Orliac. *Easter Island: Mystery of the Stone Giants.* New York: Abrams, 1995.

———. *Bois sculptés de l'île de Pâques.* Marseille, France: L. Leiris, 1995.

Porteous, J. Douglas. *The Modernization of Easter Island.* Victoria, British Columbia, Canada: University of Victoria Department of Geography, 1981.

Reynolds, Kevin, and Tim Rose Price. *Rapa Nui: The Easter Island Legend on Film.* New York: Newmarket Press, 1994.

Rosasco, Jose Luis. *Easter Island, the Endless Enigma.* Santiago, Chili: Editorial Kactus, 1991.

Routledge, Katherine Pease. *The Mystery of Easter Island.* London: Hazell, Watson, and Viney, 1919; reprinted Kempton, Ill.: Adventures Unlimited Press, 1998.

van Tilburg, JoAnne. *Easter Island: Archaeology, Ecology, and Culture.* Washington, D.C.: Smithsonian Institution Press, 1994.

4. FRENCH POLYNESIA

Académie Tahitienne. *Grammaire de la langue tahitienne.* Pape'ete, Tahiti: Académie Tahitienne (Fare Vana'a), 1986.

Adams, Henry. *Tahiti: Memoirs of Arii Taimai.* Paris, 1901; edited by Robert E. Spillner, reprinted Ridgewood, N.J.: Gregg Press, 1968.

Aldrich, John. *The French View of the Pacific: A Critique of Geopolitical Analysis.* Sydney, Australia: University of Sydney, 1988.

Aldrich, Robert. *The French Presence in the South Pacific, 1842–1940.* London: Macmillan, 1990.

Aldrich, Robert, and John Connell, eds. *France's Overseas Frontier: Les departements et territoires d'outre-mer.* Cambridge, Mass.: Cambridge University Press, 1993.

Babadzan, Alain. *Les dépouillés des dieux: Essai sur la religion tahitienne à l'époque découverte.* Paris: Éditions de la Maison des Sciences de l'homme, 1993.

Baré, Jean-François. *Huahine.* Paris: Nouvelles éditions latines, 1979.

———. *Le Malentendu Pacifique: Des premières rencontres entre polynésiens et anglais et de ce qui s'ensuivit avec les français jusqu'à nos jours.* Paris: Hachette, 1985.

———. *Tahiti, les temps et les pouvoirs; pour une anthropologie historique du Tahiti post-Européen.* Paris: Éditions de l'ORSTOM, 1987.

Barratt, Glynn. *Russia in the South Pacific. Vol 4: The Tuamotu Islands and Tahiti.* Vancouver: University of British Columbia Press, 1992.

Barrow, Terence. *The Art of Tahiti and the Neighbouring Society, Austral and Cook Islands.* London: Thames & Hudson, 1979.

Bitter, Maurice. *Histoire de Tahiti et ses îles.* Paris: J. Grancher, 1992.

Blanchet, Gilles. *La polynésie française à la croissée des chemins.* Honolulu, Hawai'i: East-West Center, 1994.

———. *A Survey of the Economy of French Polynesia, 1960–1990.* Canberra, Australia: National Centre for Development Studies, Australia National University, 1991.

Bovis, Edmond de. *Tahitian Society before the Arrival of the Europeans.* Translation and introduction by Robert D. Craig. 2d ed. Lā'ie, Hawai'i: Institute for Polynesian Studies, Brigham Young University–Hawai'i Campus, 1980.

Brousse, Robert, and others. *Atlas de Tahiti et de la Polynésie française.* 2d ed. Singapore, Singapore: Éditions du Pacifique, 1992.

Bruner, Philip L. *Field Guide to the Birds of French Polynesia.* Honolulu, Hawai'i: Bernice P. Bishop Museum, 1972.

Cadousteau, Mai-Ari'i. *Généalogies commentées des ari'i des îles de la société.* 3d ed. Pape'ete, Tahiti: Société des Études Océaniennes, 1996.

Celhay, Jean-Claude. *Plants and Flowers of Tahiti.* Pape'ete, Tahiti: Éditions du Pacifique, 1975.

Chesneaux, Jean. *Tahiti après la bombe: Quel avenir pour la polynésie?* Paris: L'Harmattan, 1995.

Chesneaux, Jean, and Nic Maclellan. *La France dans le Pacifique: de Bougainville à Mururoa.* Paris: La Découverte, 1992.

Craig, Robert D., ed. *The Marquesas Islands: Their Description and Early History, by the Reverend Robert Thomson.* 2d ed. Lā'ie, Hawai'i: Institute for Polynesian Studies, 1980.

———, trans. and ed. *Tahitian Society before the Arrival of the Europeans by Edmond de Bovis.* 2d ed. Lā'ie, Hawai'i: Institute for Polynesian Studies, 1980.

Danielsson, Bengt. *Forgotten Islands of the South Seas.* London: Allen & Unwin, 1957.

———. *Raroia: Happy Island of the South Seas.* Chicago: Rand McNally, 1953.

Danielsson, Bengt, and Marie-Thérèse Danielsson. *Poisoned Reign: French Nuclear Colonialism in the Pacific.* Ringwood, Australia: Penguin Books Australia, 1986.

———. *Moruroa, notre bombe coloniale: histoire de la colonisation nucléaire de la polynésie française.* Paris: L'Harmattan, 1993.

Danielsson, Bengt, Marie-Thérèse Danielsson, and Christian Gleizal. *Papeete, 1818–1990.* Pape'ete, Tahiti: C. Gleizal/Cobalt-Mairie de Pape'ete, 1990.

Davies, John. *History of the Tahitian Mission, 1799–1830.* Ed. by Colin Newbury. Cambridge, England: Hakluyt Society, 1961.

Deckker, Paul de, and Pierre-Yves Toullelan, eds. *La France et le Pacifique: Études.* Paris: Société française d'histoire d'outre-mer., Diffusion l'Harmattan, 1990.

Dening, Greg. *Islands and Beaches: A Discourse on a Silent Land; Marquesas, 1774–1880.* Honolulu, Hawai'i: University of Hawai'i Press, 1980; reprinted Chicago: Dorsey Press, 1988.

Deschamps, Emmanuel, and Paule Laudon. *L'archipel des Marquises.* Boulogne, France: Le Motu, 1994.

Dodd, Edward. *The Rape of Tahiti.* New York: Dodd, Mead, 1983.

Ellis, William. *Polynesian Researches: Society Islands, Tubuai Islands, and New Zealand.* 2d ed. Rutland, Vt.: Charles E. Tuttle Company, 1969.

Ellsworth, S. George, and Kathleen Clayton Perrin. *Seasons of Faith and Courage: The Church of Jesus Christ of Latter-day Saints in French Polynesia: A Sesquicentennial History, 1843–1993.* Sandy, Utah: Yves R. Perrin, 1994.

Ferdon, Edwin N. *Early Observations of Marquesan Culture, 1595–1813.* Tucscon, Ariz.: University of Arizona Press, 1993.

———. *Early Tahiti as the Explorers Saw It 1767–1797.* Tucscon, Ariz.: University of Arizona Press, 1981.

Finney, Ben R. *Polynesian Peasants and Proletarians: Socio-Economic Change among the Tahitians of French Polynesia.* Cambridge, Mass.: Schenkman, 1965.

Gleizal, Christian, ed. *Encyclopédie de la Polynésie Française.* 9 vols. Pape'ete, Tahiti: C. Gleizal/Multipress, 1986–1988.

———. *Tahiti et les îles de la société.* Paris: Éditions Nouveaux-Loisirs, 1995.

Hanson, F. Allan, and Patrick O'Reilly. *Bibliographie de Rapa, Polynésie Française.* Paris: Musée de l'Homme: Société des Océanistes, 1973.

Haupert, Yves. *Francis Sanford à coeur ouvert: les mémoires du dernier Metua: père de l'autonomie polynésienne.* Pape'ete, Tahiti: Au Vent des îles, c1998.

Henningham, Stephen. *France and the South Pacific: A Contemporary History.* Honolulu, Hawai'i: University of Hawai'i Press, 1992.

Henry, Teuira. *Ancient Tahiti.* Honolulu, Hawai'i: Bernice Pauahi Bishop Museum, 1928; reprinted New York: Kraus Reprint, 1985.

Howarth, David. *Tahiti: A Paradise Lost.* London: Harvill Press, 1983.

Jaussen, Tepano. *Dictionnaire de la langue tahitienne.* 7th ed. Pape'ete, Tahiti: Société des Études Océaniennes, 1993.

Langdon, Robert. *Tahiti: Island of Love.* 5th ed. Sydney, Australia: Pacific Publications, 1979.

Langevin, Christine. *Tahitiennes: de la tradition à l'intégration culturelle.* Paris: Harmattan, 1990.

Lee, Ida, ed. *Captain Bligh's Second Voyage to the South Sea.* London: Longmans, 1920.

Levy, Robert. *Tahitians: Mind and Experience in the Society Islands.* Chicago: University of Chicago Press, 1973.

Lewis, John J. *Wind in the Palms: Mission in the South West Pacific, 1817–1872: David Darling, George Stallworthy*. Orewa, New Zealand: College Communications, 1991.

Lockwood, Victoria S. *Tahitian Transformations: Gender and Capitalist Development in a Rural Society*. Boulder, Colo.: Lynne Rienner, 1993.

Maclellan, Nic, and Jean Chesneaux. *After Moruroa: France in the South Pacific*. Melbourne, Australia: Ocean Press, 1998.

Mazellier, Philippe, ed. *Le mémorial polynésien*. 6 vols. Pape'ete, Tahiti: Hibiscus Éditions, 1977–80.

———. *Tahiti autonome*. Pape'ete, Tahiti: P. Mazellier, 1990.

Merceron, François, and others, eds. *Dictionnaire illustré de la Polynésie: Te 'Aratai o Porinetia*. 4 vols. Pape'ete, Tahiti: Christian Gleizal/Éditions de l'Alizé, 1988.

Moorehead, Alan. *The Fatal Impact: An Account of the Invasion of the South Pacific, 1767–1840*. London: Hamish Hamilton, 1966.

Moulin, Jane Freeman. *The Dance of Tahiti*. Pape'ete, Tahiti: Christian Gleizal, Éditions du Pacifique, 1979.

Newbury, Colin. *Tahiti Nui: Change and Survival in French Polynesia, 1767–1945*. Honolulu, Hawai'i: University of Hawai'i Press, 1980.

Oliver, Douglas L. *Ancient Tahitian Society*. 3 vols. Honolulu, Hawai'i: University of Hawai'i Press, 1974.

———. *Return to Tahiti: Bligh's Second Breadfruit Voyage*. Honolulu, Hawai'i: University of Hawai'i Press, 1988.

———. *Two Tahitian Villages: A Study in Comparison*. Lā'ie, Hawai'i: Institute for Polynesian Studies, 1981.

O'Reilly, Patrick, and Edouard Reitman. *Bibliographie de Tahiti et de la Polynésie Française*. Paris: Musée de l'Homme, 1967.

O'Reilly, Patrick, and Raoul Teisier. *Répertoire biographique de la Polynésie Française*. 2 vols. 2d ed. Paris: Musée de l'Homme, 1975.

Panoff, Michel. *Tahiti Métisse*. Paris: Denoäl, 1989.

———. *Trésors des îles marquises*. Paris: Musée de l'Homme, 1995.

Poirine, Bernard. *Tahiti, du melting pot à l'explosion?* Paris: Éditions l'Harmattan, 1992.

———. *Tahiti: la fin du paradis?* Pape'ete, Tahiti: B. Poirine, 1994.

———. *Tahiti stratégie pour l'après-nucléaire: De la rente automique au développement.* 2d ed. Paris: Éditions l'Harmattan, 1996.

Pollock, Nancy J., and Ron Crocombe, eds. *French Polynesia. A Book of Selected Readings.* Suva, Fiji: Institute of Pacific Studies, 1988.

Pritchard, George. *The Aggressions of the French at Tahiti and Other Islands in the Pacific.* Ed. by Paul de Deckker. Auckland, New Zealand: Oxford University Press, 1983.

Ramsey, Meredith. *The Leeward Islands: Bora-Bora, Huahine, Raiatea, Maupiti, Tupai.* Pape'ete, Tahiti: Tiare Press, 1982.

Regnault, Jean-Marc. *La bombe française dans le pacifique: l'implantation, 1957–1964.* Pirae, Tahiti: Scoop Éditions, 1993.

Robertson, George. *An Account of the Discovery of Tahiti, from the Journal of George Robertson, Master of HMS* Dolphin. Ed. by Oliver Warner. London: Hakluyt Society, 1948. Reprint London: Folio Press, 1973.

———. *Discovery of Tahiti: A Journal of the Second Voyage of HMS* Dolphin *round the World under the Command of Captain Wallis, R.N., I the Years 1766, 1767 and 1768.* Edited by Hugh Carrington. London: Hakluyt Society, 1948; reprinted Nedelyn, Liechtenstein: Kraus Reprint, 1967.

Saura, Bruno. *Politique et religion à Tahiti.* Pirae, Tahiti: Polymages-Scoop, 1993.

———. *Pouvanaa a Oopa: père de la culture tahitienne.* Pirae, Tahiti: Au Vent des Îles, 1997.

Stillman, Amy K. *Report on Survey of Music in Mangareva, French Polynesia.* Auckland, New Zealand: University of Auckland Anthropology Department, 1987.

Teissier, Raoul. *Chefs et notables des établissements français de l'océanie au temps du protectorat, 1842–1990.* 4th ed. Pape'ete, Tahiti: Société des Études Océaniennes, 1996.

Terrell, Jennifer, ed. *Von den Steinen's Marquesan Myths.* Translated by Marta Langridge. Canberra, Australia: Australian National University, 1990.

Thomas, Nicholas. *Marquesan Societies: Inequality and Political Transformations in Eastern Polynesia.* New York: Oxford University Press, 1990.

Thomson, Robert. *The Marquesas Islands: Their Description and Early History*. Ed. by Robert D. Craig. 2d ed. Lā'ie, Hawai'i: Institute for Polynesian Studies, 1980.

Toullelan, Pierre-Yves. *Tahiti Colonial (1860–1914)*. Paris: Publications de la Sorbonne, 1987.

———. *Missionaires au quotidien à Tahiti: Les picpuciens en polynésie au XIXe siècle*. New York: E. J. Brill, 1995.

———. *Tahiti et ses archipels*. Paris: Karthala, 1991.

Toullelan, Pierre-Yves, and Bernard Gille. *Le mariage Franco-Tahitien: Histoire de Tahiti du XVIIIe siècle à nos jours*. Pape'ete, Tahiti: Éditions Polymages-Scoop, 1992.

Vernier, Henri. *Au vent des cyclones: Missions protestantes et église évangélique à Tahiti et en Polynésie française*. Pape'ete, Tahiti: Éditions Haere Po No Tahiti, 1986.

West, Francis J. *Political Advancement in the South Pacific: A Comparative Study of Colonial Practice in Fiji, Tahiti, and American Samoa*. New York: Oxford University Press, 1961.

Wheeler, Tony. *Tahiti and French Polynesia*. 4th ed. (Lonely Plant Guidebook.) Hawthorne, Victoria, Australia: Lonely Planet, 1997.

Williams, John. *A Narrative of Missionary Enterprises in the South Seas*. London: John Snow, 1837.

Zewen, Père François. *Introduction à la langue des îles Marquises*. Pape'ete, Tahiti: Éditions Haere Po No Tahiti, 1987.

5. HAWAI'I

Adler, Jacob. *Claus Spreckels: The Sugar King in Hawaii*. Honolulu, University of Hawaii Press, 1966, 1990.

Allen, Helena G. *Kalakaua: Renaissance King*. Honolulu, Hawai'i: Mutual Publishing, 1994.

———. *Sanford Ballard Cole: Hawaii's Only President, 1844–1926*. Glendale, Calif.: Arthur H. Clark Company, 1988.

Andrade, Ernest. *Unconquerable Rebel: Robert W. Wilcox and Hawaiian Politics, 1880–1903*. Niwot, Colo.: University Press of Colorado, 1996.

Armstrong, William N. *Around the World with a King.* New York: Stokes, 1904; reprinted Honolulu, Hawai'i: Mutual Publishing, 1995.

Aoudé, Ibrahim. *The Political Economy of Hawai'i.* Honolulu, Hawai'i: Department of Sociology, University of Hawai'i, 1994.

Barrère, Dorothy B. *The King's* Mahale*: The Awardees and their Lands.* Honolulu, Hawai'i: D. B. Barrère, 1994.

Bingham, Hiram. *A Residence of Twenty-One Years in the Sandwich Islands.* New York: S. Converse, 1847; reprinted Rutland, Vt.: Charles E. Tuttle Company, Inc., 1981.

Boylan, Dan, and T. Michael Holmes. *John A. Burns: The Man and His Times.* Honolulu, Hawai'i: University of Hawai'i Press, 2000.

Bradley, Harold W. *The American Frontier in Hawaii: The Pioneers, 1789–1843.* Stanford, Calif.: Stanford University Press, 1942.

Britsch, R. Lanier. *Moramona: The Mormons in Hawaii.* Lā'ie, Hawai'i: Institute for Polynesian Studies, 1989.

Buck, Sir Peter Henry. *Arts and Crafts of Hawaii.* Honolulu, Hawai'i: Bishop Museum Press, 1964.

Bushnell, Andy. *The "Horror" Reconsidered: An Evaluation of the Historical Evidence for Population Decline in Hawai'i, 1778–1893.* Honolulu, Hawai'i: A Bushnell, 1992.

Chinen, Joyce, Cathleen O. Kane, and Ida N. Yoshinaga, eds. *Women in Hawai'i: Sites, Identities, and Voices.* Honolulu, Hawai'i: Department of Sociology, University of Hawai'i, 1997.

Ching, Linda. *'Ano Lani: The Hawaiian Monarchy Years, 1810–1893.* Honolulu, Hawai'i: Hawaiian Goddesses Publishing Co., 1993.

Conroy, Hilary, and Harry Wray, eds. *Pearl Harbor Reexamined: Prologue to the Pacific War.* Honolulu, Hawai'i: University of Hawai'i Press, 1990.

Cooper, George, and Gavan Daws. *Land and Power in Hawaii: The Democratic Years.* Honolulu, Hawai'i: University of Hawai'i Press, 1990.

Craig, Robert D. *Historical Dictionary of Honolulu and Hawai'i.* Lanham, Md.: Scarecrow Press, 1998.

Cunningham, Scott. *Hawaiian Religion and Magic.* St. Paul, Minn.: Llewellyn Publications, 1994.

Daws, Gavan. *Hawaii, 1959–1989: The First Thirty Years of the Aloha State.* Honolulu, Hawai'i: Publishers Group Hawai'i, 1989.

———. *Shoal of Time: History of the Hawaiian Islands.* Honolulu, Hawai'i: University of Hawai'i Press, 1968.

Day, A. Grove. *Books about Hawaii: Fifty Basic Authors.* Honolulu, Hawai'i: University of Hawai'i Press, 1977.

———. *Hawaii and Its People.* New York: Meredith Press, 1968.

———. *History Makers of Hawaii: A Biographical Dictionary.* Honolulu, Hawai'i: Mutual Publishing of Honolulu, 1984.

Desha, Stephen. *Kamehameha and His Warrior Kekūhaupi'o.* Translated from Hawaiian by Frances N. Frazier. Honolulu, Hawai'i: Kamehameha Schools Press, 2000.

Dudley, Michael Kioni. *A Call for Hawaiian Sovereignty.* Honolulu, Hawai'i: Na Kane o ka Malo Press, 1990.

Dye, Bob, ed. *Hawai'i Chronicles: Island History from the Pages of Honolulu Magazine.* 3 vols. Honolulu, Hawai'i: University of Hawai'i Press, 1996–2000.

———. *Merchant Prince of the Sandalwood Mountains: Afong and the Chinese in Hawai'i.* Honolulu, Hawai'i: University of Hawai'i Press, 1997.

Elbert, Samuel H., ed. *Selections from Fornander's Hawaiian Antiquities and Folk-Lore.* Honolulu, Hawai'i: University of Hawai'i Press, 1959.

Ellis, William. *Polynesian Researches: Hawaii.* Rev. ed. Rutland, Vt.: Charles E. Tuttle Company, Inc., 1969.

Filipinos in Hawaii: A Bibliography. Rev. ed. Honolulu, Hawai'i: Hawai'i State Library, 1993.

Forbes, David W. *Encounters with Paradise: Views of Hawaii and Its People, 1778–1941.* Honolulu, Hawai'i: Honolulu Academy of Arts, 1992.

———. *Hawaiian National Bibliography, 1780–1900. Vol. 1: 1780–1830.* Honolulu, Hawai'i: University of Hawai'i Press, 1999.

Fornander, Abraham. *An Account of the Polynesian Race: Its Origins and Migrations and the Ancient History of the Hawaiian People to the Times of Kamehameha I.* Reprint ed. 4 vols in 1. Rutland, Vt.: Charles E. Tuttle Company, Inc., 1969.

Foster, Nelson. *Bishop Museum and the Changing World of Hawaii.* Honolulu, Hawai'i: Bishop Museum Press, 1993.

Free, David. *Vignettes of Old Hawai'i.* Honolulu, Hawai'i: Crossroads Press, 1993.

Fuchs, Lawrence H. *Hawaii Pono: A Social History.* San Diego, Calif.: Harcourt Brace Jovanovich, 1983.

Furnas, J. C. *Anatomy of Paradise: Hawaii and the Islands of the South Seas.* New York: W. Sloane Associates, 1948.

Goldstein, Donald M., and Katherine V. Dillon, eds. *The Pearl Harbor Papers: Inside the Japanese Plans.* Washington, D.C.: Brassey's 1993.

Grant, Glen. *Hawai'i Looking Back: An Illustrated History of the Islands.* Honolulu, Hawai'i: Mutual Publishing, 2000.

Hammatt, Charles H. *Ships, Furs, and Sandalwood: A Yankee Trander in Hawai'i, 1823–1825.* Ed. by Sandra Wagner-Wright. Honolulu, Hawai'i: University of Hawai'i Press, 2000.

Hartwell, Jay. *Nā Mamo: Hawaiian People Today.* Honolulu, Hawai'i: 'Ai Pōkahu Press, 1997.

Hitch, Thomas Kemper. *Islands in Transition: The Past, Present, and Future of Hawai'i's Economy.* Ed. by Robert M. Kamins. Honolulu, Hawai'i: First Hawaiian Bank, 1993.

Holmes, Tommy. *The Hawaiian Canoe.* 2d ed. Hanalei, Kaua'i: Editions Limited, 1993.

Holt, John Dominis. *Monarchy in Hawaii.* 2d rev. ed. Honolulu, Hawai'i: Ku Pa'a, 1995.

Hopkins, Jerry. *The Hula.* Hong Kong: Apa Productions, 1982.

Ii, John Papa. *Fragments of Hawaiian History.* Translated by Mary Kawena Puku'ī, ed. by Dorothy B. Barrère. 4th ed. Honolulu, Hawai'i: Bernice P. Bishop Museum, 1983.

Ikeda, Kiyoshi, and others, eds. *The Filipino American Experience in Hawaii.* Honolulu, Hawai'i: Department of Sociology, University of Hawai'i, 1991.

Interracial Marriage and Offspring in Hawai'i, 1896–1989. Honolulu, Hawai'i: Social Science Research Institute, University of Hawai'i, 1995.

Johnson, Donald D. *The City and County of Honolulu, Hawai'i: A Governmental Chronicle.* Honolulu, Hawai'i: University of Hawai'i Press, 1991.

Juvik, Sonia P., and James O. Juvik, eds. *Atlas of Hawai'i.* 3d ed. Honolulu, Hawai'i: University of Hawai'i Press, 1998.

Kaeppler, Adrienne L. *Hula Pahu. Vol. 1—Hawaiian Drum Dances.* Honolulu, Hawai'i: Bishop Museum Press, 1993.

Kamakau, S. M. *Ruling Chiefs of Hawaii.* Honolulu, Hawai'i: Kamehameha Schools Press, 1961. Rev. ed. Honolulu, Hawai'i: Kamehameha Schools Press, 1992.

———. Translated by Mary Kawena Puku'ī and edited by Dorothy B. Barrère. *Ka Po'e Kahio (The People of Old).* Reprint ed. Honolulu, Hawai'i: Bishop Museum Press, 1964, 1992

———. Translated by Mary Kawena Puku'ī, ed. By Dorothy B. Barrère. *Tales and Traditions of the People of Old (Nā Mo'olelo a ka Po'e Kahiko).* Honolulu, Hawai'i: University of Hawai'i Press, 1991.

Kamins, Robert J., Robert E. Potter, and others. *Mālamalama: A History of the University of Hawai'i.* Honolulu, Hawai'i: University of Hawai'i Press, 1998.

Kanahele, George S., ed. *Hawaiian Music and Musicians: An Illustrated History.* Honolulu, Hawai'i: University of Hawai'i Press, 1979.

———. *Emma: Hawai'i's Remarkable Queen: A Biography.* Honolulu, Hawai'i: Queen Emma Foundation, 1999.

Kent, Joel J. *Hawai'i: Islands under the Influence.* Honolulu, Hawai'i: University of Hawai'i Press, 1993.

Kimura, Yukiko. *Issei: Japanese Immigrants in Hawaii.* Honolulu, Hawai'i: University of Hawai'i Press, 1988.

Kirch, Patrick V. *Feathered Gods and Fishhooks: An Introduction to Hawaiian Archaeology and Prehistory.* Honolulu, Hawai'i: University of Hawai'i Press, 1985.

Kirk, Patrick, and Marshall Sahlins. *Anahulu: The Anthropology of History in the Kingdom of Hawaii.* 2 vols. Chicago: University of Chicago Press, 1992.

Kittelson, David J. *The Hawaiians: An Annotated Bibliography.* Honolulu, Hawai'i: University of Hawai'i, Social Science Research Institute, 1984.

Kurisu. Yasushi. *Sugar Town: Hawai'i Plantation Days Remembered.* Honolulu, Hawai'i: Watermark, 1995.

Kuykendall, R. S. *The Hawaiian Kingdom.* 3 vols. Honolulu, Hawai'i: University of Hawai'i Press, 1938, 1953, 1967.

Lebra-Chapman, Joyce. *Shaping Hawaii: The Voices of Women.* 2d ed. Honolulu, Hawai'i: Goodale Publishing, 1999.

Leib, Amos P., and A. Grove Day. *Hawaiian Legends in English: An Annotated Bibliography.* 2d ed. Honolulu, Hawai'i: University of Hawai'i Press, 1979.

Love, Robert William, Jr., ed. *Pearl Harbor Revisited.* New York: St. Martin's Press, 1995.

Lum, Arlene, ed. *Sailing for the Sun: The Chinese in Hawai'i.* Honolulu, Hawai'i: University of Hawai'i Foundation, 1989.

Lee, Samuel S. O. *Their Footsteps: A Pictorial History of Koreans in Hawaii since 1903.* Honolulu, Hawai'i: Committee on the 90th Anniversary Celebration of Korean Immigration to Hawai'i, 1993.

Lum, Arlene, ed. *Sailing for the Sun: The Chinese in Hawaii, 1789–1989.* Honolulu, Hawai'i: University of Hawai'i Press, 1989.

Macdonald, Gordon A., and others. *Volcanoes in the Sea: The Geology of Hawaii.* 2d ed. Honolulu, Hawai'i: University of Hawai'i Press, 1983.

Malo, Davida. *Hawaiian Antiquities.* New translation and edited by Malcolm Naea Chun. Honolulu, Hawai'i: Folk Press, 1987.

Mast, Robert H., and Anne B. Mast. *Autobiography of Protest in Hawai'i.* Honolulu, Hawai'i: University of Hawai'i Press, 1996.

McLean, Mervyn. *Weavers of Song: Polynesian Music and Dance.* Honolulu, Hawai'i: University of Hawai'i Press, 1999.

Miller, Char, ed. *To Raise the Lord's Banner: Selected Writings of Hiram Bingham, 1814–1869, Missionary to the Hawaiian Islands.* Lewiston, N.Y.: Edwin Mellen Press, 1988.

Moffat, Riley M., and Gary L. Fitzpatrick. *Surveying the Mahele.* Honolulu, Hawai'i: Editions Limited, 1995.

Morris, Aldyth. *Lili'uokalani.* Honolulu, Hawai'i: University of Hawai'i Press, 1993.

———. *Robert Louis Stevenson—Appointment on Moloka'i.* Honolulu, Hawai'i: University of Hawai'i Press, 1995.

Okamura, Jonathan, ed. *Filipino American History, Identity and Community in Hawaii.* Honolulu, Hawai'i: Department of Sociology, University of Hawai'i, 1996.

Osborne, Thomas J. *"Empire Can Wait"; American Opposition to Hawaiian Annexation, 1893–1898.* Kent, Ohio: Kent State University Press, 1981.

Peterson, Barbara B., ed. *Notable Women of Hawaii.* Honolulu, Hawai'i: University of Hawai'i Press, 1984.

Potter, Norris. *The Hawaiian Monarchy.* Honolulu, Hawai'i: Bess Press, 1983.

Puku'ī, Mary Kawena. *Folktales of Hawai'i (He Mau Ka'a o Hawai'i).* Honolulu, Hawai'i: Bishop Museum Press, 1995.

———. *'Olelo No'eau: Hawaiian Proverbs and Poetical Sayings.* Honolulu, Hawai'i: Bernice P. Bishop Museum, 1983.

Puku'ī, Mary K., and Samuel Elbert. *Hawaiian Dictionary: Hawaiian-English, English-Hawaiian.* Rev. ed. Honolulu, Hawai'i: University of Hawai'i Press, 1986.

Reinecke, John E. *The Filipino Piecemeal Sugar Strike of 1924–1925.* Honolulu, Hawai'i: Social Science Research Center, University of Hawai'i, 1996.

Rock, Joseph F. *The Indigenous Trees of the Hawaiian Islands.* Honolulu, privately printed, 1913; reprinted Lawai, Kaua'i: Pacific Tropical Botanical Garden, 1974.

Rose, Roger G. *Hawaii: The Royal Isles.* Honolulu, Hawai'i: Bernice P. Bishop Museum Press, 1980.

Russo, Ron. *Hawaiian Reefs: A Natural History Guide.* San Leandr, Calif.: Wavecrest Publications, 1994.

Saiki, Patsy Sumie. *Early Japanese Immigrants in Hawaii.* Honolulu, Hawai'i: Japanese Cultural Center of Hawai'i, 1993.

Sandler, Rob, and others. *Architecture in Hawaii: A Chronological Survey.* Honolulu, Hawai'i: Mutual, 1993.

Schmitt, Robert C., comp. *Firsts and Almost Firsts in Hawai'i.* Ed. by Ronn Ronck. Honolulu, Hawai'i: University of Hawai'i Press, 1995.

Schütz, Albert J. *All About Hawaiian.* Honolulu, Hawai'i: University of Hawai'i Press, 1995.

———. *The Voices of Eden: A History of Hawaiian Language Studies.* Honolulu, Hawai'i: University of Hawai'i Press, 1994.

Shallenberger, Robert J., ed. *Hawaii's Birds.* 3d rev. ed. Honolulu, Hawai'i: Hawai'i Audubon Society, 1984.

Sinclair, Marjorie Jane Putnam. *Nai'ena'ena: Sacred Daughter of Hawai'i.* Honolulu, Hawai'i: Mutual Publishing, 1995.

Spickard, Paul R., ed. *Pacific Island Peoples in Hawaii.* Social Process in Hawai'i, vol. 36. Honolulu, Hawai'i: Department of Sociology, University of Hawai'i, 1994.

Spriggs, Matthew. *Na mea 'imi i ka wa Kahiko: An Annotated Bibliography of Hawaiian Archaeology.* Honolulu, Hawai'i: Social Science Research Institute, University of Hawai'i, 1988.

St. John, Harold. *List and Summary of the Flowering Plants in the Hawaiian Islands.* Lawai, Kaua'i: Pacific Tropical Botanical Garden, 1973.

Stannard, David E. *Before the Horror: The Population of Hawai'i on the Eve of Western Contact.* Honolulu, Hawai'i: Social Science Research Institute, University of Hawai'i, 1989.

Stillman, Amy K. *Hawaiian Chants: Published and Recorded Sources and Index.* N.p., n.s., 1988.

Strength and diversity: Japanese American Women in Hawai'i. Honolulu, Hawai'i: Bishop Museum Press, 1992.

Strona, Proserfina A. *Japanese in Hawaii: A Bibliography.* Rev. ed. Honolulu, Hawai'i: Hawai'i State Library, 1993.

———. *Samoans in Hawaii: A Bibliography.* Honolulu, Hawai'i: Hawai'i & Pacific Section, Hawai'i State Library, 1987.

Sullivan, Gerard, and Gary Hawes. *The Political Economy of Hawaii.* Honolulu, Hawai'i: University of Hawai'i Press, 1985.

Takaki, Ronald T. *Pau Hana: Plantation Life and Labor in Hawaii, 1835–1920.* Honolulu, Hawai'i: University of Hawai'i Press, 1983.

———. *Raising Cane: The World of Plantation Hawai'i.* New York: Chelsea House, 1994.

Taylor, Theodore. *Air Raid—Pearl Harbor: The Story of Sunday, December 7, 1941.* San Diego, Calif.: Harcourt Brace Jovanovich, 1991.

Todaro, Tony. *The Golden Years of Hawaiian Entertainment, 1874–1974.* Honolulu, Hawai'i: Tony Todaro Publishing Company, 1974.

Trask, Haunani-Kay. *From a Native Daughter: Colonialism and Sovereignty in Hawaii.* Rev. ed. Honolulu, Hawai'i: University of Hawai'i Press, 1999.

University of Hawai'i. *Atlas of Hawaii.* 3d ed. Honolulu, Hawai'i: University of Hawai'i Press, 1998.

University of Hawai'i Library. *Current Hawaiiana: A Quarterly Bibliography.* Honolulu, Hawai'i: University of Hawai'i Library, 1944-- (quarterly).

Van Sant, John E. *Pacific Pioneers: Japanese Journeys to America and Hawaii, 1850-80.* Urbana: University of Illinois Press, 2000.

Vincent, Ramona K. *The Church of Jesus Christ of Latter-day Saints in Hawaii and Tahiti.* Honolulu, Hawai'i: University of Hawai'i Press, 1980.

Whittaker, Elvi. *The Mainland Haole: The White Experience in Hawaii.* New York: Columbia University Press, 1986.

Young, Nancy Foon. *The Chinese in Hawaii: An Annotated Bibliography.* Honolulu, Hawai'i: University of Hawai'i, Social Science Research Institute, 1973.

Yount, David. *Who Runs the University? The Politics of Higher Education in Hawai'i, 1985–1992.* Honolulu, Hawai'i: University of Hawai'i Press, 1996.

Zambucka, Kristin. *The High Chiefess, Ruth Keelikolani.* Honolulu, Hawai'i: Green Glass Productions, 1992.

6. NAURU

Demmke, Andreas, and others. *Nauru Population Profiles: A Guide for Planners and Policy-Makers.* Nouméa, New Caledonia: Secretariat of the Pacific Community, 1999.

Ellis, Albert Fuller. *Ocean Island and Nauru: Their Story.* Sydney, Australia: Angus and Robertson, 1935.

Fabricius, Wilhelm. *Nauru 1888–1900: An Account in German and English based on official records of the Colonial Section of the German Foreign Office held by the Deutsches Zentralarchiv in*

Potsdam. Trans. and ed. by Dymphna Clark and Stewart Firth. Canberra, Australia: Australia National University, 1992.

Garrett, Jemima. *Island Exiles*. Sydney, Australia: ABC Books for the Australian Broadcasting Corp., 1996.

Hambruck, Paul. *Nauru*. 2 vols. Hamburg, Germany: L. Friedrichsen, 1914–1915.

Kayser, Alois, and Karl Rensch. *Nauru Grammar*. Yarralumla, Australian Capital Territory, Australia: Embassy of the Federal Republic of Germany, 1993

Krauss, Noel L. H. *Bibliography of Nauru*. Honolulu, Hawai'i: Krauss, 1970.

Macdonald, Barrie. *In Pursuit of the Sacred Trust: Trusteeship and Independence in Nauru*. Wellington, New Zealand: New Zealand Institute of International Affairs, 1988.

McDaniel, Carl N., and John M. Gowdy. *Paradise for Sale: A Parable of Nature*. Berkeley: University of California Press, 2000.

Petit-Skinner, Solange. *The Nauruans: Nature and Supernature in an Island of the Central Pacific*. 2d edition. San Francisco, Calif.: MacDuff Press, 1995.

Pollock, Nancy. *Nauru Bibliography*. Wellington, New Zealand: Department of Anthropology, Victoria University of Wellington, 1994.

Skinner, Carlton. *Nauru, the Remarkable Community*. Santa Cruz, Calif.: Center for South Pacific Studies, University of California, 1977.

Tate, Merze. *Nauru: Phosphate and the Nauruans*. Brisbane, Australia: University of Queensland Press, 1968.

Viviani, Nancy. *Nauru: Phosphate and Political Progress*. Honolulu, Hawai'i: University of Hawai'i Press, 1970

Weeramantry, Christopher G. *Nauru: Environmental Damage under International Trusteeship*. New York: Oxford University Press, 1992

7. NEW ZEALAND

Alley, Roderic, ed. *New Zealand and the Pacific*. Boulder, Colo.: Westview Press, 1984.

Alpers, Antony. *Maori Myths and Tribal Legends.* 2d ed. Auckland, New Zealand: Longman, 1996.

Angus, Ross. *New Zealand Aspirations in the Pacific in the Nineteenth Century.* Oxford, England:Clarendon Press, 1964.

Archie, Carold. *Maori Sovereignty: The Pakeha Perspective.* Auckland, New Zealand: Hodder Moa Beckett, 1995.

Armstrong, Alan. *Games and Dances of the Maori People.* Wellington, New Zealand: Viking Seven Seas, 1986, 1992.

Awatere, Donna. *Maori Sovereignty.* Auckland, New Zealand: Broadsheet, 1984.

Aweketuku, Ngahuia Te. *Mana Wahine Maori: Selected Writings on Maori Women's Art, Culture and Politics.* Auckland, New Zealand: New Women's Press, 1991.

Barber, Laurie. *New Zealand: A Short History.* London: Hutchinson, 1990.

Barrow, Terence. *The Decorative Arts of the New Zealand Maori.* 3d ed. Wellington, New Zealand: Reed, 1972.

Bartel, Susan, ed. *Working Titles: Books that Shaped New Zealand.* Wellington, New Zealand: National Library of New Zealand, 1993.

Bassett, Judith, Keith Sinclair, and Marcia Stenson. *The Story of New Zealand.* Auckland, New Zealand: Reed Methuen, 1985.

Bateman, David. *Bateman New Zealand Encyclopedia.* 4th ed. Auckland, New Zealand: David Bateman, 1995.

Bauer, Winifred, and others, eds. *The Reed Reference Grammar of Maori.* Auckland, New Zealand: Reed Publishing, 1996.

Bawden, Patricia. *The Years before Waitangi: A Story of Early Māori-European Contact in New Zealand.* Auckland, New Zealand: Patricia Bawden (Distributed by Benton Ross, 1987).

Beaglehole, John. C. *The Discovery of New Zealand.* 2d ed. London: Oxford University Press, 1961.

Belich, James. *Making People. Vol. 1: A History of the New Zealanders From Polynesian Settlement to the End of the Nineteenth Century.* Honolulu, Hawai'i: University of Hawai'i Press, 1997.

Best, Eldon. *The Maori.* 2 vols. Wellington, New Zealand: Polynesian Society, 1924.

Biggs, Bruce. *English-Maori, Maori-English Dictionary.* Auckland, New Zealand: Auckland University Press, 1990.

Binney, Judith. *The Legacy of Guilt: A Life of Thomas Dendall.* Auckland, New Zealand: University of Auckland Press, 1968.

Binney, Judith, Judith Basset, and Erik Olssen. *The People and the Land—Te Tangata me te Whenua: An Illustrated History of New Zealand, 1820–1920.* Wellington, New Zealand: Allen & Unwin, 1990.

Bohan, Edmund. *Edward Stafford: New Zealand's First Statesman.* Christchurch, New Zealand: Hazard Press, 1994.

Brailsford, Barry. *The Tattooed Land: The Southern Frontiers of the Pa Maori.* Wellington, New Zealand: Reed, 1981.

Brake, Brian. *Te Maori: Taonga Maori (Treasures of the Māori).* Auckland, New Zealand: Reed, 1994.

Brookes, Barbara, Charlotte Macdonald, and Margaret Tennant, eds. *Women in History: Essays on European Women in New Zealand.* Sydney, Australia: George Allen & Unwin, 1986.

Brown, Bruce. *The Rise of New Zealand Labour from 1916 to 1940.* Wellington, New Zealand: Price Milburn, 1962.

Buck, Peter. *The Coming of the Maori.* 2d ed. Wellington, New Zealand: Maori Purposes Fund Board, 1966.

Bunkle, Phillida, and Beryl Hughes. *Women in New Zealand Society.* Boston, Mass.: Allen & Unwin, 1986.

Burdon, Randal M. *New Zealand Notables.* 3 vols. Christchurch, New Zealand: Caxton Press, 1941–1950.

Campbell, John Logan. *Poenamo: Sketches of Early Days in New Zealand.* London: Norgate, 1881; reprinted Auckland, New Zealand: Wilson & Horton, 1970.

Catt, Helena, and Elizabeth McLeay, eds. *Women and Politics in New Zealand.* Wellington, New Zealand: Victoria University Press, 1993.

Cauaghey, Angela. *Pioneer Families: The Settlers of Nineteenth Century New Zealand.* Auckland, New Zealand: David Bateman, 1994.

Clark, Kate McCosh. *Maori Tales and Legends.* London, D. Nutt, 1896; reprinted Dunedin: Southern Reprints, 1993.

Colless, Brian, and Peter Donovan, eds. *Religion in New Zealand Society.* 2d ed. Pamerston North, New Zealand: Dunmore Press, 1985.

Condliffe, J. B. *New Zealand in the Making: A Study of Economic and Social Development.* 2d rev. ed. London: Allen & Unwin, 1959, 1963.

———. *The Welfare State in New Zealand.* London: Allen & Unwin, 1959, 1975.

Cowan, James. *The New Zealand Wars: A History of the Maori Campaigns and the Pioneering Period.* 2 vols. Wellington, New Zealand: Government Printer, 1983.

Cox, Lindsay. *Kotahitanga: The Search for Māori Political Unity.* Auckland, New Zealand: Oxford University Press, 1993.

Dalton, B. J. *War and Politics in New Zealand, 1855-1870.* Sydney, Australia: Sydney University Press, 1967.

Davidson, Allan K. *Christianity in Aotearoa: A History of Church and Society in New Zealand.* Wellington, New Zealand: Education for Ministry, 1991.

Davidson, Janet. *The Prehistory of New Zealand.* Auckland, New Zealand: Longman Paul, 1984.

Davis, Colin, and Peter Lineham, eds. *The Future of the Past: Themes in New Zealand History.* Palmerston North, New Zealand: Department of History, Massey University, 1991.

Department of Statistics. *New Zealand Official Yearbook.* Wellington, New Zealand: Department of Statistics, 1893– (annually).

Dictionary of New Zealand Biography. 5 vols. Wellington, New Zealand: Allen & Unwin, 1990.

Donovan, Peter, ed. *Religions of New Zealanders.* Palmerston North, New Zealand: Dunmore Press, 1990.

Duff, Roger. *The Moa Hunter Period of Maori Culture.* 3d ed. Wellinton, New Zealand: E. C. Keating, Government Printer, 1977.

Dymock, Gil. *A Concise Dictionary of New Zealand Place Names.* Auckland, New Zealand: Moa Beckett, 1994.

Eldred-Grigg, Stevan. *New Zealand Working People, 1890–1990.* Palmerston North, New Zealand: Dunmore Press, 1990.

———. *The Rich: A New Zealand History.* Auckland, New Zealand: Penguin Books, 1996.

———. *A Southern Gentry: New Zealanders Who Inherited the Earth.* Wellington, New Zealand: Reed, 1980.

Ell, Gordon. *New Zealand Traditions and Folklore.* Auckland, New Zealand: Bush Press, 1994.

Ell, Sarah. *Thar She Blows: Sealing and Whaling Days in New Zealand.* Auckland, New Zealand: Bush Press, 1995.

———. *The Adventures of Pioneer Women in New Zealand: From their Letters, Diaries, and Reminiscences.* Auckland, New Zealand: Bush Press, 1992.

Evans, Patrick. *The Penguin History of New Zealand Literature.* Auckland, New Zealand: Penguin, 1990.

Fabish, Robin. *New Zealand Maori.* Auckland, New Zealand: Hodder Moa Beckett, 1995.

Firth, Raymond. *Primitive Polynesian Economy.* London: G. Routledge & Sons, 1939; reprinted New York: Norton, 1975.

Gold, Hyam, ed. *New Zealand Politics in Perspective.* 3d ed. Auckland, New Zealand: Longman Paul, 1992.

Gorst, John E. *The Maori King.* London: Macmillan, 1864; reprinted Hamilton, New Zealand: Paul's Book Arcade, 1959.

Greene, Paul F., ed. *Studies in New Zealand Social Problems.* Palmerston North, New Zealand: Dunmore Press, 1990.

Grey, Alan Hopwood. *Aotearoa and New Zealand: A Historical Geography.* Christchurch, New Zealand: Canterbury University Press, 1994.

Grey, Sir George. *Polynesian Mythology.* New York: Taplinger Publishing Company, 1970; reprinted Hamilton, New Zealand: University of Waikato Library, 1995.

Greif, Stuart William, ed. *Immigration and National Identity in New Zealand: One People, Two Peoples, Many Peoples?* Palmerston North, New Zealand: Dunmore Press, 1995.

Grimshaw, Patricia. *Women's Suffrage in New Zealand.* Auckland, New Zealand: Auckland University Press, 1987.

Gustafson, Barry. *Labour's Path to Political Independence: The Origins and Establishment of the New Zealand Labour Party 1900–1919.* Auckland, New Zealand: Auckland University Press, 1980.

Hamer, David. *The New Zealand Liberals: The Years of Power, 1891–1912.* Auckland, New Zealand: Auckland University Press, 1988.

———. *New Zealand Social History.* Auckland, New Zealand: Auckland University Press, 1980.

Hawke, G. R. *The Making of New Zealand: An Economic History.* New York: Cambridge University Press, 1985.

Hazelhurst, Kayleen M. *Political Expression and Ethnicity: Statecraft and Mobilisation in the Māori World.* Westport, Conn.: Praeger, 1993.

Holcraft, Montague Harry. *The Village Transformed: Aspects of Change in New Zealand, 1900–1990.* Wellington, New Zealand: Victoria University Press, 1990.

Holland, Martin, ed. *Electoral Behaviour in New Zealand.* Auckland, New Zealand: Oxford University Press, 1992.

Hucker, Graham. *Glimpses of New Zealand in the Nineteenth Century.* Auckland, New Zealand: Heinemann Educational, 1992.

Jackson, Gainor Wilmott. *Settlement by Sail: 19th Century Immigration to New Zealand.* Wellington, New Zealand: GP Publications, 1991.

Jackson, Hugh R. *Churches and People in Australia and New Zealand, 1860–1930.* London: Allen & Unwin, 1987.

Jackson, Keith, and Alan McRobie. *Historical Dictionary of New Zealand.* Lanham, Md.: Scarecrow Press, 1996.

James, Colin. *New Territory: The Transformation of New Zealand, 1984–1992.* Sydney, Australia: Allen & Unwin, 1992.

Johansson, Dean. *Wearing Ink: The Art of Tattoo in New Zealand.* Auckland, New Zealand: David Bateman, 1994.

Johnstone, John Campbell. *Maoria: A Sketch of the Manners and Customs of the Aboriginal Inhabitants of New Zealand.* Christchurch, New Zealand: Kiwi Publishers, 1995; reprint of publication London: Chapman and Hall, 1874.

Kawharu, Ian Hugh. *Waitangi: Maori and Pakeha Perspectives of the Treaty of Waitangi.* Auckland, New Zealand: Oxford University Press, 1989.

Kennaway, Richard, and John Henderson. *Beyond New Zealand: Foreign Policy into the 1990s.* Auckland, New Zealand: Longman Paul, 1991.

King, Jane. *The New Zealand Handbook.* 4th ed. Chico, Calif.: Moon Publications, 1996.

King, Michael. *Being Pakeha: An Encounter with New New [sic] Zealand and the Maori Renaissance.* Auckland, New Zealand: Hodder & Stoughton, 1985.

———. *God's Farthest Outpost: A History of Catholics in New Zealand.* Auckland, New Zealand: Viking, 1997.

———. *Maoriori: A People Rediscovered.* New York: Viking Press, 1989.

———. *New Zealanders at War.* Exeter, N.H.: Heinemann, 1981.

———. *Pakeha: The Quest for Identity in New Zealand.* Auckland, New Zealand: Penguin, 1991.

Kirker, Anne. *New Zealand Women Artists.* Rev. ed. Tortola, New Zealand: Craftsman House, 1993.

Krishnan, Vasantha, and others. *The Challenge of Change: Pacific Island Communities in New Zealand, 1986–1993.* Wellington, New Zealand: New Zealand Institute for Social Research and Development, 1994.

Labrum, Bronwyn. *Women's History: A Short Guide to Researching and Writing Women's History in New Zealand.* Wellington, New Zealand: Bridget Williams Books, 1993.

Leue, Holger, and Witi Ihimaera. *Aotearoa New Zealand: Faces of the Land.* Auckland, New Zealand: Reed, 1995.

Lineham, Peter J., and Anthony R. Grigg. *Religious History of New Zealand: A Bibliography.* 4th ed. Palmerston North, New Zealand: Department of History, Massey University, 1993.

Loomis, Terrence. *Pacific Migrant Labour, Class and Racism in New Zealand: Fresh off the Boat.* Aldershot, England: Gower, 1990.

Macdonald, Charlotte, Merimeri Penfold, and Bridget Williams, eds. *The Book of New Zealand Women.* Wellington, New Zealand: Bridget Williams Books, 1991.

Maori Biographies from the Dictionary of New Zealand Biography. 2 vols. Wellington, New Zealand: Bridget Williams Books, 1991.

Marais, J. S. *The Colonisation of New Zealand.* London, Oxford University Press, 1927; reprinted London: Dawsons, 1968.

Massey, Patrick. *New Zealand: Market Liberalization in a Developed Economy.* New York: St. Martin's Press, 1995.

McHugh, Paul Gerard. *The Maori Magna Carta: New Zealand Law and the Treaty of Waitangi.* Auckland, New Zealand: Oxford University Press, 1991.

McIntyre, William D. *Background to the Anzus Pact: Policy-Making, Strategy and Diplomacy, 1945–1955.* New York: St. Martin's Press, 1995.

———. *New Zealand Prepares for War: Defence Policy, 1919–39.* Christchurch, New Zealand: University of Canterbury Press, 1988.

McKinnon, Malcolm. *Immigrants and Citizens: New Zealanders and Asian Immigration in Historical Context.* Wellington, New Zealand: Institute of Policy Studies, Victoria University of Wellington, 1996.

———. *Independence and Foreign Policy: New Zealand in the World since 1935.* Auckland, New Zealand: Auckland University Press, 1993.

McLauclan, Gordon, ed. *New Zealand Encyclopedia.* 3d ed. Auckland, New Zealand: David Bateman Limited, 1992.

McLeay, Elizabeth. *Cabinet and Political Power in New Zealand.* Auckland, New Zealand: Oxford University Press, 1995.

McLintock, A. H. *Crown Colony Government in New Zealand.* Wellington, New Zealand: Government Printer, 1958.

McMillan, Neale. *Top of the Greasy Pole: New Zealand Prime Ministers of Recent Times.* Dunedin, New Zealand: McIndoe Publishers, 1993.

McNab, Robert. *From Tasman to Marsden: A History of Northern New Zealand from 1642 to 1818.* Dunedin: J. Wilkie & Company, Ltd., 1914; reprinted Christchurch, New Zealand: Cadsonbury Publications, 1996.

———, ed. *Historical Records of New Zealand.* 2 vols. Wellington, New Zealand: Government Printer, 1908–14; reprinted. Wellington, New Zealand: Government Printer, 1973.

———. *The Old Whaling Days: A History of Southern New Zealand from 1830 to 1840.* Christchurch, New Zealand: Whitcombe and Tombs, 1913.

Melbourne, Hineani. *Maori Sovereignty: The Maori Perspectives.* Auckland, New Zealand: Hodder Moa Beckett, 1995.

Miller, John Owen. *Early Victorian New Zealand: A Study of Racial Tension and Social Attitudes, 1839–1852.* New York: Oxford University Press, 1958.

Miller, Raymond, ed. *New Zealand Politics in Transition.* Auckland, New Zealand: Oxford University Press, 1997.

Milne, Robert S. *Political Parties in New Zealand.* Oxford, England:Clarendon Press, 1966.

Moon, Paul. *The Origins of the Treaty of Waitangi.* Auckland, New Zealand: Birdwood Publishing, 1994.

Morrell, W. P. *The Provisional System in New Zealand.* 2d rev. ed. Christchurch, New Zealand: Whitecombe and Tombs, 1964.

Muldoon, Robert. *Muldoon.* Wellington, New Zealand: Reed, 1977.

———. *My Way.* Wellington, New Zealand: Reed, 1981.

Mulgan, Richard G. *Democracy and Power in New Zealand: A Study of New Zealand Politics.* 2d ed. Auckland, New Zealand: Oxford University Press, 1989.

———. *Māori, Pākehā, and Democracy.* Auckland, New Zealand: Oxford University Press, 1989.

Mulgan, Richard Grant. *Politics in New Zealand.* Auckland, New Zealand: Auckland University Press and Oxford University Press, 1994.

New Zealand Ministry of Education. *Ko e Ako 'a e Kakai Pasifika: Pacific People's Education in Aotearoa New Zealand: Towards the Twenty-First Century.* Wellington, New Zealand: The Ministry, 1996.

Ngata, Hori M. *English-Maori Dictionary.* Wellington, New Zealand: Learning Media, 1995.

Nicholas, Anne. *The Art of the New Zealand Tattoo.* Auckland, New Zealand: Tandem, 1994.

O'Farrell, P. J. *Harry Holland, Militant Socialist.* Canberra, Australia: Australian National University, 1964.

Oral History in New Zealand. 4 vols. Wellington, New Zealand: National Oral History Association of New Zealand, 1992.

Orbell, Margaret. *The Illustrated Encyclopedia of Maori Myth and Legend.* Christchurch, New Zealand: Canterbury University Press, 1995.

———. *The Natural World of the Maori.* Photographs by Geoff Moon. Rev. ed. Auckland, New Zealand: David Bateman, 1996.

Oliver, W. H., and B. R. Williams, eds. *Oxford History of New Zealand.* 2d ed. Wellington, New Zealand: Oxford University Press, 1992.

Openshaw, Roger, Greg Lee, and Howard Lee. *Challenging the Myths: Rethinking New Zealand's Education History.* Palmerston North, New Zealand: Dunmore, 1993.

The Origins of the First New Zealanders. Auckland, New Zealand: Auckland University Press, 1994.

Owens, J. M. R. *Prophets in the Wilderness: The Wesleyan Mission to New Zealand.* Auckland, New Zealand: Auckland University Press, 1974.

Pearson, David. *A Dream Deferred: The Origins of Ethnic Conflict in New Zealand.* Wellington, New Zealand: Allen & Unwin, 1990.

Phillips, Jock. *A Man's Country: The Image of the Pakeha Male, a History.* Auckland, New Zealand: Penguin Books, 1996.

Race Relations in New Zealand: A Bibliography, 1970–1986. Auckland, New Zealand: Office of the Race Relations Conciliator, 1987.

Reed, Alfred Hamish. *The Story of New Zealand.* Rev. ed. Auckland, New Zealand: Fontana Silver Fern, 1974.

Rice, Geoffrey W., ed. *The Oxford History of New Zealand.* Auckland, New Zealand: Oxford University Press, 1992.

Ritchie, Jane, and James Ritchie. *Violence in New Zealand.* Wellington, New Zealand: Allen & Unwin, 1990.

Roper, Brian, and Chris Rudd, eds. *State and Economy in New Zealand.* Auckland, New Zealand: Oxford University Press, 1993.

Ross, Angus. *New Zealand Aspirations in the Pacific in the Nineteenth Century.* London: Oxford University Press, 1964.

Roth, Herbert O. *Trade Unions in New Zealand Past and Present.* Wellington, New Zealand: Reed Education, 1973.

Rudd, Chris, and Brian Roper, eds. *The Political Economy of New Zealand.* Auckland, New Zealand: Oxford University Press, 1997.

Rutherford, James. *Sir George Grey, K.C.B., 1812–1898: A Study in Colonial Government.* London: Cassell, 1961.

Ryan, Peter M. *The Reed Dictionary of Modern Maori.* Auckland, New Zealand: Reed, 1995.

Salmond, Anne. *Between Worlds: Early Exchanges between Maori and Europeans, 1773–1815.* Honolulu, Hawai'i: University of Hawai'i Press, 1997.

———. *Two Worlds: First Meetings Between Maori and Europeans, 1642–1772.* Honolulu, Hawai'i: University of Hawai'i Press, 1992.

Sargison, Patricia A. *Victoria's Furthest Daughters: A Bibliography of Published Sources for the Study of Women in New Zealand, 1830–1914.* Wellington, New Zealand: Alexander Turnbull Library, 1984.

Sharp, Andrew. *Justice and the Maori: Maori Claims in New Zealand Political Argument in the 1980s.* Auckland, New Zealand: Oxford University Press, 1990.

———. *Ancient Voyagers in Polynesia.* Berkeley: University of California Press, 1963.

———, ed. *Leap into the Dark: The Changing Role of the State in New Zealand since 1984.* Auckland, New Zealand: Auckland University Press, 1994.

Sheehan, Mark. *Maori and Pakeha: Race Relations 1912–1980.* Auckland, New Zealand: Macmillan of New Zealand, 1989.

Simmons, D. R. *The Great New Zealand Myth: A Study of the Discovery and Origin Traditions of the Maori.* Wellington, New Zealand: Reed, 1976.

Sinclair, Keith. *A Destiny Apart: New Zealand's Search for National Identity.* Wellington, New Zealand: Allen & Unwin, 1986.

———. *A History of New Zealand.* 4th rev. ed. Auckland, New Zealand: Penguin, 1991.

———. *Kinds of Peace: Maori People After the Wars, 1870–1885.* Auckland, New Zealand: Auckland University Press, 1991.

———, ed. *The Oxford Illustrated History of New Zealand.* Auckland, New Zealand: Oxford University Press, 1990; 2d ed. Auckland, New Zealand: Oxford University Press, 1996.

———. *Walter Nash.* New York: Oxford University Press, 1976.

Smith, Paul. *New Zealand at War.* Auckland, New Zealand: Hodder Moa Beckett, 1995.

Smith, S. Percy. *Hawaiki: The Original Home of the Maori.* 4th ed. Auckland, New Zealand: Whitcombe Tombs, 1921.

———. *The Lore of The Whare-wānanga: Or Teachings of the Maori College on Religion, Cosmogony, and History.* 2 pts. New Plymouth, New Zealand: Polynesian Society, 1913, 1915.

———. *Maori Wars of the Nineteenth Century: The Struggle of the Northern Against Southern Maori Tribes Prior to the Colonisation of New Zealand in 1840.* Christchurch, New Zealand: Whitcombe & Tombs, 1910; reprinted Christchurch, New Zealand: Capper Press, 1984.

Spoonley, Paul, David Pearson, and Cluny Macpherson eds. *Nga Patai: Racism and Ethnic Relations in Aotcaroa/New Zealand.* Palmerston North, New Zealand: Dunmore Press, 1996.

Starzecka, D. C., ed. *Maori: Art and Culture.* Auckland, New Zealand: D. Bateman, 1996.

Stevens, Graeme Roy. *Prehistoric New Zealand.* Rev. ed. Auckland, New Zealand: Reed, 1995.

Sturm, Terry, ed. *The Oxford History of New Zealand Literature in English.* Auckland, New Zealand: Oxford University Press, 1991.

Sutton, Doug G., ed. *The Origins of the First New Zealanders.* Auckland, New Zealand: Auckland University Press, 1994.

Webb, Raymond. *Government and the People: A Study of Politics in New Zealand.* Auckland, New Zealand: Macmillan, 1989.

Williams, Mark, and Michele Leggot, eds. *Opening the Book: New Essays on New Zealand Writing.* Auckland, New Zealand: Auckland University Press, 1995.

Wilson, John A. *The Story of Te Waharoa: A Chapter in Early New Zealand History, Together with Sketches of Ancient Maori Life and History.* London: Whitcombe and Tombs, 1907; reprinted Christchurch, New Zealand: Capper Press, 1984.

Wood, G. A. *Studying New Zealand History.* 2d ed. Dunedin, New Zealand: University of Otago Press, 1992.

Wright, Harrison M. *New Zealand 1769–1840: Early Years of Western Contact.* Cambridge, Mass.: Harvard University Press, 1959.

Young, Thomas-Durell. *ANZUS: Australian, New Zealand, and U.S. Security Relations, 1951–1986.* Boulder, Colo.: Westview Press, 1992.

8. NIUE

Berrill, Peter M. *Niue Tenure and Survey.* Christchurch, New Zealand: University of Canterbury, 1968.

Chapman, Terry. *The Decolonisation of Niue.* Wellington, New Zealand: Victoria University Press, 1976.

Chapman, Terry, and others. *Niue: A History of the Island.* Translated by Leslie Rex. Suva, Fiji: Government of Niue, 1982.

Coppell, William G. *Bibliographies of the Kermadec Islands, Niue, Swains Island and the Tokelau Islands.* Honolulu, Hawai'i: Pacific Islands Program, University of Hawai'i, 1975.

Crocombe, Marjorie T. *Two Hundred Changing Years: A Story of New Zealand's Little Sisters in the Pacific: The Cook Islands, the Tokelau Islands, and Niue Island.* Wellington, New Zealand: New Zealand Department of Education, 1962.

Government of Niue. *Niue National Development Plan, 1980–1985.* Niue: Government of Niue, 1979.

Kalauni, Solomone, and others. *Land Tenure in Niue.* Suva, Fiji: University of the South Pacific, 1977.

King, Joseph. *W. G. Lawes of Savage Island and New Guinea.* London: Religious Tract Society, 1909.

Krauss, N. L. H. *Bibliography of Niue, South Pacific.* Honolulu, Hawai'i: The author, 1970.

Loeb, Edwin M. *History and Traditions of Niue.* Honolulu, Hawai'i: Bishop Museum Press, 1926.

McDowell, David K. *History of Niue.* Wellington, New Zealand: Victoria University, 1961.

McEwen, J. M. *Niue Dictionary.* Wellington, New Zealand: Department of Maori and Island Affairs, 1970.

———. *Report on Land Tenure in Niue.* Wellington, New Zealand: New Zealand Government, 1968.

McLachlan, Sue. "Savage Island or Savage History? An Interpretation of Early European Contact with Niue." *Pacific Studies* 6, no. 1 (Fall 1982): 26–51.

Pulekula. "The Traditions of Niue-fekai." *Journal of the Polynesian Society* 12 (1903): 22–31, 85–118.

Risk, Ernest K. *The Island of Niue: Development or Dependence for a Very Small Nation.* Canberra, Australia: Australia National University Press, 1978.

Ross, Angus. *New Zealand Aspirations in the Pacific in the Nineteenth Century.* London: Oxford University Press, 1964.

Scott, Dirk. *Would a Good Man Die? Niue Island, New Zealand and the Late Mr Larsen.* Auckland, New Zealand: Hodder & Stoughton in association with Southern Cross Books, 1993.

Smith, S. Percy. *Niue: The Island and Its People.* Wellington, New Zealand: Polynesian Society, 1902; reprinteed Suva, Fiji: Institute of Pacific Studies, 1983.

Sperlich, Wolfgang B. *Tohi Vagahau Niue: Niue Language Dictionary.* Niue: Government of Niue, 1997.

Thomson, Basil. *Savage Island: An Account of a Sojourn in Niue and Tonga.* London: John Murray, 1902; reprinted Papakura, New Zealand: R. McMillan, 1984.

Whitaker, Grame. *The Niuean Language: An Elementary Grammar and Basic Vocabulary.* Alofi, Niue: University of the South Pacific Extension Center, 1982.

Yuncker, L. G. *The Flora of Niue Island.* Honolulu, Hawai'i: Bernice P. Bishop Museum Press, 1943.

9. PITCAIRN

Ball, Ian M. *Pitcairn: Children of Mutiny.* Boston, Mass.: Little, Brown, & Company, 1973.

Barrow, John. *The Mutiny of the Bounty.* London: John Murray, 1831; reprinted New York: Oxford University Press, 1989.

Belcher, Lady Diana. *The Mutineers of the Bounty and Their Descendants in Pitcairn and Norfolk Islands.* London: J. Murray, 1870; reprinted New York: AMS Press, 1980.

Christensen, Alta H. *Heirs of Exile: The Story of Pitcairn Island, Paradise of the Pacific.* Hagerstown, Md.: Review and Herald Publishing Association, 1955.

Christian, Glynn. *Fragile Paradise: The Discovery of Fletcher Christian, Bounty Mutineer.* London: Book Club Associates, 1983.

Clarke, Peter. *Hell and Paradise: The Norfolk, Bounty, Pitcairn Saga.* New York: Viking Press, 1986.

Clune, Frank. *Journey to Pitcairn.* Sydney, Australia: Angus & Robertson, 1966.

Dening, Greg. *Mr Bligh's Bad Language: Passion, Power, and Theatre on the Bounty.* Cambridge, Mass.: Cambridge University Press, 1992.

Ferris, Norman A. *Story of Pitcairn Island.* Hagerstown, Md.: Review and Herald Publishing Association, 1958.

Ford, Herbert. *Pitcairn: Port of Call.* Angwin, Calif.: Hawser Titles, 1996.

Hough, Richard. *Captain Bligh and Mr. Christian: The Men and the Mutiny.* London: Cassell, 1979.

Lummis, Trevor. *Pitcairn Island: Life and Death in Eden.* Brookfield, Vt.: Ashgate, 1997.

Marshall, David. *Breadfruit, Buccaneers and the* Bounty *Bible.* Grantham, England: Stanborough Press, 1989.

McKinney, Sam. *Bligh: A True Account of Mutiny Aboard His Majesty's Ship* Bounty. Camden, Maine: International Marine Pub. Co., 1989.

Murray, Spence. *Pitcairn Island, the First 200 Years.* La Canada, Calif.: Bounty Sagas, 1992.

Nicolson, Robert B., and Brian F. Davies. *The Pitcairners.* Sydney, Australia: Angus and Robertson, 1965; reprinted Honolulu, Hawai'i: University of Hawai'i Press, 1997.

Ross, Alan S. C. *The Pitcairnese Language.* New York: Oxford University Press, 1964.

Sargent, Charles L. *Life of Alexander Smith, Captain of the Island of Pitcairn.* Boston, Mass.: Sylvester T. Goss, 1819.

Shapiro, Harry L. *Heritage of the* Bounty*: The Story of Pitcairn through Six Generations.* New York: AMS Press, 1979.

———. *The Pitcairn Islanders.* New York: Simon & Schuster, 1968.

Young, Rosalind A. *Mutiny of the* Bounty *and the Story of Pitcairn Island, 1790–1894.* New York: Pacific Press Publishing, 1894; reprinted New York: Gordon Press, 1978.

10. SĀMOA (GENERAL)

Allardice, R. W. *A Simplified Dictionary of Modern Samoan.* Auckland, New Zealand: Polynesian Press, 1985.

Baker, Paul T., J. M. Hanna, and T. S. Baker. *The Changing Samoans: Behavior and Health in Transition.* New York: Oxford University Press, 1986.

Blanton, Casy, ed. *Picturing Paradise: Colonial Photography of Sāmoa, 1875 to 1925.* Caytona Beach, Fla.: Daytona Beach Community College, 1995.

Buck, Sir Peter H. *Samoan Material Culture.* Honolulu, Hawai'i: Bernice P. Bishop Museum, 1930.

Ellison, Joseph W. *Tusitala of the South Seas: The Story of Robert Louis Stevenson's Life in the South Pacific.* New York: Hastings House, 1953.

Franco, Robert W. *Samoan Perceptions of Work: Moving Up and Moving Around.* New York: AMS Press, 1991.

———. *Samoans in Hawaii: A Demographic Profile.* Honolulu, Hawai'i: East-West Population Institute, East-West Center, 1987.

Gilson, R. P. *Samoa, 1830–1900: The Politics of a Multi-Cultural Community.* New York: Oxford University Press, 1970.

Grattan, F. J. H. *An Introduction to Samoan Custom.* Āpia, Sāmoa: Samoa Printing & Publishing Co., 1948; reprinted Auckland, New Zealand: Macmillan, 1985.

Henry, Brother Fred. *Samoa: An Early History.* Revised by Tofa Pula and Nicholao I. Tuitelapaga. Pago Pago: American Samoa Department of Education, 1980. Reprinted as *History of Sāmoa*, Āpia, Sāmoa: Commercial Printers, 1992.

Heslin, Joseph. *A History of the Roman Catholic Church in Samoa, 1845–1995.* Āpia, Sāmoa: s.n., 1995.

Hovdhaugen, Even. *From the Land of Nafanua: Samoan Oral Texts in Transcription with Translation, Notes, and Vocabulary.* Oslo: Norwegian University Press, 1987.

Hughes, H. G. A. *Samoa: American Samoa, Western Samoa, Samoans Abroad.* Oxford, England: Clio Press, 1997.

———. *The Samoan "Imbroglio": A Select Bibliography.* Afonwen, Wales: Gwasg Gwenffrwd, 1992.

Hunkin, Alfred. *Gagana Samoa: A Samoan Language Coursebook.* Auckland, New Zealand: Polynesian Press, 1988.

Keesing, Felix M. *Modern Samoa: Its Government and Changing Life.* Facsimile ed. New York: AMS Press, 1978.

Kennedy, Paul M. *The Samoan Tangle: A Study in Anglo-German-American Relations 1878–1900.* New York: Harper & Row, 1974.

Kirk, Allan Robert. *Sāmoa's Fight for Freedom: To Write the Wrongs.* Wellington, New Zealand: Capital Letters Publishers, 1996.

Krämer, Augustin F. *Die Samoa-Inseln.* 3 vols in 2. Stuttgart, Germany: E. Nägele, 1902–03. Translated by Theodore Verhaaren, *The Samoan Islands: An Outline of a Monograph with Particular Consideration of German Sāmoa.* 2 vols. Honolulu, Hawai'i: University of Hawai'i Press, 1993–1995.

Mackensen, Gōtz. *Zum Beispiel Samoa: der Sozio-Ökonomische Wandel Samoas vom Beginn der kolonialen Penetration im Jahre 1830 bis zur Gründung des unabhängigen Staates im Jahre 1962.* Bremen, Germany: Übersee Museum, 1977.

Macpherson, Cluny, and La'avasa Macpherson. *Samoan Medical Belief and Practice.* Auckland, New Zealand: Auckland University Press, 1990.

Mangeret, A. *Mgr. Bataillon et les missions de l'océanie centrale.* 2 vols. Lyon, France: Lecoffre, 1884.

Masterman, Sylvia. *The Origins of International Rivalry in Samoa, 1845–1884.* London: G. Allen & Unwin, 1934.

Mead, Margaret. *Coming of Age in Samoa.* New York: Blue Ribbon Books, 1932.

Milner, George Bertram *Samoan Dictionary.* Auckland, New Zealand: Auckland University Press, 1993.

Moyle, Richard, ed. *The Samoan Journals of John Williams, 1830 and 1832.* Canberra, Australia: Australian National University Press, 1984.

———. *Traditional Samoan Music.* Auckland, New Zealand: Auckland University Press, 1988.

Muse, Corey, and Shirley Muse. *The Birds and Birdlore of Samoa.* Walla Walla, Wash.: Pioneer Press, 1982.

Robinson, A. C. *The Ecology of Sāmoa: An Annotated Bibliography.* Āpia, Sāmoa: South Pacific Regional Environment Programme, 1994.

Rowe, N. A. *Samoa Under the Sailing Gods.* New York: Putnam, 1930.

Runeborg, Ruth E. *Western Samoa and American Samoa: History, Culture, and Communication.* Honolulu, Hawai'i: East-West Center, 1980.

Ryden, George Herbert. *The Foreign Policy of the United States in Relation to Samoa.* New York: Octagon Books, 1933, 1975.

Schultz, Erich. *Samoan Proverbial Expressions: Alaga'upu Fa'a-Samoa.* Honolulu, Hawai'i: University of Hawai'i Press, 1989.

Setu, Fa'atulituili. *The Ministry in the Making: A History of the Church in Samoa, 1830–1900.* Suva, Fiji: Pacific Theological College, 1988.

Stair, John B. *Old Samoa or Flotsam and Jetsam from the Pacific Ocean.* London: Religious Tract Society, 1897; reprinted Papakura, New Zealand: R. McMillan, 1983.

Stevenson, Robert Louis. *A Footnote to History: Eight Years of Trouble in Samoa.* New York: C. Scribner's Sons, 1903; reprinted London: Dawsons of Pall Mall, 1967.

Stucbel, C., and Brother Herman, comps. *Tala O Le Vavau: The Myths, Legends, and Customs of Old Samoa.* Honolulu, Hawai'i: University of Hawai'i Press, 1989; reprinted Auckland, New Zealand: Pasifika Press, 1995.

Sutter, Frederic Koehler. *The Samoans: A Global Family.* Honolulu, Hawai'i: University of Hawai'i Press, 1989.

Turner, George. *Samoa: A Hundred Years Ago and Long Before.* London: Macmillan, 1884; reprinted Suva, Fiji: Institute of Pacific Studies, University of the South Pacific, 1989.

Williams, John. *A Narrative of Missionary Enterprises in the South Seas.* London: John Snow, 1837.

Wood, Alfred H. *Overseas Missions of the Australian Methodist Church. Vol. 1, Tonga and Samoa.* Melbourne, Australia: Aldersgate Press, 1975.

11. SĀMOA (AMERICAN)

Ahlburg, Dennis, and Michael J. Levin. *The North East Passage: A Study of Pacific Islander Migration to American Samoa and the United States.* Canberra, Australia: Australian National University Press, 1990.

American Sāmoa. *A 40-Year History of the Legislature of American Samoa.* Pago Pago: s.n., 1998.

Calkins, Fay G. *My Samoan Chief.* London: Frederick Muller, 1962.

Faleomavaega, Eni F. H. *Navigating the Future: A Samoan Perspective on US-Pacific Relations.* Suva, Fiji: Institute of Pacific Studies, University of the South Pacific, 1995.

———. "Some Perspectives on American Samoa's Political Relationship with the United States." *Pacific Studies* 13, no. 2 (1990): 119–123.

Fuimaono, Dennis F. *The Evolution of Jurisprudence in American Samoa.* Long Beach: California State University, 1985.

Gray, J. A. C. *Amerika Samoa: A History of American Samoa and Its United States Naval Administration.* Annapolis, Md.: US Naval Institute, 1960; reprinted New York: Arno Press, 1980.

Holmes, Lowell D. *Samoan Village: Then and Now.* 2d ed. New York: Harcourt Brace Jovanovich, 1992.

Hughes, H. G. A. *Samoa: American Samoa, Western Samoa, Samoans Abroad. World Bibliographical Series, Vol. 196.* Oxford, England, and Santa Barbara, Calif.: ABC-Clio Press, 1997.

Janes, Craig Robert. *Migration, Social Change, and Health: A Samoan Community in Urban California.* Stanford, Calif.: Stanford University Press, 1990.

Krauss, N. L. H. *Bibliography of Swain's Island, America Samoa.* Honolulu, Hawai'i: By the author, 1970.

Michal, Edward Joseph. *American Samoa or Eastern Samoa? The Potential for American Samoa to Become Free Associated with the United States.* Honolulu, Hawai'i: Pacific Islands Studies Center, University of Hawai'i, 1991.

Oakey, Betty H. *American Samoan Families in Transition: A Report.* San Francisco, Calif.: Far West Laboratory for Educational Research on Development, 1980.

Osman, Wali M. *Western Samoa Economic Report, March 1997.* Honolulu, Hawai'i: Bank of Hawai'i, 1997.

Pouesi, Daniel. *An Illustrated History of Samoans in California.* Carson, Calif.: KIN Publications, 1994.

Samoa News. Pago Pago, American Sāmoa: Tolani Teleso, 1978– (weekly).

The Samoan Times. Pago Pago, American Sāmoa: D. C. Kneubuhl, 1964– (weekly).

Shaffer, J. Robert. *American Sāmoa: 100 Years under the United States Flag.* Honolulu, Hawai'i: Island Heritage Publishing, 2000.

Setchell, William Albert. *American Samoa.* Washington, D.C.: Carnegie Institution, 1924; reprinted New York: AMS Press, 1978.

Strona, Proserfina A. *Samoans in Hawaii: A Bibliography.* Honolulu, Hawai'i: Hawai'i & Pacific Section, Hawai'i State Library, 1987.

Sutter, Frederic Koehler. *Amerika Samoa: An Anthropological Photo Essay.* Honolulu, Hawai'i: University of Hawai'i Press, 1984.

West, Francis J. *Political Advancement in the South Pacific: A Comparative Study of Colonial Practice in Fiji, Tahiti, and American Samoa.* New York: Oxford University Press, 1961.

12. SĀMOA (Formerly "Western Sāmoa")

Alailima, Fay. *Aggie Grey: A Samoan Saga.* Foreword by James A. Michener. Honolulu, Hawai'i: Mutual Publishing Company, 1988.

———. *My Samoan Chief.* Honolulu, Hawai'i: University of Hawai'i Press, 1962, 1971.

Bolabola, Cema, and others. *Land Rights of Pacific Women.* Suva, Fiji: Institute of Pacific Studies, 1986.

Côté, James N. *Adolescent Storm and Stress: An Evaluation of the Mead-Freeman Controversy.* Hillsdale, N.J.: Lawrence Erlbaum Associates, 1994.

Davidson, James W. *Samoa Mo Samoa: The Emergence of the Independent State of Western Samoa.* London: Oxford University Press, 1967.

Duranti, Alessandro. *The Samoan Fono: A Sociolinguistic Study.* Canberra, Australia: Australian National University, 1981.

———. *From Grammar to Politics: A Linguistic Anthropology in a Western Samoan Village.* Berkeley: University of California Press, 1994.

Economist Intelligence Unit. *Country Profile: Pacific Islands.* London: Economist Intelligence Unit, 1990.

———. *Fiji, Solomon Islands, Western Samoa, Vanuatu, Tonga: Country Profile, 1991–92.* London: Economist Intelligence Unit, 1991.

Fairbairn, Ian J. *The Western Samoan Economy: Prospects for Recovery and Long-Term Growth.* Canberra, Australia: Australian Government Publishing Service, 1991.

Fairbairn Pacific Consultants Pty., Ltd. *The Western Samoan Economy: Paving the Way for Sustainable Growth and Stability.* Canberra, Australia: Australian International Development Assistance Bureau, 1994.

Field, Michael J. *Mau: Samoa's Struggle Against New Zealand Oppression.* Wellington, New Zealand: A. H. and A. W. Reed, Ltd., 1984. Reprinted as *Mau: Samoa's Struggle for Freedom.* Auckland, New Zealand: Polynesian Press, 1991.

Foerstel, Lenora, and Angela Gilliam, eds. *Confronting the Margaret Mead Legacy: Scholarship, Empire and the South Pacific.* Philadelphia, Pa.: Temple University Press, 1992.

Folasā, Tupu. *Amataga ma le faavaega o le Ekalesia Metotisi Samoa, 1827–1968.* Āpia, Sāmoa: Office of the Methodist Church, 1970.

Forsyth, Claudia. *Samoan Art of Healing: A Description and Classification of the Current Practice of the Taulasea and Jojo.* San Diego, Calif.: U.S. International University, 1983.

Freeman, Derek. *Margaret Mead and Samoa: The Making and Unmaking of an Anthropological Myth.* Cambridge, Mass.: Harvard University Press, 1983.

———. *Paradigms in Collision: The Far Reaching Controversy over the Samoan Researches of Margaret Mead and Its Significance for the Human Sciences.* Canberra, Australia: Research School of Pacific Studies, Australian National University, 1992.

Government of Western Samoa. *Western Samoa's Fifth Development Plan, 1985–87.* Āpia, Sāmoa: Department of Economic Development, 1984.

———. *Western Samoa's Fourth Five-Year Development Plan, 1980–1984.* Āpia, Sāmoa: Government of Western Samoa, 1980.

———. *Western Samoa's Sixth Development Plan, 1988–1990.* Āpia, Sāmoa: Department of Economic Development, 1987.

———. *Western Samoa's Seventh Development Plan, 1992–1994.* Āpia, Sāmoa: Department of Economic Development, 1992.

Green, R. C., and Janet Davidson, eds. *Archaeology in Western Samoa.* 2 vols. Auckland, New Zealand: Auckland Institute and Museum, 1969, 1974.

Holmes, Lowell D. *Quest for the Real Samoa: The Mead/Freeman Controversy and Beyond.* South Hadley, Mass.: Bergin and Garvey Publishers, 1987.

Hughes, H. G. A. *Samoa: American Samoa, Western Samoa, Samoans Abroad.* World Bibliographical Series, Vol. 196. Oxford, England, and Santa Barbara, Calif.: ABC-Clio Press, 1997.

Kallen, Evelyn *The Western Samoan Kinship Bridge: A Study in Migration, Social Change and the New Ethnicity.* Leiden, the Netherlands: E. J. Brill, 1982.

Linkels, Ad. *Fa'a Sāmoa: The Samoan Way between Conch Shell and Disco: A Portrait of Western Sāmoa at the End of the Twentieth Century.* Tilburg, the Netherlands: Mundo Etnico Foundation, 1995.

Masterman, Sylvia. *The Origins of International Rivalry in Samoa, 1845–1884.* London: G. Allen & Unwin, 1934.

McKay, C. G. R. *Samoana: A Personal Story of the Samoan Islands.* Wellington, New Zealand: A. H. and A. W. Reed, 1968.

Meleisea, Malama. *Change and Adaptations in Western Sāmoa.* Christchurch, New Zealand: Macmillan Brown Centre for Pacific Studies, University of Canterbury, 1992.

———. *Lagaga: Short History of Western Samoa.* Suva, Fiji: University of the South Pacific, 1987.

———. *The Making of Modern Samoa: Traditional Authority and Colonial Administration in the History of Western Samoa.* Suva, Fiji: Institute of Pacific Studies, 1987.

Moors, Harry Jay. *Some Recollections of Early Samoa.* Āpia, Sāmoa: Western Samoa Historical and Cultural Trust, 1986.

Moyle, Richard M. *Fagogo—Fables from Samoa.* Auckland, New Zealand: Auckland University/Oxford University Press, 1981.

Neich, Roger. *Material Culture of Western Samoa: Persistence and Change.* Wellington, New Zealand: National Museum of New Zealand, 1985.

O le Tusi Fa'alupega o Samoa Afoa. Āpia, Sāmoa: Methodist Church in Samoa, 1985.

O'Meara, John Timothy. *Samoan Planters: Tradition and Economic Development in Polynesia.* Ft. Worth, Tex.: Holt, Rinehart, and Winston, 1990.

Reid, Barbara. *Gender, Culture, and Morality: A Comparative Study of Samoans and Pakehas in New Zealand.* Chapel Hill: University of North Carolina, 1986.

Robinson, A. C. *The Ecology of Samoa: An Annotated Bibliography.* Āpia, Sāmoa: South Pacific Regional Environment Programme, 1994.

Samoan Observer. Āpia, Sāmoa: Samoa Observer, 1979– (weekly).

Samoan Times. Āpia, Sāmoa: Fata P. Faalogo, 1967– (weekly).

Samoan Weekly. Āpia, Sāmoa: Samoa Weekly, 1977– (weekly).

Tom, Nancy Y. W. *The Chinese in Western Samoa, 1875–1985: The Dragon Came from Afar.* Āpia, Sāmoa: Western Samoa Historical and Cultural Trust, 1986.

Tu'i, Tatupa Fa'afetai Mata'afa. *Lauga: Samoan Oratory.* Suva, Fiji: Institute of Pacific Studies, 1987.

Tuimaleali'ifano, Morgan. *Samoans in Fiji.* Suva, Fiji: Institute of Pacific Studies, 1990.

Turner, George. *Samoa: A Hundred Years Ago and Long Before.* London: J. Snow, 1861; reprinted New York: AMS Press, 1979.

Wendt, Jennifer. *A Title Bestowal in Western Samoa.* Auckland, New Zealand: Longman Paul, 1987.

13. TOKELAU

Boardman, D. W. *A Tokelau-English Vocabulary.* Wellington, New Zealand: Islands Education Division, 1969.

Crocombe, Marjorie T. *Two Hundred Changing Years: A Story of New Zealand's Little Sisters in the Pacific: The Cook Islands, the To-*

kelau Islands, and Niue Island. Wellington, New Zealand: New Zealand Department of Education, 1962.

Hoëm, Ingjerd. *A Way with Words: Language and Culture in Tokelau Society.* Oslo, Norway: Institute for Comparative Research in Human Culture, 1995.

Hoëm, Ingjerd, and others. *Kupu mai te tutolu: Tokelaun Oral Literature.* Oslo, Norway: Scandinavian Press, Institute for Comparative Research in Human Culture, 1992.

Hooper, Antony. *Aid and Dependency in a Small Pacific Territory.* Auckland, New Zealand: University of Auckland, 1982.

———. "A Demographic History of the Tokelau Islands." *Journal of the Polynesian Society* 82, no. 4 (1973): 366–411.

Hovdhaugen, Even, and others. *A Handbook of the Tokelau Language.* Oslo, Norway: Norwegian University Press, 1989.

Huntsman, Judith, and Antony Hooper. *Tokelau: A Historical Ethnography.* Honolulu, Hawai'i: University of Hawai'i Press, 1996.

Iosua, Ioane, and Clive Beaumont. *An Introduction to the Tokelauan Language.* Auckland, New Zealand: C. & D. Beaumont, 1997.

MacGregor, Gordon. *Ethnology of Tokelau Islands.* Honolulu, Hawai'i: Bernice P. Bishop Museum, 1937.

Matagi Tokelau: History and Traditions of Tokelau. Translated by Antony Hopper and Judith Huntsman. Suva, Fiji: Institute of Pacific Studies, University of the South Pacific, 1991.

Office of Tokelau Affairs. *Vakai Tokelau* [Tokelau Newsletter]. Āpia, Sāmoa: Office of Tokelau Affairs, 1968–.

Palehau, Manuele. *Tokelau Tales.* Translated and edited by Judith Huntsman. Auckland, New Zealand: University of Auckland Anthropology Department, 1980.

Secretariat of the Pacific Commission. *Tokelau Population Profiles: A Guide for Planners and Policy Makers.* Nouméa, New Caledonia: Secretariat of the Pacific Community, 1998.

Thomas, Allan, Ineleo Tuia, and Judith Huntsman, eds. *Songs and Stories of Tokelau: An Introduction to the Cultural Heritage.* Wellington, New Zealand: Victoria University Press, 1990.

Tokelau Census of Population and Dwellings, 1986. Christchurch, New Zealand: Department of Statistics, 1986.

Wessen, Albert F., ed. *Migration and Health in a Small Society: The Case of Tokelau.* Oxford, England: Clarendon Press, 1992.

14. TONGA

Bain, Kenneth. *The Friendly Islands: A Story of Queen Salote and Her People.* London: Hodder & Stoughton, 1967.

———. *The New Friendly Islanders: The Tonga of King Taufa'ahau Tupou IV.* London: Hodder & Stoughton, 1993.

Baker, Lillian S., and Beatrice. *Memoirs of the Rev. Dr. Shirley Waldemar Baker, Missionary and Prime Minister.* London: Mayflower Publishing Company, 1951.

Battaille-Benguigui, Marie-Claire. *Le côté de la mer: quotidien et imaginaire aux îles Tonga, polynésie occidentale.* Bordeaux-Talence, France: Centre de recherche des éspaces tropicaux de l'université de Montaigne, 1994.

Bulu, Joel. *Joel Bulu: The Autobiography of a Native Minister in the South Seas.* London: Wesleyan Mission House, 1871; reprinted Nuku'alofa, Tonga: Friendly Islands Bookshop, 1993.

Campbell, Ian C. *Classical Tongan Kingship.* Nuku'alofa, Tonga: 'Atenisi University, 1989.

———. *Island Kingdom: Tonga, Ancient and Modern.* Christchurch, New Zealand: Canterbury University Press, 1992.

Cartmail, Keith St. *The Art of Tonga.* Nelson, New Zealand: Craig Potton Publishing, 1997.

Collocot, Ernest E. V. *Tales and Poems of Tonga.* Honolulu, Hawai'i: Bernice P. Bishop Muscum Press, 1928.

Dale, Paul W. *The Tonga book: The remarkable adventures of young William Mariner on a voyage around the world and his long sojourn in the islands of Tonga whereof he gives us a full account of those islands and the conduct of the lives of the inhabitants.* Montreux, Wash.: Minerva Press, 1996. [See also Mariner, William, below.]

Daly, Martin, compl. *Tonga. World Bibliographical Series, Vol. 217.* Oxford, England; Santa Barbara, Calif.: Clio Press, 1999.

Economist Intelligence Unit. *Country Profile: Pacific Islands.* London: Economist Intelligence Unit. 1990.

———. *Fiji, Solomon Islands, Western Samoa, Vanuatu, Tonga: Country Profile, 1991–92.* London: Economist Intelligence Unit, 1991.

Eustis, Hamilton Nelson. *The King of Tonga: A Biography.* Adelaide, Australia: Hobby Investment, 1997.

Fanua, Tupou Posesi, and Lois Wimberg Webster. *Mālō Tupou: An Oral History.* Honolulu, Hawai'i: University of Hawai'i Press, 1997.

Farmer, Sarah S. *Tonga and the Friendly Islands.* London: Hamilton, Adams & Co., 1855; reprinted Canberra, Australia: Kalia Press, 1976.

Ferdon, Edwin N. *Early Tonga as the Explorers Saw It, 1616–1810.* Tucscon, Ariz.: University of Arizona Press, 1987.

Francis, Steven. *Class Formation in the Pacific Islands of Tonga: An Investigation of Different Conceptualisations of Class Within a Hierarchial Society.* Clayton, Victoria, Australia: Department of Anthropology and Sociology, Monash University, 1990.

Gailey, Christine Ward. *Kinship to Kingship: Gender Hierarchy and State Formation in the Tongan Islands.* Austin, Tex.: University of Texas Press, 1987.

Gifford, E. W. *Tongan Myths and Tales.* Honolulu, Hawai'i: Bernice P. Bishop Museum Press, 1924; reprinted New York: Kraus Reprint, 1985.

———. *Tongan Society.* Honolulu, Hawai'i: Bernice P. Bishop Museum Press, 1929; reprinted New York: Kraus Reprints, 1971.

Grijp, Paul van der. *Islanders of the South: Production, Kinship, and Ideology in the Polynesian Kingdom of Tonga.* Leiden, the Netherlands: KITLV Press, 1993.

Groberg, John H. *In the Eye of the Storm.* Salt Lake City, Utah: Bookcraft, 1993.

Helu, 'I. Futa. *Critical Essays: Cultural Perspectives from the South Seas.* Canberra, Australia: Journal of Pacific History, 1999.

Hereniko, Vilsoni. *Woven Gods: Female Clowns and Power in Rotuma.* Honolulu, Hawai'i: University of Hawai'i Press, 1995.

Hess, Michael. *Labour Absorption in the Kingdom of Tonga: Position, Problems and Prospects.* Canberra, Australia: National Centre for Development Studies, Australian National University, 1996.

Hixon, Margaret. *Salote: Queen of Paradise.* Dunedin, New Zealand: University of Otago Press, 2000.

Huntsman, Judith. *Tonga and Samoa: Images of Gender and Polity.* Christchurch, New Zealand: Macmillan Brown Centre for Pacific Studies, 1995.

Kaeppler, Adrienne L. *Poetry in Motion: Studies of Tongan Dance.* Nukua'lofa, Tonga: Vava'u Press, 1993.

Kirch, Patrick. *Niuatoputapu: The Preshistory of a Polynesian Chiefdom.* Seattle, Wash.: Burke Museum, 1988.

Lātēkefu, Sione. *Church and State in Tonga.* Canberra, Australia: Australian National University Press, 1974.

———. *King George Tupou I of Tonga.* Nuku'alofa, Tonga: Tonga Traditions Committee, 1975.

———. *The Tonga Constitution: A Brief History to Celebrate Its Centenary.* Nuku'alofa, Tonga: Tonga Traditions Committee Publication, 1975.

Lavaka, Penelope A. *The Limits of Advice: Britain and the Kingdom of Tonga, 1900–1970.* Canberra, Australia: Australian National University Press, 1981.

Lawry, Walter. *Friendly and Feejee Islands.* 2d ed. London: Gilpin, 1850.

Lawson, Stephanie. *Tradition versus Democracy in the Kingdom of Tonga.* Canberra, Australia: Research School of Pacific Studies, Australian National University, 1994.

Linkels, Ad. *Sounds of Change in Tonga: Dance, Music and Cultural Dynamics in a Polynesian Kingdom.* 3d ed. Tilburg, the Netherlands: Mundo Étnico, 1998.

Luckcock, Janet Louisa. *Thomas of Tonga, 1797–1881: The Unlikely Pioneer.* Peterborough, England: Methodist Publishing House, 1990.

Mangeret, A. *Mgr. Bataillon et les missions de l'océanie centrale.* 2 vols. Lyon, France: Lecoffre, 1884.

Marcus, George E. *Nobility and the Chiefly Tradition in the Modern Kingdom of Tonga.* Wellington, New Zealand: Polynesian Society, 1980.

Mariner, William. *Tonga Islands: William Mariner's Account.* 5th ed. Compiled and arranged by John Martin. Nuku'alofa, Tonga: Vava'u Press, 1991.

Monfat, A. *Les Tonga ou les archipel des amis et le R. P. Joseph Chevron—Étude historique et religieuse.* Lyon, France: Witte, 1893.

Moyle, Richard. *Tongan Music.* Auckland, New Zealand: Auckland University Press, 1987.

Paongo, Kalapoli. "The Nature of Education in Pre-European to Modern Tonga." In *Tongan Culture and History,* edited by Phyllis Herda, Jennifer Terrell, and Niel Gunson, 134–144. Canberra, Australia: Australian National University, 1990.

Perminow, Arne Aleksej. *The Long Way Home: Dilemmas of Everyday Life in a Tongan Village.* Oslo, Norway: Scandinavian University Press, 1993.

Poulsen, Jens. *Early Tongan Prehistory: The Lapita Period on Tongatapu and Its Relationship.* 2 vols. Canberra, Australia: Australian National University Press, 1987.

Rutherford, Noel. *Shirley Baker and the King of Tonga.* New York: Oxford University Press, 1971; reprinted Auckland, New Zealand: Pasifika Press, 1996.

———, ed. *Friendly Islands: A History of Tonga.* Melbourne, Australia: Oxford University Press, 1977.

Schneider, Thomas. *Functional Tonga-English, English-Tongan Dictionary.* 2d ed. Mt. Waverly, Victoria, Australia: Dellasta Pacific, 1995.

Shumway, Eric B. *Intensive Course in Tongan.* Rev. ed. Lā'ie, Hawai'i: Institute for Polynesian Studies, 1988.

———. *Tongan Saints: Legacy of Faith.* Lā'ie, Hawai'i: Institute for Polynesian Studies, 1991.

Small, Cathy A. *Voyages: From Tongan Villages to American Suburbs.* Ithaca, N.Y.: Cornell University Press, 1997.

Tanham, George Kilpatrick. *The Kingdom of Tonga.* Santa Monica, Calif.: Rand Corporation, 1988.

Thistlethwaite, Robert, and others. *The Kingdom of Tonga: Action Strategy for Managing the Environment.* Āpia, Sāmoa: South Pacific Regional Environment Program, 1993.

Thompson, Richard H., and ‘Ofa Thompson. *The Student's English-Tongan and Tongan-English Dictionary*. Nuku‘alofa, Tonga: Friendly Islands Bookshop, 1996.

Thomson, Basil. *The Diversions of a Prime Minister*. Edinburgh, Scotland: Blackwood, 1894; reprinted London: Dawsons, 1968.

———. *Savage Island: An Account of a Sojourn in Niue and Tonga*. London: John Murray, 1902.

Tonga Chronicle. Nuku‘alofa, Tonga: Government Information Office, 1965– (weekly).

Tonga Parliamentary Bulletin. Nuku‘alofa, Tonga: Vava‘u Press, 1984– (daily during parliamentary sessions).

Tu‘inukuafe, Edgar. *An Introduction to the Tongan Language*. Auckland, New Zealand: Pacific Islanders Educational Resource Centre, 1992.

Turner, J. G. *The Pioneer Missionary: Life of the Rev. Nathaniel Turner, Missionary in New Zealand, Tonga, and Australia*. London: Wesley Conference Office, 1872.

Vason, George. *An Authentic Narrative of Four Years' Residence at Tonga-taboo . . . in 1796*. London: Longman, Hurst, Rees, 1810.

West, Thomas. *Ten Years in South-Central Polynesia: Being Reminiscences of a Personal Mission to the Friendly Islands and Their Dependencies*. London: James Nisbet and Company, 1865.

Whistler, W. Arthur. *Tongan Herbal Medicine*. Honolulu, Hawai‘i: Isle Botanica, 1993.

Williams, John. *A Narrative of Missionary Enterprises in the South Seas*. London: John Snow, 1837.

Wood, Alfred H. *Overseas Missions of the Australian Methodist Church. Vol. 1, Tonga and Samoa*. Melbourne, Australia: Aldersgate Press, 1975.

Wood-Ellem, Elizabeth. *Queen Salote of Tonga: The Story of an Era 1900–1965*. Auckland, New Zealand: Auckland University Press, 1999.

15. TUVALU

Besnier, Niko. *Literacy, Emotion and Authority: Reading and Writing on a Polynesian Atoll.* Cambridge, Mass.: Cambridge University Press, 1995.

———. *Tuvaluan: A Polynesian Language of the Central Pacific.* London and New York: Routledge, 2000.

Chambers, Keith Stanley. *Unity of Heart: Culture and Change in a Polynesian Atoll Society.* Prospect Heights, Ill.: Waveland Press, 2001.

Crocombe, Ron. *Land Tenure in the Atolls: Cook Islands, Kiribati, Marshall Islands, Tokelau, Tuvalu.* Suva, Fiji: Institute of Pacific Studies, 1987.

Faaniu, Simati, and others. *Tuvalu: A History.* Suva, Fiji: University of the South Pacific, 1983.

Fairbairn, Te'o Ian. *Tuvalu: Economic Situation and Development Prospects.* Canberra, Australia: Australian Inernational Development Assistance Bureau, 1993.

Geddes, W. H., and others. *Atoll Economy: Social Change in Kiribati and Tuvalu: Islands on the Line.* Canberra, Australia: Australian National University Press, 1982.

Habtemariam Tesfaghiorghis. *The Implications of Population Growth for Tuvalu.* Canberra, Australia: National Centre for Development Studies, Australian National University, 1994.

Institute of Pacific Studies. *Tuvalu: A History.* Suva, Fiji: Institute of Pacific Studies, 1983.

Koch, Gerd. *The Material Culture of Tuvalu.* Suva, Fiji: Institute of Pacific Studies, University of the South Pacific, 1984.

Lane, John. *Tuvalu: State of the Enviroment Report, 1993.* Āpia, Sāmoa: South Pacific Regional Environment Programme, 1994.

Laracy, Hugh, ed. *Tuvalu: A History.* Suva, Fiji: Institute of Pacific Studies, 1983.

Macdonald, Barrie. *Cinderellas of the Empire: Towards a History of Kiribati and Tuvalu.* Canberra, Australia: Australian National University Press, 1982.

McQuarrie, Peter. *Strategic Atoll: Tuvalu and the Second World War.* Christchurch, New Zealand: Macmillan Brown Centre for Pacific Studies, University of Canterbury, 1994.

Munro, Doug. "The Lagoon Islands: A History of Tuvalu, 1820–1908." Ph.D. dissertation, Macquarie University, Sydney, 1982.

Munro, Doug, Suamalie N. T. Iosefa, and Niko Besnier. *Te Tala o Niuoku: The German Plantation on Nukulaelae Atoll, 1865–1890.* Suva, Fiji: Institute of Pacific Studies, University of the South Pacific, 1990.

Noricks, Jay S. *A Tuvalu Dictionary.* 2 vols. New Haven, Conn.: Human Relations Area Files, 1981.

Roberts, R. G. "Te Atu Tuvalu: A Short History of the Ellice Islands." *Journal of the Polynesian Society* 67, no. 3 (1958): 394–423.

Rodgers, K. A. "An Annotated Bibliography of the Natural History of Tuvalu (Ellice Islands)." *Pacific Science* 39, no. 1 (January 1985): 100–130.

———. *The Biology and Geology of Tuvalu: An Annotated Bibliography.* Sydney, Australia: Australian Museum, 1988.

Tuvalu. *Report on the 1991 Population Census of Tuvalu.* Funafuti, Tuvalu: Government of Tuvalu, 1992.

16. WALLIS AND FUTUNA

Angleviel, Frédéric. *Les missions à Wallis et Futuna au XIXe siècle.* Bordeaux-Talence, France: Le Centre de Recherche des Espaces Tropicaux de l'Université Michel de Montaigne, 1994.

Bluzy, Raymond, and Olivier Rauch. *La Nouvelle-Calédonie, la Polynésie Française, Wallis et Futuna: Géographie.* Nouméa, New Caledonia: CTRDP, 1990.

Burrows, Edwin Grant. *Ethnology of Uvea (Wallis Island).* Honolulu, Hawai'i: Bernice P. Bishop Museum, 1937.

———. *Ethnology of Futuna.* Honolulu, Hawai'i: Bernice P. Bishop Museu, 1936; reprinted New York: Kraus Reprint Co., 1971.

———. *Songs of Uvea and Futuna.* Honolulu, Hawai'i: Bernice P. Bishop Museum Press, 1945.

Dougherty, Janet W. D. *West Futuna-Aniwa: An Introduction to a Polynesian Outlier Language.* Berkeley: University of California Press, 1983.

Frimigacci, Daniel. *Aux temps de la terre noire: Ethnoarchéologie des îles Futuna et Alofi.* Paris: Peeters, 1990.

Gantelet, Pascale, and Philippe Maesse. *Images de la population de Wallis et Futuna: Principaux résultats de recensement 1990.* Paris: Institution Nationale de la Statistique et des Études Économiques, 1992.

Goddard, Philippe. *Wallis et Futuna.* 2d ed. Nouméa, New Caledonia: Éditions d'Art Calédoniennes, 1991.

Mangeret, A. *Mgr. Bataillon et les missions de l'océanie centrale.* 2 vols. Lyon, France: Lecoffre, 1884.

Mayer, Raymond. *Les transformations de la tradition narrative à l'île Wallis ('Uvea).* Paris: Société des Océanistes, 1976.

O'Reilly, Patrick. *Bibliographie méthodique, analytique et critique des îles Wallis et Futuna.* Paris: Musée de l'Homme, 1964.

———. "Chronologie de Wallis et Futuna." *Journal de la Société des Océanistes* 19 (1963): 12–45.

Poncet, Alexandre. *Histoire de l'île Wallis: Le protectorat français.* 2 vols. Paris: Musée de l'Homme, publication #23, 1972.

Renaud, George J.-L. *Les l'îles Wallis: Histoire et ethnologie.* N.p., s.n., 1983.

Rensch, Karl H. *The Language of Wallis Island.* Mawson, New South Wales: Archipelago Press, 1995.

———. *Tikisionalio Fakauvea-Fakafalani: Dictionnaire Wallisien-Française* (Wallisian-French Dictionary). Canberra, Australia: Australian National University Department of Linguistics, 1984.

Roux, Jean-Claude. *Wallis et Futuna: Espaces et temps recomposée: chroniques d'une micro-insularitée.* Bourdeaux-Talence, France: Université Michel de Montaigne, 1995.

Thierry, Agostini, and others. *101 mots pour comprendre Wallis et Futuna.* Nouméa, New Caledonia: Éditions île de lumière, 1999.

Thomas, Allan. *Hgorofutuna: Report of a Survey of the Music of West Futuna, Vanuatu.* Auckland, New Zealand: Department of Anthropology, University of Auckland, 1992.

ABOUT THE AUTHOR

ROBERT D. CRAIG holds a bachelor's degree (1962) and a master's degree (1964) from the University of Cincinnati, Ohio. After studying in Europe for two semesters, he continued his graduate work at the University of Utah, where he finished his Ph.D. in 1966.

He currently lives outside of San Diego, California, and is retired emeritus professor of history from Alaska Pacific University in Anchorage. His interest in the Pacific comes from his teaching in Hawai'i and Guam for over 16 years and from his many travels to the various island nations of the South Pacific for over 30 years. He has worked for three Pacific research centers—the Institute for Polynesian Studies in Hawai'i, the Micronesian Area Research Center in Guam, and the Pacific Rim Studies Center in Anchorage—and has had the distinction of having founded two scholarly journals—*Pacific Studies* in Hawai'i (1979–) and *Pacifica* (1989–1991) in Anchorage.

His most prominent book publications include the *Historical Dictionary of Oceania* (1981), the *Dictionary of Polynesian Mythology* (1989), the *Historical Dictionary of Honolulu and Hawai'i* (1998) and numerous other shorter works, monographs, and research papers.

His retirement from full-time teaching in 1998 ended a 32-year distinguished university career that garnered him numerous teaching, research, and service awards. In 1992, the U.S. National Council for Advancement and Support of Education (CASE) named him Alaska Professor of the Year and nominated him for the prestigious CASE 1992 U.S. Professor of the Year.

His retirement plans include the continuation of his research and writing on Polynesian subjects—history, mythology, and culture—and the return to some of his research interests from graduate school days—medieval history and Old-French literature.